Slavery in Classical Antiquity

Views and Controversies about Classical Antiquity
General Editor: M. I. Finley

Also published:
The Language and Background of Homer
Edited by G. S. Kirk

Alexander the Great: the Main Problems
Edited by G. T. Griffith

Plato, Popper and Politics
Edited by Renford Bambrough

In preparation:
The Crisis of the Roman Republic
Edited by Robin Seager

Slavery in Classical Antiquity

Views and Controversies

Edited by
M. I. FINLEY

*Reader in Ancient Social and Economic History
in the University of Cambridge*

HEFFER/*Cambridge*

BARNES & NOBLE/*New York*

Acknowledgements for permission to use material
reproduced in this volume are due to:

The Economic History Society
The Editor, *The Polish Review*
J. C. B. Mohr Verlag
Franz Steiner Verlag
Harvard University Press
The Editor, *The Philosophical Review*
Editions Montchrestien
The Editor, *Journal of Roman Studies*
The Editor, *Hermathena*
The Editor, *Annales*

Photographically reprinted in England for W. Heffer & Sons Ltd, Cambridge
by Lowe and Brydone (Printers) Ltd, London, N.W.10
First published in this form 1960
Reprinted 1964
Reprinted with supplement to bibliography 1968

SBN 85270 012 1 (*cloth*)
SBN 85270 013 X (*paper*)

PREFACE

It is a fact, I believe, that students of antiquity are at present investigating slavery more systematically, and debating its issues more fully, than ever before. This is a welcome development, but it creates a problem. Text-books, said R. G. Collingwood in the introduction to *The Idea of History*, "always describe not what is now being thought by real live historians, but what was thought by real live historians at some time in the past when the raw material was being created out of which the text-book has been put together". In this field text-books hardly exist, and it is not unfair to the few there are to suggest that they do not adequately reveal current thinking on the subject, precisely at a time when it is active and fluid.

This volume has the clearly defined objective of bringing together a number of articles which present the main issues, debate them, suggest new approaches, or argue a thesis or theses. Neither date of publication nor accessibility in the original form was taken into consideration in making the selection. The main test was simply whether or not a particular article would help in significant measure to clarify some important aspect or implication of ancient slavery. Some duplication was unavoidable. Insofar as it reveals how the same evidence provokes different interpretations or emphases, this duplication is a good thing. Otherwise it is an inevitable condition of any anthology of this kind, and a serious effort has been made to avoid an excessive amount.

Since the volume is intended for university students above all, another criterion was also necessary, namely, language. All but three of the articles are in English, and the choice of those three—two in French and one in German—reflects the realities of university life today. The language barrier explains the absence of any contribution on one or two subjects which I very much wanted to include (most obviously, perhaps, the possible effects of Christianity on Roman slavery). Furthermore, in the interest of students (and their teachers, too, for that matter), it was decided to print the volume photographically. Whatever aesthetic objections may be aroused by different type-faces and margins will surely be overcome by the very considerable reduction in price, as against a complete reprinting. There is the added compensation that this process insures absolutely accurate reproduction of the original text, with the identical pagination for purposes of reference and citation.

Formal acknowledgements have been made elsewhere in the volume, but I should like here to express my personal appreciation of the readiness with which authors and publishers consented to the reproduction of their articles. The selection and the Bibliographical Essay are entirely my responsibility.

M. I. FINLEY.

31 July, 1959.

CONTENTS

The pagination of the present volume is given in square brackets, top centre of the page.

I

SLAVERY IN THE ANCIENT WORLD

By A. H. M. JONES

I

A S the subject of this paper is the economic importance of slavery, little need be said of domestic servants. It should, however, be emphasized that the proportion of slaves absorbed by domestic service must at all periods have been considerable, for, by and large, personal servants were always slaves, and they were employed in numbers which by modern standards seem very lavish. Moralists continually denounce the luxury of the rich who counted them by the hundred or even the thousand, and if their figures are suspect, we have the well attested case of Pedanius Secundus, prefect of the city under Nero, whose town house was served by a staff of 400.[1] Slaves were, moreover, employed by persons of relatively humble means. In the fourth century B.C., according to Demosthenes, even the poorest of those who paid the war tax, peasant farmers with a holding of six or seven acres, might well own a maidservant.[2] In the fourth century A.D., private soldiers in the Roman army quite commonly owned a slave or two:[3] S. Martin is commended by his biographer for his asceticism in restricting himself to one slave batman.[4] For academic readers, Libanius' plea for his four lecturers is perhaps the most illuminating evidence which can be quoted for the high standard of domestic service prevalent in antiquity. They were, according to Libanius, miserably paid. Those who had a house laboured under a heavy mortgage; others lived in lodgings 'like cobblers'. They could barely afford to marry, and congratulated themselves if they had only one child. They owed money to the baker, and had to sell their wives' trinkets to meet the bill. These unfortunates could afford only three slaves, or even two, who were insolent to their masters because they had not many fellow servants.[5]

Slaves were also commonly employed throughout antiquity in secretarial and managerial posts. In fifth-century Athens, Nicias entrusted his mining interests to a slave, for whom he is alleged to have paid the fantastic price of one talent.[6] In fourth-century Athens, bank managers were often slaves or freedmen of the owners: Archestratus entrusted his bank to his slave Pasion, whom he

---

[1] Tacitus, *Annals*, XIV, 43.
[2] Dem[osthenes], XXIV, 197; cf. my *Athens of Demosthenes* (Cambridge, 1952), pp. 9–11.
[3] *Cod[ex] Theod[osianus]*, VII, xiii, 16, xxii, 2. [4] Sulpicius Severus, *Vita S. Martini*, 2.
[5] Lib[anius], *Or[atio]*, XXXI, 11. [6] Xen[ophon], *Mem[orabilia]*, II, v, 2.

freed and to whom he ultimately bequeathed the business, and Pasion in his turn, when he retired, leased the bank to his freed slave Phormio.[1] This habit of employing slaves in managerial positions of trust sometimes resulted in curious anomalies. In the early imperial fleet the ratings were free provincials, but the captains of the ships were slaves of the emperor, and the admirals his freedmen.[2] The bailiff or agent of a farm or estate was commonly a slave of the owner, but the working tenants whose rents he collected and whose work he supervised were under the Principate commonly free men.[3]

The reason why slaves and freedmen were preferred for posts of this kind was that self-respecting free men were unwilling to accept positions in which they had to obey the orders of an employer. The point is well put in a dialogue reported by Xenophon between Socrates and a certain Eutherus.[4] Eutherus had lost his property overseas owing to the war, and was reduced to earning his living as a manual labourer. Socrates warns him that his strength will fail with advancing age and no one will be willing to hire him, and suggests that he seek employment as a works manager or estate agent of a wealthy man. Eutherus is shocked: 'I would find it hard to endure slavery' he replies, and after further argument sums up his attitude: 'I absolutely refuse to be liable to be called to account by anyone.' This is a particularly interesting case; Eutherus not only preferred manual labour to blackcoated employment, he was willing to hire his labour to an employer, but not to forfeit his independence by accepting a position which involved personal service to a master.

Employers no doubt also preferred to use in positions of trust men whose characters they knew, and on whose obedience they could rely; slaves could be chastised if they disobeyed instructions, and freedmen had formed the habit of executing their masters' orders. Cicero approved the old custom (still prevalent in his own day) whereby magistrates appointed as their secretaries (*accensi*) their own freedmen, 'to whom they used to give orders not very differently than to their slaves'.[5] During the early Principate this practice produced a glaring anomaly. The emperor's secretaries and accountants (*ab epistulis, a libellis, a rationibus*) became inevitably Secretaries of State and Ministers of Finance, and yet as inevitably these posts had to be filled by imperial freedmen; no Roman of standing would have demeaned himself by becoming the emperor's personal servant. The aristocracy bitterly resented the power and wealth of Pallas, Narcissus and the other great imperial freedmen, but the problem was insoluble until eventually, after over a century had passed, these secretarial posts acquired sufficient status to rank as public offices and to be acceptable to members of the equestrian order—though never to senators.[6]

II

The slave manager or agent is an interesting figure, but it is slave workmen with whom this paper is concerned. What were their numbers at various times and places, compared with the numbers of the free working population? How

[1] Dem. xxxvi, 4–7, 43 *et seq.*; cf. *Econ. Hist. Rev.* viii (1955), 152, n. 8.

[2] The evidence is given in C. G. Starr, *The Roman Imperial Navy* (Ithaca, N.Y., 1941), pp. 32, 44, 69. *Pace* Professor Starr, I think that the inscriptions which he cites show that the trierarchs were often Imperial slaves.

[3] W. E. Heitland, *Agricola* (Cambridge, 1921), pp. 361 *et seq.*; see *Dig[est]*, xxxiii, vii, 20, § 3 for a farm bequeathed with its (slave) *actor* and the arrears of its (free) *coloni*.

[4] Xen. *Mem.* ii, viii, 1–5.   [5] Cicero, *Epistulae ad Quintum fratrem*, i, i, 13.

[6] A. M. Duff, *Freedmen in the Early Roman Empire* (Oxford, 1928), pp. 143 *et seq.*

were they obtained, by breeding or by purchase, and what did they cost? On what kind of work were they employed and under what conditions? What was the relative cost to the employer of servile and free labour, and how did their standard of living compare?

It is easier to ask these questions than to answer them. Reliable population statistics for the ancient world are extremely rare, and there are no trustworthy figures for numbers of slaves. It is however possible to make a rough estimate for Athens in the latter part of the fourth century B.C. We know that the adult male citizens numbered 21,000 and the adult male resident foreigners 10,000. This implies a total adult free population of both sexes of 60,000 or more, and a total free population including children of at least twice that figure. We also know the amount of corn grown in and imported into Attica, and the annual consumption which was considered normal for a man. We can thus calculate the corn consumed by the free population, and by deducting this amount from the total available find how much was left to feed slaves. The maximum possible number of slaves who could have been maintained is on this calculation about 20,000, or one slave to every three adult free persons.[1] A considerable number of the slaves must have been domestic servants. If, as Demosthenes implies, most of the citizens liable to payment of war tax, who numbered about 6,000, owned a servant girl, this would account for say 5,000.[2] Resident foreigners on this basis would have owned another 2,500, and there were, of course, many more prosperous families, both citizen and alien, which had larger domestic staffs. It would probably not be an overestimate to allocate 10,000, or half the slave population, to domestic service, leaving 10,000 to industry and agriculture, or one to three free adult males.

We hear little of agricultural slavery, and slaves were in fact probably little employed on the land. Most of Attica was cultivated by small peasant proprietors who had no need for slave labour, even if they could have afforded it. There was a small class of wealthier landlords who did not work their own land, but their estates often consisted of a number of scattered farms, some of which were let to free tenants. Only the home farm where the landlord resided was normally cultivated by slaves.[3]

Slaves were more commonly employed in industry. To begin at the bottom end of the social scale, a cripple, pleading for the continuation of his public assistance, declares: 'The craft which I practise cannot help me much. I already (he is getting on in years) find difficulty in doing the work myself, and I have not yet been able to acquire anyone to take it over.'[4] As Xenophon puts it, 'those who can, buy slaves so as to have fellow workers'.[5] That is, craftsmen who could afford it bought slaves and trained them as assistants, hoping ultimately to retire and live in their declining years on the proceeds of their work. Socrates cites five contemporaries, including a miller, a baker and a clothier, who lived in some affluence on the labour of their slaves.[6] Industrial slaves were also one of the recognized forms of investment for the wealthy; Socrates couples them with land and house property as possible sources of unearned income.[7] We occasionally meet with comparatively large industrial slave establishments. Demosthenes' father owned thirty-two cutlers and twenty bed-makers.[8] Pasion, besides his bank, had acquired before he died land to the value of 20 talents

[1] *Econ. Hist. Rev.* VIII (1955), 142–3.   [2] See p. 185, n. 2 *supra*.
[3] *Past and Present* I (1952), 20–1; *Econ. Hist. Rev.* VIII (1955), 144, 150–1.
[4] Lysias, XXIV, 6.   [5] Xen. *Mem.* II, iii, 3.
[6] *Ibid.* II, vii, 3–6.   [7] *Ibid.* III, xi, 4.   [8] Dem. XXVII, 9.

and a shield factory which brought in a talent a year.[1] The brothers Lysias and Polemarchus owned another shield factory comprising nearly 120 slaves.[2] This is by far the largest industrial establishment of which we know, and was probably exceptional. It had attained this size at the end of the Peloponnesian War, when there had been a prolonged and heavy demand for armaments, and its owners were foreigners, and therefore precluded from investing their money in land or house property. The average wealthy citizen in normal times, to judge by the half dozen estates which Isaeus describes in his speeches, put most of his money into land and houses, and rarely owned more than a dozen industrial slaves.[3]

Industrial slaves might be mere hands, fed and clothed by their owner. Demosthenes senior's slaves were apparently of this type. They seem to have worked in his house, for no factory building is included in the estate, and he bought the raw materials—Demosthenes includes in the valuation of the estate the stock of ivory and iron in hand:[4] he also marketed the finished products.[5] It was, however, also a common practice for owners of industrial slaves to let them work independently, collecting from them a fixed rent and allowing them to keep for themselves whatever they earned in addition. Thus Timarchus owned a little factory of nine or ten shoemakers, whose foreman paid him 3 obols a day and the other hands 2 obols each.[6] Such industrial slaves, who 'lived apart', as the Athenians expressed it, seem to have formed a substantial part of the population; they could on occasion be included in the call-up to man a fleet, together with resident foreigners.[7] Such a slave could be sold as a going concern, with his assets and liabilities—and the latter might exceed the former, as Epicrates found to his cost. Being enamoured of a boy he was bamboozled into buying his father Midas and his brother too and the perfumery which Midas ran, with its stock and outstanding debts. He paid 40 minae ($\frac{2}{3}$ talent) and discovered too late that there were 5 talents owing to sundry creditors.[8]

The great majority of Athenian industrial slaves worked in the silver mines of Laurium. The number fluctuated greatly. In the fifth century, before the occupation of Deceleia by the Spartans in 413, the mines were very intensively worked. Xenophon, writing two generations later, implies that at that period well over 10,000 slaves were employed in them,[9] and this is not impossible. In the fifth century the free population, both citizen and foreign, was much larger than in the fourth, and the total number of slaves was likewise larger; according to Thucydides over 20,000 slaves, mainly industrial, escaped during the Deceleian War.[10] From 413 till about 340 the mines were neglected; Xenophon implies that in his day the number of slaves employed in them was very small, since he thought they could easily absorb 6,000 or even 10,000 additional workers.[11] From the 330's the mines were again very actively exploited, but we have no reliable figures for the number of slaves employed.

Some mining entrepreneurs owned their slaves: we know of one who possessed thirty with a workshop for crushing and smelting the ore, and who raised his working capital to buy concessions from the state by loans on their security.[12]

[1] *Idem*, xxxvi, 4–5, 11.
[2] Lysias, xii, 19.
[3] *Econ. Hist. Rev.* viii (1955), 151, n. 1.
[4] Dem. xxvii, 10, 30–3.
[5] *Ibid.* 19–22.
[6] Aeschines, *in Timarchum*, 97.
[7] Dem. iv, 36.
[8] Hypereides, v, 5 *et seq.*
[9] Xen. *Vect[igalia]*, iv, 25.
[10] Thucydides, vii, 27, 5.
[11] Xenophon's evidence is confirmed by the inscriptions, see *Hesperia*, xix (1950), 189 *et seq.*
[12] Dem. xxxvii, 4 *et seq.*

Other entrepreneurs hired their slaves. This was according to Xenophon a common practice in the fifth century. Nicias is said to have owned 1,000 slaves whom he leased to a mining entrepreneur for 1 obol a day, the lessee feeding them and replacing casualties, and two other wealthy Athenians are said to have exploited gangs of 600 and 300 slaves in the same way.[1] Xenophon recommended that the state should go into the business in a large way. It was, according to him, highly profitable. He does not state what unskilled labourers cost, but he does say that if the state bought 1,200 initially, and used the resulting income to build up its stock, in five or six years it would possess 6,000.[2] This calculation, assuming that Xenophon was capable of working out the sum involved in compound interest, is based on a price of between 125 and 150 drachmae. There is some corroborative evidence that this is a plausible figure. Xenophon elsewhere speaks of slaves being worth very different sums, one 2 minae, another not half a mina, others five or ten (these must be skilled men).[3] Demosthenes in a forensic speech mentions a slave being sold for 2 minae,[4] and in another of two being valued at 2½ minae[5] (these were agricultural labourers; the price of 125 drachmae agrees closely with the figure for miners). Finally in 414–413 a batch of sixteen slaves, the confiscated property of an alien residing in the Peiraeus, fetched 2,552 drachmae when auctioned.[6] These included a boy who was sold for only 72 drachmae, but some, who fetched figures like 300 or 240, were doubtless skilled men, and most will have been of superior quality to miners. The average price is nevertheless only 160 drachmae each.

A rent of an obol a day (60 drachmae a year) for a slave costing 125 or 150 drachmae would give the owner a net return of at least 40 per cent per annum, or perhaps nearly 50 per cent, on his capital. This does not allow for periods of unemployment, for Xenophon insists that the silver mines have a virtually inexhaustible capacity for absorbing labour. Nor does it allow for amortization; though the lessee replaced casualties, the time would come when some of the men would grow too old to find a hirer. But if a slave had an average useful life of twenty years it would not at the low prices prevailing make much difference. To amortize a slave worth 150 drachmae would require 7½ drachmae a year, and if this sum is deducted from his rent of 60 drachmae a year, the return drops from 40 to 35 per cent.

The lessee seems also to have done well out of the transaction. The Eleusis accounts of 329 and 326 B.C. show that the state paid 1½ drachmae a day for unskilled labour and allowed 3 obols (½ drachma) a day for feeding public slaves, also unskilled labourers.[7] On these figures a mining entrepreneur would pay 9 obols a day for free labour, as against 4 obols (3 for food and 1 for hire) for slave labour; he would also have to make some allowance for replacement of clothes and for making good casualties, but the margin seems ample for this. In Xenophon's day the figures may have been rather lower, for prices rose rapidly in the second half of the fourth century. Demosthenes in 351 reckoned the cost of feeding a standing army, partly citizen and partly mercenary, at only 2 obols a day.[8] This figure is rather suspect, as he is trying to persuade the

[1] Xen. *Vect.* iv, 14–15.
[2] *Ibid.* iv, 23.
[3] Xen. *Mem.* ii, v, 2.
[4] Dem. xli, 8.
[5] *Idem*, liii, 1.
[6] M. N. Tod, *Greek Historical Inscriptions*² (Oxford, 1948), no. 79.
[7] *I[nscriptions] G[raecae]*, ii–iii², 1672, ll. 4–5, 42–3, 117–18, 141–2.
[8] Dem. iv, 28.

people that his project will not be too expensive, but he can hardly have proposed giving less than a slave ration to soldiers without making himself ridiculous. On the other hand, wages at the end of the fifth century were only 1 drachma a day.[1] On this basis the cost of free labour would be 6 obols as against 3 for servile.

Skilled slave craftsmen do not seem to have brought in quite so high a return. Demosthenes declares that his father's cutlers were worth 5 or 6 minae each, or at the lowest reckoning 3 minae, and that his group of thirty-two or thirty-three brought in a net income of 30 minae a year. On the lowest valuation the return is 30 per cent, on the higher figures 15 or 20 per cent. He does not state the value of the twenty bed-makers, but as they were held as a pledge for a loan of 40 minae, they must have been worth well over 2 minae each. They brought in a net income of 12 minae a year, which is 30 per cent on the amount of the loan for which they were pledged, but less on their real value.[2] Timarchus' shoemakers who paid him 2 obols a day will have brought him in 120 drachmae a year each, or 40 per cent, if they cost only 3 minae, from 20 to 25 per cent if they cost 5 or 6. As one could normally get 12 per cent on loans with good security, such as mortgages, investment in skilled industrial slaves does not seem to have been very profitable, when allowance is made for amortization, which was a more serious matter when valuable skilled slaves were concerned, and for market risks. Demosthenes' guardians alleged, whether truly or not, that since his father's death the slaves had often been idle as their products were unsaleable.[3]

III

It is often stated that the competition of slave labour depressed the standard of living of free workers. It is impossible to disprove this statement, since we cannot know how much free workers would have earned if there had been no slaves, but the probabilities are against it. A slave craftsman 'living apart' was in no position to undercut his free neighbour, since he had not only, like him, to maintain himself and his family, if any, but also to pay his rent to his master. There is no evidence that owners of slave factories undercut free craftsmen. They seem to have preferred to sell their products at prevailing prices, and make as large a profit as they could: Demosthenes' guardians did not claim that they had sold off the products of his factory cheap, owing to the alleged glut, but that they did not sell them at all, or alternatively suspended the slaves' work. With hired labour the case was rather different. Where there was continuous employment, as in the mines, slave labour, whether owned by the entrepreneur or hired by him from a big slave owner like Nicias, was so much cheaper than free that it displaced it altogether. We hear of poor Athenians working their own claims with their own hands,[4] but never of hired free miners. But in casual employment, such as building or harvesting,[5] hired slaves and free men were employed indifferently. We do not know what the practice of private employers was, but the Athenian state, as the temple building accounts prove, paid the same rate (which was two or three times the cost of maintaining a slave) to

---

[1] *IG*, 1², 373–4, analysed by R. H. Randall in *American Journal of Archaeology*, LVII (1953), 199–210.

[2] Dem. xxvii, 9.   [3] Dem. xxvii, 19–21.

[4] Xen. *Vect.* iv, 22; Dem. xlii, 20.

[5] See Dem. liii, 19–21 and lvii, 45 for hired slaves and free persons in harvesting. For building, see next note.

free workers or hired slaves[1]. Slave owners who hired out their slaves evidently preferred to make á handsome profit by charging full current wage rates for their services rather than to undercut free workmen: they had after all to cover themselves against the periods of unemployment inevitable in casual work, when the slaves would be earning nothing but still had to be fed.

The reason that unskilled slave labour was so profitable to the owner was that slaves were fantastically cheap. The price of an unskilled man was, we have seen, from 125 to 150 drachmae. The cost of feeding him was, at Demosthenes' figure of 2 obols a day, 120 drachmae a year, or at the rate of 3 obols actually paid in 329 by the Athenian state to its slave labourers 180 drachmae a year: and a slave had to be clothed and shod as well as fed. A slave, that is, cost initially about a year's keep at the outside. Slave merchants could hardly have made a profit unless they acquired their wares for nothing or next to nothing and sold them very rapidly. Piracy and kidnapping were in fact common at this period, and there were large backward and unsettled areas nearby, where continual inter-tribal warfare produced a glut of prisoners. It was only in such conditions that slave labour was cheap enough to play the not inconsiderable role that it did in Athenian economy. Yet even here it was only when the slave was put to work as an unskilled labourer in the mines that he undercut the free man.

IV

Another time and place where slavery played an important role was Italy and Sicily during the last two centuries of the Republic. It was a period of constant wars, ruthlessly conducted, which threw many thousands of prisoners on to the market. It was also a period when piracy flourished unchecked until it became so intolerable a nuisance that in 67 B.C. Pompey was voted a vast fleet and army to clear the seas. He did so temporarily, but during the civil wars that followed piracy revived. Slaves should have been dirt cheap and very plentiful. Price figures are unfortunately almost entirely lacking for the western Mediterranean. After the battle of Cannae (216 B.C.) Hannibal offered to release his prisoners on the following scale of ransoms: 500 quadrigati for a Roman cavalryman, 300 for a Roman infantryman, 200 for an Italian ally, and 100 for a slave.[2] This scale is incidentally a warning against using ransoms as equivalent to slave prices; a free captive (or his relatives) could be expected to pay substantially more (according to his status) for his freedom than his commercial value. The figure for slaves is presumably roughly the current market price. In silver content 100 quadrigati were equivalent to about 150 Athenian drachmae, so that the price is low even by Athenian standards. In the eastern Mediterranean we have the Delphic manumission records for the last two centuries B.C. Here, out of about 700 prices, some 58 per cent range from 3 to 4 minae and another 14 per cent up to 5. Above 5 minae (mostly 6, 8 or 10) are 12 per cent, and below 3 minae (mostly 2–2½) are 14 per cent.[3] These figures represent select slaves of good quality, who alone would be likely to earn their manumission, the overwhelming majority adults. It is not improbable also that manumission prices were higher than the market rate; for masters were in a strong bargaining position and slaves might have been willing to pay more for their freedom than they would fetch on the open market. Taking these

---

[1] *IG*, I², 373–4. See p. 190, n. 1 *supra*.   [2] Livy, xxii, 52 and 58.
[3] A. Calderini, *La manomissione e la condizione dei liberti in Grecia* (Milan, 1908), p. 214.

factors into account, the figures suggest a range of slave prices not dissimilar from that prevailing at Athens in the fourth century B.C. where skilled adults cost 3 to 5 minae.

As at Athens in the fifth and fourth centuries B.C. servile labour was employed on a large scale in the mines: Polybius records that in his day 40,000 worked in the great silver mines near Carthagena in Spain.[1] According to Diodorus, who draws his information from a contemporary source, Posidonius, the slaves were ruthlessly driven, and only the hardiest lived long.[2] This implies that the supply was abundant and very cheap. There were however limits beyond which the employment of slave labour became unprofitable. Strabo tells us of a realgar mine in Paphlagonia where the mortality among the workers was so high, owing to the poisonous atmosphere, that the contractors, although they used the dregs of the slave market (slaves sold off because of their crimes), often abandoned their operations.[3]

The novelty of this period is the extension of slave labour in a big way to agriculture. The reasons for this are well known. The Roman aristocracy, both senatorial and equestrian, were acquiring vast money fortunes from the exploitation of the empire, and investing them in land. The peasant proprietors of Italy were hard hit by long term military service, and were compelled to sell their plots. Great estates thus grew up at the expense of small holdings, and as slaves were very cheap, the owners used them in preference to free labour. It is impossible to estimate how far the process went. The peasant proprietor was certainly never eliminated in Italy, but the reduction in their numbers was sufficiently serious to alarm the more thoughtful members of the aristocracy. The succession of agrarian laws, begun by Tiberius Gracchus, did something to check the process, but the great servile revolt under Spartacus shows that agricultural slaves must still have been very numerous in Italy in the 70's.

Cato's and Varro's treatises on agriculture imply that landlords used slave labour for all types of farming, for arable, vineyards, oliveyards and cattle ranches alike, but that they also hired labour for the peak periods, the harvest, the vintage and the olive-picking:[4] Varro also recommends the use of hired labour on unhealthy farms.[5] It appears then that the maintenance of a slave was a sufficiently serious item in the landlord's budget to make him keep a small permanent staff only, and that the cost of a slave was high enough to make frequent replacements uneconomic. Not all great landlords cultivated their estates with slave labour: in the Civil War Domitius manned six ships with his shepherds, who were slaves, and with his free tenants (coloni).[6] There seems to have been a considerable landless rural population, presumably dispossessed peasants, who continued to make a living as hired labourers, mainly in the harvest and vintage season. Tiberius Gracchus was able to command an overwhelming majority of voters when he proposed his land distribution bill in the winter, but, we are told, when he stood for re-election in the summer and tried to call on the rural voters, they did not respond, being busy with the harvest, and he was defeated.[7] It was from this class that the armies of the late Republic

---

[1] Cited by Strabo, III, 147. [2] Diodorus, v, 36.
[3] Strabo, XII, 562.
 See W. E. Heitland, Agricola (Cambridge, 1921), pp. 164 et seq., 178 et seq.
[5] Varro, de re rustica, I, 17.
[6] Caesar, de bello civili, I, 34 and 56. Varro (op. cit. I, 2, 17; II, 3, 7) also alludes casually to tenancy agreements. [7] Appian, Civil Wars, I, 14, 2–3.

must have been largely recruited, particularly after Marius introduced voluntary enlistment and waived the minimum property qualification for service.[1]

The wars of Augustus in Spain, Germany, the Alpine areas and Illyricum and Pannonia put large numbers of prisoners on the slave market, but with the cessation of great wars of conquest after his death this source of slaves dried up. From the beginning of the Principate the establishment of law and order within the empire cut off the other main source of supply, piracy and brigandage. Most slaves must have been bred during this period. This proposition is not susceptible of proof, but there are some indications in its favour. Of the slaves whose provenance is known the great majority come from within the empire, usually from the same area in which they lived, and few from beyond the frontiers.[2] The law took an increasing interest in the offspring of slaves. By the *senatusconsultum Claudianum* of A.D. 52, if a free woman cohabited with a slave, his owner was empowered to claim her (and her subsequent offspring) as his slave.[3] The legal position of infants who were exposed and brought up as slaves became an important issue: Trajan upheld the old principle that their free status was unprejudiced, but other emperors ruled that the parents could not reclaim them or could do so only if they repaid the cost of their upbringing.[4] In the *familia Caesaris*, the great body of imperial slaves and freedmen who filled the lower grades of the bureaucracy, hereditary service seems to have been the normal rule. Countless tombstones record freedmen of Augustus whose sons are also freedmen of Augustus, and must have been born in servitude. The emperor apparently did not free his slaves until they had produced slave sons to succeed them in the service.[5]

Home bred slaves must in the nature of things be rather expensive articles. The master has to allow his slave enough to keep his wife, who may be economically superfluous, and his children, who will be of little use until they reach their 'teens, and many of whom, under ancient conditions, will have died before reaching working age. Cato's ideal olive farm and vineyard were manned by twelve and sixteen male workers respectively, of whom only one, the bailiff, was allowed a wife.[6] The food and clothing bill would have been doubled or trebled, and no more work done, if he had allowed all his hands to keep a family to maintain the human stock of the farm.

In these circumstances one could *a priori* expect slaves to become scarce and dear. The recorded prices of slaves are in fact high. In Dacia in the middle of the second century a girl of six fetched 205 denarii, a woman (a Cretan) 420, and a man (a Greek) 600.[7] At the same period a boy of seven (from beyond the Euphrates) was sold at Seleucia of Syria for 200, a girl of twelve (a Phrygian) at Side of Pamphylia for 350 and an adult woman (from Marmarica) at Ravenna for 625 denarii.[8] The literary allusions are consistent with the documents. Petronius[9] speaks of 300 denarii as a bargain price for a sharp-witted Jewish boy, Horace[10] quotes 500 drachmae as a typical price for an ordinary

---

[1] Cf. Appian, *op. cit.* i, 29, 4; Sallust, *Jugurtha*, 73, 6.

[2] M. Bang in *Mitteilungen des kaiserlichen deutschen archaeologischen Instituts, Römische Abteilung*, XXV (1910), 223–55.

[3] Tacitus, *Annals*, XII, 53.

[4] Pliny, *Ep[istulae]*, x, 65–6.   [5] *Journal of Roman Studies*, XXXIX (1949), 43.

[6] Cato, *de re rustica*, 10, 11, cf. Varro, *de re rustica*, i, 18.

[7] S. Riccobono, *F[ontes] I[uris] R[omani ante Justiniani]²* (Florence, 1943), III, 87, 89, 88.

[8] *Op. cit.* III, 132–4.   [9] *Satyricon*, 68.

[10] *Satires*, II, vii, 43. At this date denarius and drachma are equivalent, except in Egypt where four Alexandrian drachmae were equal to one denarius.

B

slave of poor quality, and Martial[1] records a bid (refused) of 600 denarii for a prostitute. This is a consistent range of prices, which prevails throughout the empire with one exception, Egypt. Here we find one comparable price, a home born youth of seventeen sold at Alexandria in A.D. 154 for 2,800 local drachmae (=700 denarii).[2] The other prices (eight adults) range from 1,500 to 1,000 drachmae (=375–250 denarii).[3] The export of home born slaves from Egypt was prohibited by the Roman government[4] and the local demand was low—almost only for domestic service. Egypt was thus, in this as in many other things, economically segregated from the rest of the empire, and followed its own rules.

The range of prices from the rest of the empire indicate that 500 to 600 was a normal price for an unskilled adult. In fact we know that much larger sums were paid for skilled men: Horace[5] quotes 2,000 denarii for a handsome boy, educated in Greek, and Columella,[6] writing under Nero, recommends paying the same sum for a trained vinedresser. The figure of 500 to 600 denarii is then comparable with the 125 to 150 drachmae paid for an unskilled slave at Athens. In silver content 600 denarii are equivalent to 450 drachmae, so that the Roman price reckoned in silver is about three times the Athenian. But the purchasing power of the denarius was much higher than that of the drachma. Wheat at Athens was cheap at 5 drachmae to the medimnus,[7] in the Roman empire at 2 sesterces to the modius:[8] that is 5 drachmae would buy the same quantity as 3 denarii. The minimum ration allowance allowed by Demosthenes for his proposed standing away was 2 obols a day or 120 drachmae a year. A Roman soldier had 60 denarii a year deducted from his pay for rations.[9] On this basis a slave in the second century cost eight to ten times his annual keep as against a year or a year and a quarter's keep in fourth-century Athens.

V

Columella, writing a handbook for the gentleman farmer under Nero, still recommends the use of slaves in the home farm, but advises letting outlying properties to free tenants, especially if they are arable.[10] For vineyards he appears to assume that slave labour will be used, expensive though it is.[11] Pliny, a generation later, often speaks of his troubles with his tenants: they demand remissions of rent, but nevertheless fall into arrears, he thinks of letting his farms on a share of the crop instead of a fixed money rent, he has difficulty in finding suitable tenants.[12] He never speaks of slaves, and says in fact that he nowhere used chained slaves.[13] As, however, he sold the crops of his vineyards to contractors[14] he must have cultivated these by direct labour, which probably means slaves. The third-century lawyers reveal a similar mixture:

[1] vi, 66, 9.   [2] *Journal of Egyptian Archaeology*, XVII (1931), 4.
[3] *Aegyptische Urkunden aus den staatlichen Museum zu Berlin, Griechische Urkunden* (= *BGU*), III, 805; IV, 1114, 1128. *Oxyrhynchus Papyri* (= *P. Oxy.*), 95. *Aegyptus*, XIII (1933), 230. *Griechische Papyrusurkunden der Hamburger Staats- und Universitätsbibliothek*, 63. *Sammelbuch Griechische Urkunden aus Aegypten*, 6016. *P. Col. inv.* 512 (unpublished, cited by W. L. Westermann. *The Slave Systems of Greek and Roman Antiquity* (Philadelphia, 1955), p. 101, n. 116).
[4] *BGU*, v, 65–7, 69.   [5] *Epodes*, II, ii, 5.
[6] *Ibid.* III, 3, 6.   [7] Dem. XXXIV, 39.   [8] *Econ. Hist. Rev.* v (1953), 295.
[9] H. M. D. Parker, *The Roman Legions* (Oxford, 1928), p. 217.
[10] Columella, I, 7, 8.   [11] *Idem*, III, 3, 6.
[12] Pliny, *Ep.* III, 19; VII, 30; IX, 37; X, 8; cf. IX, 36.
[13] *Ibid.* VII, 19.   [14] *Ibid.* VIII, 2; cf. IX, 20.

the bequest of an estate might include agricultural slaves,[1] and also the arrears of free tenants.[2] They also show that the slaves commonly had families.[3] One gains the general impression that slaves were used on the home farm attached to a residential villa and for more highly skilled jobs, like vinedressing, but that ordinary arable farming was left to free tenants: and, moreover, that agricultural slaves were normally bred.

This evidence applies mainly to Italy. For the provinces our evidence is very scanty save for two areas, Egypt and Africa. In Egypt, where agricultural slavery had never existed, the land continued to be cultivated by free peasants as tenants either of the state, the temples, or private landlords. In Africa we know from literary and legal sources of private landlords who owned agricultural slaves,[4] but a series of inscriptions reveal that on the great imperial estates the head tenants (conductores) sublet most of the land in small lots to free working tenants (coloni). They must have kept some land in hand, no doubt cultivating it with slaves, for the coloni, in addition to their rent—a share, normally a third, of the crop—owed labour services—six to twelve days a year at the three peak periods of ploughing, hoeing and harvest.[5]

There is a change in mining also. Some mines and quarries were worked by convict labour: it is significant that damnatio ad metallum under the Principate becomes a common alternative to the death penalty, especially for the lower classes.[6] But free labour was also employed. We possess a number of second-century indentures in which free men leased their labour for six months or a year in the Dacian gold mines: in the only specimen where all the relevant figures are preserved the rate of pay is 70 denarii plus food for six months.[7] This is equivalent to 200 denarii a year, or two-thirds of what a private in the army received at that period. In the Lex Metalli Vipascensis of Hadrianic date the mines are no longer leased as a whole to contractors (conductores) who employ large gangs of slaves, but individual shafts are let or sold by the resident imperial agent (procurator) to tenants (coloni) who appear to be working miners, often grouped in partnerships, sometimes employing slave or hired labour.[8]

On the other hand slaves seem to have been extensively used in commerce and industry, in Italy at any rate. This is implied by the elaborate rules which were evolved to define the legal responsibility of owners for their slaves' commercial transactions. The law held the owner, unless he expressly and publicly disclaimed responsibility, liable in full for the debts and contracts of his institor, the slave whom he put in charge of a shop or business.[9] If the owner had disclaimed responsibility, creditors had two alternative remedies, the actio peculii and the actio tributoria.[10] Under the former they could recover from the slave's peculium, the sum which was by his master's consent under his control; but the master in this case had a prior claim to recover debts owing to himself by his slave. Under the latter, all creditors, including the owner, could recover in proportion to their claims from the merces peculiaris, the stock of the business

---

[1] Dig. xxxiii, vii, 3, § 1; 8; 12, §§ 2–9, 35, 37, 46; 18, §§ 6–7, 11, 13; 19; 20, §§ 3, 5–6, 9, etc.
[2] Ibid. xxxii, 78, § 3; 91, pr. §1; 97; 101, § 1; xxxiii, ii, 32, § 7; vii, 20, pr. §§ 1, 3; 27, § 1.
[3] Ibid. xxxiii, vii, 12, §§ 7, 33. Trimalchio is represented as breeding slaves on a vast scale on his estates (Petronius, Satyricon, 53).
[4] Apuleius, Apologia, 93 (400 slaves, most probably agricultural, being associated with lands, crops and stocks), cf. 17 and 47 for allusions to agricultural slaves; Herodian, vii, iv, 3; Dig. xxxiii, vii, 27, § 1.   [5] FIR, i, 100–3.
[6] This penalty is first recorded under Trajan (Pliny, Ep. x, 58) and Hadrian (Pomponius in Dig. xl, iv, 46).
[7] FIR, iii, 150.   [8] FIR, i, 104.   [9] Dig. xiv, iii.   [10] Dig. xiv, iv.

which the slave carried on, which might be less than the *peculium*, as it did not include the slave's personal assets.

It cannot be necessarily deduced from these legal rules that the conditions for which they provided were widespread, but their evidence is supported, for Italy and to a lesser extent for southern Gaul and Spain, by that of the inscriptions, which show a very large number of freedmen engaged in industry and trade. Some of these freedmen were former domestic slaves, who learned a craft or opened a shop after manumission in order to support themselves,[1] but it seems likely that the majority of them started as slave *institores*, and purchased their *merces peculiaris* together with their freedom. It must, however, be stressed that the evidence which we possess is geographically limited. In Egypt, where our knowledge, thanks to the papyri, is fullest, industrial slavery is almost unknown. In general we find only free independent craftsmen, apart from one allusion to free hired labour in the weaving industry.[2] Elsewhere in the East evidence is scanty, but we know that at Tarsus, a great centre of the linen industry, the weavers were free men, too poor indeed to afford the 500 drachmae fee required for inscription on the local citizen register, but according to Dio Chrysostom[3] otherwise worthy of the citizenship.

It would seem that under the Principate the price of slaves was too high to allow their employment in unskilled labour, but that it was now relatively more profitable to use them in skilled jobs, in agriculture, for instance, as vinedressers, and as craftsmen in industry and agents in trade. This development would have been helped by the growing practice of breeding slaves; for the son of a skilled slave could be early apprenticed to his trade. It may reasonably be doubted whether the employment of slave labour, even in skilled work, was very profitable at this period, and its prevalence in Italy and the neighbouring provinces may be due to special causes. In these areas resided the great majority of Roman senators and *equites*, who filled the lucrative administrative and military posts throughout the empire. There was thus a continuous and considerable inflow of money, in the form of salaries and of less legal perquisites, into Italy, southern Gaul and Spain, and this money sought investment. It went mostly into land, but the amount of land was limited, and prices rose to exorbitant heights. Almost the only alternative investment was slaves, and even if they were not a very profitable investment they brought in something.

From the third century onwards public security deteriorated. In many parts of the empire brigandage became rife; the Isaurians, for instance, continually raided eastern Asia Minor and northern Syria. Constant border warfare brought in its crop of barbarian prisoners, and barbarian invaders carried off thousands of Roman citizens, whom they had sold back to the empire as slaves. Such persons could reclaim their freedom if they could repay their purchasers the price that they had paid for them, but for many this must have been impossible and they remained slaves. Nevertheless the demand for slaves still exceeded the supply, especially at a great centre of consumption like Rome. Symmachus, an immensely wealthy senator, went to the trouble of asking the praetorian prefect of Italy, then resident on the Danube, to buy him twenty slaves for use as stable boys, 'because on the frontier it is easy to find slaves and the price is usually tolerable'.[4] Slaves were normally bred, and there seems to have been a heavy demand for foundlings and for newborn babies (*sanguino-*

---

[1] *Dig.* xxxviii, i, 16.
[2] *P. Oxy.* 1414.
[3] xxxiv, 21–3.
[4] Symmachus, *Epistulae*, ii, 78.

lenti) sold by their parents. This practice was by now legal,[1] and the sale of older children though illegal was widespread.[2]

In these circumstances slave prices might have been expected to fall somewhat from the high level prevailing in the second century A.D., and in fact they seem to have done so. In a schedule of prices, which Justinian laid down for the compensation payable to the joint owners of a slave whom one of the partners had manumitted, a child (up to ten) is valued at 10 solidi, an unskilled adult (male or female over ten) at 20 solidi, and a skilled man or woman at 30: substantially higher prices are assigned to eunuchs and to specialists such as notaries and doctors.[3] This schedule seems from the meagre evidence available to have been realistic. A Gallic boy of fourteen was sold at Ascalon in 359 for 18 solidi.[4] Palladius[5] tells a story of a man who sold himself for 20 solidi, and Leontius[6] of another who fetched as much as 30 in a similar transaction. As against this high price S. Remigius records in his will that he bought a man for only 14 solidi 'to prevent his being killed'.[7] A Visigothic Law[8] provides an interesting commentary on the price of 10 solidi at which Justinian assessed children under ten, and on the cost of breeding slaves. Parents were entitled to recover children whom they had exposed or sold as infants on payment of one solidus for each year of the child's age up to a maximum of ten. This, it is explained, was to cover his maintenance while he was not yet productive; after ten he was deemed to earn his keep by his work. Slave breeders had to reckon with heavy mortality, both during the first ten years and later, so that the commercial price of 20 solidi for any slave over ten was not so excessive as it might seem. But the wide margin between the cost of breeding slaves and their market price suggests that they had a rarity value. The standard price for an unskilled adult, 20 solidi, was equivalent in gold value to a little over 300 denarii, and four or five times the contemporary ration allowance (*annona*) of a soldier.[9] Slave prices had thus dropped to about half in real value of what they were in the peaceful days of the second century A.D., but were still four or five times as high as in Athens of the fourth century B.C.

In the mines slavery seems by the fourth century to have been extinct; some convict labour was still employed, notably Christian recusants in the Great Persecution,[10] but *metallarii* in the codes are assumed to be free men. In agriculture the codes show that slaves still existed side by side with free tenants. In industry the state weaving mills and dyeworks were manned by public slaves:[11] so also were the mints[12] and the imperial transport service, the *cursus publicus*.[13] In private industry on the other hand slaves seem to have been rare. We hear of one man of means, Thalassius of Antioch, who owned a slave-manned knife factory, precisely like Demosthenes, as Libanius pointed out,[14] and of

---

[1] *Fragmenta Vaticana*, 34, *Cod. Theod.* V, x, 1.
[2] *Cod. Theod.* III, iii, 1; XI, xxvii, 2; Val[entinian], *Nov*[ella], xxxiii; cf. Rufinus. *Historia Monachorum*, 16; Zosimus, II, 38; Lib. *Or.* XLVI, 23; Cassiodorus, *Variae*, VIII, 33.
[3] *Cod*[ex] *Just*[inianus], VII, vii, 1.   [4] *FIR*, III, 135.
[5] *Lausiac History*, 83.
[6] *Life of John the Almoner*, 22. The compensation payable for the murder of an unskilled slave (a ploughman or swineherd) is also 30 solidi in the *Lex Romana Burgundiorum*, ii, 6 (*M*[*onumenta*] *G*[*ermaniae*] *H*[*istorica*], *Legum Sectio* I, II, 127), but here a penal element may enter into the price.
[7] *MGH, Scriptores rerum Merovingicarum* III, 339.
[8] *Lex Visigothorum*, IV, iv, 3 (*MGH, Legum Sectio* I, I, 194).
[9] Val. *Nov.* xiii, 3; *Cod. Just.* I, xxvii, i, §§ 22–38.
[10] Eusebius, *Ecclesiastical History*, VIII, 12, etc.   [11] *Cod. Theod.* x, xx, 2, 3, 5, 7, 9.
[12] *Ibid.* x, xx, 10.   [13] *Ibid.* VIII, v, 58.   [14] Lib. *Or.* XLII, 21.

humble persons in the province of Moesia, who though landless might qualify for the decurionate by their wealth in slaves.[1] In general, however, industry was carried on by free craftsmen of humble status grouped in guilds.[2]

What is abundantly clear from the sources is that slavery on the land and in the state industries was hereditary. The laws are much concerned with regulating the tangles which resulted from intermarriage between such slaves and free persons.[3] In the Diocletianic persecution some Christians were as a penalty enslaved and drafted into the state weaving mills,[4] but apart from this there is no hint that the government ever thought of adding to its hereditary stock. Landlords might sometimes restock a derelict farm with slaves,[5] but this was exceptional; indeed the prefect of the city once persuaded the Roman senators to contribute to famine relief by pointing out how disastrous it would be if they were forced to buy slaves to replace their starving peasants.[6] It would seem that on some estates a hereditary servile population had been established: we hear of agricultural slavery mainly in Italy,[7] and some western provinces,[8] where it was no doubt a survival from the conditions of the late Republic and early Principate. The state similarly was able to maintain its slave establishments by breeding. In private industry there was not the same continuity of ownership and the units were too small for hereditary groups to be established.

VI

During this period the social and legal status of slaves and free persons both on the land and in the state industries tended to be assimilated. On the one hand owing to the acute shortage of manpower the government tended to 'freeze' workers in essential occupations, together with their children.[9] On the other hand slaves in the hereditary groups were allowed to hold property, and bequeath it to their children. In the state industries it is difficult to find other than technical differences between the *fabricenses* or arms manufacturers, who were legally soldiers, and the workers in the mints, weaving mills and dyeworks, who were legally slaves. Both were bound with their children to their trades; *fabricenses* were branded to facilitate their detection if they escaped. Both could hold and bequeath property.[10] In agriculture the free tenant was tied with his children to his plot of land from the reign of Diocletian, and later legislation forbade him to alienate his private property without his landlord's consent,[11] and deprived him of his right to bring civil actions against his landlord.[12] Valentinian I prohibited the sale of agricultural slaves apart from the land

---

[1] *Cod. Theod.* xii, i, 96.

[2] See my article, 'The economic life of the towns of the Roman Empire', *Recueils de la Société Jean Bodin*, vii (1955), 177 *et seq.*

[3] For the state industries see *Cod. Theod.* x, xx, 3, 5, 10, 15, 17 for mixed marriages and also viii, v, 58 and x, xx, 16 for wives and children. For agricultural slaves see Val. *Nov.* xxxi,6; *Cod. Just.* xi, xlviii, 21 for mixed marriages; cf. *Cod. Theod.* ii, xxv, 1; *Cod. Just.* xi, xlviii, 7, lxviii, 3 and 4 for families.

[4] Eusebius *Vita Constantini*, ii, 34.   [5] *Cod. Theod.* v, xiii, 4.

[6] Ambrose, *de officiis*, iii, 47.

[7] *Vita Melaniae Junioris*, 10 and 18 (*Analecta Bollandiana*, viii (1889), 27, 33, xxii (1903), 13); letter of Pope Pelagius in P. Jaffé, *Regesta Pontificum Romanorum*[2] (Leipzig, 1885), i, 127, no. 956 (656).

[8] E.g. Orosius, vii, 40 for Spain, and *Lex Gundobada*, 54 (*MGH, Legum Sectio* I, ii, 88) for Gaul.

[9] See my *Ancient Economic History* (1948), pp. 12 *et seq.*

[10] On the *fabricenses* see *Cod. Theod.* x, xxii, on the other groups, *ibid.* x, xx.

[11] *Cod. Theod.* v, xix, 1.   [12] *Cod. Just.* xi, l, 2.

which they cultivated.[1] They possessed their *peculia* or private property, which they could not alienate but which normally passed to their children.[2] Slave and free peasants intermarried freely, and the only practical distinction between them was that the status of their children followed different rules in mixed marriages.

If one may draw any general conclusions from this rather inadequate evidence, it would appear that gang slavery in its crudest form, the use of bought slaves for unskilled labour, flourished only in rather exceptional circumstances, when, owing to the prevalence of wars and piracy, prices stood at a rock bottom level, and then only in work in which they could be continuously employed. In these circumstances slaves tended to replace free labour. At Athens there is no evidence that this caused unemployment among the free population, or that it reduced wages in occupations, such as building, where slave and free unskilled labour were employed concurrently. In Italy, under the late Republic, on the other hand, peasants were thrown out of work by the increasing use of agricultural slaves. In the settled conditions of the Principate gang slavery tended to die out and did not revive in the later empire despite growing insecurity and a consequent fall in the price of slaves. Where agricultural slavery survived it was a heritage of the past, and the social and economic position of slaves on the land had become indistinguishable from that of free persons.

In skilled industrial employment, where the capital value of a slave depended less on his initial price and more on the cost of training him, the use of slaves did not vary so much according to the state of the slave market. In this sphere the profits of the master were not so great, both because of the relatively high capital value of trained slaves, and because it was generally found advisable to give such slaves economic incentives which brought their condition close to that of the free craftsman. As a result slaves do not seem to have competed with free persons by cutting prices. In skilled employments also the use of servile labour seems to become rare in the later empire, except in the large state factories, where the slaves were a hereditary class scarcely distinguishable from free persons.

Jesus College, Cambridge

---

[1] *Ibid.* xi, xlviii, 7. This rule was revoked in Italy by Theoderic (*Edictum*, 142).

[2] Letters of Pope Gelasius (fr. 28 in A. Thiel, *Epistolae Romanorum Pontificum genuinae* (Brunsberg, 1867) and of Pope Pelagius (Migne, *Patrologia Latina*, lxix, 418)) mention apparently substantial *peculia* of agricultural slaves of the Roman Church. One had the temerity to make a will; this was disregarded by the Pope, who, however, allowed his property to pass to his sons.

II

SLAVERY AND THE ELEMENTS OF FREEDOM
IN ANCIENT GREECE

By WILLIAM LINN WESTERMANN

It is a privilege to be permitted to present before this distinguished audience the following problem which has long and deeply enlisted my interest and attention. Of what type was the Greek institution of slavery? What were the characteristics peculiar to it which induced Alfred Zimmern, many years ago, to write an article which posed this question as its title: "Was Greek Civilization Based on Slave Labor?" [1] Zimmern deserves great credit for having raised the problem in this new form as to how slavery presented itself to the inhabitants of the Greek city-states of the Mediterranean area. His argument is that Greek civilization did not display those conditions "which are the natural result of a system of slave labour." [2] The specific conditions which underlie slavery, or develop from it, as he gives them, are taken directly from J. E. Cairnes's book upon "Slave Power." [3] It must be understood that Cairnes restricts slavery as an economic institution to one form, one structure, with unvarying characteristics and a fixed set of requirements necessary for its continuation. This he did despite the fact that he knew, and specifically asserted, that ancient slavery is not to be compared with modern Negro slavery, which was the especial field of his observations.

Out of his observations of American Negro slavery as social and economic organism Cairnes abstracted a list of tendencies which, he claimed, were typical of slave societies. The slave system of any locality is, however, invariably an inextricable part of, and an expression of, that culture within which it exists. In its own degree it helps to determine the cultural coloration of its time and place; but to a far greater extent it tends to reflect the general features of the total culture. The differences which the slave institution may develop in any two contemporary and neighboring slave states may be

---

[1] First printed in *The Sociological Review* II (1909), pp. 1-19, 159-176. It was reprinted, without significant change, in his book of essays entitled *Solon and Croesus*, London, 1928.

[2] Zimmern, *Solon and Croesus*, p. 119.

[3] J. E. Cairnes, *The Slave Power*, 3d edition, New York, 1863. The conditions which must result from slavery are stated by Zimmern, *op. cit.* pp. 110-113. The ones selected are to be found in Cairnes, *op. cit.*, pp. 39-40, 50-55, 60, 76 *et passim*.

so great that, as systems, they are morphologically incomparable and their social impacts and results completely different. In antiquity, for example, the differences between contemporary forms of enslavement appear conspicuously in the slave situations as known to us at Athens in its "classical" period of the fifth and fourth centuries B.C. and in the Cretan town of Gortyn at the same time.[1]

Having taken the "typical" conditions set up by Cairnes as requirements in a true slave state, and not finding these in the Greek world, Zimmern concluded that Greek society was not a slave society.[2] Yet there is no doubt in his mind that the Greeks kept slaves.[3] He attempts to get himself out of this contradiction by a process of re-defining enslavement under two forms, chattel slavery and apprentice slavery. The chattel slave he regards as a possession, something owned, which itself cannot own. As soon as a slave is permitted to own property or make a contract, says Zimmern, he is no longer a chattel. He becomes a human being; and as such he has escaped from bondage.

There has seldom been in history, I should say, any slave-holding community in which the theoretical slave—that is, a thing totally devoid of legal personality and without possessions of his own—has really existed in the actual practise of that community. Only in the confinement of prisons can men be totally deprived of all their freedoms, and hence totally enslaved. This inability to coerce human beings into a situation of total slave subjection produces a fundamental contradiction inherent in the very structure of the institution of slavery. It was this inescapable contradiction which compelled Aristotle to acknowledge that a dichotomy existed between the freedom of man in nature and the enslavement of man in law.

Zimmern is to be credited with calling attention to the fact that the slaves of the Greeks lived close to the border of that wide space which exists between slavery and freedom. His phrase "apprentice

---

[1] These are the two systems best known to us from Greece of the fifth and fourth centuries B.C. For the type of slavery existing in the Dorian community of Gortyn see Augustus C. Merriam's translation of the Code of Gortyn, with explanatory notes, in *American Journal of Archaeology* I (1885) pp. 325-350 and the text, translation and commentary upon this code by Josef Kohler and Erich Ziebarth, *Das Stadtrecht von Gortyn*, Göttingen, 1912. The commentary by Franz Bücheler and Ernst Zitelmann in *Rheinisches Museum* XL (1885), *Das Recht von Gortyn*, is less satisfactory.

[2] Zimmern, *Solon and Croesus*, pp. 119, 161.

[3] *Ibid.*, p. 119.

2

slavery"[1] is unfortunately chosen. The idea probably came to him from his observation of the Abolition Act as applied in the British colonies in the West Indies beginning August 1, 1834. This provided for an actual change of status of the negro slaves of the West Indies from slavery into apprenticeship and out of apprenticeship into the status of free men.[2] By coining the phrase "apprentice slavery" Zimmern provided himself with an escape from the dilemma of a non-slave society which kept slaves; but the avenue of escape leads the reader into a state of mental confusion where two totally incompatible things are merged. Apprenticeship is a method of teaching some manual dexterity or mental skill by the age old process of imitation, instruction and directed practise. Apprentice status is always contractual, whether by an indenture or verbal agreement. Slavery is a status in which the enslaved can make no contract for himself.[3]

The dominant form of Greek city-state slavery was non-praedial, meaning that it was not agricultural slavery either of the plantation or of the ranch type. Its foremost characteristic was its extensive use in the handicrafts. The practical results of this fact were simple ones. The skilled workmen in the industrial city-states, because of the type of the urban residences of the time, lived apart from their masters. This is a matter of deduction from archaeological observations. There are, it is true, but few Greek city-states of the fifth or fourth centuries which have been preserved for excavation. In the best example of such cities known to us the houses, even those of the well-to-do town residents, furnished rooms for "no more than three slaves—household servants:"[4] No example of slave barracks has, to my knowledge, been found in any of the older Greek cities so far excavated; and there is no mention known to me in Greek literature of any barracks for those slaves who were held in private ownership.

---

[1] *Ibid.*, pp. 120-121. It is clear from the fifth edition of his excellent study called the *Greek Commonwealth*, Oxford, 1931, pp. 393-396 and the notes, that Zimmern had moved forward toward a clearer understanding both of the theory and of the practise of Greek slavery between the time when he first presented the problem of Greek slavery and the republishing of his book.

[2] W. L. Burn, *Emancipation and Apprenticeship in the British West Indies*, London, 1937. For the terms of the bill of emancipation and the discussion of it see pages 118-120.

[3] It should be said here for the British abolitionist law makers that they did not employ the self-contradicting term "apprentice slavery."

[4] Sterling Dow in his review of D. M. Robinson and J. Walter Graham, *Excavations at Olynthus*, Part VIII. The review appeared in the *Am. Historical Review* XLIV (1939) p. 581.

3

The Greek phrase applied to these workers who lived away from their masters was χωρὶς οἰκοῦντες.[1] This is to be understood in its simple and most literal meaning. They "lived apart" from their owners, that is to say, in other residences.

Another descriptive phrase applied to these workmen was μισθοφοροῦντα σώματα, "pay-bringers" if one is to be literal. Living where they could these were the fellows who frequented the Anakeion, the temple of the Dioscuri on the north side of the Acropolis, as their special hangout.[2] The degree of supervision and control to which these unfree workmen would be submitted would vary with the individual slave owner. Since these "pay earners" were incapable of letting out their own services under a legally binding contract, this must always have been done by the owner. There is some reason to believe, however, that the degree of freedom granted the unfree "pay-earners" in the search for work and in their conduct of their jobs was very large.

Highly instructive for the kind of life followed by these slaves is a single brief paragraph about an Athenian politician named Timarchus. It is his slaves which interest us, not his political or personal morality, both of which have been griveously befouled by the orator Aeschines.[3] Timarchus inherited, along with a house south of the Acropolis and a plot of land at Alopeke, eleven or twelve slaves. Nine or ten of these were "leather cutters." This may mean that all of them were shoe makers. At any rate, Timarchus leased their craft skill to a single shop owner who paid him three obols per day for their use as a group. Each of these craftsmen slaves brought to Timarchus a return of two obols per day out of their wages. The rest of what they earned was their own.[4]

---

[1] The manumitted slaves whose place of residence is recorded in the φιάλαι ἐλευθερικαί inscriptions of I G II, 2, 1, nos. 1553-1578 lived in different demes of Attica.. Xenophon in the pamphlet on The Revenues IV 49-50 expected that a populated city, with valuable building lots, would arise around the silver mines where his thousands of state owned slaves would live. He has no thought of concentration came or barrack's life.

[2] Immanuel Bekker, Anecdota Graeca I (Berlin 1814) 212, 12, s. v. 'Ανακεῖον: Διοσκούρων ἱερὸν, οὗ νῦν οἱ μισθοφοροῦντες δοῦλοι ἑστᾶσιν.

[3] Timarchus prosecuted Aeschines for treason while on an embassy to Philip II of Macedon. See Demosthenes or. XIX, On the Embassy, hypothesis 2, 10. For Aeschines' lowest aspersions upon the moral character of Timarchus, see his or. I, Against Timarchus, 47-57.

[4] Aeschines, ibid., 97. The technical terms for this is ἕκαστος - - - - ἀποφορὰν ἔφερει. ἀποφορά is regularly employed; and it is legally exact in the sense that the slaves did not "pay" him. That verb would be ἀποδιδοῦναι. They merely "brought away" for him (ἀποφέρειν) so much income per day.

4

Two more highly specialized workers belonging to Timarchus remain to be considered. One of these was a woman slave "skilled in working Amorgos cloth," who carried into the market the fine products of her loom.[1] It is not possible to determine who furnished this skilled craft worker with her raw materials. Probably she bought the goods herself. Certainly she wove the cloths and sold them in the market. The chances are that she sold them to a local dealer, not to the ultimate consumers. This is the best deduction from the phrase, "she carried them into the market." The second of these two slaves was a male, an embroiderer. Nothing is said about his work.

This entire group of "pay bringers" has been made to live and move before our minds by a group of shattered inscriptions long known and much disputed as to some of their meanings. These seem to present lists recording the offerings of silver bowls dedicated to the god in accordance with a law which was passed at Athens, apparently before the death of Lycurgus in 323 B.C.[2] Three classes of Attic residents appear in these lists. The slaves are distinguished by having no father's name given. They are recorded as living in a certain town or deme.[3] The second class is that of the metics, or resident aliens. Their distinguishing mark in these lists is that they invariably are said to be from a certain deme, "from Ceramicus" or "living in Ciriadae,"[4] which, again, indicates the actual location of their domiciles.[5] Sometimes their patronymics are given, sometimes not. The third class comprises the Athenian citizens, always distinguishable by their deme registration. This would, in some cases, also indicate their places of residence, but not always, because the Athenian citizen inherited his deme connection and retained it throughout his life no matter where his residence might be. For my purpose of proving cases where slaves lived elsewhere than their owners, the citizen slave owners cannot be decisive. For

---

[1] *Ibid.* 97, ἔτι δὲ πρὸς τούτοις γυναῖκα ἀμόργινα ἐπισταμένην ἐργάζεσθαι καὶ ἔργα λεπτὰ εἰς τὴν ἀγορὰν ἐκφέρουσαν.

[2] I G II¹ 1553-1578. Fragments of the law itself seem to be preserved at the beginning of no. 1560 according to A. Wilhelm in *Sitzungsberichte der Wiener Akademie, Phil.-hist. Klasse,* vol. 165 (1911). *Abhandlung* VI p. 9.

[3] E. g. I G II 2¹, 1553, 18-19: Πλίννα ἐμ Πειραί(ωι) οἰκοῦσα.

[4] In the latter case the phrasing is the same as that for the slaves. I G II, 2¹, 1567, 16: Ἡγήμονα Ἡγησίππου ἐκ Κερ(αμείκου); 1576, 42-3, Σωτηρίδην ἐγ Κειριά(δαι) οἰκοῦντα.

[5] "*Heimatsbezeichnung*", Von Wilamowitz-Moellendorff in *Hermes* XXII (1887) p. 115.

this reason the cases of metic slave holders alone are used. The very fact that the demal residence of these slaves is recorded is, in itself, proof that they usually lived elsewhere than their masters. Otherwise the master's residence would suffice for both master and slave. The following examples will be enough to prove the point:[1]

(I G II, 2, 1)	Slave		Metic Owner	
	Name	Residence	Name	Residence
1553, 18-20	Plinna	Piraeus	Astynomus	Oe
1567, 15-6	Lysias	Piraeus	Hegemon	Ceramicus
1569, 3-7	Mania	Collytus	{Cerycides {Aristocles	A Theban Cydathene
1570, 85-6	Olympis	Melite	————emus	Collytus
1576, 40-3	Eutychus	Alopeke	Soterides	Ciriadae

A papyrus recently published, may here be quoted because it throws a beam of light upon the high degree of actual freedom of movement enjoyed by these slaves who lived where they desired and paid in a quantum of their earnings to their masters. It comes from Egypt and from the first century A.D.[2] Nevertheless it is, in my judgment, fairly representative of the liberties accorded to the "pay-bringers" of Athens in the fifth and fourth centuries B.C.

A young man named Nilus writes, presumably from Alexandria, to his father who lived up the river at Oxyrhynchus. At the time of writing he was hearing lectures and studying with tutors, with whom he was not satisfied. It is the method of financing his education which is so striking. He claims that he has become despondent to the point where his health has been affected; and he states the reason, somewhat cryptically. People who do not bring in any money, (he says) and do not do anything to correct that fact, ought not to mix in his affairs. Then he becomes specific: "For earlier, Heracles—may the wretch die wretchedly—was useful, bringing in some obols day by day; but now when he was imprisoned by Isidorus, as he deserved to be, he has fled and gone up the river, as I believe, to you. Understand that he is a person who will not ever hesitate to intrigue against you. For he was not ashamed to spread reports joyfully in the city about the matter in the theater and to

---

[1] The source is *Inscriptiones Graecae* II (2d ed.) 2, 1, 1553-1578.

[2] *Oxyrhynchus Papyri* XVIII, London, 1941, 2190, 37-55.

chatter lies such as a prosecutor in court would not tell, and that too when he suffered nothing that he deserved, but when he was released did everything like a free man. Nevertheless, if you do not send him (back) you will be able to turn him over to a carpenter, perhaps. For I hear that a young man makes (ποιεῖ) two drachmas a day. Or bind him to some other work at which he will earn more money, so that his pay, when collected, may be sent to us from time to time. For you know that Diogas, too, is learning his letters."

The man Heracles certainly was a slave and a typical "pay-earner." Obviously carpentry was a trade at which he had some proficiency and earning power. He had been sent away with two lads, and his earnings above his own expenses were assigned to them as a part of their support during their period of study.[1]

Two peculiarities of Greek city-state slavery distinguish it, by the looseness of its structure, from any other system of bondage known to me. The first is displayed for us most clearly in its practise at Athens.[2] It is the custom of purchase by the city-state of slaves who were employed in its bureaucratic services. This was, in itself, not unusual in antiquity. The Romans used *servi publici,* both in imperial and in municipal services, upon a wide scale.[3] But where else than in Greece will one find a purchased group of public slaves used as a police force, armed, and with powers of arresting the free? In the attempt to conceive a Negro police force in our southern states before slavery was abolished one may find a measuring rod for the immense disparities which may exist between one form of slavery and another. The second peculiarity is the existence of benefit clubs called *eranoi,* a social institution peculiar to the Greeks alone in antiquity, although it followed them in their emigrations into other lands. One of these types of club advanced money to slaves which they, in turn, used for the purchase of their

---

[1] The provision sometimes appears in the Delphic manumission documents that the freedman or freedwoman is to make maintenance payments to the manumittor, to his wife or to his children during the fixed term of his obligatory services, called the *paramone.* See the monthly payments in kind (wheat and wine)* in Collitz-Baunack, *Sammlung der griech. Dialekt-Inschriften* II, no. 1884, 12-14. Compare also *ibid.* 1731, 8; 1884, 10-12; and the manumissions with bondage service restrictions, including maintenance payments, published by G. Colin in *Bull. Corr. Hell.* XXII (1898), no. 32, 5 and 104, 9-10. In Colin's no. 32, line 5, I would supply in the *lacuna* τροφείαν, without hesitation, where Colin has supplied βρέφος.

[2] The public slaves of Greece have been fully discussed by O. Jacob, *Les Esclaves Publics à Athènes,* Bibliothèque de la Faculté de Philosophie et Lettres de l'Université de Liége, fasc. XXXV, Liége, 1928.

[3] *Léon Halkin, Les esclaves publics chez les Romains,* Brussels, 1897.

freedom. This practise was already developed in Attica in the fourth century B.C. In the lists of the silver bowl dedications by emancipated slaves which were cited above, no less than fourteen examples of such loans appear.[1] Since the manumissions of the freedmen or freedwomen of these documents remained subject to voidance through legal process so long as the debt to the loaning group was not repaid,[2] these *eranoi*, as clubs, seem more analogous to temporary loan associations than to any other organization that occurs to me.[3]

In the case for which Demosthenes wrote the prosecuting speech against the morally reprehensible, but charming, slave prostitute, Neaera, the girl had been bought out of a bordello in Corinth by two young men. When they wished to marry they did not want her about in some bawdy house in the town. They proposed that she buy her freedom and leave the city. Neaera, thereupon, collected contributions from some of her lovers, "bringing together an *eranos* for her freedom." The head of her benefit club was an Athenian named Phrynion who took the money already collected and made up the remainder required for the manumission price.[4]

Let us place beside the literary evidence which I have already cited two cases attested by the Athenian silver bowl dedications of the late fourth century. The astonishing ease of manumission for industrial workers will thereby become even more clear.

"Nicias, dealer in frankincense, dwelling in Piraeus, having defeated Philocrates the Eleusinian, son of Epicrates, and an association of contributors (the loan group) headed by Theophrastus, son of Bathylus, of the deme of Cholargus, (has dedicated) a bowl worth 100 drachmas."[5]

---

[1] This is specifically stated in Collitz-Baunack, S.G.D.I, II, 2317, 9-10, of about 50 B.C.: εἰ δὲ μὴ καταφεῖϱ(αι), ἅ τε ὠνὰ ἄκυϱος ἔστω καὶ δουλευέτω Νίκαϱχς 'Αϱιστο(τέ)λει.

[2] The temporary nature of these loan ἔϱανοι is illustrated in S.G.D.I, II 1791. The slave is to pay the ἔϱανος, or loan, to the name of his owner in two payments at four months intervals "until the loan club runs out" (ἄχϱι κα λήξη ὁ ἔϱανος).

[3] I 'G ,II, 2d ed., 2, 1, 1553, 9-10 and 22-23; 1556, 28; 1557, 106; 1558, 40 ff.; 1559, 26-31; 1566, 28; 1568, 20 and 23; 1569, 19-20; 1570, 25-6, 58-9 and 61-2; 1571, 10.

[4] Demosthenes, oration LIX, *Against Neaera*, 29-32.

[5] I G II, 2, 1, 1558, 37-43. See Franz Poland, *Geschichte des griechischen Vereinswesens*, Leipzig, 1909, pp. 28-9. I do not believe in his translation of καὶ κοινὸν ἐϱανιστῶν as meaning "and Company." That would be, simply, καὶ μετόχους. Erich Ziebarth, *Das griechische Vereinswesen*, Leipzig, 1896, p. 159 is certainly wrong in his statement that these κοινά had actually owned the slaves who were manumitted.

Nicias was the slave. He had run a retail incense shop as a "pay-bringing" slave and no doubt, continued in that business after he became a freedman. Eventually, we may surmise, he paid off his debt to the *eranos* group of Theophrastus and Company.

Again: "Bion, gem engraver, living in Melite (deme), having defeated Chaerippus, son of Chaeredemus of (the deme) Halae, and an association of contributors headed by Chaerippus of Halae, (has dedicated) a bowl worth 100 drachmas."[1]

In this case the owner of the skilled gem worker, Bion, had himself formed the manumission loan group. Presumably he was its largest contributor since it bears his name.

What sort of slavery is this? What are its characteristics? Western scholars bring with them fixations upon the subject which derive from Negro slavery. In seeking answers to these questions, therefore, we must first discard all of the paraphernalia of modern slavery and all of the cannelized habits of thought upon slavery which we moderns carry about with us. What did the Greeks think of the slave system with which they were familiar? If we can ascertain that, we can, at least, try to see the slave structure as it appeared to them and think about it as they would think.

To the Greeks slavery was one of many forms of bondage and not, necessarily, the worst of these. Isocrates said that the Spartans enslaved the souls of their Perioeci no less than they enslaved those of their slaves, (meaning the Helots). [2] Aristotle speaks more exactly to our purpose, which is to determine the rigidities and the flexibilities of the Greek idea of slavery. These, if we can isolate and examine them, should reflect the flexibilities and rigidities of the system which gave birth to their idea of it. Aristotle says: "The (free) workman in the meaner handicrafts has a kind of limited slavery."[3] His point is that the slave may, by association with his master, partake of his quality of excellence, his *areté*. The free workman, who has no such association of dependence, is in this respect worse off, in his limited slavery, than the full slave.

However we may define the word "slave," slavery is a status which carries with it a series of limitations upon the options, or

---

[1] *Ibid.* no. 1559, 26-31.
[2] Isocrates, *Panathenaicus*, 178.
[3] Aristotle, *Politics*, I 13 (= 1260 a). Jowett in his *Politics of Aristotle*, Oxford, 1885, p. 25 has given an imprecise idea of the adjective ἀφωρισμένην by translating it "a special and separate" slavery.

choices, permitted to the enslaved person. This is exactly the way in which the Greeks envisaged slavery. In the Delphic inscriptions recording slave manumissions which are to be found in volume II of Collitz-Baunack, *Sammlung der griechischen Dialekt-Inschriften,* four liberties of the person are constantly reiterated as comprising the substance of the freedom which the present freedman had not enjoyed before his emancipation. These are highly significant.

1. He is to be his own representative, his own master, in all legal matters, without need of intervention of a second party. This is the legal expression of freedom.

2. He is not subject to seizure as property. Said otherwise: No one dares lay a hand upon him.

3. He may do what he desires to do.

4. He may go where he desires to go. Or, in a variant form, he may live where he desires to live.[1]

These are the four elements of liberty of the individual which to the Greek mind distinguished the non-slave from the enslaved. Reversing this, as one may look at a transparency in a window from the back as well as from the front, the major personal restrictions which determine full slave status are these:

1. In all legal actions the slave must be represented by his master or by some other person legally empowered by the owner.

2. He is subject to having hand laid upon him by anybody. That is, he is subject to seizure and arrest (the *manus injectio* of the Latin). This would apply, with particular emphasis to fugitive slaves.[2]

---

[1] P. Foucart, *L'affranchisement des esclaves,* Paris, 1867, pp. 10-11, made these observations quite clearly; but the consequences have never been drawn from the observations. With slight differences of wording in the manumission documents the formulas repeat themselves: (1) κυριεύων αὐτοσαυτοῦ, Collitz-Baunack, *Sammlung der griechischen Dialekt-Inschriften* II (Göttingen 1899 — S.G.D.I.) no. 2049, 7; 2065, 10. (2) ἐλεύθερος ὢν καὶ ἀνέφαπτος τὸν πάντα χρόνον, no. 2049, 7-8, or ἀνέφαπτος ἀπὸ πάντων τὸν πάντα βίον, as in no. 2065, 4. (3) ποιέουσαν ὅ κα θέλει, no. 2117, 4; cf. 1684, 6; 1685, 4; 1686, 7, etc. (4) ἀποτρέχουσα οἷς κα θέλει, no. 1686, 7; 1687, 4-5; or, more precisely, οἰκέουσα καὶ πολιτεύουσα εἴ κα αὐτὰ θέλει, no. 1844, 7. S.G.D.I. II no. 1780, 6-8, which falls in the period 170-157/6 B.C., is a splendid example of statement of the four elements of freedom: ἐφ' οἷτε ἀνεφάπτο[υς] εἶμεν καὶ αὐτὰν καὶ τὰ παιδάρια ἀπὸ πάντων τὸν πάντα βίον, ποιοῦντας ὅ κα θέλωντι καὶ οἰκεούσας εἴ κα θέλωντι καὶ ἐρπούσας οἷς κα θέλωντι. εἰ δέ τις ἐφάπτοιτο τοῖς τρίοις, ἔστω ὁ παρατυχὼν συλέων ὡς ἐλευθέρους.

[2] This is expressed in two formulas—S.G.D.I. II 1910 of about 156-151 B.C.: εἰ δέ τίς κα ἐφάπτηται ἐπὶ καταδουλώσει Κλεοῦς, βέβαιον παρεχόντω, and S.G.D.I. II 1909, (177 B.C.), 12-13: καὶ ὁ θέλων συλέων ἐπ' ἐλευθερίαι.

3. He cannot do what he wishes, but must do what his master orders. This means that freedom of choosing his activities is denied to him.

4. He cannot go to those persons or places to which he may wish to go, live in the domicile in which he desires to live, or determine his *polis* residence and affiliation.

These four major freedoms of men found their best expression for antiquity in the formulas devised and stated by the astute priests of the Delphian Apollo in the terms of the manumission by fictitious sale to the god whom they served. These may be briefly summarized in this form: To be one's own master (κυριεύων). To be protected against seizure (except by due process of law). [1] To have freedom of action. To have freedom of movement. In the Delphic manumission documents which I have checked, numbering over 750, the Greek verb used in expressing two of these freedoms, namely those of action and of mobility, is ἐθέλειν never βούλεσθαι. The new freedoms are the abilities to fulfill emotional desires, those things which one's heart prompts one to do. This is the essential meaning of ἐθέλειν whereas βούλεσθαι would invoke the rational elements of planning and of provision for carrying out that plan. οὐκ ἐθέλειν denotes a longing to do something without the right or the will power to accomplish it. What the slave does is, therefore, done unwillingly (ἄκων). What the free man does he does of his own volition (ἕκων). [2]

As displayed in the institution of the slave police at Athens, in the *choris oikountes,* the slave craftsmen of the industrial towns who lived their lives apart from their owners, and in the accepted formulae of the Delphic manumissions, slavery was not separated from freedom by a sharp dividing line. This is the essential of the freedman status, of the condition of the ἐξελεύθερος in the Greek, of the *libertus* in Latin legal terminology. It is well known, obvious and generally accepted by scholars. What has *not* been sufficiently noted is that, to the Greek mind, freedom was not a unit but some-

---

[1] ἀνέφαπτος. The Latin terminus technicus corresponding to this is *incolumis.*
[2] For the semantics of these two verbs consult Richard Maschke, *Die Willenslehre im griechischen Recht,* Berlin, 1926, pp. 2-10. I have checked the manumission documents in S.G.D.I II 1684-2342, and those published by G. Colin in *Bulletin de Correspondence Hellenique* XXII (1898), pp. 9-140. I find that the verb consistently used in connection with freedom of action and freedom of movement is ἐθέλειν.

thing divisible. They broke it down into four common denominators: its legal recognition; the unassailable quality which it granted to the manumitted; the right of choice of action, or activity; the right to move where one wished.[1] It is important to note that freedman status was not only divisible in itself. Each of the three remaining freedoms, once the legal status was fixed, could be broken into, or impinged upon. A freedman might be in possession of any one, or any two, of the three elements other than legal recognition which were the necessary components of complete freedom.[2] He might be possessed of only a part of any one of these three elements. Any one of these three might be restricted in its relation to himself. But if he was a freedman at all, the restrictions imposed must be legalized, either by a law of the city-state or by a legally recognized contract.

This statement is susceptible of definite proof, by analysis of some 170 Delphic manumission documents containing clauses by virtue of which the emancipated slave was still subject, legally, to certain bondage restrictions.[3] These restrictions were imposed upon his freedom for a fixed term of years or for a flexible period often dependent upon the life expectancy of the manumittor. Their result was to make illusory in some degree a liberty which was unquestionably and legally granted. These are the manumissions with bondage arrangements termed *paramone* by the Greeks. Recognition of the divisibility of freedom settles for me a long controversy as to whether the paramonist, the freedman under bondage limitations, was still a slave or a free man during the term of his bonded services. Several of the Romanistic legalists have decided that the freedman obligated to *paramone* services was actually of slave status. The *paramone* clauses of the manumission document, under this view, introduced conditions which suspended the grant of

---

[1] This problem of the right to move might be termed "the kinetics" of bondage and of free status.

[2] In S.G.D.I. no. 2140 all of the four factors of freedom are specifically mentioned as granted to the freedwoman despite the fact that she remained a bonded servant.

[3] I have not included several cases in which the choice is given of working out one's freedom by *paramone* or of paying it out in money, under the system of borrowing from an *eranos* group.

freedom.[1] This is wrong. By the manumittor's sale to the god and by the act of the slave in entrusting this sale to the god the slave became free.[2] The error arose through the fact that the four elements of freedom were not understood. The slave became *legally* free by the act of sale to the god. Of the other three elements of freedom (freedom from attack or summary arrest, freedom of action, and freedom of movement) the ex-slave had, in these cases, only partial control. Hence his *eleutheria* must again be asserted as becoming operative at the end of the term of his obligatory services. Often this is stated with specific enumeration of all the four elements of personal liberty.[3] This I can only assert here, after a rather exhaustive survey of the material involved. Its proof must await more detailed study and another opportunity for its presentation.

By isolating these four freedoms I have found a way, I believe, which will lead to a deeper understanding of the structure of the slave system of the Greek society of which this slave structure was a necessary and accepted part. Theirs was a society in which a man could be part free and part slave, ἡμίδουλος. Aristotle, in a passage which has been unnecessarily questioned and corrected, tells us that Clisthenes after the casting out of the tyrants "enrolled in the tribes

---

[1] See Moritz Bloch, *Die Freilassungsbedingungen der delphischen Freilassungs-inschriften*, Strassburg, 1914, pp. 27-29. His references to older scholars include Ernst Curtius, *Anecdota Delphica*, Berlin, 1843, p. 40, who decided that the slaves manumitted with *paramone* conditions were *statu liber sed non sui iuris;* L. Mitteis, *Reichsrecht und Volksrecht* (1891) p. 388 who called the liberty of the freedman a *suspensiv-bedingte Freiheit";* and L. Beauchet, *Droit privé de la Republique Athénienne*, Paris, 1897, II p. 495.

The more recent discussions of the Greek bondage services required after manumission, the *paramone* services, are those of Josef Partsch in a review of Sachau's *Syrische Rechtsbücher in Ztsch, der Savigny-Stiftung, Rom. Abt.* XXIII (1907), pp. 423-440; of Paul Koschaker in *Abhandlungen der Sächsischen Akademie, hist.-phil, Klasse* XLII (1931), no. 1, and Ernst Schönbauer, *Ztsch. Sav-Stift., Rom. Abt.*, LIII (1933), pp. 422-450.

Georges Daux, *Delphes au IIe et au Ier Siècle*, pp. 46-60 (in *Bibliothèque des Écoles Françaises d' Athènes et de Rome*, 1936, no. 140) has made no advance over the conclusions regarding the free or slave status of the paramonist as presented by Koschaker. See particularly the long note of Daux, *ibid.* p. 57.

[2] So Henri Wallon correctly decided long ago by virtue of his approach to slavery as a social and economic institution. See his *L'esclavage dans l'antiquité*, 2d ed., Paris, 1879, I p. 340. But the ex-slave did not become a hierodoule, as Wallon thought.

[3] The second grant of the freedoms made after the term of the *paramone*, would, I believe, be more correctly regarded as a mere extinction of the agreement regarding the bonded services. In SGDI 2144, it is clearly stated that the death of the owner releases a girl, already free, from the *paramone* services.

13

many foreigners and slave metics."[1] Now the χωρὶς οἰκοῦντες of the Greek industrial towns became clear to me. Legally they were slaves, of course; but *de facto* only partly δοῦλοι because they lived where they wished. The fourth freedom was already theirs. In the letter from Oxyrhynchus to his father the student Nilus used a significant phrase about the slave who was his "paybringer": ὡς ἐλεύθερος πάντα ποιῶν. "He did everything like a free person."[2] This pay-earning slave was free, in one at least, of the four elements which constituted enslavement, probably in two of them. Certainly he had some degree of choice as to the nature of his work. Presumably he could live where he wished in the city in which he happened to be employed.

Of these four personal liberties of the free man the option of mobility has been most neglected, though it is of the greatest importance. The freedom to go where the former slave wished to go persisted into the time of the Langobardic law in the form of a symbol of Lombard manumission. The slave who was to be freed was taken to a crossroad and thence might start out in any one of four directions.[3] Thomas Hobbes in his *De Cive* has, in fact, reduced his definition of slavery to the terms of deprivation of this one freedom alone. With his remarkable insight, and in his lucid Latin, he has assigned gradations to liberty, regarding it as major or minor according as the space in which it operates is greater or smaller.[4] To him the free man is that person who is subservient only to the state. This corresponds to the "limited freedom" which Aristotle assigns to the free artisan if he works at some "banausic" trade. To Hobbes the slave is that person who is subservient to a fellow man as well as to the state. In the Cyropaedia[5] Xenophon has expressed quite distinctly the idea of the third freedom, namely that of action: "We must differentiate ourselves from our slaves insofar as slaves serve their masters without their own will. But we, if we desire to be free, must of our own will do what appears to be most worth while."

---

[1] Aristotle, *Politics* III 1, 10 (1275 b): ξένους καὶ δούλους μετοίκους.The change of Niehbur to ξένους, μετοίκους καὶ δούλους, and similar changes are unnecessary.

[2] P. Oxy. XVIII 2190, 48-9. In the manumission documents from Delphi this is constantly phrased: ποέοντα ὅ κα θέλη. See, for example, S.G.D.I. II no. 1695, 6.

[3] See Munroe Smith, *The Development of European Law* (New York 1928), p. 11. For its transition into Anglo-Saxon Law cf. *Leges Henrici I regis*, ch. 78, in Felix Liebermann, *Gesetze der Angelsachsen*, Halle 1903 vol. 1, p. 594.

[4] Thomas Hobbes, *De Cive* IX 9. The idea is quoted with approval by Pufendorf in *De Jure Naturae* 944.

[5] Xenophon, *Cyropaedia* VIII 1, 4.

14

This has been an attempt to approach slavery in Greek society by way of the slave ideology of the Greeks themselves as this is disclosed in the formulas originated and repeated through centuries by the powerful priesthood of Apollo at Delphi. Its chief results may be stated as follows:

Greek society was, of course, a slave society. Its slavery was of a type unfamiliar to Europeans and Americans of the last two centuries. It had no color line. (Therefore, *pace Aristoteles,* it had no single and clearly defined slave race or slave caste.) The person enslaved might well be one-quarter free, or three quarters free, depending upon the personal inviolability and the options of activity and movement which might actually be granted him. Herein lies the explanation of the fact that the Greeks could conceive of "debtor slaves, who are free" and "free slaves of the unprivileged classes," σώματα λαϊκὰ ἐλεύθερα.[1] In the metic class of the city-states the manumitted slave found a group into which, as freedman, he merged easily, without effort on his part or opposition from the group which he entered. There was an astonishing fluidity of status in both directions, from slavery to freedom as from freedom to slavery. This it is which, in large measure, explains the absence of slave revolts in the Greek classical period. Why should an enslaved person revolt if thereby he merely gains that which he might so easily obtain by the simple process of borrowing money for his emancipation and repaying that money?

As labor, slave workmen had a marked advantage over free labor in that the slave craftsmen were usually exempt from all levies for military service; and they were not distracted from their occupations by the many civic duties which engrossed the time of the citizens. Economic competition between the slave and the free laborer seems to have been a negligible problem, at least at Athens where we know Greek slavery best. This may be explained, perhaps, by the fact that the economic organization of the Greek world was, on the whole, an expanding one in the fifth and fourth centuries. The lack of complaints about the condition of the slaves in the fifth and fourth centuries is the best proof of a condition of equilibrium between contentment and discontent attained among them.

---

[1] ὑποχρέων σωμάτων ὅσα ἂν ἐλεύ[θε]ρα ὄντα in P. Col. Inv. 480 (Westermann. *Upon Slavery in Ptolemaic Egypt)* and σώματα λαϊκὰ ἐλεύθερα in *Papyrus Erzherzog Rainer Inv.* 24,552, published by Herbert Liebesny in *Aegyptus* XVI (1936) 257-291. See also Westermann, *Enslaved Persons Who are Free* in *Am. Journal of Philology* LIX (1938), 1-30.

Otherwise there would have been slave revolts such as did occur under the more maleficent latifundian system of Sicily and Italy in the first two centuries B.C. In the ancient situation slave labor never became exclusive in the labor market, nor even its dominant feature, except upon the *latifundia* of Sicily and Italy. Ancient society does not appear to me to have been particularly self-conscious about its slaves. Certainly it was never hysterical, not even emotionally excited about the slave institution. I fail to find any background of fear of slavery in its literature or in its life. No moral horror of the institution appears such as developed in the eighteenth and nineteenth centuries in the west. In this sense ancient society did not develop a social slave mentality. There is no equivalent in ancient Greek literature for the many speeches and pamphlets written by modern slave owners upon the economic validity of the slave institution.

Upon the basis of its particular type of slavery ancient society attained a notably high level of culture. The decline of this culture was roughly contemporary with the displacement of a free-and-slave labor system by an enforced and immobile working class, the colonate upon the land and compulsory labor under the guild system in the handicrafts. We come back to the problem of mobility, the fourth of the four freedoms of the Greek manumissions. *Libertas — nihil aliud est quam absentia impedimentorum motus,* said Hobbes.[1] When by legal enactments a society imposes personal immobility upon great masses of men, then you have, indeed, created a system more deadly in its rigidity than the loose structure of Greek slavery ever was.

---

[1] Thomas Hobbes, *De Cive* IX 9.

III

Wege zur Menschlichkeit in der antiken Sklaverei

von Professor Dr. phil. JOSEPH VOGT

Wenn es mir nach altem Brauch zukommt, mein Amt mit einem
Vortrag aus meinem Fachgebiet anzutreten, so möchte ich einen
Problemkreis erörtern, der mich seit einer Reihe von Jahren be-
schäftigt und der, wie ich glaube, zu den grundlegenden Fragen
meiner Wissenschaft gehört. Auf dem weiten Feld der Geschichte
des Altertums stellt die griechisch-römische Antike den Bezirk dar,
der uns im historischen Ablauf der Reiche und Kulturen des Mit-
telmeergebiets noch am nächsten steht und in seinem menschlichen Wert als Urbild, stets gegenwärtig bleibt. Die Sklaverei, als
ein wesentliches Element in der gesellschaftlichen Struktur der
Antike, ist seit langer Zeit – zuerst im Zusammenhang mit der
modernen Antisklavereibewegung – eindringend erforscht worden.
Aus einer Preisaufgabe der Pariser Académie des sciences morales
et politiques von 1837 ist die erste umfassende Monographie über
den Gegenstand von Henri Wallon hervorgegangen [1]. In den folgenden Jahrzehnten sind einzelne Gebiete der antiken Gesellschaft
und Wirtschaft auf Grund eines fortdauernd anwachsenden Quel-
lenmaterials genauer untersucht worden. Der Vortrag von Eduard
Meyer über die Sklaverei im Altertum [2] kann als ein richtung-
weisender Entwurf gelten. Die Darstellungen von W. L. Westermann [3] bringen die mannigfachen Aspekte und Wandlungen des
Instituts zum Vorschein. Was uns aber fehlt, ist ein anschauliches

---

[1] H. Wallon, Histoire de l'esclavage dans l'antiquité, 2. Aufl., Paris 1879.
[2] Ed. Meyer, Die Sklaverei im Altertum, Kleine Schriften, I 1924, S. 169 ff.
[3] W. L. Westermann, Art. Sklaverei RE Suppl. VI 894 ff. (1935) und The Slave
Systems in Greek and Roman Antiquity., Mem Am. Philos. Soc. 40 (1955).

Bild der Funktionen, die die Sklaverei im Organismus der antiken
Gesellschaft innegehabt hat, und eine kritische Würdigung ihrer
Rolle für Entstehung, Entfaltung und Untergang der Kultur. Die
marxistische Wissenschaft bringt der Sklaverei ein besonderes
Interesse entgegen, sie vermag sie aber nur im Zusammenhang der
materiellen Produktion und der Klassenbildung zu fassen und ver-
fällt so, wie die rege sozialgeschichtliche Forschung in den kom-
munistisch regierten Ländern zeigt, mehr und mehr einem läh-
menden Schematismus. In dieser Lage scheint es mir geboten, die
Darstellung der Sklaverei in der antiken Gesellschaft in den Rahmen der verschiedenen Rechtsverhältnisse von Dienstbarkeit ein-
zuordnen, ihren Anteil am Produktionsprozeß und am Kultur-
schaffen für möglichst viele Gebiete exakt festzustellen, die Men-
talität der bürgerlichen Schichten und die Gesinnung der Sklaven
genauer zu untersuchen. Im Rahmen der Mainzer Akademie der
Wissenschaften und der Literatur habe ich Mitarbeiter bei diesen
Forschungen gefunden. Siegfried Lauffer hat die Bergwerkssklaven
von Laureion behandelt [1], Franz Bömer hat sich der Religion der
Sklaven zugewandt [2]; über die Quellen der antiken Sklaverei geben
die Studien zur Kriegsgefangenschaft und zur Sklaverei in der
griechischen Geschichte von Gisela Micknat [3] und die bevorstehen-
den Untersuchungen von Franz G. Maier über den hellenistischen
Seeraub, von Hans Volkmann über die Versklavung der Einwohner-
schaften eroberter Städte Auskunft. Ich selbst habe dort die
Fragwürdigkeit einer harmonisierenden Betrachtung von Griechentum und Humanität aufzuzeigen gesucht und an der Struktur der antiken Sklavenkriege die These von einer kommunisti-
schen Internationale des Altertums zurückgewiesen [4]. Von jüngeren
Mitgliedern des Arbeitskreises sind Beiträge über das Bild des unfreien Menschen im griechischen und römischen Schrifttum, über
die Sklaven im antiken Kriegsdienst, über die unfreie Bevölkerung

---

[1] S. *Lauffer*, Die Bergwerkssklaven von Laureion, Akademie der Wissenschaften
und der Literatur, Abhandlungen der geistes- und sozialwissenschaftl. Klasse
1955, 12 und 1956, 11.
[2] F. *Bömer*, Untersuchungen über die Religion der Sklaven in Griechenland und
Rom, I: Die wichtigsten Kulte und Religionen in Rom und im lateinischen Westen,
ebenda 1957, 7.
[3] G. *Micknat*, Studien zur Kriegsgefangenschaft und zur Sklaverei in der griechischen Geschichte, I. Homer, ebenda 1954, 11.
[4] J.*Vogt*, Sklaverei und Humanität im klassischen Griechentum, ebenda 1953, 4,
und Struktur der antiken Sklavenkriege, ebenda 1957, 1.

in der römischen Revolution, über die Funktion der Sklaven in der Erziehung und im künstlerischen Leben zu erwarten. Wenn diese und noch andere Fragen geklärt sind, wird man wohl darüber urteilen können, ob die antike Sklaverei – medizinisch gesprochen – einen lebbaren Zustand gebildet und wie sie die Kultur beeinflußt hat.

Nach diesem Einblick in die Werkstatt möchte ich auf einige überraschende Erscheinungen zu sprechen kommen, die zwar nur einen kleinen Ausschnitt aus dem ganzen Phänomen ausmachen, uns aber einige Kategorien der Bedientensklaverei in besonderer menschlicher Nähe zu den Freien zeigen. Es kann natürlich nicht davon die Rede sein, daß das Institut der Sklaverei als solches die Menschlichkeit gefördert habe. Wenn selbst Platon nichts dagegen eingewandt hätte, daß ein Mensch als Besitzstück wie ein Maultier auf dem Markt gekauft und verkauft wird, wenn Vedius Pollio, ein Freund des Kaisers Augustus, seine Sklaven bestrafen durfte, indem er sie in den Fischteich warf als Futter für seine Muränen, ohne sich dadurch strafbar zu machen, so ist wohl klar, daß dieses ganze System allem, was wir mit Menschlichkeit meinen, schroff widersprach. Griechische Sophisten haben dies offen ausgesprochen und sich darauf berufen, daß die Natur niemand zum Sklaven gemacht habe. Die stoische Philosophie hat allen Menschen Anteil an der Weltvernunft zugebilligt und daraus die Ideale des Weltstaats und der Humanität gewonnen. Ohne feste Bindung an eine der großen Schulen hat sich »der Gedanke von der sittlichen Freiheit auch des rechtlich Unfreien« eine gewisse Anerkennung verschafft[1]. Diese Lehren haben im Lauf von Jahrhunderten die Sklaverei zwar nicht aufzuheben vermocht, aber doch gemildert. Indes geht es hier nicht um Philanthropia und Humanitas, diese hohen Werte antiken Denkens. Ich möchte vielmehr zeigen, wie in der griechischen und noch mehr in der römischen Gesellschaft die Sklaven an bedeutsamer Stelle Aufgaben zu verrichten hatten, bei denen sie ihre Herren in der ganzen Schwachheit der menschlichen Natur zu betreuen hatten, nämlich als Säuglinge, als Kinder und als Kranke, und wie bei solcher Begegnung abseits aller Theorie Innigkeit, Treue und Freundschaft erwuchsen, fast möchte man sagen: Menschlichkeit wider Willen. Die Ammen, die Pädagogen und die Leibärzte der hohen Herren verdienen unsere Aufmerksamkeit, nicht weil es uns gelüstete, die antike Welt aus der Diener-

[1] Dazu W. *Richter*, Seneca und die Sklaven, Gymnasium 65 (1958) S. 196 ff.

perspektive zu betrachten, sondern weil hier deutlich wird, daß ein radikales System nur bestehen kann, indem es sich an den empfindlichsten Stellen einschränkt. Natürlich könnte man diese Beobachtung auch an anderen Berufen der Haussklaven anstellen, an den Sekretären, Kammerdienern und Köchen etwa. Doch wir halten uns an langdauernde und gut bezeugte Einrichtungen, die dem Schutz des gefährdeten Lebens selbst dienten.

Mit dem Mütterchen Eurykleia beginnt die lange Reihe der Ammen, die als unfreie Dienerinnen in griechischen und römischen Familien die Kinder des Hauses gestillt und gepflegt haben. Gewiß gab es immer auch Mütter, die sich ihre Kinder nicht wegnehmen ließen, aber in der Stadt war doch die Regel, daß man das Kind für die Zeit des Stillens – zwei Jahre zumeist – der Amme (τίτθη) und für die Pflege der folgenden Jahre der Wärterin (τροφός) übergab, also Sklavinnen anvertraute, die zudem meist ausländischer Herkunft waren. Nicht als ob man diese Dienste geringgeschätzt hätte; erzählte doch der Mythos davon, daß die Sprößlinge der Götter ihre erste Ernährung und Pflege von den Nymphen selbst empfangen haben. Als das griechische Denken mit den Sophisten daran ging, das Leben nach der Vernunft zu ordnen, entwarf es, wie uns im großen Zusammenhang Werner Jaeger gezeigt hat, die Grundlagen einer Erziehung, die mit der Pflege des Säuglings begann, dann die Spielzeit regelte und mit dem 7. Jahr zum Lernen in der Schule hinführte. Platon hat im 5. Buch der Politeia und umfassend im 7. Buch der Gesetze die Erziehung in den aufeinanderfolgenden Stufen der Pflege (τροφή) und der Bildung (παιδεία) behandelt und die Auffassung vertreten, daß die erzieherische Formung des Menschen schon beim Kind im Mutterleibe zu beginnen habe und daß sie entscheidende Bedeutung erlange beim Kleinkind, das geformt werden müsse wie Wachs, solange es weich ist [1]. In der Erziehungslehre, die sich in den Schulen der hellenistischen Philosophie als eine besondere Wissenschaft entfaltete, war die Anweisung über die Amme ein äußerst wichtiges Kapitel. Wir sehen dies noch an den letzten Brechungen der Theorien, die wir bei Quintilian und Tacitus, bei Favorin und Plutarch und in der Frauenheilkunde des Soran vorfinden. Da wird nachdrücklich betont, daß die Mutter die natürliche Ernähre-

---

[1] *Platon*, Nom. VI 789 a–e und das Folgende.

rin des Kindes sei, daß sie allein mit wahrer Sympathie sich der
Aufgabe widme, daß dies alles von der Vorsehung so eingerichtet sei.
Einzelne gehen weiter, argumentieren physiologisch, daß mit der
Muttermilch auch der Charakter sich vererbe, und verlangen dann
folgerichtig die Ablehnung der Amme überhaupt. Die Ärzte, die
sich an die realen Verhältnisse halten, geben genauere Vorschriften
für die Auswahl der Amme; Soran verlangt, daß es eine Griechin
sein müsse, Oreibasios bevorzugt Frauen von thrakischer oder
ägyptischer Herkunft.

Es dürfte damit klar sein, daß die Frage in ihrer ganzen Bedeutung stets gegenwärtig war. Aber auch dies ist sicher, daß die Erziehungslehre in ständiger Polemik mit der Erziehungspraxis
stand – ein Verhältnis, das offenbar zum Wesen dieser Wissenschaft
gehört. Es blieb dabei, daß die Frauen der Adelshäuser und der
wohlbestellten Bürgerfamilien sich nicht der Mühe des Stillens
unterzogen. Wir besitzen in hellenistischen Papyri Ammenver-
träge, in denen Sklavinnen und verarmte Bürgerfrauen zum
Ammendienst eingestellt werden. Auch in die römische Welt drang
dieser Brauch im Zug der allgemeinen Hellenisierung ein. Gewiß
hat hier die gute, alte Zeit, in der der Sohn nicht »in der Kammer
einer gekauften Amme, sondern im Schoß und Busen der Mutter«
erzogen wurde, lang gedauert; die römische Mutter hat höheren
Rang und stärkere Wirkung als die griechische. Aber Bildung und
Luxus bereiteten auch hier der Amme und der Wärterin den Weg,
und es verstand sich, daß in einer Gesellschaft, die zweisprachig
wurde, die *Graecula ancilla* willkommen war [1].

Sklavinnen waren es also, die in der antiken Welt die Kindheit
der Helden und Könige, der Dichter und Philosophen betreut
haben. Sie haben sie gewickelt und in Schlaf gewiegt, mit Amule-
ten und Sprüchlein gegen bösen Spuk gesichert, mit Fabeln und

---

[1] *Tacitus*, Dial. 28 f. – Über die Amme bei Griechen und Römern orientieren –
abgesehen von den alten Handbüchern – W. *Schubart*, Die Amme im alten Alexan-
drien, Jahrb. f. Kinderheilkunde 70 (1909) S. 82 ff.; W. *Braams*, Zur Geschichte des
Ammenwesens im klassischen Altertum, Jenaer medizin.-hist. Beitr. 5 (1913);
G. *Herzog-Hauser*, Art. Nutrix RE XVII 1491 ff. (1937). – Grundlegend für die
Geschichte der Erziehungslehre, besonders auch für die Wandlungen der Vorschriften für das Ammenwesen sind W. *Schick*, Favorin περὶ παίδων τροφῆς und die
antike Erziehungslehre, Leipzig 1912 und F. *Glaeser*, De Pseudo-Plutarchi libro περὶ
παίδων ἀγωγῆς, Diss. philol. Vindobon. XII 2, 1918; vgl. auch das Nachwort zu
Plutarch, Kinderzucht, griechisch und deutsch bei Ernst Heimeran, München
1947.

Geschichten unterhalten, mit Ammenmärchen, wie man leichthin sagt, während doch Platon die Macht dieser Erzählungen kennt, die »den Kindern wie Liederzauber an das Ohr schlagen, sie erheiternd und wieder ernst stimmend«[1]. Die ganze Fülle des Spielzeugs, wie wir es auf Bildern sehen und in Terrakotta greifen können, haben die Kinderfrauen zum Leben gebracht. Als Barbarinnen, wie man damals sagte, als urwüchsige Geschöpfe, wie wir sie verstehen möchten, haben sie alle diese Jahre durchwoben, in der das Leben nichts anderes war als Spielerei (παιδιά). Den Philosophen der Antike lag es ganz fern, das Kind um seiner selbst willen zu entwickeln. Wenn es trotzdem ein volles Kindsein gab, dann wurde dies zumeist den Ammen und den Kindermädchen verdankt.

Wie dieser Sklavendienst in das Leben der Erwachsenen hineingewirkt, was er für die Kultur im ganzen bedeutet hat, können wir nur bruchstückhaft ermessen. Favorin sagt, daß die Mutter, die ihr Kind weggebe, es von der natürlichen Liebe ausschließe und zu vergessen beginne, und daß das Kind seine Liebe ganz der Amme zuwende[2]. Ähnlich wird es mit der Wärterin gegangen sein. An der menschlichen Aufgabe, die ihnen hier einmal gestellt war, sind die Sklavinnen gewachsen, sie haben mit ihren Zöglingen eine seelische Verbundenheit gewonnen, die oft das ganze Leben anhielt. Dafür haben wir Zeugnisse genug. Es war schmerzlich für die treue Wärterin, wenn der Knabe heranwuchs und dem Sportplatz und dem Forum überlassen werden mußte[3]. Sie mochte sich oft trösten, wenn sie nun freigelassen wurde und im Haus ihre Versorgung fand als die treue Dienerin, wie sie, auch in kritischer Lage der Familie ergeben, in einer pseudodemosthenischen Rede erscheint[4]. Was die andere Seite betrifft, so gehörte Güte, ja Fürsorge für die Behüter der eigenen Kindheit zum Wohlverhalten des gebildeten Menschen, Cicero weiß davon, und der jüngere Plinius bestätigt es, indem er seiner Amme nach langem, treuem Dienst ein kleines Grundstück schenkt[5]. Es ruht auf dieser Lebenserfahrung,

---

[1] *Platon*, Nom. X 887 d.
[2] Bei *Gellius*, Noct. Att. 12, 1, 21 ff.
[3] *Frontonis* et *M. Aurelii* ep. S. 103 (Naber).
[4] *Demosth.* 47, 55 ff.
[5] *Cicero*, Lael. 74; *Plinius*, ep. 6, 3. Über den humanitären Zug in der gebildeten Gesellschaft der Kaiserzeit *A. M. Duff*, Freedmen in the Early Roman Empire, Oxford 1928, S. 99 f.

wenn Amme und Wärterin in der dramatischen Dichtung zu
Pflegemüttern ihrer Zöglinge und zu Vertrauten ihrer Herrinnen
werden, am bedeutendsten in der klassischen Tragödie der Griechen. Aischylos läßt in den Choephoren (734 ff.) die Amme des
Orest in dem Augenblick sprechen, als sie die Nachricht von seinem
Tod vernommen hat. Ein Zeugnis für die vielen, die stumm bleiben
mußten, ist diese Klage, in der die Trauer um den lieben Toten sich
mit der Erinnerung an das mühevolle, überraschungsreiche Geschäft
der Säuglingspflege verbindet. Die Sklavin ist es hier, die trauert,
während die Mutter über die Todesnachricht frohlockt. Das ist in
der tragischen Fabel begründet, wie sich versteht, und doch will
es etwas Allgemeines besagen, wenn wir bedenken, wie selten es
einer griechischen Mutter der klassischen Zeit gegeben war, »das
unverständige Wesen wie ein Tierchen zu pflegen«. Natürlich
bleibt dieser Monolog doch eine einfältige Ammenrede. Die Ver-
traute aus dem Sklavenstand ist in der Tragödie ja nicht Partnerin
im vollen Sinn, auch wenn sie in ein Geheimnis eingeweiht wird.
Behaftet mit der Angst und Schwachheit des Durchschnittsmen-
schen steht sie außerhalb des tragischen Bereichs und hat keinen
Anteil an Verantwortung und Schicksal[1]. Allein, daß es diese
Treue im Kleinen gab, um die die Dichter wissen, war ein köst-
licher Besitz in einer Welt, die so kraß vom Egoismus beherrscht
war. Das bezeugen uns reizvolle Vasenbilder und Terrakottafigu-
ren, besonders aber die Denkmäler, die die Ammen und Kinderfrauen im Totenkult erhalten haben. Seien es Grabstelen mit
Relief oder schlichte Inschriften nur, die »die tüchtige Amme« mit
dem Namen nennen: diese Weihungen erheben die Sklavin in den
Kreis der Verwandten[2]. Was immer in der Literatur über die ge-
schwätzige, trunksüchtige und schmutzige Alte kursieren mochte,
hier sprechen so viele Menschen und in so warmen Tönen – der
hohe Beamte, der sogar das Konsulat erreicht hat, *nutrici et mam-*

---

[1] Vgl. Sklaverei und Humanität im klassischen Griechentum, Abh. Ak. d. Wiss.
u. d. Lit. 1953, 4 S. 175 ff. – Zur literarischen Gestalt *H. Ahlers,* Die Vertrauen-
rolle in der griechischen Tragödie, Diss. Gießen 1911.
[2] Einige Beispiele bei *A. T. Klein,* Child Life in Greek Art, New York 1932, S. 2
und die Tafeln. – Das schöne Material bei *A. Conze,* Attische Grabreliefs, *F. Winter,*
Die antiken Terrakotten und in andern Sammelwerken sollte einmal eine mono-
graphische Darstellung finden. Vgl. die Interpretation der Grabstele der Pyraichme
τίττη (sic) χρηστή aus Athen durch *S. Karouzos,* Hellenika 15 (1957) S. 311 ff.
(Hinweis von *Friedrich Matz*).

mulae bene merenti [1] –, daß wir nicht zweifeln können, wo die Stimme des echten Lebens erklingt. Es läge nahe, von dieser Gestalt der antiken Gesellschaft den Blick über Jahrhunderte und Kontinente hinweg zu jener *black mammy* zu wenden, der alten Amme und Kinderfrau, die in der amerikanischen Negersklaverei als angesehenes Mitglied der herrschaftlichen Familie begegnet und nach der Emanzipation bis heute im Leben wie in der Dichtung weiterwirkt [2]. So ergiebig der Vergleich wäre, wir müssen uns hier auf die Zeugen des Altertums beschränken. Fern jeder Rücksicht auf Sippe und Partei, auf Polis und Schulgemeinschaft, worin sich sonst der Ehrgeiz erschöpft, bekennen sie etwas von der Wahrheit, die in dem spanischen Sprichwort liegt: »Die Hand, die die Wiege bewegt, bewegt die Welt.«

Neben den Ammen werden oft die Pädagogen genannt. Damit kommen wir zu einem Sklavenberuf, der in männlicher Prägung noch tiefer in das öffentliche Leben hineingeragt hat. Worum es sich handelt, mag zunächst ein Wort Platons nahelegen: »Ohne Hirten dürfen weder Schafe noch sonstiges Vieh gelassen werden, also auch Knaben nicht ohne Knabenführer, so wenig wie Sklaven ohne Herren. Es gibt kein Tier, das so schwer zu leiten wäre wie ein Knabe.«[3] Dieses schwierige Geschäft kam, wie Platon dann ausführt, dem Pädagogen zu, der dem Knaben, wenn er von der Wärterin und Mutter losgekommen war, in seinem kindischen Gebaren und Unverstand zu wehren hatte. Ein freier Hellene war für diese Aufgabe kaum zu haben, er wollte sein eigener Herr sein, nicht als Angestellter dienen und dafür noch schlecht bezahlt werden. So griff man zu den Sklaven und nahm einen treuen Diener des Hauses, oft genug einen alten, für andere Arbeiten unbrauchbaren Sklaven. Auch hier denkt man an den Negersklaven im amerikanischen Süden, der oft zum Intimus der Kinder wurde und in der literarischen Gestalt des »Onkel Remus« berühmt werden

[1] *Dessau*, Inscriptiones Lat. selectae 8532.
[2] Meinem Kollegen *R. Haas* verdanke ich den Hinweis auf *J. W. Parkhurst*, The Rôle of the Black Mamij in the Plantation Household, Journ. of the Negro Hist. 23 (1938) S. 349 ff. und *A. W. Calhoun*, A Social History of the American Family from the Colonial Times to the Present, II New York 1945 S. 282 f. Bekannt ist die Negermagd Dilsey in William Faulkners »The Sound and the Fury« (1929), die im Zusammenbruch der Weißen die heile Welt repräsentiert.
[3] *Platon*, Nom. VII 808 d.

sollte[1]. Natürlich hat die philosophische Erziehungslehre diese Heranziehung von minderwertigen Sklaven barbarischer Herkunft scharf kritisiert, die Einwände gehen von der Schule Platons und von dem Peripatetiker Hieronymos bis zu Plutarch[2]. Aber auch hier erwies sich die Theorie als machtlos. Selbst in den ersten Häusern behalf man sich mit Sklaven als Aufsehern, die die Jungen zu begleiten und zu betreuen hatten, wenn sie mit dem siebenten Jahr zur Schule gingen. Sogar von dem großen Perikles erzählte man die Geschichte, er habe, als einmal ein Sklave vom Baum herabfiel und sich ein Bein brach, gesagt: »Nun ist eben ein Pädagoge aus ihm geworden.«[3] Wie ständhaft diese Knabenführer ihre Pflicht erfüllten, zeigt die reizvolle Szene am Schluß des platonischen Lysis (223). Da melden sich, nachdem Sokrates lange, allzulange in der Palästra diskutiert hat, die Knabenaufseher, um ihre Jungen rechtzeitig heimzubringen, und schelten so nachdrücklich in ihrem schlechten Griechisch, daß Sokrates sich geschlagen gibt und die Gesellschaft auflöst. So wird der Geist nach seinem Höhenflug von barbarischen Dienern auf den so notwendigen Boden des Animalischen herabgeholt. Ebenso gutmütig brummend, wie Platon hier die Aufseher zeichnet, erscheinen diese oft auf Vasenbildern und in der Kleinplastik: fremdländische Typen, kahlköpfig, mit struppigem Bart und langem Stock[4] – beinahe wie Straßenausgaben des Sokrates.

Auch Rom hat diesen Sklavenberuf gekannt. In den ersten Jahrhunderten freilich, als man in italischer Abgeschlossenheit leben durfte, übernahm der Vater selbst den Jungen, nachdem die Mutter seine Kindheit betreut hatte, und führte ihn in die strenge Welt der Sitte und des Gemeinwesens ein. Aber mit der römischen Expansion in die weite Welt wurden Politik und Bildung so differenziert, daß der Hausvater Hilfe und Ablösung suchen mußte. Da traf es sich gut, daß man Griechen als Kriegsgefangene einbrachte und als Hausklaven erwerben konnte. Diesen griechischen

---

[1] *J. Chandler Harris*, Uncle Remus, His Songs and Sayings, 1881, dazu *Calhoun* a. O. S. 281 ff., 311.

[2] *Platon*, Alkib. I 121 c ff.; Hieronymos bei Stobaios, Ecl. II S. 233 (Wachsmuth); *Plutarch*, De lib. educ. 4 A B. – Einige Bemerkungen zur antiken Kritik am sklavischen Pädagogen bei *R. H. Barrow*, Slavery in the Roman Empire, London 1928, S. 39 ff.

[3] Stobaios a. O.

[4] *A. Klein* a. O. S. 28 ff. und die S. 25 Anm. 3 genannten Sammelwerke.

27

D

Sklaven, denen auch freie Hellenen zur Seite treten konnten, übertrug man nun den Unterricht der Jugend in allen Abstufungen und erst recht die persönliche Betreuung, die der Schule zur Seite ging. Ein griechisch sprechender Aufseher *(custos)* gehörte jetzt zum römischen Haus; in der Komödie sind die *servi paedagogi* so geläufig, daß wir die Übernahme der Sache und der Bezeichnung noch in das 3. Jahrhundert setzen können. Später kommt der Ausdruck *monitor* auf, der deutlich zeigt, worauf es bei der Knabenführung vor allem ankam. Mit *comes* und *rector* benannte man dagegen den Hofmeister der Jünglinge, und es war nicht selten, daß ein *monitor,* der sich bewährt hatte, die Freiheit erhielt und in den höheren Rang eines *comes* aufstieg; selbst in die Berufe der gelehrten Erziehung *(litterator, grammaticus, rhetor)* sind einzelne Pädagogen vom Sklavenstand aus eingedrungen. In der entschieden männlich geformten römischen Welt hatten die Frauen eine angesehene Stellung, daher auch die Mädchen einen besseren Anteil an Erziehung und Bildung als bei den Griechen. So gab es hier, zahlreicher als in Hellas, auch Pädagogen für Mädchen, ja es fehlte auch die *paedagoga* nicht [1].

Aufgabe und Stellung des Pädagogen waren in Hellas und Rom im wesentlichen gleich. Er begleitete den Jungen zur Schule, trug das Schulzeug, wachte über ihn auf der Straße, die ja in der antiken Stadt für Jungen gefährlicher war als für Mädchen, er hatte ihm gutes Benehmen und Sittsamkeit beizubringen. Mit dem Unterricht hatte er nichts zu tun, höchstens daß er hin und wieder die Schulaufgaben beaufsichtigte und in dieser Funktion Repetitor oder gar – um in der Sprache der Tübinger akademischen Erziehung zu reden – Repetent werden konnte. In dieser, so einfach aussehenden Betreuung lag aber ein klarer, erzieherischer Auftrag, denn nicht von den Wissenschaften, sondern vom menschlichen Umgang erwartete man die Formung der Persönlichkeit, wie schon das heroische Vorbild, die vielgerühmte Freundschaft zwischen Achill und seinem Pädagogen Phoinix, erkennen läßt. So ist es verständlich, daß man an dem Unwissen der Pädagogen weniger An-

---

[1] Zeugnisse über die Stellung des Pädagogen bei *E. Schuppe,* Art. Paidagogos RE XVIII 2375 ff. (1942); über die römischen Verhältnisse *Barrow* a. O. S. 88 ff. und R. *Boulogne,* De plaats van de paedagogus in de romeinse cultuur, Diss. Utrecht 1951. Dazu die Darstellungen der griechischen und römischen Erziehung von *P. Girard, A. Gwynn* und vor allem *H.-I. Marrou,* Geschichte der Erziehung im klassischen Altertum, Freiburg 1957.

stoß nahm als an ihrer Halbbildung[1], und daß die Theoretiker vom Aufseher vor allem einen zuverlässigen Charakter forderten. Für die Erziehung von Kindern ein kindertümliches Verfahren zu verlangen, lag damals ganz fern; so mochte man es geradezu begrüßen, daß die Pädagogen zumeist alte Männer waren. Aber die Gefahr, die in der Heranziehung von Sklaven, überwiegend ausländischen Sklaven, zu diesem Geschäft lag, ist von Einsichtigen immer wieder zum Bewußtsein gebracht worden. »Es ist eine arge Sache, daß ein Freier von einem Sklaven beherrscht wird«, sagt Sokrates in Platons Lysis (208 c), und in dem pseudoplatonischen ersten Alkibiades (121 c–122 b) holt er zu einer schweren Kritik dieses fahrlässigen athenischen Erziehungssystems im Vergleich mit der wohlüberlegten Aufzucht und Unterweisung der Prinzen am persischen Königshof aus. Das Risiko, das darin lag, einen Angehörigen der verachteten Unterschicht zum Erzieher zu berufen, illustriert eine Anekdote von dem Philosophen Aristipp. Als dieser auf die Frage, was er für die Erziehung eines Sohnes verlange, den Preis von tausend Drachmen nannte, meinte der sparsame Vater, dafür könne er ja einen Sklaven kaufen. Worauf Aristipp: »Dann wirst du eben zwei Sklaven haben.«[2] Die herabziehende Wirkung des Sklaven als Erziehers befürchten auch weiterblickende Römer, nur daß bei ihnen noch die dünkelhafte Geringschätzung der *Graeculi* hinzutritt (vgl. Tac. dial. 29). Vor allem mußte bei so ungleichem Gespann in der Erziehung doch die Frage aufkommen, wie sich überhaupt Führung und Gehorsam, Vertrauen und Hingabe bilden konnten. »Bist du mein Sklave oder bin ich der deine?« antwortet der junge Herr bei Plautus auf die Vorhaltungen seines Pädagogen[3]. Dieses Dilemma konnte der Stock wahrlich nicht beheben.

Und doch haben, wenn wir die Zeugnisse der Jahrhunderte überschauen, die sklavischen Pädagogen die Herausforderung aufgenommen und als Anstandslehrer der griechischen und. römischen Jugend ihre Schuldigkeit getan. So mißlich ihre Stellung war, sie hatten den Vorteil, Zöglinge von so kindlichem Alter zu übernehmen, daß der soziale Abstand nicht von vornherein ein persönliches Nahverhältnis ausschloß. Väter und Mütter traten wenig in

---

[1] *Quintilian,* Inst. orat. 1, 1, 8 f.
[2] *Plutarch,* De lib. educ. 4 F.
[3] *Plautus,* Bacch. 162.

Wettbewerb, so fiel den Pädagogen eine ähnliche Chance zu wie den Ammen. Ihre Schützlinge riefen sie in der Lallsprache der Kinder mit den Kosenamen *tata* und *tatula, papas* und *nonnus* und blieben oft für das ganze Leben bei dieser zärtlichen Benennung [1]. Von dieser menschlichen Verbundenheit zeugt auch die dichterische Gestalt des Pädagogen als Vertrauten der Helden in der Tragödie, der jungen Herren im Lustspiel. Der treue Diener, voll Erfahrung und Güte, greift stärker in die Handlung ein als die Amme, wenn auch bei ihm ein letzter, unüberbrückbarer Abstand gegenüber dem Herren besteht. Gewiß hören wir auch Stimmen, die den Pädagogen als groben Kerl und elenden Schulmeister kennzeichnen, doch überwiegt das Urteil, daß seine Leistung, mochte sie auch unbequem sein, doch dankenswert sei. Der junge Mann atmete auf, wenn er den Mahner los wurde: *tandem custode remoto* [2], aber er mußte sich, wenn er ehrlich war, sagen, daß er gerade an diesem Widerstand groß geworden war. Der Dichter Martial (11, 39) mag hier für viele sprechen; ich übersetze das Epigramm:

> Meine Wiege hast du bewegt, Charidemus, vor Zeiten,
> Hast den Knaben bewacht, unzertrennlich von ihm.
> Nun ist der Bart mir geschoren und schwarz wird dabei das Tüchlein,
> Schon beklagt sich die Maid über der Lippen Stich.
> Aber für dich blieb ich klein: dich fürchtet unser Verwalter,
> Unser Kassier und das Haus, alles hat Angst vor dir.
> Spielen gestattest du nicht und lieben ist uns verboten,
> Nichts läßt du mir, doch dir läßt du alles erlaubt.
> Immerfort wird getadelt, vermahnt, geklagt und geseufzet,
> Und nach der Rute gar greifen möchte dein Zorn.
> Habe ich tyrischen Schmuck angelegt und gesalbt meine Haare,
> Rufst du laut: »Niemals hätt' es der Vater getan!«
> Und du zählt beim Wein mit gerunzelter Stirn uns're Becher,
> Gleich als wäre der Krug dir aus der Kammer geraubt.
> Laß das! Unerträglich ist mir ein freigelassener Cato.
> Daß ich ein Mann jetzt bin, sagt meine Freundin dir.

Ja gewiß, wenn das Mädchen auftrat, mußte der alte Erzieher weichen, aber es war trotz allem ein Abschiednehmen voll Achtung, und dies bedeutet eben doch keine Trennung. Unter den Gebildeten ist es die allgemeine Überzeugung, daß neben den Eltern die Ammen und die Pädagogen als Erzieher ehrerbietige Liebe ver-

---

[1] *K. Zacher*, Zu den Juvenalscholien, Rhein. Mus. 45 (1890) S. 537 ff.; *W. Heraeus*, Kleine Schriften (Idg. Bibl. III 17), 1937, S. 158 ff.; *Boulogne* a. O. S. 56.
[2] *Horaz*, Ars 161.

dienen[1]. In der geschichtlichen Überlieferung wird es zur Regel, in der Lebensbeschreibung großer Männer auch deren Pädagogen zu nennen, so daß mit Themistokles, Alkibiades und Alexander, mit Cato Uticensis und Augustus auch ihre Sklavenerzieher in die Geschichte eingegangen sind. Wenn Augustus, bereits im Besitz der großen Macht, seinen Pädagogen durch ein Staatsbegräbnis ehrte[2], so bedeutet dies die Dankesbezeugung für menschliche Förderung und zugleich die öffentliche Anerkennung des Sklavendienstes für den Staat. Für die einfachen Menschen sprechen Grabschriften, die die Zöglinge ihren Pädagogen und manchmal diese ihren Zöglingen gesetzt haben. »Ihrem Hofmeister und Lehrer«, paedagogo suo καὶ καθηγητῇ, sagt Claudia[3], und bringt damit eine Erfahrung zum Ausdruck, die nicht selten gewesen sein kann. Denn die Sprache selbst, die Bedeutungsgeschichte des Wortes *paedagogus*, hat die Leistung des Knabenführers auf ihrer Höhenlinie festgehalten. Wenn Seneca jene Vorbildgestalt bezeichnen will, die den Jünger der Philosophie im Gewissen verpflichtet, dann greift er zum Wort *paedagogus*, und wenn er die erzieherische Aufgabe des Philosophen umreißt, dann nennt er ihn *paedagogus generis humani*. In ähnlichem Sinn wird in der christlichen Glaubenslehre das Gesetz des Alten Testaments als Pädagoge, als Erzieher der Menschen zum Mündigwerden in Christus verstanden[4]. Es ist aber nicht so, als ob in dieser späten Zeit aus dem Bedeutungsgehalt des Wortes die Erinnerung an den sklavischen Träger des Namens verschwunden wäre. Nein, es ist gerade der Verstand des Dieners, die Treue des Ungelehrten, die Strenge des Ausländers, was diese verpflichtende Kraft gewonnen hat. Kaiser Julian, einer der letzten Hellenen, versichert uns, daß er seinem Pädagogen Mardonios, der einmal als Sklave aus dem Skythenland gekommen war, dann freilich auch Literatur und Philosophie gelernt hatte, die etwas derbe, stumpfe, asketenhafte Tugend verdanke, die er sein eigen nennt[5]. Darin also dürfen wir die geschichtliche Rolle der Sklaven als Erzieher erkennen, daß sie es verstanden haben, in eine über-

---

[1] *Cicero*, Lael. 74; *Seneca*, Ep. 60, 1; *Plinius*, Ep. 5, 16, 3. Vgl. *Cicero*, Brut. 210.
[2] *Cassius Dio* 48, 33, 1.
[3] *Dessau*, Inscriptiones Lat. selectae 4999.
[4] *Seneca*, Ep. 11, 9; 25, 6; 89, 13. – *Paulus* im Galaterbrief 3, 24, dazu *Bertram*, Theolog. Wörterbuch z. NT., V S. 619 f.
[5] *Julian*, Misopogon 351 f.; dazu *J. Bidez*, Julian der Abtrünnige, München 1940, S. 24 ff. und die Anmerkung S. 379.

zivilisierte Gesellschaft einen Schuß von Natürlichkeit und Vitalität zu bringen und für die Formung junger Menschen nutzbar zu machen. Das gilt auch für die meisten der griechisch sprechenden Pädagogen in der römischen Welt. Diesen kam es allerdings besonders zustatten, daß sie ihren Zöglingen bei der Erlernung des Griechischen behilflich sein und so einen leichteren Weg zu einer geistigen Gemeinschaft finden konnten.

Und schließlich die Sklaven als Ärzte. Hier haben wir ein besonders erregendes Phänomen vor uns, indes läßt es sich kürzer fassen, denn es betrifft nur Rom und die römische Welt. Die Griechen, die von früher Zeit an sowohl eine handwerkliche Heilpraxis als auch eine Krankenheilung beim Tempel der Gottheit kannten, haben – das gehört zu ihren großen Leistungen – die wissenschaftliche Medizin hervorgebracht: die auf exakter Naturbeobachtung und rationalem Denken beruhende Heilkunde. Diese Wissenschaft und Kunst, die vom klassischen Zeitalter an eng mit der Philosophie verbunden war, blieb den freien Bürgern vorbehalten, und es verstand sich dabei, daß die Ärzte auch die Behandlung kranker Sklaven übernahmen. Platon entwirft in eine ideale Zukunft hinein die Möglichkeit, daß Ärzte ihre Sklaven in die Heilkunst einführen und sie im Dienst von Sklavenpatienten verwenden[1]. Es hat aber, wie die literarischen Zeugnisse und die zahlreichen Inschriften lehren, in der griechischen Welt, auch im hellenistischen Zeitalter, so gut wie keine Sklaven als Ärzte gegeben; wo einer vorkommt, ist er Gehilfe des freien Arztes[2].

Ganz anders hat sich die Heilkunst bei den Römern entwickelt. Das gepriesene Altrom hat sich mit jener Volksmedizin begnügt, deren Hausmittel noch Cato empfiehlt. Die wissenschaftliche Heilkunde wurde, wie die Wissenschaft und Literatur überhaupt, von Kriegsgefangenen aus dem hellenistischen Osten nach Rom gebracht. Vornehme Römer haben es sich etwas kosten lassen, heilkundige Sklaven zu kaufen oder einen begabten Mann ihrer Sklavenfamilie als Arzt ausbilden zu lassen. Der *servus medicus* war der Arzt im eigenen Haus, er begleitete den Herrn, wenn dieser in die Provinz oder in den Krieg ging. Verdiente Sklavenärzte wurden

---

[1] *Platon*, Nom. IV 720 a–e und IX 857 cd.
[2] *L. Cohn-Haft*, The Public Physicians of Ancient Greece, Smith College, Studies in History 42 (1956) S. 3, 14 f. (Hinweis von *Hans Diller*).

freigelassen und erhielten so die Möglichkeit, ihre Kunst selbstän-
dig auszuüben. Spätestens seit 200 v. Chr. sind auch freie Griechen
als Ärzte in den Westen eingewandert, zumal da die Stadt Rom seit
Sullas Zeit zum Mittelpunkt aller Künste und Wissenschaften
wurde. Lehre und Praxis der in Rom tätigen griechischen Ärzte
bilden von nun an den wesentlichen Teil der Geschichte der griechischen Medizin. Durch Caesar und Augustus erhielten diese ausländischen Ärzte das Bürgerrecht, durch Vespasian die Immunität
und das Korporationsrecht. So bildete sich ein römischer Ärztestand, dessen hervorragendste Vertreter als Leibärzte am kaiserlichen Hof erscheinen, der aber auch im römischen Heer, in der
Arena und im Theater, in den Berufsvereinen und in den Stadtge-
meinden lohnende Aufgaben erhielt [1]. In diesem weiten Bereich
finden wir durch Jahrhunderte nur wenige geborene Römer als
Ärzte. Zwar galt der Arztberuf für Bürger, die nicht dem Sena-
toren- und Ritterstand angehörten, als anständiger Broterwerb,
und selbst Männer der Oberschicht konnten für etwaige ärztliche
Leistung ein freiwillig gebotenes Honorarium entgegennehmen.
Die Tendenz der kaiserlichen Politik ging ausdrücklich auch dahin,
die Berufe des Arztes und des Lehrers den Freien zu sichern. Aber
es blieb dabei, daß man die Heilkunst zumeist den zugewanderten
freien Griechen, daneben den Sklaven und Freigelassenen vorwie-
gend östlicher Herkunft überließ. Nicht nur für Rom, sondern auch
für die Provinzen sind in der Kaiserzeit durch Inschriften Hun-
derte von solchen, aus der Unfreiheit aufgestiegenen Ärzten bekannt, Männer, die durch ihre Arbeit zu Wohlstand gelangt sind
und für ihre Verdienste gerühmt werden [2].

Diese weitgehende römische Enthaltung von medizinischer
Wissenschaft und ärztlicher Tätigkeit hat natürlich tiefe Gründe.

---

[1] Die Entwicklung der Medizin in Rom ist wiederholt dargestellt worden, so von
M. *Albert*, Les médecins grecs à Rome, Paris 1894 (meist ohne Stellenangaben);
Th. Meyer, Geschichte des römischen Ärztestandes, Habilitationsschrift Jena
1907; *T. Clifford Allbutt*, Greek Medicine in Rome, London 1921 (weitschweifig).
Beste Zusammenfassung bei *P. Diepgen* Geschichte der Medizin, I Berlin 1949.
[2] Über den standesgemäßen Charakter des Arztberufs *Cicero*, Off. 1, 150 f. – Zur
rechtlichen und sozialen Stellung der Ärzte *Duff* a. O. S. 119 f.; *R. Herzog*, Urkun-
den zur Hochschulpolitik der römischen Kaiser, SB Preuss. Ak. 1935, S. 967 ff.;
K. H. Below, Der Arzt im römischen Recht, Münchener Beiträge zur Papyrus-
forschung und ant. Rechtsgeschichte 37 (1953), bes. S. 57 ff., dazu *U. v. Lübtow*,
Gnomon 29 (1957) S. 616 ff. – Reiches personengeschichtliches Material bei
H. Gummerus, Der Ärztestand im römischen Reich nach den Inschriften, Soc.
Scient. Fenn., Comm. Hum. Litt. III 6, 1932.

Der wissenschaftliche Charakter der Heilkunde hat in einem Volk, in dessen Begabung das methodische und systembildende Denken schwach entwickelt war, nicht anziehend gewirkt. Das Handwerkliche einer Praxis, die leicht in augenscheinliche Abhängigkeit von den Patienten führte, hat eher abgestoßen. Dazu kam die ungünstige Konstellation, unter der man die wissenschaftliche Heilkunde zuerst kennenlernte: daß sie von diesen Griechen, die politisch überwunden, aber geistig überlegen waren, so anmaßend und undurchsichtig vertreten wurde! Das finstere Mißtrauen Catos, der diesen auf Geldmachen erpichten, betrügerischen Griechen geradezu eine Verschwörung gegen das Leben der Menschen in Italien zugeschrieben hat, ist bekannt[1]. Doch zwei Jahrhunderte später erfolgt beim älteren Plinius[2] ein noch schlimmerer Ausbruch römischen Ressentiments. Er nimmt Catos Einwände wieder auf und verstärkt mit den Erfahrungen, die man inzwischen mit den Hof- und Modeärzten gemacht hat, mit allem Nachdruck die römische Abwehrhaltung: diese Ärzte machen Geschäfte mit Menschenleben, sie treiben ein lügnerisches Gewerbe, sie experimentieren, ohne einer Prüfung unterworfen zu sein, nur ihnen ist es erlaubt, in völliger Sicherheit vor Bestrafung einen Menschen umzubringen! In der modernen Forschung hat man dem sonst so soliden wissenschaftlichen Beobachter und Sammler Plinius diesen Ausfall schwer verübelt. Zweifellos stellt er ein weiteres Zeugnis römischer Beschränktheit dar, und doch begegnet uns hier zugleich eine tiefe Einsicht in die Schäden der Zivilisation, die durch die Einrichtung der vielen sklavischen Hilfsdienste den Menschen sich selbst entfremdet hat. Am Ende seiner grimmigen Polemik faßt Plinius zusammen (29, 1, 19): »Es geschieht uns recht so. Denn niemand hat Interesse dafür, was zu seinem Heil nötig ist. Wir wandeln auf fremden Füßen, wir lesen mit fremden Augen, wir grüßen nach fremdem Gedächtnis, wir leben durch fremde Leistung. Die natürlichen Dinge haben ihren Wert verloren, und mit ihnen sind auch die wahren Gehalte des Lebens untergegangen. Nichts als das Vergnügen halten wir für unseren Besitz.« Das also ist es, was Plinius so erregt, daß die Sklaven uns die natürlichen Leistungen des Organismus abnehmen: die Sänftenträger die Arbeit der Füße, die Vorleser die Funktion der Augen, die Namenrufer die Leistung des

---

[1] *Cato,* Ad Marcum fil. 1 (Jordan S. 77).
[2] *Plinius,* Nat. Hist. 29, 1, 1–28.

Gedächtnisses, die Ärzte die Gesundheitspflege; seine Liste hätte
noch viel, viel länger sein können! In der mannigfaltigen antiken
Kulturkritik ist es ein erstaunlicher Fall, daß hier als ein Ergebnis
der Sklaverei die Selbstentfremdung des Menschen erkannt wird –
ein frühes Vorspiel der Entdeckung desselben Prozesses im System
der mechanischen Sklaven in der modernen Industriegesellschaft.

In der schwierigen Lage, in der sich so die Medizin in der römischen Welt befand, scheint sich kein Weg zur Menschlichkeit zu
öffnen. Sklaven als Hausärzte der römischen Großen und der Kaiser haben sich wiederholt in die Verbrechen der Politik verstricken
lassen [1]. Andere haben sich entgegen allen Regeln ihrer Kunst den
Patienten so gefügig gezeigt, daß der große Arzt Galen sich hef-
tig entrüstet: »Was immer man von ihnen verlangt, sie gehorchen
nach Sklavenart im Gegensatz zu jenen alten, unter Ärzten ge-
priesenen Nachkommen des Asclepius, die über ihre Kranken
herrschen wollten wie Feldherrn über ihre Soldaten und Könige
über ihre Untertanen, ihnen aber nicht gehorchten und dienten nach
der Gewohnheit der Geten, Tibier, Phryger und Thraker, die man
kauft.«[2] Und doch haben die besten Vertreter des Berufs, mochten
sie Sklaven oder Freigelassene sein, sich an die Weisung des Hippo-
krates gehalten, daß der Kranke und der Arzt sich gemeinsam der
Krankheit entgegenstellen müssen [3], und haben von Mensch zu
Mensch gesprochen und gewirkt. Cicero rühmt nicht nur das Wissen, die Verläßlichkeit und Güte des freien Arztes Asclapon, er be-
klagt auch den Tod des Sklaven Alexion, weniger weil er in ihm
einen guten Arzt verloren habe, als weil er um dessen Liebe,
Menschlichkeit und Charme ärmer geworden sei. Und Seneca
kommt zu der Erkenntnis, daß der Arzt und der Lehrer nicht mit
Lohn abzutun seien, weil sie in ihren Berufen uns zu Freunden werden. [4] Ganz allgemein vertritt dieser auf das Praktische abzielende
Moralist in dem berühmten 47. Brief die Auffassung, daß Herren

---

[1] Beispiele bei *Albert* a. O. S. 101 ff.; über ein ähnliches Verhalten freier Ärzte
R. Herzog, Nikias und Xenophon von Kos, Hist. Zeitschr. 29 (1922) S. 189 ff.
[2] *Galen*, Meth. med. I 1 (X S. 4 Kühn). – Das überlieferte Τίβιοι steht wohl für
Θίβιοι; zu diesen Pontosbewohnern, aus deren Gebiet Sklaven ausgeführt sein
sollen, vgl. *Ziegler* RE VI A 272.
[3] *Galen*, In Hippocr. epid. VI comm. IV 4, 9 (XVII B S. 147 Kühn), vgl. *J. Il-
berg*, N. Jbb. f. d. klass. Alt. 15 (1905) S. 310.
[4] *Cicero*, Fam. 13, 20; Att. 15, 1 a, 1. – *Seneca*, Benef. 6, 16; Ep. 47; Benef. 3,
18 ff.

und Sklaven von Natur aus gleich sind und daß Sklaven nicht
nach Art ihrer Dienstleistung, sondern nach ihrem Charakter zu
bewerten sind. Er weiß davon, daß auch der Sklave als sittliche
Persönlichkeit zum Wohltäter an seinem Herrn werden kann, daß
er – dies ist entscheidend – der Tugend fähig ist. In dem Wertbe-
griff *humanitas* tritt bei ihm das Bildungsmoment zurück, um der
praktischen Menschenliebe, der sozialen Gesinnung Raum zu
geben[1].

Es ist ganz offenkundig, daß in dieser römischen Atmosphäre,
die so wesentlich durch die Berührung der Völker und die Mischung
der Stände bestimmt war, die ärztliche Standesethik das Gepräge
einer inneren Haltung gewonnen hat. Weder der Eid des Hippo-
krates noch die hippokratischen Schriften des 5. und 4. Jahrhunderts kennen, wie man neuerdings nachgewiesen hat, die sittliche
Pflicht der Menschenliebe[2], und wenn einer der öffentlichen Ärzte
der hellenistischen Zeit wegen unentgeltlicher Behandlung der
Kranken gelobt wird, so ist dies deutlich eine Ausnahme[3]. Erst in
der römischen Kaiserzeit hat Scribonius Largus im Vorwort seines
pharmazeutischen Handbuchs es klar ausgesprochen, daß der Arzt,
dessen Kunst allen in gleicher Weise zukomme, ein Herz voll Er-
barmen und Menschlichkeit haben müsse (*plenus misericordiae et
humanitatis animus*)[4]. Der Autor, der am Britannienfeldzug des
Kaisers Claudius teilgenommen hat, weiß auch um die Pflichten des
Soldaten und des guten Bürgers (Z. 34), römische Denkweise ist
ihm also vertraut; es spricht aber doch einiges dafür, daß er ebenso
Freigelassener war wie der hohe Gönner, dem er seine Schrift ge-
widmet hat, C. Julius Callistus, der mächtige Sekretär des Kaisers
Claudius. Dieser Kaiser, der bei der Nachwelt als der Diener seiner

---

[1] *J. Lichy*, De servorum condicione quid senserit L. Annaeus Seneca, Diss. Mün-
ster 1927; *G. J. tenVeldhuys*, De misericordiae et clementiae apud Senecam philos.
usu atque ratione, Diss. Utrecht 1935; *M. Pohlenz*, Die Stoa, I Göttingen 1948 S.
315 f. – In der S. 21 genannten, eindringenden Untersuchung vertritt *W. Richter*
die Auffassung, daß in der Stellungnahme Senecas zur Sklavenfrage in ep. 47
nicht nur und vielleicht überhaupt nicht stoische Gedanken zur Geltung kommen.

[2] *K. Deichgräber*, Die ärztliche Standesethik des hippokratischen Eides, Quellen
und Studien zur Geschichte der Naturwissenschaften und der Medizin 3 (1933)
S. 35 f.; *L. Edelstein*, The Professional Ethics of the Greek Physician, Bull. Hist.
Med. 30 (1956) S. 391 ff.

[3] *Cohn-Haft* a. O. S. 32 ff.

[4] Ausgabe und Interpretation des Vorworts bei *K. Deichgräber*, Professio Medici,
Abh. Ak. d. Wiss. u. d. Lit. 1950, 9; die genannte Formulierung Z. 29 ff.

Freigelassenen galt, hat immerhin das Gesetz erlassen, daß die kranken Sklaven, die von ihren Herren auf die Tiberinsel ausgesetzt werden, die Freiheit erhalten sollten[1]. Ich möchte glauben, daß in diesem Fall die ehemaligen Sklaven mitgewirkt haben, in der ärztlichen Ethik wie in der kaiserlichen Gesetzgebung dem Geist der Humanität den Sieg zu verschaffen. In der folgenden Zeit ist der so lange verleugnete soziale Auftrag des Arztberufs mehr und mehr erkannt worden. In einem philosophischen Gedicht über die Pflichten des Arztes, das Paul Maas aus Fragmenten einer athenischen Inschrift rekonstruiert hat und das einem sonst unbekannten Philosophen des 2. Jahrhunderts namens Sarapion gehört, wird gesagt, der Arzt müsse zuerst seinen Sinn heilen und sich selbst helfen, dann werde er wie ein Gott gleichermaßen Retter sein von Sklaven und Armen, Reichen und Herrschern und allen ein Bruder[2]. »Die Ärzte sind die natürlichen Anwälte der Armen«, ist ein Wort von Rudolf Virchow[3]. In der Antike ist dieser Gedanke noch im Vorhof des Christentums wenigstens angebahnt worden.

Damit sind wir am Ende einer Betrachtung, die skizzenhaft ist und ihre Ausführung im einzelnen noch erhalten wird. Sie hat uns in Bereiche geführt, die der Historiker nur selten betritt, und doch dürfte es klar sein, daß jene Haupt- und Staatsaktionen, die unser Interesse zumeist auf sich ziehen, den guten Gang der täglichen Dienste und das Wirken der stillen Kräfte des Lebens voraussetzen. Der aristokratische Mensch der antiken Kultur, der nichts höher schätzte als Unabhängigkeit und Muße, lud so viel an Arbeit, als nur eben anging, besonders die schwere Arbeit in den Plantagen, Bergwerken und Fabriken, aber auch jeden mühseligen Dienst im Haus den Sklaven auf und vollbrachte sein schöpferisches geistiges Werk in einer exklusiven Gesellschaft, von der es geradezu hieß: viel Sklaven, viel Feinde *(quot servi, tot hostes)*[4]. Die Gebrechlichkeit dieser sozialen Struktur erweist sich kaum

---

[1] *Sueton*, Claud. 25, 2; *Cassius Dio* 60, 29, 7. Vgl. *Duff* a. O. S. 34, 194; *A. Momigliano*, L'opera dell'imperatore Claudio, Collana Storica 41 (1932) S. 129 ff.

[2] *J. H. Oliver – P. L. Maas*, An Ancient Poem on the Duties of a Physician, Bull. Hist. Med. 1 (1939) S. 315 ff.; *Edelstein* a. O. S. 415.

[3] Die medizinische Reform, Eine Wochenschrift, Berlin 1848/9, S. 2.

[4] *Festus* 349, 23 Lindsay; *Macrobius*, Sat. 1, 11, 13.

irgendwo klarer als in der Tatsache, daß in der Haussklaverei ein
so wesentlicher Teil der Kinderpflege, der Jugenderziehung und
des Gesundheitsdienstes den Sklaven übertragen war. Doch hier
geschah es nun, daß diese Unterdrückten, indem sie Menschen an-
vertraut erhielten, aus ihrer Sklavenexistenz herausgehoben wurden. Die Wärterinnen, die Erzieher und die Ärzte sind an ihren
Aufgaben gewachsen, haben mit ihren Herren menschlichen Kon-
takt gewonnen und so in den gefährlichsten Zonen die ständischen
Schranken überwunden. Manche von ihnen haben in aller Form
die Freiheit erlangt, allerdings ohne dann als Freigelassene den
Kampf gegen ein System aufzunehmen, das als solches unverrück-
bar feststand. Andere sind, obwohl rechtlich in der Unfreiheit ver-
harrend, faktisch zu Partnern im gesellschaftlichen Leben der
Freien geworden. »Wer klug als Sklave dient, hat an der Herr-
schaft teil«, so hat einer, der aus der Sklaverei aufgestiegen war,
seine Erfahrung zusammengefaßt[1]. Am meisten aber will es besagen, daß fort und fort auch bei den Unterdrückern der Panzer
der harten Herzen durchstoßen und Menschlichkeit erfahren
wurde. Aus einer tiefen, unzerstörbaren Schicht des Humanen
heraus hat sich in einem kleinen, doch entscheidenden Bereich eine
Art Selbstreinigung des schmutzigen Systems vollzogen und die
Wahrheit in Erinnerung gebracht, daß der Mensch für den Menschen etwas Heiliges ist[2]: *homo sacra res homini*.

---

[1] *Publilius Syrus*, Sent. 586.
[2] *Seneca*, Ep. 95, 33.

IV

WAS GREEK CIVILIZATION BASED ON SLAVE LABOUR?[1]

I.

Two generalizations may be made at the outset. First: at all times and in all places the Greek world relied on some form (or forms) of dependent labour to meet its needs, both public and private. By this I mean that dependent labour was essential, in a significant measure, if the requirements of agriculture, trade, manufacture, public works, and war production were to be fulfilled. And by dependent labour I mean work performed under compulsions other than those of kinship or communal obligations.[2] Second: with the rarest of exceptions, there were always substantial numbers of free men engaged in productive labour. By this I mean primarily not free hired labour but free men working on their own (or leased) land or in their shops or homes as craftsmen and shop-keepers. It is within the framework created by these two generalizations that the questions must be asked which seek to locate slavery in the society. And by slavery, finally, I mean roughly the status in which a man is, in the eyes of the law and of public opinion and with respect to all other parties, a possession, a chattel, of another man.[3]

How completely the Greeks always took slavery for granted as one of the facts of human existence is abundantly evident to anyone who has read their literature. In the Homeric poems it is assumed (correctly) that captive women will be taken home as slaves, and that occasional male slaves – the victims of Phoenician merchant-pirates – will also be on hand. In the seventh century B.C., when Hesiod, the Boeotian "peasant" poet, gets down to practical advice in his *Works and Days,* he tells his brother how to use slaves properly; that they will be available is simply assumed.[4] The same is true of Xenophon's

---

[1] This is a slightly enlarged and revised version of a paper read at the triennial meeting of the Joint Committee of Greek and Roman Societies in Cambridge on 11 August 1958. No effort has been made to annotate fully or to provide more than a handful of modern references. I am grateful to Professors A. H. M. Jones and M. Postan in Cambridge, and Mr G. E. M. de Ste. Croix of New College and Mr P. A. Brunt of Oriel College, Oxford, for much helpful criticism.

[2] I also exclude the "economic compulsion" of the wage-labour system.

[3] It is obviously not a valid objection to this working definition to point out either that a slave is biologically a man none the less, or that there were usually some pressures to give him a little recognition of his humanity, such as the privilege of asylum or the de facto privilege of marriage.

[4] I believe that the ἔριθος and perhaps the θῆς of ll. 602–3 were slaves, from the context, peculiar as that use of the two words may be. But even if one rejects my interpretation of these two lines, slaves are so repeatedly taken for granted in the poem that it is incorrect to

146   [54]

manual for the gentleman farmer, the *Oeconomicus*, written about 375 B.C. A few years earlier, an Athenian cripple who was appealing a decision dropping him from the dole, said to the Council: "I have a trade which brings me in a little, but I can barely work at it myself and I cannot afford to buy someone to replace myself in it."[5] In the first book of the Pseudo-Aristotelian *Oeconomica*, a Peripatetic work probably of the late fourth or early third century B.C., we find the following proposition about the organization of the household, stated as baldly and flatly as it could possibly be done: "Of property, the first and most necessary kind, the best and most manageable, is man. Therefore the first step is to procure good slaves. Of slaves there are two kinds, the overseer and the worker."[6] Polybius, discussing the strategic situation of Byzantium, speaks quite casually of "the necessities of life – cattle and slaves" which come from the Black Sea region.[7] And so on.

The Greek language had an astonishing range of vocabulary for slaves, unparalleled in my knowledge.[8] In the earliest texts, Homer and Hesiod, there were two basic words for slave, *dmos* and *doulos*, used without any discoverable distinction between them, and both with uncertain etymologies. *Dmos* died out quickly, surviving only in poetry, whereas *doulos* remained the basic word, so to speak, all through Greek history, and the root on which were built such words as *douleia*, "slavery". But Homer already has, in one probably interpolated passage, the word (in the plural form) *andrapoda*, which became very common, and seems to have been constructed on the model of *tetrapoda*.[9] Still another general word came into use in the Hellenistic period, when *soma* ("body") came to mean "slave" if not otherwise qualified by an adjective.

These words were strictly servile, except in such metaphors as "the Athenians enslaved the allies". But there was still another group which could be used for both slaves and freemen, depending on the context. Three of them are built on the household root, *oikos* – *oikeus*, *oiketes*, and *oikiatas* – and the pattern of usage is variegated, complicated, and still largely unexamined. In Crete, for example, *oikeus* seems to have been a technical status term more like "serf" than any other instance known to me in Greek history. It was archaic even in Crete, however, and it dropped out of sight there in post-fifth-century documents. Elsewhere these *oikos*-words sometimes meant merely "servant" or "slave" generically, and sometimes, though less often, they indicated narrower

imply a balanced alternative, as does W. L. Westermann, The Slave Systems of Greek and Roman Antiquity (Philadelphia 1955), 4, when he writes: "The peasant of modest means of the type of Hesiod might well have slaves but he also used hired labour."

[5] Lysias 24.6.
[6] Ps.-Aristotle, Oec. 1.5.1,1344a22.
[7] Polyb. 4.38.4.
[8] I am not considering the local helotage words here, although the Greeks themselves customarily called such people "slaves".
[9] Homer, Il. 7.475.

distinctions, such as house-born slave (as against purchased) or privately owned (as against royal in the Hellenistic context).[10]

If we think of ancient society as made up of a spectrum of statuses, with the free citizen at one end and the slave at the other, and with a considerable number of shades of dependence in between, then we have already discovered two lines of the spectrum, the slave and the serf-like *oikeus* of Crete. At least four more can easily be added: the helot (with such parallels as the *penestes* of Thessaly); the debt-bondsman, who was not a slave although under some conditions he could eventually be sold into slavery abroad; the conditionally manumitted slave; and, finally, the freedman. All six categories rarely, if ever, appeared concurrently within the same community, nor were they equal in importance or equally significant in all periods of Greek history. By and large, the slave proper was the decisive figure (to the virtual exclusion of the others) in the economically and politically advanced communities; whereas helotage and debt-bondage were to be found in the more archaic communities, whether in Crete or Sparta or Thessaly at an even late date, or in Athens in its pre-Solonian period. There is also some correlation, though by no means a perfect one, between the various categories of dependent labour and their function. Slavery was the most flexible of the forms, adaptable to all kinds and levels of activity, whereas helotage and the rest were best suited to agriculture, pasturage, and household service, much less so to manufacture and trade.

II.

With little exception, there was no activity, productive or unproductive, public or private, pleasant or unpleasant, which was not performed by slaves at some times and in some places in the Greek world. The major exception was, of course, political: no slave held public office or sat on the deliberative and judicial bodies (though slaves were commonly employed in the "civil service," as secretaries and clerks, and as policemen and prison attendants). Slaves did not fight as a rule, either, unless freed (although helots apparently did), and they were very rare in the liberal professions, including medicine. On the other side, there was no activity which was not performed by free men at some times and in some places. That is sometimes denied, but the denial rests on a gross

---

[10] The terminology needs systematic investigation in terms of a range of unfree and semi-free statuses. I have given only some examples. On the regional and dialectal variations, see Erika Kretschmer, "Beiträge zur Wortgeographie der altgr. Dialekte. 1. Diener, Sklave", Glotta XVIII (1930), 71–81. On the interchangeability of the terms in classical Athenian usage, see Siegfried Lauffer, Die Bergwerkssklaven von Laureion (2 vols., Akad. Wiss. Mainz, Abh. Geistes- u. Sozialwiss. Kl. 1955, no. 12; 1956, no. 11), I 1104–8; cf. E. L. Kazakevich, "The Term δοῦλος and the Concept 'Slave' in Athens in the Fourth Century B.C." (in Russian), VDI (1956), no. 3, pp. 119–36, summarized in Bibl. Class. Or. II (1957), 203–205. (A former student, Mr. Jonathan Frankel, kindly abstracted the latter article for me.)

error, namely, the failure to differentiate between a free man working for himself and one working for another, for hire. In the Greek scale of values, the crucial test was not so much the nature of the work (within limits, of course) as the condition or status under which it was carried on.[11] "The condition of the free man," said Aristotle, "is that he does not live under the restraint of another."[12] On this point, Aristotle was expressing a nearly universal Greek notion. Although we find free Greeks doing every kind of work, the free wage-earner, the free man who regularly works *for* another and therefore "lives under the restraint of another" is a rare figure in the sources, and he surely was a minor factor in the picture.[13]

The basic economic activity was, of course, agriculture. Throughout Greek history, the overwhelming majority of the population had its main wealth in the land. And the majority were smallholders, depending on their own labour, the labour of other members of the family, and the occasional assistance (as in time of harvest) of neighbours and casual hired hands. Some proportion of these smallholders owned a slave, or even two, but we cannot possibly determine what the proportion was, and in this sector the whole issue is clearly not of the greatest importance. But the large landholders, a minority though they were, constituted the political (and often the intellectual) elite of the Greek world; our evidence reveals remarkably few names of any consequence whose economic base was outside the land. This landholding elite tended to become more and more of an absentee group in the course of Greek history; but early or late, whether they sat on their estates or in the cities, dependent labour worked their land as a basic rule (even when allowance is made for tenancy).

[11] See A. Aymard, "L'idée de travail dans la Grèce archaïque", J. de Psych. XLI (1948), 29–45.

[12] Rhet. 1.9, 1367a32.

[13] This statement is not invalidated by the occasional sally which a smallholder or petty craftsman might make into the labour market to do three days' harvesting or a week's work on temple construction; or by the presence in cities like Athens of a substantial number of men, almost all of them unskilled, who lived on odd jobs (when they were not rowing in the fleet or otherwise occupied by the state), those, for example, who congregated daily at Κολωνὸς μίσθιος (on which see A. Fuks, in Eranos XLIX, 1951, 171–73). Nowhere in the sources do we hear of private establishments employing a staff of hired workers as their normal operation. Public works are frequently adduced as evidence to the contrary, but I believe without sufficient cogency. In the first place, the more common practice seems to have been a contract with an entrepreneur (even if he worked alone), not hire for wages; see P. H. Davis, "The Delian Building Accounts", Bull. Corr. Hell. LXI (1937), at pp. 110–20. Second, such evidence as we have – most fully from Delos – argues that such work was spasmodic and infrequent, and quite inconceivable as a source of livelihood for any but a handful of men. All this is consistent with the view that most of the craftsmen appearing in the accounts were independent masons and carpenters who occasionally accepted a job from the state just as they accepted orders from private clients. The key to the whole question is the absence of entrepreneurs whose regular labour force consisted of hired free men.

In some areas it took the form of helotage, and in the archaic period, of debt-bondage, but generally the form was outright slavery.

I am aware, of course, that this view of slavery in Greek agriculture is now strongly contested. Nevertheless, I accept the evidence of the line of authors whom I have already cited, from Hesiod to the pseudo-Aristotelian *Oeconomica*. These are all matter-of-fact writings, not utopias or speculative statements of what ought to be. If slavery was not the customary labour form on the larger holdings, then I cannot imagine what Hesiod or Xenophon or the Peripatetic were doing, or why any Greek bothered to read their works.[14] One similar piece of evidence is worth adding. There was a Greek harvest festival called the Kronia, which was celebrated in Athens and other places (especially among the Ionians). One feature, says the Atthidographer Philochorus, was that "the heads of families ate the crops and fruits at the same table with their slaves, with whom they had shared the labours of cultivation. For the god is pleased with this honour from the slaves in contemplation of their labours."[15] Neither the practice nor Philochorus' explanation of it makes any sense whatever if slavery was as unimportant in agriculture as some modern writers pretend.

I had better be perfectly clear here: I am not saying that slaves outnumbered free men in agriculture, or that the bulk of farming was done by slaves, but that slavery dominated agriculture insofar as it was on a scale that transcended the labour of the householder and his sons. Nor am I suggesting that there was no hired free labour; rather that there was little of any significance. Among the slaves, furthermore, were the overseers, invariably so if the property was large enough or if the owner was an absentee. "Of slaves," said the author of the *Oeconomica*, "there are two kinds, the overseer and the worker."

In mining and quarrying the situation was decisively one-sided. There were free men, in Athens for example, who leased such small mining concessions that they were able to work them alone. The moment, however, additional labour was introduced (and that was the more common case), it seems normally to have been slave. The largest individual holdings of slaves in Athens were workers in the mines, topped by the one thousand reported to have been leased out for this purpose by the fifth-century general Nicias.[16] It has been suggested, indeed, that at one point there may have been as many as thirty thousand slaves at work in the Athenian silver mines and processing mills.[17]

[14] Scholars who argue that slavery was unimportant in agriculture systematically ignore the *Hausvaterliteratur* and similar evidence, while trying to prove their case partly by weak arguments from silence (on which see G. E. M. de Ste. Croix in Class. Rev., n. s. VII, 1957, p. 56), and partly by reference to the papyri. One cannot protest strongly enough against the latter procedure, since the agricultural regime in Ptolemaic and Roman Egypt was not Greek; see M. Rostovtzeff, The Social & Economic History of the Hellenistic World (3 vols., Oxford, repr. 1953), I 272–77.

[15] Philochorus 328 F 97, ap. Macrob. Sat. 1.10.22.

[16] Xenophon, Poroi 4.14.   [17] See Lauffer, op. cit., II 904–16.

E

Manufacture was like agriculture in that the choice was (even more exclusively) between the independent craftsman working alone or with members of his family and the owner of slaves. The link with slavery was so close (and the absence of free hired labour so complete) that Demosthenes, for example, could say "they caused the *ergasterion* to disappear" and then he could follow, as an exact synonym and with no possible misunderstanding, by saying that "they caused the slaves to disappear".[18] On the other hand, the proportion of operations employing slaves, as against the independent self-employed craftsmen, was probably greater than in agriculture, and in this respect more like mining. In commerce and banking, subordinates were invariably slaves, even in such posts as "bank manager." However, the numbers were small.

In the domestic field, finally, we can take it as a rule that any free man who possibly could afford one, owned a slave attendant who accompanied him when he walked abroad in the town or when he travelled (including his military service), and also a slave woman for the household chores. There is no conceivable way of estimating how many such free men there were, or how many owned numbers of domestics, but the fact is taken for granted so completely and so often in the literature that I strongly believe that many owned slaves even when they could not afford them. (Modern parallels will come to mind readily.) I stress this for two reasons. First, the need for domestic slaves, often an unproductive element, should serve as a cautionary sign when one examines such questions as the efficiency and cost of slave labour. Second, domestic slavery was by no means entirely unproductive. In the countryside in particular, but also in the towns, two important industries would often be in their hands in the larger households, on a straight production for household consumption basis. I refer to baking and textile making, and every medievalist, at least, will at once grasp the significance of the withdrawal of the latter from market production, even if the withdrawal was far from complete.[19]

It would be very helpful if we had some idea how many slaves there were in any given Greek community to carry on all this work, and how they were divided among the branches of the economy. Unfortunately we have no reliable figures, and none at all for most of the *poleis*. What I consider to be the best computations for Athens suggest that the total of slaves reached 80–100,000 in peak periods in the fifth and fourth centuries B.C.[20] Athens had the largest population in the classical Greek world and the largest number of slaves.

[18] Dem. 27.19,26; 28.12; see Finley, Studies in Land and Credit in Ancient Athens (New Brunswick 1952), 67. For another decisive text, see Xen. Memorab. 2.7.6.

[19] On the importance of the domestic slave as nursemaid and pedagogue, see Joseph Vogt's rectoral address, "Wege zur Menschlichkeit in der antiken Sklaverei", Univ. Tübingen Reden XLVII (1958), 19–38. (Dr V. Ehrenberg kindly called my attention to this publication.)

[20] Lauffer, op. cit., II 904–16.

Thucydides said that there were more slaves in his day on the island of Chios than in any other Greek community except Sparta,[21] but I suggest that he was thinking of the density of the slave population measured against the free, not of absolute totals (and in Sparta he meant the helots, not chattel slaves). Other places, such as Aegina or Corinth, may at one time or another also have had a higher ratio of slaves than Athens. And there were surely communities in which the slaves were less dense.

More than that we can scarcely say about the numbers, but I think that is really enough. There is too much tendentious discussion of numbers in the literature already, as if a mere count of heads is the answer to all the complicated questions which flow from the existence of slavery. The Athenian figures I mentioned amount to an average of no less than three or four slaves to each free household (including all free men in the calculation, whether citizen or not). But even the smallest figure anyone has suggested, 20,000 slaves in Demosthenes' time[22] – altogether too low in my opinion – would be roughly equivalent to one slave for each adult citizen, no negligible ratio. Within very broad limits, the numbers are irrelevant to the question of significance. When Starr, for example, objects to "exaggerated guesses" and replies that "the most careful estimates. . . . . reduce the proportion of slaves to far less than half the population, probably one third or one quarter at most",[23] he is proving far less than he thinks. No one seriously believes that slaves did all the work in Athens (or anywhere else in Greece except for Sparta with its helots), and one merely confuses the issues when one pretends that somehow a reduction of the estimates to only a third or a quarter of the population is crucial.[24] In 1860, according to official census figures, slightly less than one third of the total population of the American slave states were slaves. Furthermore, "nearly three-fourths of all free Southerners had no connection with slavery through either family ties or direct ownership. The 'typical' Southerner was not only a small farmer but also a nonslaveholder."[25] Yet no one would think of denying that slavery was a decisive element in southern society. The analogy seems obvious for ancient Greece, where, it can be shown, ownership of slaves was even more widely spread among the free men and the use of slaves much more diversified, and where the estimates do not give a ratio significantly below the

[21] Thuc. 8.40.2.
[22] A. H. M. Jones, Athenian Democracy (Oxford 1957), 76–79; cf. his "Slavery in the Ancient World", Econ. Hist. Rev., 2nd ser., IX (1956), at p. 187.
[23] C. G. Starr, "An Overdose of Slavery", J. Econ. Hist. XVIII (1958), at pp. 21–22.
[24] It is remarkable how completely Starr misses this point in his very belligerent article. Although he says over and over again that slavery was not "dominant" or "basic" in antiquity, I can find no serious argument in his article other than his disproof of the view that slaves did all the work.
[25] Kenneth M. Stampp, The Peculiar Institution: Slavery in the Ante-Bellum South (New York 1956), 29–30.

American one. Simply stated, there can be no denial that there were enough slaves about for them to be, of necessity, an integral factor in the society.

There were two main sources of supply. One was captives, the victims of war and sometimes piracy. One of the few generalizations about the ancient world to which there is no exception is this, that the victorious power had absolute right over the persons and the property of the vanquished.[26] This right was not exercised to its full extent every time, but it was exercised often enough, and on a large enough scale, to throw a continuous and numerous supply of men, women, and children on to the slave market. Alongside the captives we must place the so-called barbarians who came into the Greek world in a steady stream – Thracians, Scythians, Cappadocians, etc. – through the activity of full-time traders, much like the process by which African slaves reached the new world in more modern times. Many were the victims of wars among the barbarians themselves. Others came peacefully, so to speak: Herodotus says that the Thracians sold their children for export.[27] The first steps all took place outside the Greek orbit, and our sources tell us virtually nothing about them, but there can be no doubt that large numbers and a steady supply were involved, for there is no other way to explain such facts as the high proportion of Paphlagonians and Thracians among the slaves in the Attic silver mines, many of them specialists, or the corps of 300 Scythian archers (slaves owned by the state) who constituted the Athenian police force.

Merely to complete the picture, we must list penal servitude and the exposure of unwanted children. Beyond mere mention, however, they can be ignored because they were altogether negligible in their importance. There then remains one more source, breeding, and that is a puzzle. One reads in the modern literature that there was very little breeding of slaves (as distinct from helots and the like) among the Greeks because, under their conditions, it was cheaper to buy slaves than to raise them. I am not altogether satisfied with the evidence for this view, and I am altogether dissatisfied with the economics which is supposed to justify it. There were conditions under which breeding was certainly rare, but for reasons which have nothing to do with economics. In the mines, for example, nearly all the slaves were men, and that is the explanation, simply enough. But what about domestics, among whom the proportion of women was surely high? I must leave the question unanswered, except to remove one fallacy. It is sometimes said that there is a demographic law that no slave population ever reproduces itself, that they must always be replenished from outside. Such a law is a myth: that can be said categorically on the evidence of the southern states, evidence which is statistical and reliable.

[26] See A. Aymard, "Le partage des profits de la guerre dans les traités d'alliance antiques," Rev. hist. CCXVII (1957), 233–49.   [27] Herod. 5.6.

III.

The impression one gets is clearly that the majority of the slaves were foreigners. In a sense, they were all foreigners. That is to say, it was the rule (apart from debt bondage) that Athenians were never kept as slaves in Athens, or Corinthians in Corinth. However, I am referring to the more basic sense, that the majority were not Greeks at all, but men and women from the races living outside the Greek world. It is idle to speculate about proportions here, but there cannot be any reasonable doubt about the majority. In some places, such as the Laurium silver mines in Attica, this meant relatively large concentrations in a small area. The number of Thracian slaves in Laurium in Xenophon's time, for example, was greater than the total population of some of the smaller Greek city-states.

No wonder some Greeks came to identify slaves and barbarians (a synonym for all non-Greeks). The most serious effort, so far as we know, to justify this view as part of the natural arrangement of things, will be found in the first book of Aristotle's *Politics*. It was not a successful effort for several reasons, of which the most obvious is the fact, as Aristotle himself conceded, that too many were slaves "by accident," by the chance of warfare or shipwreck or kidnapping. In the end, natural slavery was abandoned as a concept, defeated by the pragmatic view that slavery was a fact of life, a conventional institution universally practised. As the Roman jurist Florentinus phrased it, "Slavery is an institution of the *ius gentium* whereby someone is subject to the *dominium* of another, contrary to nature."[28] That view (and even sharper formulations) can be traced back to the sophistic literature of the fifth century B.C., and, in a less formal way, to Greek tragedy. I chose Florentinus to quote instead because his definition appears in the *Digest*, in which slavery is so prominent that the Roman law of slavery has been called "the most characteristic part of the most characteristic intellectual product of Rome."[29] Nothing illustrates more perfectly the inability of the ancient world to imagine that there could be a civilized society without slaves.

The Greek world was one of endless debate and challenge. Among the intellectuals, no belief or idea was self-evident: every conception and every institution sooner or later came under attack – religious beliefs, ethical values, political systems, aspects of the economy, even such bedrock institutions as the family and private property. Slavery, too, up to a point, but that point was invariably a good distance short of abolitionist proposals. Plato, who criticized society more radically than any other thinker, did not concern himself much with the question in the *Republic*, but even there he assumed the continuance of slavery. And in the *Laws*, "the number of passages...that deal

[28] Dig. 1.5.4.1.
[29] W. W. Buckland, The Roman Law of Slavery (Cambridge 1908), v.

with slavery is surprisingly large" and the tenor of the legislation is generally more severe than the actual law of Athens at that time. "Their effect, on the one hand, is to give greater authority to masters in the exercise of rule over slaves, and on the other hand to accentuate the distinction between slave and free man."[30] Paradoxically, neither were the believers in the brotherhood of man (whether Cynic, Stoic, or early Christian) opponents of slavery. In their eyes, all material concerns, including status, were a matter of essential indifference. Diogenes, it is said, was once seized by pirates and taken to Crete to be sold. At the auction, he pointed to a certain Corinthian among the buyers and said: "Sell me to him; he needs a master."[31]

The question must then be faced, how much relevance has all this for the majority of Greeks, for those who were neither philosophers nor wealthy men of leisure? What did the little man think about slavery? It is no answer to argue that we must not take "the political theorists of the philosophical schools too seriously as having established 'the main line of Greek thought concerning slavery'."[32] No one pretends that Plato and Aristotle speak for all Greeks. But, equally, no one should pretend that lower-class Greeks necessarily rejected everything which we read in Greek literature and philosophy, simply because, with virtually no exceptions, the poets and philosophers were men of the leisure class. The history of ideology and belief is not so simple. It is a commonplace that the little man shares the ideals and aspirations of his betters – in his dreams if not in the hard reality of his daily life. By and large, the vast majority in all periods of history have always taken the basic institutions of society for granted. Men do not, as a rule, ask themselves whether monogamous marriage or a police force or machine production is necessary to their way of life. They accept them as facts, as self-evident. Only when there is a challenge from one source or another – from outside or from catastrophic famine or plague – do such facts become questions.

A large section of the Greek population was always on the edge of marginal subsistence. They worked hard for their livelihood and could not look forward to economic advancement as a reward for their labours; on the contrary, if they moved at all, it was likely to be downward. Famines, plagues, wars, political struggles, all were a threat, and social crisis was a common enough phenomenon in Greek history. Yet through the centuries no ideology of labour appeared,

---

[30] Glenn R. Morrow, Plato's Law of Slavery in Its Relation to Greek Law (Univ. of Illinois Press 1939), 11 and 127. Morrow effectively disproves the view that "Plato at heart disapproved of slavery and in introducing it into the *Laws* was simply accommodating himself to his age" (pp. 129–30). Cf. G. Vlastos, "Slavery in Plato's Thought", Philos. Rev. L (1941), 293: "There is not the slightest indication, either in the *Republic*, or anywhere else, that Plato means to obliterate or relax in any way" the distinction between slave and free labour.

[31] Diogenes Laertius 6.74. On the Cynics, Stoics, and Christians, see Westermann, op. cit., pp. 24–25, 39–40, 116–17, 149–59.   [32] Westermann, op. cit., p. 14 n. 48.

nothing that can in any sense be counterpoised to the negative judgments with which the writings of the leisure class are filled. There was neither a word in the Greek language with which to express the general notion of "labour", nor the concept of labour "as a general social function."[33] There was plenty of grumbling, of course, and there was pride of craftmanship. Men could not survive psychologically without them. But neither developed into a belief: grumbling was not turned into a punishment for sin – "In the sweat of thy face shalt thou eat bread" – nor pride of craftsmanship into the virtue of labour, into the doctrine of the calling or anything comparable. The nearest to either will be found in Hesiod's *Works and Days*, and in this context the decisive fact about Hesiod is his unquestioning assumption that the farmer will have proper slave labour.

That was all there was to the poor man's counter-ideology: we live in the iron age when "men never rest from toil and sorrow by day, and from perishing by night"; therefore it is better to toil than to idle and perish – but if we can we too will turn to the labour of slaves. Hesiod may not have been able, even in his imagination, to think beyond slavery as *supplementary* to his own labour, but that was the seventh century, still the early days of slavery. About 400 B.C., however, Lysias' cripple could make the serious argument in the Athenian *boule* that he required a dole because he could not afford a slave as a *replacement*.[34] And half a century later Xenophon put forth a scheme whereby every citizen could be maintained by the state, chiefly from revenues to be derived from publicly owned slaves working in the mines.[35]

When talk turned to action, even when crisis turned into civil war and revolution, slavery remained unchallenged. With absolute regularity, all through Greek history, the demand was "Cancel debts and redistribute the land". Never, to my knowledge, do we hear a protest from the free poor, not even in the deepest crises, against slave competition. There are no complaints – as there might well have been – that slaves deprive free men of a livelihood, or compel free men to work for lower wages and longer hours.[36] There is nothing

[33] See J.-P. Vernant, "Prométhée et la fonction technique", J. de Psych. XLV (1952), 419–29; "Travail et nature dans la Grèce ancienne", J. de Psych. LII (1955), 18–38.

[34] Lys. 24.6: τὸν διαδεξόμενον δ'αὐτὴν οὔπω δύναμαι κτήσασθαι.

[35] Xen. Poroi 4.33; cf. 6.1. The best examples of Utopian dreaming in this direction are, of course, provided by Aristophanes, in Eccl. 651–61 and Plut. 510–26, but I refrain from stressing them because I wish to avoid the long argument about slavery in Attic comedy.

[36] This generalization stands despite an isolated (and confused) passage like Timaeus 566 F 11, ap. Athen. 6.264D, 272B, about Aristotle's friend Mnason. Periander's prohibition of slave ownership (Nicolaus of Damascus 90 F 58) sounds like another of the traditional tyrant's measures designed (as Nicolaus suggests) to keep the citizens of Corinth occupied. If there is any truth in it, the "slaves" may actually have been debt-bondsmen, for the background of Periander's programme was an archaic rural one; see Édouard Will, Korinthiaka (Paris 1955), 510–12.

remotely resembling a workers' programme, no wage demands, no talk of working conditions or government employment measures or the like. In a city like Athens there was ample opportunity. The *demos* had power, enough of them were poor, and they had leaders. But economic assistance took the form of pay for public office and for rowing in the fleet, free admission to the theatre (the so-called theoric fund), and various doles; while economic legislation was restricted to imports and exports, weights and measures, price controls.[37] Not even the wildest of the accusations against the demagogues – and they were wholly unrestrained as every reader of Aristophanes or Plato knows — ever suggested anything which would hint at a working-class interest, or an anti-slavery bias. No issue of free versus slave appears in this field of public activity.[38]

Nor did the free poor take the other possible tack of joining with the slaves in a common struggle on a principled basis. The Solonic revolution in Athens at the beginning of the sixth century B.C., for example, brought an end to debt bondage and the return of Athenians who had been sold into slavery abroad, but not the emancipation of others, non-Athenians, who were in slavery in Athens. Centuries later, when the great wave of slave revolts came after 140 B.C., starting in the Roman west and spreading to the Greek east, the free poor on the whole simply stood apart. It was no issue of theirs, they seem to have thought; correctly so, for the outcome of the revolts promised them nothing one way or the other. Numbers of free men may have taken advantage of the chaos to enrich themselves personally, by looting or otherwise. Essentially that is what they did, when the opportunity arose, in a military campaign, nothing more. The slaves were, in a basic sense, irrelevant to their behaviour at that moment.[39]

In 464 B.C. a great helot revolt broke out, and in 462 Athens dispatched a hoplite force under Cimon to help the Spartans suppress it. When the revolt ended, after nearly five years, a group of the rebels were permitted to escape, and it was Athens which provided them refuge, settling them in Naupactus. A comparable shift took place in the first phase of the Peloponnesian War. In

[37] There is, of course, the argument of Plutarch, Pericles 12.4–5, that the great temple-building activity in fifth-century Athens was a calculated make-work programme. I know of no similar statement in contemporary sources, and the notion is significantly missing in Aristotle, Ath. Pol. 24.3. But even if Plutarch is right, public works at best provided supplementary income (see n. 13) and they made use of slave labour, thus serving as further evidence for my argument. Nor could Plutarch's thesis be applied to many cities (if any) other than Athens.

[38] I doubt if any point can be made in this context of the fact that citizens and slaves worked side by side in the fields and workshops and on public works, or that they sometimes belonged to the same cult associations. Such phenomena are widespread wherever slavery existed, including the American South.

[39] See Joseph Vogt, Struktur der antiken Sklavenkriege (Mainz Abh. 1957, no. 1), 53–57; cf. E. A. Thompson, "Peasant Revolts in Late Roman Gaul and Spain", Past & Present, no. 2 (1952), 11–23.

425 the Athenians seized Pylos, a harbour on the west coast of the Peloponnese. The garrison was ꞓ small one and Pylos was by no means an important port. Nevertheless, Sparta was so frightened that she soon sued for peace, because the Athenian foothold was a dangerous centre of infection, inviting desertion and eventual revolt among the Messenian helots. Athens finally agreed to peace in 421, and immediately afterwards concluded an alliance with Sparta, one of the terms of which was: "Should the slave-class rise in rebellion, the Athenians will assist the Lacedaemonians with all their might, according to their power."[40]

Obviously the attitude of one city to the slaves of another lies largely outside our problem. Athens agreed to help suppress helots when she and Sparta were allies; she encouraged helot revolts when they were at war. That reflects elementary tactics, not a judgment about slavery. Much the same kind of distinction must be made in the instances, recurring in Spartan history, when helots were freed as pawns in an internal power struggle. So, too, of the instances which were apparently not uncommon in fourth-century Greece, but about which nothing concrete is known other than the clause in the agreement between Alexander and the Hellenic League, binding the members to guarantee that "there shall be no killing or banishment contrary to the laws of each city, no confiscation of property, no redistribution of land, no cancellation of debts, no freeing of slaves for purposes of revolution."[41] These were mere tactics again. Slaves were resources, and they could be useful in a particular situation. But only a number of specific slaves, those who were available at the precise moment; not slaves in general, or all slaves, and surely not slaves in the future. Some slaves were freed, but slavery remained untouched. Exactly the same behaviour can be found in the reverse case, when a state (or ruling class) called upon its slaves to help protect it. Often enough in a military crisis, slaves were freed, conscripted into the army or navy, and called upon to fight.[42] And again the result was that some slaves were freed while the institution continued exactly as before.

[40] The relevant passages in Thucydides are 4.41, 55, 80; 5.14; 5.23.3; 7.26.2. The "slave-class" (ἡ δουλεία) here meant the helots, of course. In my text in the pages which follow immediately (on slaves in war), I also say "slaves" to include the helots, ignoring for the moment the distinction between them.

[41] Ps.-Demosthenes 17.15. For earlier periods, cf. Herod. 7.155 on Syracuse and Thuc. 3.73 on Corcyra (and note that Thucydides does not return to the point or generalize about it in his final peroration on *stasis* and its evils).

[42] See the material assembled by Louis Robert, Etudes épigraphiques et philologiques (Bibl. Éc. Hautes Ét. 272, Paris 1938), 118–26. Xenophon, Poroi 4.42, uses the potential value of slaves as military and naval manpower as an argument in favour of his proposal to have the state buy thousands of slaves to be hired out in the mines. Cf. Hypereides' proposal after Chaeronea to free all the Athenian slaves and arm them (see fragments of his speech against Aristogeiton, Blass no. 18, and Ps.-Plut., Hyper. 848F–849A).

In sum, under certain conditions of crisis and tension the society (or a sector of it) was faced with a conflict within its system of values and beliefs. It was sometimes necessary, in the interest of national safety or of a political programme, to surrender the normal use of, and approach to, slaves. When this happened, the institution itself survived without any noticeable weakening. The fact that it happened is not without significance; it suggests that among the Greeks, even in Sparta, there was not that deep-rooted and often neurotic horror of the slaves known in some other societies, which would have made the freeing and arming of slaves en masse, for whatever purpose, a virtual impossibility. It suggests, further, something about the slaves themselves. Some did fight for their masters, and that is not unimportant.

Nothing is more elusive than the psychology of the slave. Even when, as in the American South, there seems to be a lot of material – autobiographies of ex-slaves, impressions of travellers from non-slaveholding societies, and the like – no reliable picture emerges.[43] For antiquity there is scarcely any evidence at all, and the bits are indirect and tangential, and far from easy to interpret. Thus, a favourite apology is to invoke the fact that, apart from very special instances as in Sparta, the record shows neither revolts of slaves nor a fear of uprisings. Even if the facts are grante d– and the nature of our sources warrants a little scepticism – the rosy conclusion does not follow. Slaves have scarcely ever revolted, even in the southern states.[44] A large-scale rebellion is impossible to organize and carry through except under very unusual circumstances. The right combination appeared but once in ancient history, during two generations of the late Roman Republic, when there were great concentrations of slaves in Italy and Sicily, many of them almost completely unattended and unguarded, many others professional fighters (gladiators), and when the whole society was in turmoil, with a very marked breakdown of social and moral values.[45]

At this point it is necessary to recall that helots differed in certain key respects from chattel slaves. First, they had the necessary ties of solidarity that come from kinship and nationhood, intensified by the fact, not to be underestimated, that they were not foreigners but a subject people working their own lands in a state of servitude. This complex was lacking among the slaves of the Greek world. The Peripatetic author of the *Oeconomica* made the sensible recommendation that neither an individual nor a city should have many slaves of the same nationality.[46] Second, the helots had property rights of a kind: the law, at least, permitted them to retain everything they produced beyond the fixed deliveries to their masters. Third, they outnumbered the free population on a scale without parallel in other Greek communities. These are the peculiar factors, in my opinion, which explain the revolts of the helots and the persistent

---

[43] See Stampp, op. cit., pp. 86–88.

[44] Ibid., pp. 132–40.   [45] Vogt, Sklavenkrieg.

[46] Ps.-Arist., Oec. 1.5,1344b18; cf. Plato, Laws 6.777C–D; Arist., Pol. 7.9.9, 1330a 25–28.

Spartan concern with the question, more than Spartan cruelty.[47] It is a fallacy to think that the threat of rebellion increases automatically with an increase in misery and oppression. Hunger and torture destroy the spirit; at most they stimulate efforts at flight or other forms of purely individual behaviour (including betrayal of fellow-victims), whereas revolt requires organization and courage and persistence. Frederick Douglass, who in 1855 wrote the most penetrating analysis to come from an ex-slave, summed up the psychology in these words:

"Beat and cuff your slave, keep him hungry and spiritless, and he will follow the chain of his master like a dog; but feed and clothe him well, – work him moderately – surround him with physical comfort, – and dreams of freedom intrude. Give him a *bad* master, and he aspires to a *good* master; give him a good master, and he wishes to become his *own* master."[48]

There are many ways, other than revolt, in which slaves can protest.[49] In particular they can flee, and though we have no figures whatsoever, it seems safe to say that the fugitive slave was a chronic and sufficiently numerous phenomenon in the Greek cities.[50] Thucydides estimated that more than 20,000 Athenian slaves fled in the final decade of the Peloponnesian War. In this they were openly encouraged by the Spartan garrison established in Decelea, and Thucydides makes quite a point of the operation. Obviously he thought the harm to Athens was serious, intensified by the fact that many were skilled workers.[51] My immediate concern is with the slaves themselves, not with Athens, and I should stress very heavily that so many skilled slaves (who must be presumed to have been, on the average, among the best treated) took the risk and tried to flee. The risk was no light one, at least for the barbarians among them: no Thracian or Carian wandering about the Greek countryside without credentials could be sure of what lay ahead in Boeotia or Thessaly. Indeed, there is a hint that these particular 20,000 and more may have been very badly treated after escaping under Spartan promise. A reliable fourth-century historian attributed the great Theban prosperity at the end of the fifth century to their having purchased very cheaply the slaves and other booty seized from the Athenians during the Spartan occupation of Decelea.[52] Although there is no

[47] Note that Thucydides 8.40.2 makes the disproportionately large number of Chian slaves the key to their ill-treatment and their readiness to desert to the Athenians.

[48] My Bondage and My Freedom (New York 1855), 263–64, quoted from Stampp, op. cit., p. 89.

[49] Stampp, op. cit., ch. III: "A Troublesome Property", should be required reading on this subject.

[50] I am prepared to say this despite the fact that the evidence is scrappy and has not, to my knowledge, been properly assembled. For mass flights in time of war, see e.g. Thuc. 7.75.5; 8.40.2.

[51] Note how Thucydides stressed the loss in anticipation (1.142.4; 6.91.7) before actually reporting it in 7.27.5.   [52] Hellenica Oxyrhynchia 12.4.

way to determine whether this is a reference to the 20,000, the suspicion is obvious. Ethics aside, there was no power, within or without the law, which could have prevented the re-enslavement of fugitive slaves even if they had been promised their freedom.

The *Oeconomica* sums up the life of the slave as consisting of three elements: work, punishment, and food.[53] And there are more than enough floggings, and even tortures, in Greek literature, from one end to the other. Apart from psychological quirks (sadism and the like), flogging means simply that the slave, as slave, must be goaded into performing the function assigned to him. So, too, do the various incentive plans which were frequently adopted. The efficient, skilled, reliable slave could look forward to managerial status. In the cities, in particular, he could often achieve a curious sort of quasi-independence, living and working on his own, paying a kind of rental to his owner, and accumulating earnings with which, ultimately, to purchase his freedom. Manumission was, of course, the greatest incentive of all. Again we are baffled by the absence of numbers, but it is undisputed that manumission was a common phenomenon in most of the Greek world. This is an important difference between the Greek slave on the one hand, and the helot or American slave on the other. It is also important evidence about the degree of the slave's alleged "acceptance" of his status.[54]

IV.

It is now time to try to add all this up and form some judgment about the institution. This would be difficult enough to do under ordinary circumstances; it has become almost impossible because of two extraneous factors imposed by modern society. The first is the confusion of the historical study with moral judgments about slavery. We condemn slavery, and we are embarrassed for the Greeks, whom we admire so much; therefore we tend either to underestimate its role in their life, or we ignore it altogether, hoping that somehow it will quietly go away. The second factor is more political, and it goes back at least to 1848, when the *Communist Manifesto* declared that "The history of all hitherto existing society is the history of class struggles. Free man and slave, patrician and plebeian, lord and serf, guild-master and journeyman, in a word, oppressor and oppressed, stood in constant opposition to one another...." Ever since, ancient slavery has been a battleground between Marxists and non-Marxists, a political issue rather than a historical phenomenon.

---

[53] Ps.-Arist., Oec. 1.5,1344a35.

[54] The technical and aesthetic excellence of much work performed by slaves is, of course, visible in innumerable museums and archaeological sites. This is part of the complexity and ambiguity of the institution (discussed in the following section), which extended to the slaves themselves as well as to their masters.

Now we observe that a sizable fraction of the population of the Greek world consisted of slaves, or other kinds of dependent labour, many of them barbarians; that by and large the elite in each city-state were men of leisure, completely free from any preoccupation with economic matters, thanks to a labour force which they bought and sold, over whom they had extensive property rights, and, equally important, what we may call physical rights; that the condition of servitude was one which no man, woman, or child, regardless of status or wealth, could be sure to escape in case of war or some other unpredictable and uncontrollable emergency. It seems to me that, seeing all this, if we could emancipate ourselves from the despotism of extraneous moral, intellectual, and political pressures, we would conclude, without hesitation, that slavery was a basic element in Greek civilization.

Such a conclusion, however, should be the starting-point of analysis, not the end of an argument, as it is so often at present. Perhaps it would be best to avoid the word "basic" altogether, because it has been preempted as a technical term by the Marxist theory of history. Anyone else who uses it in such a question as the one which is the title of this paper, is compelled, by the intellectual (and political) situation in which we work, to qualify the term at once, to distinguish between a basic institution and the basic institution. In effect what has happened is that, in the guise of a discussion of ancient slavery, there has been a desultory discussion of Marxist theory, none of it, on either side, particularly illuminating about either Marxism or slavery. Neither our understanding of the historical process nor our knowledge of ancient society is significantly advanced by these repeated statements and counter-statements, affirmations and denials of the proposition, "Ancient society was based on slave labour." Nor have we gained much from the persistent debate about causes. Was slavery the cause of the decline of Greek science? or of loose sexual morality? or of the widespread contempt for gainful employment? These are essentially false questions, imposed by a naive kind of pseudo-scientific thinking.

The most fruitful approach, I suggest, is to think in terms of purpose, in Immanuel Kant's sense, or of function, as the social anthropologists use that concept. The question which is most promising for systematic investigation is not whether slavery was the basic element, or whether it caused this or that, but how it functioned.[55] This eliminates the sterile attempts to decide which was historically prior, slavery or something else; it avoids imposing moral judgments on, and prior to, the historical analysis; and it should avoid the trap which I shall call the free-will error. There is a maxim of Emile Durkheim's that "The voluntary character of a practice or an institution should never be

[55] Cf. Vogt, "Wege zur Menschlichkeit", pp. 19–20: "What we lack is a clear picture of the functions maintained by slavery in the organism of ancient society, and a critical evaluation of its role in the rise, development, and decline of the culture."

assumed beforehand."[56] Given the existence of slavery – and it is given, for our sources do not permit us to go back to a stage in Greek history when it did not exist – the choice facing individual Greeks was socially and psychologically imposed. In the *Memorabilia* Xenophon says that "those who can do so buy slaves so that they may have fellow workers."[57] That sentence is often quoted to prove that some Greeks owned no slaves, which needs no proof. It is much better cited to prove that *those who can*, buy slaves – Xenophon clearly places this whole phenomenon squarely in the realm of necessity.

The question of function permits no single answer. There are as many answers as there are contexts: function in relation to what? And when? And where? Buckland begins his work on the Roman law of slavery by noting that there "is scarcely a problem which can present itself, in any branch of law, the solution of which may not be affected by the fact that one of the parties to the transaction is a slave."[58] That sums up the situation in its simplest, most naked form, and it is as correct a statement for Greek law as for Roman. Beyond that, I would argue, there is no problem or practice in any branch of Greek life which was not affected, in some fashion, by the fact that many people in that society, even if not in the specific situation under consideration, were (or had been) slaves. The connection was not always simple or direct, nor was the impact necessarily "bad" (or "good"). The historian's problem is precisely to uncover what the connections were, in all their concreteness and complexity, their goodness or badness or moral neutrality.

I think we will find that, more often than not, the institution of slavery turned out to be ambiguous in its function. Certainly the Greek attitudes to it were shot through with ambiguity, and not rarely with tension. To the Greeks, Nietzsche said, both labour and slavery were "a necessary disgrace, of which one feels *ashamed*, as a disgrace and as a necessity at the same time."[59] There was a lot of discussion: that is clear from the literature which has survived, and it was neither easy nor unequivocally one-sided, even though it did not end in abolitionism. In Roman law "slavery is the only case in which, in the extant sources...., a conflict is declared to exist between the *Ius Gentium* and the *Ius Naturale*."[60] In a sense, that was an academic conflict, since slavery went right on; but no society can carry such a conflict within it, around so important a set of beliefs and institutions, without the stresses erupting in some fashion, no matter how remote and extended the lines and connections may be from the original stimulus. Perhaps the most interesting sign among the Greeks can

[56] E. Durkheim, The Rules of Sociological Method, transl. from 8th ed. (repr. Glencoe, Ill., 1950), 28.

[57] Xen., Mem. 2.3.3.   [58] Op. cit., p. v.

[59] The Greek State: Preface to an Unwritten Book, in Early Greek Philosophy & Other Essays, transl. by M. A. Mügge (London & Edinburgh 1911), 6.

[60] Buckland, op. cit., p. 1.

be found in the proposals, and to an extent the practice in the fourth century B.C., to give up the enslavement of Greeks.[61] They all came to nought in the Hellenistic world, and I suggest that this one fact reveals much about Greek civilization after Alexander.[62]

It is worth calling attention to two examples pregnant with ambiguity, neither of which has received the attention it deserves. The first comes from Locris, the Greek colony in southern Italy, where descent was matrilineal, an anomaly which Aristotle explained historically. The reason, he said, was that the colony was originally founded by slaves and their children by free women. Timaeus wrote a violent protest against this insulting account, and Polybius, in turn, defended Aristotle in a long digression, of which unfortunately only fragments survive. One of his remarks is particularly worth quoting: "To suppose, with Timaeus, that it was unlikely that men, who had been the slaves of the allies of the Lacedaemonians, would continue the kindly feelings and adopt the friendships of their late masters is foolish. For when they have had the good fortune to recover their freedom, and a certain time has elapsed, men, who have been slaves, not only endeavour to adopt the friendships of their late masters, but also their ties of hospitality and blood; in fact, their aim is to keep them up even more than the ties of nature, for the express purpose of thereby wiping out the remembrance of their former degradation and humble position, because they wish to pose as the descendants of their masters rather than as their freedmen."[63]

In the course of his polemic Timaeus had said that "it was not customary for the Greeks of early times to be served by bought slaves."[64] This distinction, between slaves who were bought and slaves who were captured (or bred from captives), had severe moral overtones. Inevitably, as was their habit, the Greeks found a historical origin for the practice of buying slaves – in the island of Chios. The historian Theopompus, a native of the island, phrased it this way: "The Chians were the first of the Greeks, after the Thessalians and Lacedaemonians, who used slaves. But they did not acquire them in the same manner as the latter; for the Lacedaemonians and Thessalians will be found to have derived their slaves from the Greeks who formerly inhabited the territory which they now possess, ... calling them helots and *penestae*, respectively. But

---

[61] See F. Kiechle, "Zur Humanität in der Kriegführung der griechischen Staaten", Historia VII (1958), 129–56, for a useful collection of materials, often vitiated by a confusion between a fact and a moralizing statement; and even more by special pleading of a familiar tendency, as in the argument (p. 140 n. 1) that reports of mass enslavement or massacre must not be taken too literally because some always managed to escape, or in the pointless discussion (pp. 150–53) of the supposed significance of Polybius' use of ἀναγκάζουσιν instead of κελεύουσιν in 5.11.3.

[62] See Rostovtzeff, op. cit. I 201–208.

[63] Polyb. 12.6a (transl. by E. S. Shuckburgh).

[64] 566 F 11, ap. Athen. 6.264C; cf. 272 A–B.

the Chians possessed barbarian slaves, for whom they paid a price."[65] This quotation is preserved by Athenaeus, whose *floruit* was about 200 A.D. and who went on to comment that the Chians ultimately received divine punishment for their innovation. The stories he then tells, as evidence, are curious and interesting, but I cannot take time for them.

This is not very good history, but that does not make it any less important. By a remarkable coincidence Chios provides us with the earliest contemporary evidence of democratic institutions in the Greek world. In a Chian inscription dated, most probably, to the years 575–550 B.C., there is unmistakable reference to a popular council and to the "laws (or ordinances) of the *demos*".[66] I do not wish to assign any significance other than symbolic to this coincidence, but it is a symbol with enormous implications. I have already made the point that, the more advanced the Greek city-state, the more it will be found to have had true slavery rather than the "hybrid" types like helotage. More bluntly put, the cities in which individual freedom reached its highest expression – most obviously Athens – were cities in which chattel slavery flourished. The Greeks, it is well known, discovered both the idea of individual freedom and the institutional framework in which it could be realized.[67] The pre-Greek world – the world of the Sumerians, Babylonians, Egyptians, and Assyrians; and I cannot refrain from adding the Mycenaeans – was, in a very profound sense, a world without free men, in the sense in which the west has come to understand that concept. It was equally a world in which chattel slavery played no role of any consequence. That, too, was a Greek discovery. One aspect of Greek history, in short, is the advance, hand in hand, of freedom *and* slavery.

Jesus College, Cambridge.   M. I. FINLEY

---

[65] 115 F 122, ap. Athen. 6.265B–C.

[66] For the most recent discussion of this text, see L. H. Jeffery in Annual of the Brit. Sch. Athens, LI (1956), 157–67.

[67] It is hardly necessary to add that "freedom" is a term which, in the Greek context, was restricted to the members of the *koinonia*, always a fraction, and often a minor fraction, of the total male population.

V

ATHENAEUS AND THE SLAVES OF ATHENS

By William Linn Westermann

IN THE calculation of the population of the Athenian state made by Demetrius of Phalerum "the returns for the slave population . . . have not come down to us, but the number of the slaves perhaps equalled the citizens and aliens combined." [1] Many years have passed since Professor Ferguson suggested this ratio as a possible proportion between slaves and free in the city-state of Athens late in the fourth century B.C. It would mean that bond and free were about equal, one to one. Since that time his views may well have changed. As at the time when it was penned, this view would even now be regarded as a judiciously balanced estimate, characteristic of the good judgment and temperance which have been so consistent a quality of that scholarship which the friends and pupils of Professor Ferguson have wished to honor through these studies. If the more drastic estimate which eventually is presented in this paper differs from his own, it is offered without polemical intent, as a problem vital to the consideration of the history and culture of the city-state of Athens which has so long enlisted the interest and scholarly ability of Professor Ferguson.

Inquiries into the number of slaves in Attica have been made many times.[2] There is little new evidence contemporary with the special period of the fifth and fourth centuries before Christ [3] to

---

[1] W. S. Ferguson *Hellenistic Athens* (1911) 54. Through combination of Diodorus XVIII 74. 3 with the report of this population estimate as it has come down to us, Felix Jacoby, *Fragmente der griechischen Historiker*, II D 245, p. 813, under *Stesikleides*, would date the ἐξετασμός of Demetrius in 317–316 B.C. Ferguson placed it shortly after 311 B.C. Because of an obvious mistake in the text a positive conclusion as to date is not possible.

[2] For a summary of the modern attitudes and discussions of the numbers of slaves see Rachel L. Sargent, *The Size of the Slave Population at Athens*, University of Illinois Studies in the Social Sciences XII no. 3 (1924), 13–43.

[3] It is one of those disappointments inherent in the luck of excavations that the American excavations of the Agora at Athens have thrown no new light upon the slave system of the city.

F

present and evaluate. In discussing the slave problem in Greece Alfred Zimmern has said: "the same evidence is marshalled; the same references and footnotes are transferred, like stale tea-leaves, from one learned receptacle to another."[1] Partly true; but it should be said in praise of the persistence of pedantry — not in blame. Every ambitious actor must at some time stage his own conception of Hamlet. In like manner every student of the greatness of Athens, of the causes which made its people so vibrant a force in the moulding of Greek culture, must make his own decision, so far as he can, upon this matter of the numerical relation of the slave population to the free. For upon that decision, in some degree, depends an important judgment regarding the total character of Athenian society and its vaunted individual freedom and liberty. Was it a slave state, in its total spirit, or was it really free? One cannot evade the issue or conjure it away by re-defining Greek slavery upon general assumptions regarding its nature and its effects. Every slave system is an integral part of that social and economic organism in which it is embedded. In every social system of which it is a part slavery determines in some measure the nature of that system and is itself, in some degree, modified by the total social system. In no two state organisms is it ever quite the same.

In one of his assumptions Zimmern was not well informed. As a matter of record there was available when he wrote a large amount of new information upon ancient slavery. This information has been considerably increased since he wrote his article.[2] It consists of documentary and contemporary evidence upon slavery itself and upon related forms of bondage, which derives

[1] Alfred Zimmern, *Solon and Croesus* (1928), p. 106.

[2] Cf. Zimmern's statement of ten "distinctive features" of a slave system of labor, *op. cit.* 110–113. Five may be accepted as correct, so far as generalizations are correct; but the remaining five are either incorrect or questionable. Who needs to be told in these days that theoretical economics do not guide us to an understanding of society's problems? Zimmern's distinction between chattel-slavery and apprentice-slavery (p. 120) has no meaning to me. Slavery is a system under which some human beings are chattels. Where this fundamental legal and social fact does not exist another relationship between human groups has arisen which is not slavery.

from the lands and peoples of the pre-Greek cultures and from the extensions of Greek civilization, in hybrid forms of cultural expression, into the Hellenistic and Roman phases of antiquity.[1] Refreshed with new knowledge and new points of view one moves backward from the later period into the two centuries of Athenian leadership. So doing, one may question with revived interest the old facts and the old falsehoods; and one finds that they have taken on new meanings. The old tea-leaves, quite suddenly, are no longer stale.

In 1423 the ardent Italian collector of Greek manuscripts, Giovanni Aurispa, brought back the one manuscript of the *Deipnosophists* of Athenaeus which is the source of all later manuscripts and editions of that work.[2] It was this, our good luck, which introduced into the study of ancient slavery all the difficulties which face us regarding the relative proportion of enslaved and free in antiquity. Were it not for the rambling and antiquarian table-talk of these dining-club professors of Athenaeus we would have had to deal, predominantly, with comprehensible and credible numbers of slaves — fifties, hundreds, and thousands, instead of thousands, myriads and hundreds of thousands.

Athenaeus, a "culture Greek"[3] of Naucratis in Egypt, put together this work, of the symposium type, somewhere near the close of the second century of our era. Despite obvious and demonstrable blunders in copying made by Athenaeus or by his amanuensis[4] it is impossible to dismiss him summarily. So much of his material

[1] The new materials from Hellenistic and Roman times will be found in synthetic presentation, interwoven with the old, in the article "Sklaverei" in Pauly-Wissowa-Kroll, *Realencyclopädie*, Supplementband VI, cols. 893–1068. A large amount of new information upon slavery in the Neo-Babylonian Kingdom has been assembled at the Oriental Institute of the University of Chicago. At the time of this writing it has not yet been published.

[2] Wilhelm von Christ — Wilhelm Schmid, *Geschichte der griech. Literatur*, 5th ed. (1913) II 2. 628.

[3] The phrase was coined, so far as I know, by W. W. Tarn in his *Hellenistic Civilization*.

[4] E.g. in XI 500 c Dercyllidas is called a "Scythian." Actually he was called a "Sisyphus." *Vide* Xen. *Hell*. III 1. 8 and Jules Nicole in *Bibl. de l'École des Hautes Études, Sciences Phil. et Hist*. LXXIII (1887) p. 29. In II 44 c where Athenaeus should be speaking of a certain Sostratus he places instead Philinus who

is right that one must specifically prove him to be wrong or fantastic if one wishes to discard his alleged facts at any point. In Book VI 272–273 a, Athenaeus cites several passages upon the number of slaves owned by individuals in the past and of slaves resident in certain city-states. Among these is this statement: "Ctesicles says, in the third book of his *Chronica*, that during the one hundred and ——teenth [1] Olympiad an investigation [2] was held at Athens by Demetrius of Phalerum of those inhabiting Attica; and the Athenians were found to be 21,000, the metics 10,000 and the servants (οἰκετῶν in the text) forty myriads (400,000)." The context makes it certain that by οἰκέται Athenaeus means slaves; and we would not be warranted in doubting that the numbers were correctly copied from Ctesicles' *Chronica*. If we are to accept this number the enslaved persons of the Athenian state about 317–308 B.C. surpassed the free by about four to one. About the same ratio, according to further citations given by Athenaeus, would hold for Corinth and Aegina. The entire group of his quotations dealing with slave numbers is presented with the obvious intent of proving this single point, that the slaves in ancient Greece, that is 500 years before his time, greatly outnumbered the free. To discredit his proofs one must necessarily analyze the entire set of citations, because one must concede that they make a formidable group of alleged facts, which in their totality become impressive through the array of their numerical similarities.

Timaeus of Sicily is first cited as stating that it was not customary among the Greeks to possess slaves. Probably Timaeus said that the Greeks, in olden times (presumably referring to Homeric times, as shown by τὸ πάλαιον), did not use purchased slaves as personal attendants. [3] Athenaeus then points out that

---

was, in reality, the source of the information about Sostratus. See K. Funk in *Philologus*, Supplementband X (1905–1907) 641 n. 233.

[1] There is a lacuna in the text at this point. The manuscript has only καὶ δεκάτηι πρὸς ταῖς ἑκατόν.

[2] The word used is ἐξετασμός, from ἐξετάζειν, not ἀπογραφία, which would be used to designate a formal census.

[3] See Athenaeus VI 264 c. Polybius, book XII, is quoted by Athenaeus, VI

Timaeus' statement is inconsistent with another of his statements that Mnason of Phocis owned more than 1,000 slaves, and with still another citation, from the third book of the "Histories" of Timaeus, to the effect that Corinth was so prosperous that it possessed forty-six myriads of slaves (460,000). After this follows the quotation from Ctesicles about Demetrius of Phalerum and his 400,000 slaves at Athens. From a monograph of Aristotle upon the *Polity of the Aeginetans*, which is now lost, comes the information that there were 470,000 slaves in their state. Out of Sicilian and Italian history of the second and first centuries B.C., without statement of his sources, Athenaeus offers the information that more than a million slaves were put to death in the slave revolts, and that Spartacus caused "a large number" of slaves to rise and that daily they "poured in" to join him.

The numbers which he advances for individual property in slaves are so chosen that they consistently support the general idea of these masses of enslaved persons in the Greek city-states. There is the affirmation, quoted above, about Mnason of Phocis and his more than 1,000 slaves. From the pamphlet *Upon the Revenues*, ascribed to Xenophon,[1] Athenaeus quotes a reference to the effect that Nicias (the general of the Sicilian expedition) had a thousand slaves and leased them for work in the silver mines to Sosias, a Thracian, on an arrangement by which each rented slave brought in an obol a day.[2] The slave investment of Nicias is later supported by a quotation from Posidonius regarding a slave revolt in Attica which occurred about 103–102 B.C.[3] Posidonius "says that they murdered the guards at the mines, captured the fortress at Sunium

---

272 b, in refutation of the first statement. This part of the twelfth book of Polybius is lost except in the citation by Athenaeus.

[1] The question of the authorship, whether actually written by Xenophon or not, does not vitally affect the discussion of slave numbers given in the *Revenues*. I however, have not been favorably impressed with the contention of W. Schwahn in *Rheinisches Museum* LXXX (1931) 258–259, that it is not from Xenophon's hand, nor by his arguments which would assign it to Eubulus, finance minister at Athens, or to one of his followers. See Adolf Wilhelm's able discussion of the *Revenues* of Xenophon in *Wiener Studien* LII (1934) 18–19, 37–38.

[2] The statement is a fairly exact abridgement of Xenophon, *Upon the Revenues* 4.14.

[3] W. S. Ferguson in *Klio* IV (1904) 12 and in *Hellenistic Athens* 427 n. 4 and 428 n. 1.

and caused havoc in Attica for some time."[1] This incident might easily have been caused by a total of 500 or 1,000 slaves if they were a determined lot. In fact a similar riot of the slaves in the Attic mines had occurred about thirty years earlier (ca. 130 B.C.) and their numbers are given as "over one thousand."[2] As a figure derived from an ancient source this is fairly definite. At best the slave revolt at Athens, as taken from Posidonius, has no validity as proof that Nicias three hundred years earlier owned a thousand slaves.

It is these "Attic myriads of slaves who worked the mines" which bother Athenaeus, as they have, since his time, bothered everybody who is interested. He returns to the task of bolstering up his Attic myriads. "Each of the Romans . . . has owned prodigious numbers of them. For very many have owned ten thousand and twice ten thousand" which they keep as attendants when they go out. If we begin with the numbers given by Athenaeus about the slaves of the time nearest his own life it becomes immediately apparent that this clipper of interesting data, a bookworm living in Egypt, had no personal knowledge of the Roman Empire in its western part. It is also significant that his dining professors, as they talk about their own time, do not cite references.

Let us begin with those numbers which have actually been transmitted to us by ancient authorities other than Athenaeus for the period of the empire. The writers of the Augustan Histories were credulous enough, in all conscience. But even their credulity never swallowed more than two or three thousand slaves in any one man's possession. Proculus, a robber chieftain of the Maritime Alps in the Ligurian district when he was declared Imperator in 280 A.D. "is said to have armed 2,000 of his own slaves."[3] He was a robber chieftain and might well have armed 2000 followers. But one doubts that they were slaves, because the Emperor Tacitus himself, when he manumitted all the slaves of his urban household, nevertheless kept within the provisions of the Caninian Law which did not permit the freeing of more than one hundred slaves

---

[1] Athenaeus VI 272 f.
[2] Diodorus XXXIV 2. 19: καὶ κατὰ τὴν Ἀττικὴν ὑπὲρ χιλίων.
[3] *Scriptores Historiae Augustae, Firmus* 12. 2.

by any one person.[1] The actual evidence as to numbers of slaves owned by the most powerful families of the Empire, as recorded in the ancient literature and as estimated from epigraphical sources, has been assembled in Pauly-Wissowa-Kroll *Realencyclopädie* Supplementband VI 1000–1002. These data indicate that Seneca's description of a household of conspicuous wealth, where it mentions the "trained cohort of slaves,"[2] sets the upper limit of slave numbers which one can ascribe even to the richest Romans of the early Empire. Taking the legion at its full complement of 6,000 this would place the highest number of slaves in individual possession at about 600.

So much for Athenaeus' ten and twenty thousand slaves owned by the Romans of his time. If we turn to the west at the time of the Republic he betrays his gullibility much more quickly. The total numbers of slaves and poor free persons engaged in the great slave revolts in Sicily and Italy, according to the ancient authorities, are as follows. In Sicily in the revolt of 135–132 B.C. the total numbers ran to 70,000,[3] in the uprising of 104–101 B.C. 3,500 in Italy[4] and certainly not more than 50,000 to 100,000 in Sicily;[5] under Spartacus in Italy in 72–71 B.C. possibly 120,000 men.[6] Out of a total number of slaves and free, in the major slave uprisings, which did not surpass 300,000, Athenaeus has relentlessly slain a million.[7]

---

[1] *Script. Hist. Aug., Tacitus* 10 .7.

[2] Seneca *Epistulae Morales* 110. 17. I reject the 4,116 slaves which Isidorus, a freedman of Gaius Cornelius, is alleged to have enumerated in his will at his death in 8 B.C., Pliny *N. H.* XXXIII 135. The number of small cattle there ascribed to Isidorus, namely 257,000, is somewhat more than one-half of the total of sheep and goats owned in the province of Umbria at the present time. Furthermore it would require about 400 square miles of grazing land to feed Isidorus' sheep and goats alone.

[3] This total recorded by Livy *Epitome* LVI, is more credible than the 200,000 given by Diodorus XXXIV–V 2. 18.

[4] Diodorus XXXVI 2. 6.

[5] The suppression of this revolt was carried out by a Roman army of 17,000 men: Diodorus XXXVI 8. 1.

[6] Appian *Bella Civilia* I 14. 117. The number handed down in the text of Velleius Paterculus II 30. 6 has obviously been corrupted in transmission.

[7] Athenaeus VI 272 f.

Athenaeus may be entirely credible on fish and cakes, but it does seem sensible to eliminate him as an independent source upon the institution of slavery. We must grant, however, that his direct quotations, where he gives his sources, may be quite accurate as quotations, though not so as to fact. For, as we have seen, his quotation about the thousand slaves owned by Nicias is given substantially as it stands in Xenophon *Upon the Revenues*. Let us first dispose of the four hundred and seventy thousand slaves of the Aeginetans. The number purports to come from Aristotle's *Polity of the Aeginetans*. Wherever the mistake lay [1] this figure is jettisoned by common sense and by common consent. Aegina is eight miles long by six miles wide. In 1928 it boasted 8,832 inhabitants.[2] A rough calculation, if we were to accept the number, would give Aegina, in Aristotle's time, a population density of almost twelve thousand to the square mile, counting slaves alone.[3] The most rational guess that we have of the population in the Cyclades islands in antiquity — that of Julius Beloch — allows them about one hundred twenty-five persons per square mile.[4]

Athenaeus is completely out of the picture as an independent witness for masses of slaves owned by wealthy men of Roman times or for the tens of myriads of slaves whom he places among the populations of the Greek city-states of the fourth century B.C. The statement ascribed to Aristotle regarding the 470;000 slaves in Aegina must be disregarded as physically impossible. For the slave numbers in hundreds of thousands we are forced back upon three witnesses of the Hellenistic and earlier Greek periods: first, upon Ctesicles in the *Chronica*, or the investigation of Demetrius of Phalerum, for the 400,000 in Attica; second, upon Timaeus of Sicily for the thousand owned by Mnason of Phocis and the 460,000 possessed by the Corinthians; third, upon the Xenophontic pamphlet *Upon the Revenues* for a thousand slaves

---

[1] It is as difficult to imagine that this number actually appeared in the Aristotelian study as to suppose that Demetrius of Phalerum actually reported that there were 400,000 slaves in Attica.

[2] *Annuaire Statistique de la Grèce* IV, Athens, 1933, p. 43.

[3] Rachel L. Sargent *Slave Population* 20 note 60, 31.

[4] 48 to the square kilometer, as given by Beloch, *Bevölkerung der griechisch-römischen Welt* 506; cf. 84–85.

personally owned by Nicias, six hundred belonging to Hipponicus, and three hundred to Philemonides.

Professor Ferguson himself, in *Hellenistic Athens* p. 54 and note 3, briefly but completely disposed of the slave figures which reputedly go back to the investigation of Demetrius, by assuming that the numbers of the slaves actually recorded in the ἐξετασμός of the Phalerian have not come down to us. If Athenaeus used the very text of Ctesicles' *Chronica*, rather than a quotation from it culled from some later author, and if this text was sound, the fault lay with Ctesicles. There is no possibility of checking upon the reports from Timaeus about Mnason of Phocis and the slaves of Corinth. But if the numbers for Athens are of no value, those for Corinth must be discarded with them. Setting aside for the moment the *Chronica* of Ctesicles and its four hundred thousand Attic slaves, let us approach the statement about the private ownership at Athens of one thousand, of six hundred, and of three hundred slaves by Nicias, Hipponicus, and Philemonides respectively. The first two of these slave owners were well known as exceedingly rich men according to the standards of wealth of their time.[1]

Known instances of family fortunes of the time make it quite certain that capital sums in private hands were sufficient to enable single men of outstanding wealth to purchase as many as a thousand slaves if they concentrated upon this form of investment. According to the reputed wealth of Nicias his investment in slaves would have constituted a third of his entire fortune.[2] Such a fortune must, of course, be regarded as highly exceptional.[3]

---

[1] Xenophon *Upon the Revenues* 4. 14–15. Regarding Hipponicus, note the Athenian jibes directed at him and several of his ancestors because of the sources of their fortunes, in Pauly-Wissowa-Kroll *Realencyclopädie* VIII 1907–1909, *Hipponikos* 1, 2, 3.

[2] According to Lysias, 19. 47–48, the fortune of Nicias was thought to have been 100 talents, that of Callias 200 talents. It should be noted in both of these cases that the evidence available to Lysias was not entirely convincing even to himself. This is apparent from his use of προσεδοκᾶτο in the one case, and ὥς φασι in the other.

[3] The ancient information upon the size of fortunes in Attica in the fifth and fourth centuries in relation to alleged investment in slaves will be found conveniently stated in Sargent *Slave Population* 49–56, 96–100.

If we were to accept at face value the statement of these amazing numbers of slaves owned by Nicias, Hipponicus and Philemonides, as handed down *only* in Xenophon's plan for increasing the state revenues,[1] we would still be unable to arrive at any figure for the total slave population which would make their number exceed that of the free residents of Attica. For it is clear that Xenophon has selected and grouped the highest numbers that he could find and that he regards them as rare and extraordinary cases. Athenian slave labor was predominantly used in the mines at Laurium or as skilled labor in handicraft shops in the city. Intrinsically, under the conditions of economic use of slave labor in Attica, the maintenance by single persons of so many unfree workmen is not credible. Under the plantation system in the southern sections of the United States, which made actual sustenance of the slaves a relatively easy matter, I have found but few instances of ownership of more than 700 negroes by any one planter, whether his main crop was tobacco, cotton or sugar.[2] The slaves owned and employed upon the Brazilian sugar plantations, exclusive of the military forces used as guards on these estates, averaged about 300.

If the evidence of Xenophon in regard to private ownership of

---

[1] The number does not appear in Plutarch *Nicias* 4. Plutarch contents himself with a πλῆθος ἀνδραπόδων. Probably he doubted Xenophon's thousand slaves as much as I do.

[2] In South Carolina just before the Civil War a planter named Burnsides is reputed to have owned more than 1,000 slaves; but this figure is not established by a census report. Where great slave concentrations in single ownership occur they are likely to be on several non-contiguous estates. The numbers of slaves actually owned by the outstanding plantation proprietors in the United States may be illustrated by the following list: In 1790 in South Carolina, William Blake, 695; Ralph Izard, 604; Nathaniel Heyward, 433; William Washington, 393; and three members of the Horry family, respectively, 340, 229 and 222 slaves. See Ulrich Phillips, *American Negro Slavery*, New York, 1918, pp. 95–6. At Mt. Vernon in 1821 Bushrod Washington had 90 slaves. In 1832 the larger plantations in Virginia customarily maintained from 50 to 100 slaves. See Fr. Bancroft, *Slave Trading in the Old South*, Baltimore, 1931, pp. 15–6. This was a sufficient number on any plantation to stamp the owner as an aristocrat, a large planter of honored position, Bancroft pp. 345–6. In 1858 the wealthiest cotton grower in Georgia, Joseph Bond, owned 566 slaves, *ibid.* 353. Compare the 235 slaves of General Gadsden sold in 1859 at Charleston, South Carolina, according to Bancroft, p. 182.

slaves is open·to doubt on general consideration of the difficulties
of slave maintenance, it is still further weakened upon close
analysis of his text. He is arguing that the Athenian state could
buy up a large number of slaves and help to replete the state
income by renting them out, as the "wage-earning" slaves
(μισθοφοροῦντα σώματα) were constantly leased to entrepreneurs by
private owners. In citing his examples of large incomes derived
from the slave-renting system he betrays the scanty nature of his
information. "For long ago, I presume, we who have been interested have heard that Nicias, son of Niceratus, owned in the
silver mines a thousand men which he leased out to Sosias, the
Thracian, on the basis that he pay an obol per day net for each
slave and keep the number always equal.[1] Hipponicus also owned
six hundred slaves let out in the same manner who brought in a
mina net per day, and Philemonides three hundred who brought
in a half mina. And others owned slaves in accordance, I suppose,
with their (financial) ability." [2] No source is given. So far as
Xenophon is concerned it is hearsay from a long time ago (πάλαι;
and note the doubting δήπου). What has he to say of the silver-
mine workers of his own time? "But why speak of matters of long
ago? For now there are many men in the mines rented out thus."
Either the numbers of rented slave laborers in the Laurian mines
in his day were too few to suit his argument, or he had no knowledge of the number. In either case why believe him on hearsay
about matters of fifty-five years earlier?

Two hundred years ago the number of four hundred thousand
slaves for Athens was summarily rejected by the French scholar,
Charles Rollin, who reduced them to forty thousand by the
arbitrary method of assuming an error in the text of Athenaeus.[3]
In 1752 David Hume in his essay upon *The Populousness of Ancient*

[1] The modern editions read here παρέχειν instead of παρεῖχεν of the manuscripts. See Rudolph Herzog in *Festgabe für Hugo Blümner*, Zürich, 1914, pp. 475–
6. Herzog's idea, that Sosias was a slave bailiff, owned by Nicias, may be correct.

[2] Xenophon *Upon theRevenues* 4. 14–15. The rate of interest on investment,
namely an obol net per day on each slave, is the same throughout.

[3] In the edition of his *Histoire ancienne des Egyptiens, des Carthaginois, des
Assyriens*, etc., IV 409, published at Amsterdam in 1735, Rollin merely states that
the 400,000 of Athenaeus are "a manifest error." See also the English translation

Nations adopted this drastic reduction of Rollin and gave ten reasons for so doing.[1] Hume's arguments are thoroughly sound although his reasoning is entirely general and *a priori* in character. In 1817 the great German classicist August Boeckh came to the defense of Athenaeus. His authority was great enough to re-establish faith in the traditional four slaves at Athens to every free person and the corresponding predominance of slaves over the free at Corinth and Aegina.[2] In support of this reaction he advanced a difficult fragment from the Athenian fourth century orator Hyperides[3] in which Hyperides urged that "more than 150,000 from the silver mines and those throughout the rest of the country, then those indebted to the public treasury, the dis-franchised and the metics" should be conscripted for military service; but this fragment, which appears in a quotation by the tenth-century lexicographer Suidas,[4] is so late and the text in

---

The *Ancient History of the Egyptians, Carthaginians, Assyrians* etc., of the same year (London 1735), IV 302, where the note appears with the phrase as just quoted.

[1] *Essays Moral, Political and Literary*, edited by T. H. Green and Grose, London, 1898, I 419–21.

[2] August Boeckh, *Die Staatshaushaltung der Athener*, 3rd ed., Berlin, 1886, I 47–52. He assumes that the relation of the free to the slave population can be placed at 27 to 100, or about 1 to 4 (p. 49). His next statement, that the same relation on the American sugar plantations stood at one free to six slaves, may be true of single plantations; but the comparison between American sugar plantations and the ancient city-states is entirely misleading. In 1850 in the state of Louisiana, where sugar culture was most highly developed in the United States, there were 100 free persons to every 96 slaves. In South Carolina the ratio was 140 slaves to 100 free and in Georgia 124 to 100 free. These are the highest slave numbers known to me in any of the states of the South. See *U. S. Bureau of Census: A Century of Population Growth*, Washington, 1909, p. 140.

Boeckh was followed in England by H. F. Clinton, *Fasti Hellenici*, Oxford, 1841, II 480, and in Germany by B. Büchsenschütz, *Besitz und Erwerb im griechischen Altertume*, Halle, 1869, pp. 140–2, and by the eminent German classicist, Friederich Blass. See his essay upon the *Soziale Zustände in Athen im 4ten Jahrhundert*, Kiel, 1885, p. 9. Jakob Burckhardt, *Griechische Kulturgeschichte*, Berlin, 1898, I 158, although he found it difficult to adjust his conception of Greek culture to such a preponderance of slaves, could not bring himself to an outright break with the statements of Athenaeus.

[3] In the third edition of *Hyperidis Orationes Sex* by C. Jessen, Leipzig, 1917, it appears as fragment 7. 29.

[4] Suidas I 1, p. 279. 22–25 (ed. Adler, Leipzig, 1928).

itself so doubtful that it should not be regarded as admissible evidence in an attempt to determine, even roughly, the ratio of slaves to free in Attica.[1]

The passage of Athenaeus regarding the relatively vast number of slaves in Greek city-states must be dropped *in toto* and, with it, any attempt to re-establish the results of the investigation of the population of Attica, so far as it relates to the numbers of the slaves, except as estimates based upon contemporary indications. The alleged numbers of the slaves privately owned by Nicias, Hipponicus and Philemonides are also, in my judgment, of no historical value, other than to prove that these three were wealthy men who were reputed to have had heavy investments in "wage-earning slaves" (μισθοφοροῦντα σώματα). The one hundred fifty thousand slaves from the mines of Attica, supposedly recorded by Hyperides, must go. With these figures all of the testimony is exhausted, which would warrant the conclusion that Greek society in the fifth and fourth centuries, and particularly that of Athens, was predominantly slave ridden. There were no slave revolts in Greek lands until the second half of the second century B.C., such as marked the history of western plantation slavery from 200 B.C. to 71 B.C. The two revolts which did occur, in 130 B.C. at Delos and Athens and 103–102 B.C. in Athens alone, were backwashes of the great western slave outbreaks of the same periods. The Greek insurrections do not give the impression that large numbers were involved.[2] There is no piece of Greek city-state legislation which betrays any great fear of slave revolts

[1] This number of 150,000 slaves is rejected by Beloch, *Bevölkerung* 98–9 (who would amend it to 40,000 or 50,000) and by Ettore Cicotti, in *Rendiconti dell' Istituto Lombardo*, Series II vol. XXX (1897), pp. 657–9. Attempts to make use of this fragment by arbitrary emendation are unsatisfactory, as stated by Cicotti in the study cited above, p. 668, and by A. W. Gomme, *Population of Athens* 21–2, in criticism of Beloch's emendation.

The story need not be retold of the growing tendency among modern scholars since 1890 to abandon Athenaeus' figures and cut down the estimates of the ratio of slaves to free in Greece, including Athens. See Sargent *Slave Population* 35–42.

[2] These revolts are dealt with, much in this sense, by Professor Ferguson in *Hellenistic Athens* 378–9 and 427–8.

such as lurks constantly in the consciousness of every society in which the slaves equal the free or exceed them in number.

There is one instance known to me from the classic Greek world in which a public fear of revolution involving the emancipation of slaves and their use in class warfare has been predicated. This was in the League of the Hellenes established by Philip II of Macedon at Corinth in 338 B.C. The constitution of the League provided that the central organization and its policing force should see to it that, among the constituent members, there would be "no executions and banishments contrary to the laws established in the city-states, no confiscations of property nor redistributions of land, no abolition of debts and no freeing of slaves for the furthering of revolutionary movements." [1] These were provisions designed by Philip of Macedon for the preservation of social order, as against revolutionary disorder, within the separate city-state members of the League. It is true that the separate state entities gave over to a police force of the federation the power of enforcement of order and obviously with the object of preserving the propertied interests of each community against radical changes. But it is going too far toward modernism to see, back of these conservative proposals, the threatening "horrors of class warfare." [2] Class warfare was, admittedly, a constant factor in the political life of the city-states of the fourth century which had to be met or endured. So far as the slaves were concerned the city-states merely agreed to make it illegal to permit slave-owners to manumit their slaves for enlistment in the contending ranks in local revolutions. It is not an indication of unrest among the slaves as servile groups — rather, in fact, the contrary.

The most exact information available upon the number of the slave population at Athens toward the close of the fifth century lies in a remark made by Thucydides. It is the more trustworthy because it has no intention of proving that the slave numbers were either large or moderate. As observer he was careful; and, above all, he was rational in his outlook and sober in his judgments;

---

[1] Demosthenes *On the Agreements with Alexander*, 17. 15.

[2] This is the attitude of Robert von Pöhlmann in his *Geschichte der sozialen Frage und des Sozialismus* (2d ed., 1912) I 420–1.

and he knew his Athens. He tells us that the permanent occupation by the Spartans in 413 B.C. of a fortified place at Decelea near Athens did great damage to the Athenians, and that, because of the destruction of property and loss of men which this occupation brought about, the war turned out badly for them. In describing the damage which the Decelean garrison caused by its constant presence *through the remaining years of the war* he states that more than 20,000 slaves "had deserted"[1] and that the greater part of these were handicraftsmen. This has no further meaning than that Thucydides had heard this estimate of the number of the runaway slaves during an eight year period. There is no way of knowing whose estimate it was; but, obviously, Thucydides thought it a reasonable one. The majority of these, he believed, were handicraftsmen. Possibly we may assume that the artisans among them numbered 13,000 or 14,000, as Gomme has suggested.[2] It seems reasonable enough that the majority were

[1] Thucydides VII 27. 5: πλέον ἢ δύο μυριάδες ηὐτομολήκεσαν, καὶ τούτων πολὺ μέρος χειροτέχναι. It is clear from the tenor of this entire section that Thucydides has in mind the gradual and constant attrition of Athenian strength down to the end of the war. This is expressed in the imperfect tense, πολλὰ ἔβλαπτε τοὺς 'Αθηναίους and in the aorist, ἐκάκωσε τὰ πράγματα, "it brought their affairs to a bad end." The pluperfect, ηὐτομολήκεσαν, is retrospective, from the standpoint of the end of the war. Cf. Eduard Schwartz *Das Geschichtswerk des Thukydides* (2d ed., 1929) 200, and W. Schadewaldt *Die Geschichtsschreibung des Thukydides* (1929) 8, 21. Failure to note this fact has vitiated Rachel Sargent's use of the passage (*Size of the Slave Population at Athens*, p. 88), when she assumes that, *at the time of the occupation* of Decelea, 20,000 slaves deserted, all in the single year 413 B.C. Also her statement that the majority of these were from the mines is not warranted by the promise of Alcibiades in Thuc. VI 91. 7. Alcibiades stated that slaves would come over and that the Athenians would lose the revenues of the Laurian mines. There is no suggestion that these two results of the occupation of Decelea were to be connected one with the other.

This evidence of Thucydides received a surprising confirmation in 1908 through the publication of a newly discovered fragment of an historian of the fourth century B.C. which states that, after they had joined the Spartans in the occupation of Decelea, the Thebans became prosperous through taking over slaves and other war booty at a low price. See Grenfell and Hunt, *Oxyrhynchus Papyri* V (1908) no. 8 col. 13. 28–33, reprinted by F. Jacoby, *Fragmente der griechischen Historiker*, Berlin, 1923–1930, II A p. 26 (no. 66 col. 12. 4).

[2] A. W. Gomme *The Population of Athens in the Fifth and Fourth Centuries B.C..*

handicraftsmen, in view of the war situation and the constant need, before and after Decelea, of the manufacturing of war materials, both offensive and defensive. Distributed over the eight years from the first occupation of Decelea to the end of the war the slave desertions would be at the rate of about 2,500 per year.

In two cases the numbers of slaves owned by individual residents of Athens at about this time are known. In 414 B.C. the property of a resident alien named Cephisodorus was confiscated. He owned sixteen slaves.[1] In 404 B.C., when their properties were confiscated in the oligarchic revolution, the orator Lysias and his brother owned one hundred and twenty slaves including their domestic servants, attendants, and handicraftsmen employed in a shield-making establishment which they ran.[2]

For the fourth century we are only a little better off in respect to slave numbers, if at all, than in the fifth century. In elaborating his project for increasing the revenues of the Attic state Xenophon proposed, among other ideas, that the Attic state should make an immediate purchase of 1,200 slaves whom it was then to lease out to the owners of the silver mine pits at Laurium as mining laborers. Out of the profits of the enterprise these were to be increased by gradual purchase over a space of five or six years until a total of 6,000 should be reached, with the idea, contemplated under the plan, of an eventual total of 10,000 state-owned slaves.[3] Most important is Xenophon's dream that eventually the state would own three slaves for every Athenian citizen.[4] This implies that Xenophon could conceive a total of about 60,000 to 65,000 slaves in public ownership, when those in private ownership must necessarily have shrunk to a small number because of the competition of the state's slaves. Xenophon, therefore, thought of the slaves in terms of about a third or a quarter of the total

[1] The information is exact since it is from an original document of that year: Dittenberger *Sylloge Inscriptionum Graecarum* (3d ed.) I no. 96.

[2] Lysias 12 *Against Eratosthenes* 8, 19. See Hasebroek *Trade and Politics in Ancient Greece* 72–3 (= *Staat und Handel* 76).

[3] Xenophon *Upon the Revenues* 4. 23–4. For the gradual process of purchasing, *ibid.* 4. 38.

[4] *Ibid.* 4. 17.

population.[1] For the slave population of Syracuse in Sicily we have
a confirmation of this estimate. This is found in a statement of
Diodorus that Dionysius I in 396 B.C. freed enough slaves in that
state to man sixty war vessels.[2] Julius Beloch has estimated that
this number indicates that the Syracusan territory had at least
12,000 slaves capable of bearing arms. His conclusion as to the
entire population of the Syracusan territory resulted in an ap-
proximate total of 250,000 inhabitants.[3] This would indicate for
Syracuse also a ratio of slaves to free population of about one to
four.

In the eyes of Plato about fifty would be the limit of the number
of slaves owned by a wealthy citizen of Athens. In the *Republic*,
when discussing the constant terrors which surround tyrants, he
has Socrates says: "Suppose that one of the gods should snatch
up out of the state a man who had fifty slaves or more and place
him, with his wife and children and his slaves and the rest of his
property, in a desert place where no free man could help him.
How terrible and how great his fear would be for himself, his
children and his wife that they would be killed by his slaves?"[4]
Plato's idea of the number of slaves which a wealthy man might
be expected to possess is borne out with singular exactness by the
actual number owned by the orator Demosthenes. In his prosecu-
tion of the guardian of his estate he disclosed to the court that his
father had left him an establishment for the manufacture of
knives and swords with thirty-two or thirty-three slaves and a
workshop for making couch frames with twenty slave workmen

---

[1] The number of the citizens in 355 B.C. is not known. Beloch's doubtful figure
of 21,000 citizens in 400 B.C. (*Bevölkerung* 74) or Gomme's equally questionable
22,000 (*Population of Athens* 26) have been taken arbitrarily as the basis of this
ratio.

[2] Diodorus XIV 58. 1.

[3] Beloch *Bevölkerung* 280–1.

[4] Plato *Republic* 578 e. The statement that it is to be a *wealthy* citizen appears
in 578 d. In Plato's State of the *Laws*, which was designed as an agrarian society,
supported primarily by slave labor in agricultural production, one-third of the food
produced was to be assigned to the slaves, one-third to the artisans and alien
residents, the other third to the free men, *Laws* VIII 848 a. This implies that
about one-third of the population would be servile in status.

G

trained to this trade.[1] Another Athenian of the same time, a certain Timarchus, had inherited eleven or twelve slaves, including nine or ten leather workers, a woman linen weaver and a leather embroiderer.[2]

The observation that a considerable part of the Attic population had no slaves at all is even more important than the figures given above in proving that the exaggerated numbers which Athenaeus gives must be abandoned.[3] The statement should be obvious for the poorer classes of the city;[4] and it is definitely proven for the disabled citizen workman for whom Lysias wrote a speech in defense against an action which was brought for the withdrawal of a state dole formerly received by him. The cripple asserted that he could not afford to keep a slave to help him in his trade.[5] It is also to be proven in the case of people of enough means so that they became involved in litigation over estate inheritances. One case will be enough to illustrate the fact. One member of the group involved in the complicated litigation did not inventory any slaves in his property. Stratocles, a brother of the defendant in the case, inherited through the death of a daughter a property valued at two and a half talents, or 15,000 drachmas in silver. It is listed as consisting of real estate, sixty sheep, a hundred goats and other equipment; but no slaves appear.[6] The inventory

[1] Demosthenes 27 *Against Aphobus* I 9 for the knife makers and 24 for the twenty couch makers. In Demosthenes, 37 *Against Pantaenetus* 4, a loan was made to a mine owner on the security of his mine pit and thirty slaves which he owned.

[2] Aeschines 1 *Against Timarchus* 97.

[3] Sargent, *Slave Population* 101, evidently recognized the value of this negative evidence, but applied the method only with reference to the slaves in handicraft shops.

[4] A. W. Gomme, *Population of Athens* 21, has correctly concluded that the number of domestic slaves in the homes of the lowest class, the thetes, would be negligible because of the expense of keeping them.

[5] Lysias 24 *In Defense of the Cripple* 6. In the property inherited by the Athenian, Diodotus, in Lysias 32 *Against Diogeiton* 5, amounting to the considerable sum of 7 talents, 40 minas, and 2,000 drachmas, no slave is mentioned.

[6] Isaeus 11 *On the Estate of Hagnias* 40–1. The defendant and his brother had sufficient means to care for themselves, but not enough to subject them to the liturgical services which fell upon the well-to-do. Since the number of the sheep and goats inherited by the daughter of one of the two men is enumerated, I judge

of his estate at the time of his death is also given. The estimated total then was put at 33,000 drachmas, made up of real property, interest-bearing loans, furniture, sheep, barley, wine, and nine hundred drachmas in silver. Not a single slave appears.

Two extracts from the literature of the period may serve to clinch the argument. In the *Ecclesiazusae* of Aristophanes, produced in 392 B.C., in her proposal for collective ownership of property the feminist Praxagora wants to put an end to a situation in which one person has many slaves and another has not even a single attendant.[1] In respect to the working classes of the population Xenophon makes the significant remark — "*those who can do so* buy slaves so that they may have fellow workmen."[2]

All of the evidence which is really significant points toward the conclusion that in Attica the slaves did not comprise more than a third of the total population, possibly not more than a fourth. It must be granted that this statement is no more than a reasonable suggestion. For the Peloponnesus, outside of Sparta and its Helot population, a much smaller ratio of slaves must be postulated because of the statement ascribed to Pericles[3] that the Peloponnesians, in contrast to the Athenians, did their own work. Even Athenaeus, who is responsible for the long-established belief in the huge masses of slaves at Corinth, Aegina, and Athens, else-

---

that if the estate had possessed slaves they would be given. I am assuming that the slave inventory of the estate, if there were any slaves, would not be included under the item of "remaining equipment." Cf. the further enumeration of the items in the property, *ibid.* 43. Some of the property, it is true, was not declared in the inventory. Again, however, I do not believe that slave holdings could be concealed in the declaration.

No slaves appear in the modest property holding of Dicaeogenes in Isaeus 5. 22–3, 29, nor in the dowry of a daughter in 8 *On the Estate of Ciron* 8. In the *Cyropaedia* I 1. 1 Xenophon says that some families kept in their homes a considerable number of slaves, others very few. There is no way of determining what proportion of the families in Athens had some slaves and what part owned "very few."

[1] Aristophanes *Ecclesiazusae* 593.

[2] Xenophon *Memorabilia* II 3. 3.

[3] Thucydides I 141. 3. From Thucydides III 15 it becomes clear that the Peloponnesian allies of Sparta were loth to undertake military operations during the harvest season because their citizens would at that time be engaged in getting in their crops.

where states that the most of the Greeks, except the Chians, originally tended to use conquered Greeks in helotage rather than
have slaves.[1] No Greek writer of this period has uttered any
complaint against a supposed influx of slaves such as was expressed
so freely at Rome in the first century of the Christian era. For
Chios we have the authority of Thucydides that it contained more
slaves than any other Greek state except Sparta.[2] It should be
clear that Thucydides' comparison is between the number of
slaves at Chios and the number of *Helots* at Lacedaemon. Actually we know very little about the number of the Helots. The
best guess available puts the minimum at 60,000. If this be somewhere near the truth, Beloch's rough estimate of about 100,000
slaves at Chios may be near the mark.[3] It is fairly certain that in
other Greek communities than those which were centers of handicraft production the slave ratio fell considerably below any per-
centage which may be established for Athens.

Without question the Greek city-states of the fifth and fourth
centuries B.C., and among them notably Athens, used slave labor
upon a fairly large scale. But the slaves were employed at the
same work as the free, usually side by side with them, and apparently without prejudice or friction. In any sense which implies either that the enslaved population predominated over the
free or that the Greek city-states displayed the mentality of a slave-
ridden society, Greek culture was not founded upon slavery.

[1] Athenaeus VI 265 b, c.
[2] Thucydides VIII 40. 2.
[3] For the Helot figures see Beloch *Bevölkerung* 147; for the Chian slaves, *ibid*. 2.
The total population of Chios was estimated in 1932 at about 80,000.

VI

GREEK THEORIES OF SLAVERY FROM HOMER TO ARISTOTLE

ROBERT SCHLAIFER

I. THE EVIDENCE

THE first theories of any political and social institution are to be found long after it has been first established, when its validity and justice are first attacked and then defended. To this rule slavery is no exception. Before the attacks begin, there is no conscious theorizing; there is only a state of mind, a habit of thought, in regard to slaves, which can be learned from incidental remarks and from the treatment accorded the slave; both of these can be well observed in the Homeric poems, where the relations of the master and his slave are more clearly depicted than by any other classical Greek author except Euripides. Somewhat later than the heroic period the general attitude toward the servile members of society crystallized in the form of law; the extant parts of the laws of two states, Athens and Gortyna, afford excellent evidence for our problem. In the great period of Greek literature innumerable references in all sorts of writers illuminate this popular, unconscious attitude.

The beginning of conscious theory is to be found in the teachings of the Sophists, of whose writings and doctrines only the merest scraps remain, and with whom Plato does not choose to debate this question. There is, consequently, no systematic statement of the problem until the *Politics* of Aristotle, with which this account will be concluded.

II. INTRODUCTORY: HELLENIC NATIONALISM

The Greek theories of slavery after the heroic period can be understood only in the light of two contributing factors: the rise of a pan-Hellenic nationalism and the growth of disdain for menial occupations. Neither of these has left the slightest trace in Homer, who, as Thucydides [1] was the first to notice, has no common name for Greeks or for barbarians. The foundations of this nationalism were laid in the eighth century, when, with the rise of the great national festivals, all of non-Greek blood were excluded. The formation of political and religious leagues, the meeting of pilgrims from all parts of Greece at the great oracles — these and similar gatherings caused the Greeks to realize that they were one in blood, spirit, and heritage. It was during the eighth century that there arose the use of 'Hellenes' as a common appellation for all Greeks and 'barbarians' as a category in which all others were included. The feeling of distinction between these two must have been greatly strengthened through continual observation of the barbarian by the many colonists of the seventh century.

Not until the Persian wars, however, is there any evidence that this feeling of national unity involved a belief in national superiority. This struggle, in which almost all the Greeks participated as a nation and which resulted in the complete defeat of almost all the known foreign peoples, headed by a king hitherto believed invincible, caused a great surge of national pride. This was the sentiment which the poet Aeschylus expressed in his *Persae* (472) and which he chose to place on his tombstone; [2] this was the sentiment which held Greece together for seventeen years more in a pan-Hellenic league. And then, as the glory of Salamis and Plataea receded into the past and as clashes with the Great King became less frequent, a new factor, consciousness of superiority in the arts and sciences, kept national pride alive. Their very language was felt by the Greeks to be superior [3] — Aristophanes [4] uses βάρβαρος to mean 'incapable of speech.' After the shameful dealings by both sides with the Great King at the close of the Peloponnesian war, after the national humiliation of the peace of Antalcidas, this cultural superiority was — and was sometimes admitted to be[5] — all that remained on which to support Greek pride and

---

[1] 1, 3, 3.

[2] Anon. *Vit. Aesch.*; Plut. *De Exil.* 13 (*Mor.* 604f); Athen. 14, 23, 627cd.

[3] Dion. Hal. *Rhet.* 11, 4; K. J. F. Roth, *Bemerk. üb. d. Sinn . . . d. Wortes Barbar* (Nürnberg, 1814), pp. 8-9.

[4] *Av.* 199.   [5] Isoc. 15, 293-294.

conceit. Βάρβαρος, when used adjectivally, now assumed the more comprehensive significance of 'gauche';[1] Hellenism was recognized to be a thing of the spirit rather than of blood.[2] But not for a century, until the time of Eratosthenes,[3] were the full implications of this admission realized; in the fifth and fourth centuries the general view was that a Greek *ipso facto* possessed this superior culture and that a non-Greek was incapable of receiving it.

Besides this realization of their superior *Kultur*, there was another factor in the composition of the Greek attitude toward the barbarian — the ready submission of the latter to absolute monarchy, a state which the Greek habitually termed δουλεία. This accusation against the barbarian, first uttered by Aeschylus in his *Persae*,[4] was repeated by Herodotus;[5] its general acceptance is shown by the fact that although Euripides himself refuses to admit its justice,[6] yet he puts it in the mouths of two of his characters.[7]

From these two beliefs, that in a superior *Kultur* and that in the actual slavery of the barbarian in his political state, two conclusions naturally followed: first, that barbarians were by nature fitted only for slavery and hence that it was not only the privilege but even the duty of Greeks to enslave them;[8] second, that a Greek was by nature designed for freedom. Neither of these conclusions is found in Herodotus, but both were a matter of common belief by the end of the fifth century. In the fourth century two new phenomena appear in connection with them: the frequent preaching that these beliefs should be realized in a great national crusade against the enemy,[9] and the attempt to state in technical

---

[1] E.g. in [Dem.] 26, 17.

[2] Isoc. 4, 50. Cf. the use of ὁμόφωνοι instead of συγγενεῖς in [Plat.] *Menex.* 241e.

[3] Strab. 1, 4, 9, p. 66.

[4] 241-242.

[5] 7, 135, 3; cf. 6, 44, 1.

[6] Cf. Th. Gomperz, *Griechische Denker*[4] (Berlin & Leipzig, 1922-31), II, p. 15.

[7] *Hel.* 276; *Iph. Aul.* 1400-1401.

[8] Isoc. 4, 131-132; 181-182; cf. 34-37.

[9] 'Nonnulli' *ap.* Isoc. 5, 120; Gorg. frg. 1; Isoc. *Ep.* 9, 19 (to Archidamus); 3, 5 (to Philip); *Or.* 4, 182; cf. 158; Dem. 14, 32. These dreams of a crusade were attributed to the great leaders of an earlier time, e.g. to Cimon by Theopompus *ap.* Plut. *Cim.* 18, 5; see J. Kärst, *Gesch. d. Hellenismus*[2] (Leipzig, 1917-26), I, pp. 151,

philosophical language the difference between the Greek and the barbarian φύσις. The explanation was simply the assertion that the barbarian failed to possess, or possessed in undue proportion, some essential part of the soul. By Plato the Orientals were supposed to be lacking in τὸ θυμοειδές and to have an excess of τὸ φιλοχρήματον; in addition they, together with all barbarians, lacked τὸ φιλομαθές, a possession of the Greeks alone.[1] Aristotle apparently thought that the deficiency of the Orientals in courage and of the Northerners in intelligence was due to climatic causes.[2] To both Plato and Aristotle the barbarian lacked the governing element of the soul, Plato's θεῖον ἄρχον, Aristotle's τὸ βουλευτικόν.[3] Such a conclusion suited admirably the various reports and travellers' tales brought back from the East and accorded still better with the nature of the barbarian slave as it could be observed at home. It is true that some, whose names are much less highly regarded than these two, held a more intelligent view of the origin of the slavelike nature of the barbarian, namely, that it was caused by long subjection to slave-like domination. Thus, as Isocrates says,[4] οὐ γὰρ οἷόν τε τοὺς οὕτω τρεφομένους καὶ πολιτευομένους οὔτε τῆς ἄλλης ἀρετῆς μετέχειν οὔτ' ἐν ταῖς μάχαις τρόπαιον ἱστάναι τῶν πολεμίων. But regardless of the cause, subjection to tyranny, the equivalent of slavery, was considered the mark of the barbarian:

ἰὼ τυραννὶ βαρβάρων ἀνδρῶν φίλη.[5]

By the time of Aristotle, however, there had arisen a large body of contrary opinion, which maintained that the popular prejudice

---

514–515. The general acceptance in the early fourth century of the justice and desirability of such a crusade is shown by the fact that Isocrates' *Panegyric* is an argument concerning its leadership only: see sec. 66.

[1] Plat. *Rep.* 435e–436a.
[2] H. Newman, *The Politics of Arist.* (Oxford, 1887–1902), III, pp. 363–364.
[3] Plat. *Rep.* 590cd; Arist. *Pol.* 60a12. In both these passages the element is denied not to barbarians as such, but to slaves. Since, however, as will be shown, both Plato and Aristotle held that all barbarians are φύσει δοῦλοι, the statement made in the text is legitimate.
[4] Isoc. *Or.* 4, 150; cf. the whole passage 150–151; also 5, 124.
[5] Tragici incert. frg. 359 Nauck.²

against the barbarian was entirely unjustified. In the seventh and sixth centuries the tyrannies and the Orphic cults had begun to lay the foundations for cosmopolitanism: [1] the former had pursued a policy of foreign, including non-Greek, alliances; members of the tyrannic families had sometimes taken foreign names; and they had not restricted the immigration of barbarians. The Orphic cults were open to all men, not to Greeks alone, and Orpheus himself was supposed to have been a Thracian. But with the fall of the tyrannies in the sixth century and the decline of the Orphic cults in the fifth, there was little to check the intensification of nationalism after the Persian wars. [2]

It was inevitable, however, that with the spread of the 'enlightenment' a school should arise to deny the categorical division of mankind into Greeks and barbarians. Hellenism, as has been shown, was gradually becoming a thing of the spirit and therefore tended to break the bounds of nationality and race. The chief attention of philosophy was to virtue, knowledge, and similar ethical qualities, and sooner or later it was bound to be recognized that many barbarians possessed these virtues to a great degree. The first signs of the new cosmopolitanism are found in Euripides, who reflects so many of the ideas of the 'enlightenment.' Although for dramatic reasons he often lets his characters express the opposite view, [3] it is clear that his own sentiments are shown in the fragment: [4]

τὸν ἐσθλὸν ἄνδρα, κἂν ἑκὰς ναίῃ χθονός,
κἂν μήποτ' ὄσσοις εἰσίδω, κρίνω φίλον.

Democritus had already said: [5] ἀνδρὶ σοφῷ πᾶσα γῆ βατή· ψυχῆς γὰρ ἀγαθῆς πατρὶς ὁ ξύμπας κόσμος, and the fact that Lysias [6] rages against

[1] Gomperz, I, p. 113.
[2] There may be a slight trace of cosmopolitan spirit in Pind. *Nem.* 6, 1–2; it is to be remembered that Pindar was a citizen of a Medizing state.
[3] E.g. the famous words of Jason to Medea (Eur. *Med.* 533–544), words which almost any Greek might have used, and yet which are obviously intended to arouse disgust in the audience.
[4] Frg. 902 N². Cf. frgg. 777 and 1047.
[5] Frg. 247 ed. H. Diels, in *Die Frag. d. Vorsokrat.*⁵ (Berlin, 1934–), II, p. 194.
[6] 31, 6.

ὅσοι δὲ φύσει μὲν πολῖταί εἰσι, γνώμῃ δὲ χρῶνται ὡς πᾶσα γῆ πατρὶς αὐτοῖς ἐστιν ἐν ᾗ ἂν τὰ ἐπιτήδεια ἔχωσιν, shows that the argument, although adopted perhaps for base reasons, was quite widespread. Hippias' assertion [1] that in matters of law and custom universality was the only true criterion of goodness amounted to a flat denial that any nation could be peculiarly excellent. In rejecting[2] the validity of distinctions of birth, Lycophron must certainly have drawn the obvious inference that there was no distinction between Greek and barbarian. Finally, the Sophist Antiphon states categorically:[3] φύσει πάντα πάντες ὁμοίως πεφύκαμεν καὶ βάρβαροι καὶ Ἕλληνες εἶναι . . . οὔτε βάρβαρος ἀφώρισται ἡμῶν οὐδεὶς οὔτε Ἕλλην. Even Plato, in his Statesman, reversed the position he had earlier taken in the Republic and adopted Antiphon's theory: it is as ridiculous, he says, to divide mankind into Greeks and non-Greeks as into Phrygians and non-Phrygians.[4] Although he returned in the Laws to his old view, he remained open-minded enough to admit that certain barbarian regulations were preferable to those of his favorite states, Sparta and Crete.[5]

The Cynics, denying the significance of everything not contained in the individual himself, refused, of course, all value or importance to the state: μόνην τε ὀρθὴν πολιτείαν εἶναι τὴν ἐν κόσμῳ.[6] But, it must be remembered, 'der leitende Gedanke dieses cynischen Kosmopolitismus ist weit weniger die Zusammengehörigkeit und Verbindung aller Menschen, als die Befreiung des Einzelnen von den Banden des Staatslebens und den Schranken der Nationalität.'[7] And yet, while Aristotle was engaged in writing his Politics, in which he upheld the old nationalistic spirit, Alexander was disregarding his advice to act toward the Greeks as a leader, toward the barbarians as a master, and was establishing in fact a world

[1] Gomperz, I, p. 336; E. Zeller, Die Philosophie d. Griechen in ihrer geschichtl. Entwick. (Leipzig, 1919-23), I, ii⁸, p. 1397, n. 2.
[2] Stob. ed. Wachsmuth et Hense (Berlin, 1884-1912) 4, 29, 24.
[3] Antiph. Soph. ed. L. Gernet (with Antiph. Or.) (Paris, 1923), 1, frg. 5 = Pap. Oxy. XI, no. 1364, vv. 275-292 (p. 100).
[4] Polit. 262c-e. Cf. Gomperz, II, p. 448.
[5] Legg. 674a.
[6] Diog. Cyn. ap. Diog. Laer. 6, 72.
[7] Zeller, II, i⁵, pp. 325-326.

state.[1] Thus at the end of the period under discussion the situation was rapidly becoming that which obtained at the beginning. A feeling of the distinction between Greek and barbarian, arising gradually between the eighth and sixth centuries, had developed in the fifth and fourth into a belief in Hellenic superiority, only to find almost immediately opponents among the Sophists and later among the Cynics, whose ideal was in fact partially realized in the empire of Alexander.

III. INTRODUCTORY: BANAUSIC OCCUPATIONS

The idea that certain occupations were menial and beneath the dignity of a freeman is not found in the earliest Greek literature, but its rise and its prevalence at any given time are unfortunately difficult to determine. The attempt, however, must be made, for this idea is the chief cause of the Greek attitude toward slaves which resulted in the most commonly held of all the later theories, that of the natural slave. In Homer and Hesiod there appears no prejudice against any honest means of gaining a livelihood; it is a common observation that the wives and daughters of Homer's Zeus-reared kings spend their days in the humblest of household tasks. According to Hesiod only those mortals who devote themselves to useful toil will receive the favor of the gods,[2] and in some states this attitude persisted well into the sixth century. Solon, who, himself a merchant,[3] became the highest magistrate and lawgiver extraordinary in the crisis of the Athenian state, in his poems describes the artisans as sons of Athena and Hephaestus.[4] It was only at a relatively late date that the feast of the χαλκεῖα ceased to be a festival of the whole people and became exclusively for artisans.[5] Until the tyrannies, in fact, there was almost no slave

[1] Plut. De Alex. Fort. 1, 6 (Mor. 329b).

[2] Op. et D. 298-309. Cf. Hym. Hom. 20, where Hephaestus and Athena are said to have raised mankind from barbarism by teaching them the arts.

[3] Plut. Sol. 2, 1.

[4] Sol. ed. E. Diehl, Anthol. Lyr. Graeca (Leipzig, 1925), frg. 1, 49-50. Cf. Plat. Legg. 920d.

[5] Suid. s.v. χαλκεῖα. These remarks on the situation in Athens are derived from P. N. Ure, The Origin of Tyranny (Cambridge, 1922), p. 16.

labor at all in those states which had not been conquered during the dark ages.[1]

The change in attitude, then, began only with the disruption of the old order brought about by the conquest of much of Greece by the Dorians, who when they had settled in a new land forced the subject population to tend to the supply of the necessities of life and devoted themselves exclusively to military occupations.[2] It was, of course, inevitable that once labor had become reserved to an inferior class, whether slave or serf, it should soon come to be regarded as degrading in itself. This contempt naturally extended to the tillers of the soil as well as to artisans and tradespeople, while on the other hand in states where there was no ruling and exploiting class there is until the fifth century no evidence for a prejudice against any form of labor.

At no time did the tiller of the land in any state of the latter type fall from high esteem in the popular mind. The attitude in Athens is well shown by Euripides' line:[3]

$$αὐτουργός — οἵπερ καὶ μόνοι σώζουσι γῆν,$$

and Aristophanes' respect for the small farmer is well known. The basis of this high opinion is easy to understand: farming not only rendered the body fit for service as a hoplite but also required intelligence and initiative, not merely the brute force which the slave or day laborer contributed. The average Greek — not the member of the *Demos* alone but also the politically moderate of the higher classes.— probably believed that these αὐτουργοί were the only possible basis for a well-governed democracy.

An oligarchically minded person, however, who believed that the system of Sparta was at least very near to the ideal, would naturally disagree with this view and would wish to establish in his state also an exploiting class, whose only difference from the Laconian was to be devotion to the more philosophical life of politics, rather than the life of war. Xenophon, who was as aristocratic

[1] B. Büchsenschütz, *Besitz u. Erwerb im griech. Alterthume* (Halle, 1869), pp. 321, 341, 193 (cited by Ure, *op. cit.*, p. 22, n. 6).

[2] Newman, *Pol. of Arist.*, I, pp. 99-100.

[3] *Or.* 920.

as Plato or Aristotle but less intellectual and therefore could not have imagined spending all his time at politics and philosophizing, occupies the middle ground between the common view and that of the two great philosophers. In one passage[1] he speaks of agriculture in terms of the highest praise. His ideal, however, is really that of the gentleman farmer who supervises his estate but works in the field only occasionally, for pleasure and exercise. Ischomachus' estate certainly required slaves, but Xenophon would probably have allowed the αὐτουργός to be a citizen, although perhaps without all the privileges of the upper class.

Plato classes the peasant with the manual laborer. In his *Republic* all the productive classes are to be members of the third estate, which, while free in name, is really slave. Although it is true that these people are not to be enslaved — indeed, the taking of their liberty by the governors is the first sign of the decline of his ideal state[2] — yet the fact that they are to have no share in the government of the city shows that Plato is really extending the usual notion of the worthlessness of βάναυσοι for political purposes to include the peasants also. In the *Laws*,[3] too, agriculture as well as industry and commerce is strictly forbidden to the citizen. Aristotle[4] follows Plato exactly in this: the cultivators of the soil, εἰ δεῖ κατ' εὐχήν, should be slaves; if this ideal cannot be realized, then serfs should be used, but never freemen.

These views concerning peasants were, as has been shown, rare in the more enlightened states of Greece. For the banausic occupations, however, all but the βάναυσοι themselves had only contempt from the early fifth century on.[5] Several factors contribute to produce this attitude, none of which can actually be illustrated by citations, but which may nevertheless be assumed with some confidence. First was the growth of the hoplite system, which

---

[1] Xen. *Oec.* 6, 9; cf. 4, 4; 5, 1–17; 6, 10.

[2] *Rep.* 547bc.   [3] 806de.   [4] *Pol.* 30a25 ff.

[5] E. Meyer, *Die Sklaverei im Altertum*, in vol. I² of *Kleine Schriften* (Halle, 1924), p. 200, disputes this, but his conclusion is really only another form of statement for the same fact. Cf. Dem. 18, 258; Ar. *Ach.* 478–479; *Thes.* 387; *Ran.* 840. Many artisans preferred mercenary service abroad to continuing at their occupations — Agesilaus' army was composed chiefly of this class: Plut. *Ages.* 26; Polyaen. 2, 1, 7.

received its test in the closing years of the sixth and the beginning of the fifth centuries.[1] Second, the plunder of the Persian wars made many more citizens financially independent, thus increasing the numbers of the class which could look down upon the petty workers and shop-keepers.[2] Last of all, many prisoners of the wars were enslaved and the increased wealth made it possible to purchase still others, so that as slaves became widely employed the idea spread that the tasks at which they were put were unfit for a freeman.

The first of these causes, the importance of the hoplite army, was the only one which was recognized by the Greeks, and when they came to justify their scorn of the βάναυσος, this formed an important part of their argument. For if one was forced to sit all day, sometimes even in front of a fire, one's body soon became incapable of strenuous service in heavy armor. When the body became weakened, the soul too lost its vigor and courage[3] and soon was lost to every virtue.[4] The result would be that in case of an invasion the τεχνῖται would, if they had their choice, flee before the enemy.[5] It may be, but it is unlikely, that Socrates, who was a stone-mason in his youth, drew the obvious distinction between harmful trades and crafts and those, such as brick-laying, which were as beneficial as farming.[6] A further objection raised against the banausic oc-

[1] Newman, *Pol. of Arist.*, I, p. 100.

[2] W. Drumann, *Die Arbeiter u. Communisten in Griechenland u. Rom* (Königsberg, 1860), p. 46 (cited by Ure, *Orig. of Tyr.*, p. 19).

[3] Plat. *Rep.* 495de; Xen. *Oec.* 4, 2; *Mem.* 4, 2, 22; Arist. *Pol.* 37b8 ff.

[4] Plat. *Rep.* 590c; 495d; Arist. *Pol.* 28b39 ff.

[5] Xen. *Oec.* 6, 6-7.

[6] From Xen. *Mem.* 1, 2, 56-57, Gomperz (II, p. 63) and Zeller (II i[5], p. 170) conclude that Socrates, more radical than Plato, believed that any honest means of earning a living was honorable. Socrates, however, had said (Xen. *Oec.* 4, 2-3) αἱ γε βάναυσικαὶ καλούμεναι . . . καταλυμαίνονται . . . τὰ σώματα . . . . τῶν δὲ σωμάτων θηλυνομένων καὶ αἱ ψυχαὶ πολὺ ἀρρωστότεραι γίγνονται. When he says, then, in the passage under consideration (Xen. *Mem.* 1, 2, 57) τοὺς μὲν ἀγαθόν τι ποιοῦντας ἐργάζεσθαι . . . καὶ ἐργάτας [ἀγαθοὺς] εἶναι, and τὸ μὲν ἐργάτην εἶναι ὠφέλιμόν τε ἀνθρώπῳ καὶ ἀγαθὸν εἶναι, he can scarcely mean by ἀγαθόν τι any occupation with the effects on body and soul of αἱ βάναυσικαὶ καλούμεναι (sc. τέχναι). It may be, therefore, that he is here distinguishing a certain class of trades as non-banausic. It is to be observed, however, that Plato and Xenophon, as well as Eurip-

cupations was the fact that they left the citizen insufficient leisure for intercourse with his friends or, more important, for attending to the business of the city.[1] In any case, it simply would not be fitting (πρέπον) for the citizen to have to bother with the necessities of life.[2] For still another reason, according to Plato, and in spite of the fact that it was intrinsically useful and good, trade was not to be practiced by the citizen: it causes or encourages men to pursue their appetites beyond the measure of reason.[3]

With the growing importance of industry there was, to be sure, a tendency for the artisan and commercial class to rise somewhat in the estimation of their fellow-citizens, but one must not over-estimate this rise. In Corinth, where probably — although this is disputed[4] — Periander had, in order to encourage free labor, forbidden the purchase of slaves,[5] artisans were least scorned.[6] But it is to be noted that Herodotus says ἥκιστα δὲ Κορίνθιοι ὄνονται τοὺς χειροτέχνας — he does not say οἱ δὲ Κορίνθιοι οὐκ ὄνονται . . ., and if there was disdain in Corinth, there must have been contempt else-where. Only an extreme democracy gave the βάναυσοι a share in the government,[7] and even here it was only the more successful βάναυσοι. The Thetes at Athens were never made eligible to the higher offices, although they were enfranchised and admitted to the courts in the sixth century. Their service in the navy, an impor-tant but never a respected branch of the Greek military service, connected them still more closely with slaves.[8] For no matter how

---

ides, make no such distinction, but class all crafts and trades together: Plat. *Rep.* 495d; Xen. *Oec.* 4, 2; Eur. frg. 635 N². Cf. Newman, *Pol. of Arist.*, I, p. 103. Cf. Soc. *ap.* Xen. *Mem.* 3, 7, 5–6. It is perhaps more probable that Socrates' real view is that of Dem. 57, 45: πολλὰ δουλικὰ καὶ ταπεινὰ πράγματα τοὺς ἐλευθέρους ἡ πενία βιάζεται ποιεῖν.

[1] Xen. *Oec.* 4, 3; Plat. *Legg.* 846de; 807c; Arist. *Pol.* 37b14; 29a1.
[2] Newman, *Pol. of Arist.*, I, p. 117.
[3] *Legg.* 918b–919b.
[4] G. Busolt, *Griechische Geschichte* (Gotha, 1893–1904), I², p. 646.
[5] Heraclid. 5, 2 in Müller, *F H G*, II, p. 213; Nicol. Dam. frg. 59 Müller, *F H G*, II, p. 393. This and the above reference are from Ure, *Orig. of Tyr.*, p. 192.
[6] Hdt. 2, 167.
[7] Arist. *Pol.* 77b1 ff.
[8] Cf. Plat. *Legg.* 706b–d.

much pride the moderately well-to-do citizen might take in the navy as a whole, his attitude toward the individual sailor was much the same as the attitude in most modern countries toward common privates or seamen. Thus a theory of the equal merit and value of all occupations never reached an articulate expression in Greece. Even the Sophists, of whom there seemed always to be at least one to uphold any conceivable theory, are not recorded as having proclaimed this equality, although Prodicus showed more sympathy for the despised classes than was common.[1] The prejudice against workers, which had arisen first in the states ruled by exploiting aristocracies, where it extended to all forms of manual labor, had in the other states of Greece, although restricted to banausic occupations, spread so rapidly during the fifth century that by 400 B.C. it was and remained universal.

IV. The Legal Theory

'Das Institut der Sklaverei beruht darauf, dass es zwischen verschiedenen Stämmen ein ursprüngliches rechtliches Verhältnis nicht gibt noch geben kann. . . . Wo [religiöse] Voraussetzungen fehlen, ist der Kriegszustand das natürliche Verhältnis zwischen zwei Stämmen; mit dem Stammfeinde, den man in seine Gewalt bekommt, sei es im Kriege, sei es durch Raub oder List, kann man daher machen, was man will. . . . Auch der Stammgenosse kann in dies Verhältnis durch einen Rechtsakt hinabgestossen werden, etwa wegen Schulden oder wegen eines Verbrechens, so gut wie der Stamm ihm das Leben nehmen kann: dadurch wird er aus der Stammgemeinschaft ausgestossen und den Stammfremden gleichgestellt.'[2] That a foreigner could always be enslaved is too well known to require illustration;[3] it remains to examine the causes of enslavement of citizens and the legal status of all slaves.

---

[1] Prodicus in Mullach, *F P G*, II, p. 139a (cited by Ure, *Orig. of Tyr.*, p. 19).

[2] Meyer, *Sklaverei*, p. 177.

[3] The only apparent exception is Lycurgus' law of ca. 333, which provided μηδενὶ ἐξεῖναι Ἀθηναίων μηδὲ τῶν οἰκούντων Ἀθήνησιν ἐλεύθερον σῶμα πρίασθαι ἐπὶ δουλείᾳ ἐκ τῶν ἀλισκομένων ἄνευ τῆς τοῦ προτέρου δεσπότου γνώμης: [Plut.] *Vit. X Orat.* 7 *Lycurg.* 12 (*Mor.* 841f). It seems certain, however, that the interpretation of M. H. E. Meier, *De vit. Lycurg.*, etc. (Halis, 1847), p. 40, is correct, viz. that this law ap-

In both Athens and Gortyna, the only states of which we have knowledge, great precautions were taken lest a citizen should be illegally enslaved, but in this as in other laws relating to slaves Gortyna is more advanced. Although the seizing and selling of a freeman was in Athens an offense punishable by death,[1] still there was no provision by which the wrongly enslaved person might institute proceedings in his own behalf, and there were no means for preventing the owner of the slave from making away with him before the trial. In Gortyna, on the contrary, enslavement did not automatically involve loss of all civil rights, a principle of which we shall see further illustrations. Here, in case suit was brought on behalf of a slave claiming his enslavement had been illegal, the owner was compelled under penalty of a five-stater fine to produce him at the trial.[2]

The causes for which a freeman might legally be enslaved varied in the different states of Greece. The chief of these, of course, was debt. In most states the mere fact that a debt was unpaid was itself sufficient reason for enslavement;[3] in Athens before Solon's time, however, enslavement followed only if the debtor's body had been pledged as security.[4] There is, of course, no difference between the latter type of enslavement and simple self-sale, which was fairly common in early times in Athens and elsewhere,[5] especially

---

plies only to the fugitives of one state. But even if the other interpretation (e.g. Tarn, *C A II*, VI, p. 443), that it was a general law forbidding enslavement of Greeks, is correct, still it is only an extension of the meaning of *Stammgenosse* from 'fellow-citizen' to 'fellow-Hellene': cf. above, pp. 166 ff.

[1] Dem. 4, 47; Lycurg. ed. B. et S. frg. 61; Arist. *Resp. Ath.* 52, 1.

[2] *Code of Gortyna* 1, 1 ff.; 10, 25 ff.; E. Zitelmann, *Das Recht von Gortyn, Rh. Mus.* XL (1885), Anhang, p. 79.

[3] Diod. Sic. 1, 79, 5; Isoc. 14, 48. Apparently the Athenian oligarchs of 403 passed a regulation to that effect: Lys. 12, 98.

[4] Plut. *Sol.* 13, 2; *De vitand. Aer. al.* 4, 1 (*Mor.* 828f); Arist. *Resp. Ath.* 2, 2.

[5] The sale could be for a limited time, indeterminate, or permanent. The cases most closely resembling forfeiture for debt are those where the cause of the sale was poverty, e.g. Hes. *Op. et D.* 600–603; Hdt. 8, 137, 1–2. A case of self-sale for another motive is Eur. *Alc.* 1–2 and Schol. Cf. Daremberg et Saglio, *Dictionnaire des antiquités*, etc., IV, p. 1261a; H. Wallon, *Histoire de l'esclavage dans l'antiquité*[2] (Paris, 1879), I, p. 70.

H

since Greek mortgages took the form of sales with option of re-purchase. The same principle is involved in the sale of children by their father; [1] namely, that a man's soul and body, and those of all persons under his parental authority, were his to do with as he pleased. But since society can for the general interest restrict the rights of the individual, Solon prohibited both the use of the body as security [2] and the sale of oneself or one's children into slavery.[3] An apparent exception in Athens is the fact that a ransomed pris-oner remained the slave of his redeemer until the ransom was re-paid. But this was not really a case of enslavement by a fellow-citizen: it was the purchase of a slave made by the foreigner with the stipulation that the prisoner had the option of redeeming him-self at the price which the ransomer had paid for him.[4]

In Gortyna the absence of any provision for enslavement for debt leads one to believe that it was not permitted. Here again the case of the ransomed prisoner seems, but is not, an exception: it was a loan to the prisoner of the money to ransom himself; apparently a fee or interest could be charged on this loan, and if the loan and interest were not paid, the ransomed person was delivered over to the ransomer for detention but was not made a slave.[5]

The enslavement of a metic or freedman for non-compliance with certain regulations [6] is based on the general theory of the right to enslave all foreigners and is not a case of penal enslavement, for such a penalty is out of all proportion to the crime involved, e.g.,

---

[1] Plut. *Sol.* 13, 3.

[2] Plut. *Sol.* 15, 3; *De vitand. Aer. al.* 4, 1 (*Mor.* 828f).

[3] Plut. *Sol.* 13, 3. An exception was made in the case of an unmarried girl who had been detected in relations with a man: *ib.* 23, 2, but this is really criminal rather than civil legislation.

[4] Dem. 53, 11. This stipulation of the right to purchase oneself at a fixed price is akin to the right of a slave to demand resale if mistreated: Poll. 7, 13 (who quotes Ar. frg. 567 K. (I, p. 536) and Eupolis frg. 225 K. (I, p. 319)); Luc. *Dial. D.* 24, 2; Plut. *De Superstit.* 4 (*Mor.* 166d); Wallon, *Esclavage*, I, p. 314. In such a case there must have been some provision to keep the owner from preventing the sale by demanding an exorbitant price.

[5] *Code* 6, 46 ff. 'Detention' (εἶναι ἐπὶ τῷ ἀλλυσαμένῳ): Zitelmann, p. 166. The fact that the amount was reclaimable only if the ransom was originally requested by the prisoner shows that the transaction was really a loan.

[6] Harpoc. *s.vv.* μετοίκιον; ἀποστασίου; [Dem.] 25, 57; Suid. *s.v.* ἀποστασίου.

non-payment of a twelve-drachma tax. The non-compliance with
the regulation ended the tenuous legal position of the metic or
freedman, and he was then subject to the same treatment as any
enemy.

Of cases of enslavement under criminal rather than civil juris-
diction there are only two recorded. The first is the permission
under Solon's legislation, already mentioned,[1] for the father to sell
his daughter who had been detected in illegal sexual relations. The
other is a law of Halicarnassus of *ca.* 457,[2] providing a settlement
of a recent revolution and ordering that anyone attempting to
repeal the law should be banished and his property confiscated,
but if his property was not worth ten staters, he should be sold outside of Halicarnassus as a slave.[3]

Such are the various ways by which a freeman, through law and
not through violence, could become a slave. It remains to consider
the legal position of the slave, the most striking characteristic of
which is his lack of legal personality. In Athens this lack was most
clearly manifested in the fact that the slave could not bring suit [4]
or, ordinarily, be sued [5] in his own name; in this he was no different
from the foreigner or metic, both of whom had to transact business
through a representative. In suits for damages where the master
was alleged to have ordered the act and was sued directly the case
was simply one of agency and was not at all peculiar to slavery
When the slave was sued in his own name the penalty was whipping,[6]
but the master must have been responsible for restitution of damages if, as was probable, the slave was incapable of this.[7] At Syrus

[1] Above, p. 178, n. 3.

[2] W. Dittenberger, *Sylloge Inscr. Gr.*[3] (Leipzig, 1915-21), 45, 32 ff.

[3] The provision that the sale must be outside Halicarnassus was probably only
to prevent civil discord; it was too early for the sentiment against the enslavement
of Greeks by Greeks. Cf. the similar practice of the Thracians: Hdt. 5, 6, 1.

[4] [Dem.] 53, 20; cf. Plat. *Gorg.* 483b.

[5] J. H. Lipsius, *Das attische Recht*, etc. (Leipzig, 1905-08), pp. 794 ff. If the slave,
however, was alleged to have done the damage *sua sponte*, the suit was brought
against him directly, but the owner was attacked in the pleading: Lipsius, *op. cit.*,
pp. 795-796; Dem. 37, 50-51; cf. below, n. 7.

[6] Dem. 22, 55; 24, 167.

[7] Hyperid. ed. Blass[3], 5, 22; Lipsius, *Att. Recht*, p. 660. This is the explanation
of the phrase τὸν κύριον διώκειν in Dem. 37, 51; cf. 55, 31.

the slave was whipped and the master was fined one hundred drachmas for a certain class of offenses.[1] At Andania the slave was both whipped and nominally fined,[2] although that the master was responsible for the payment of the fine is seen from the provision that if it was not paid he had to compound it by turning over the slave to work it out or else be liable for double the amount.[3]

The exact identity of the bases of the legal positions of the slave, metic, and foreigner is again shown by the laws concerning murder. The intentional killing of a foreigner or metic, or a slave belonging to another person, was not an offense against human law, for none of these classes possessed rights for the protection of which the state was liable. Yet the taking of a human life was blamable before the gods, no matter whose it was, and the Greek state took care not to offend the gods. Hence such a murder, being like the involuntary killing of a citizen, was tried before the same special court of the *Ephetae* on the Palladium and punished in the same way, by exile.[4] Moreover, in order that the offense might not go unpunished, since Athens had no public prosecutor, the owner of the slave was obliged by law to prosecute the case.[5] Nor was this principle violated in the least in the case of one who murdered his own slave.[6] Since it was inevitable that occasions should arise when the killing of a slave was necessary, the state took no action in such a case, but the underlying idea of responsibility is the same; here, however, the individual is left to his own conscience.[7] The Spartans alone of all the Greeks denied this fundamental assumption of the sinfulness of all murder.[8]

This view of the law of murder gives us the clue to the interpretation of the law of personal injury. The slave had no political right which was violated in his murder; neither was any political

---

[1] Ditt. *Syll.*², 680.   [2] Ditt. *Syll.*³, 736, 76 ff.

[3] Lipsius, *Att. Recht*, p. 660, holds that there was a similar provision at Athens for composition by the surrender of the slave, citing Xen. *Hell.* 2, 4, 41. It seems certain, however, that this passage proves the opposite, for if there had been such a provision, Thrasybulus would have compared the Athenians to slaves, not dogs.

[4] Lipsius, *op. cit.*, p. 605: Schol. 2 in Aeschin. 2, 87; Isoc. 18, 52; Arist. *Resp. Ath.* 57, 3; cf. Eur. *Hec.* 291–292.

[5] [Dem.] 47, 70; 72.   [6] Isoc. 12, 181.
[7] Antiph. 6, 4.   [8] Isoc. 12, 181.

right violated when he was physically attacked. Since there was no religious sanction against mere injury inflicted on a man, whether citizen or not, it can be assumed that in general the prohibitions against injuring a slave were in no sense based on any right whatever inherent in him, but on the owner's right of protection' for his property, the need of preserving order and educating the citizens in moral excellence,[1] and the continual fear of a revolt. The law forbidding ὕβρις against anyone, whether citizen or foreigner, slave or free, is preserved;[2] the penalty varied from a light fine to death. There was, of course, no protection for the slave against his owner except the religious one of asylum.[3]

Torture of slaves,[4] although usually made much of, is in reality quite unimportant. The state could, in a matter of public concern, demand any slave for torture;[5] since it could subject any foreigner to the same treatment,[6] this is merely an additional illustration of the fact that the bases of the legal positions of the slave and the foreigner were the same.[7] The fact that a private citizen could at will torture his own slave [8] is only a part of his complete powers, based on the slave's lack of any legal rights. And torture was used against slaves in Greece, not 'weil ihnen die Fähigkeit sittlicher Selbstbestimmung abgeht,'[9] but for the same reason that it has always been used against all except those whose political rights

---

[1] The latter reason is specifically given by Aeschin. 1, 17; Dem. 21, 46. Cf. Plato's reason for the same provision in his ideal state: *Legg.* 777de.

[2] Dem. 21, 47. Its authenticity is vindicated by Lipsius, *Att. Recht*, pp. 421–422, comparing Aeschin. 1, 15.

[3] Thalheim in Pauly-Wissowa, *Realencyclopädie*, etc., s.v. Δοῦλοι: Poll. 7, 13 (cf. above, p. 178, n. 4); Ar. *Eq.* 1312; *Thesm.* 224; cf. Eur. *Herac.* 259–260. The right of demanding resale was religious and could be exercised only in the sanctuary of the Theseum: Poll. *l.c.*; Luc. *Dial. D.* 24, 2.

[4] The entire subject is treated by Lipsius, *Att. Recht*, pp. 888–895.

[5] Andoc. 1, 22; 64.

[6] The principle is stated by Lys. 13, 27. Specific cases: Lys. 3, 33; 13, 54; Dem. 18, 133; Antiph. 1, 20; 5, 49; Thuc. 8, 92, 2; others cited by Lipsius, *Att. Recht*, p. 894, n. 118; p. 895, n. 122.

[7] Until the archonship of Scamandrius (date unknown) even citizens could be tortured by the state: Andoc. 1, 43; cf. [Dem.] 29, 39.

[8] Lys. 1, 16; Dem. 40, 15; 48, 16; 48, 18.

[9] L. V. Schmidt, *Die Ethik d. alt. Griechen* (Berlin, 1882), II, p. 215.

prevented it, namely, because it was thought the surest method of attaining the truth.[1]

The slave in Athens, then, is a man, and possessed of all the characteristics inherent in a man as such. He has none of the privileges, rights, and immunities of the citizen and in this he is exactly like the foreigner or metic. He has no legal personality, for this is a peculiarity of the citizen. Hence the foreigner, in becoming a slave, lost nothing, but merely came under the physical control of a master. In the case of the enslavement of a citizen, the loss of rights is to be considered separately and as a prior act to the enslavement, for the rights could be taken without enslavement. Since the slave has no legal rights, the force of the master can be used in any way the latter desires, unless some other specific factor prevents. Thus it is a mistake to insist too strongly on the analogy between the slave and the beast: while the *relations* of master and slave were practically those of owner and property, still this does not necessarily imply any similarity between the slave and other forms of property, a fact of which the average Greek never lost sight.[2] The emphasis placed by various theorists on the mutual advantage of the relation[3] shows this most clearly. It must be kept in mind that there is little difference in theory between the free foreigner and the slave; the only real difference is that the one is in point of fact under the physical control of a master.

The great contrast between the Gortynian system and the Athenian is that the former grants to the slave certain personal privileges which are now thought of as belonging by right to the human being *qua* human, and not to the citizen only. It is, however, impossible to determine·whether this status and these privileges were granted in recognition of a right, as an expedient making for easier control of the slave population, or simply out of pure

---

[1] Dem. 30, 37; Lycurg. 1, 29. But cf. Arist. *Rhet.* 76b32 ff.

[2] Aristotle comes the closest to denying this, but in so doing, as will be shown, he involves himself in great difficulties; and in admitting that friendship, even if only the analog of true friendship (*Eth. Eud.* 42a28 ff.), can exist between master and slave (*Pol.* 55b12 ff.; *Eth. Nic.* 61b5 ff.), he admits this distinction between the slave and other forms of property.

[3] Below, p. 187.

humanitarianism. In most respects, e.g., the responsibility of the master for damages done by a slave,[1] the slave's representation in court and in all formal acts elsewhere by the master,[2] and the frequent repetition in various cases of the provision that the witnesses required must be free,[3] the law is the same as the Athenian.

But there are considerable differences. The slave was permitted to acquire more property in his own right than was usual at Athens, for fines were provided up to one hundred staters.[4] This property was apparently not subject to confiscation by the master,[5] as it was under Roman and Athenian law. The slave had even a right of inheritance in his master's property if other heirs were lacking,[6] 'eine Bestimmung, die neu und hochbedeutsam ist.'[7] Most important of all, however, is the fact that in Gortyna the slave is granted full family rights. The slave family was not merely a permitted union, but a full legal entity[8] with regular marriage.[9] The father is the head during his life, and his sons assume control on his death; daughters belong to the family as long as they are unmarried; after marriage they enter the family of their husbands.[10] The sanctity of this slave family is recognized and, if only by small penalties, protected.[11] Finally, no restrictions were placed on slave marriages: if two slaves belonged to different masters, the consent of the latter was not necessary to marriage,[12] and a slave could marry even a free woman.[13] 'In der Hauptsache gleiches Recht wie für die freien Familien gilt auch für die Häuslerfamilien, nur dass hier überall die Gewalt des Hausvorstandes, weil derselbe Häusler ist, durch seinen Herrn ausgeübt wird.'[14] Although this,

---

[1] *Code* 7, 10 ff.; cf. Zitelmann, pp. 167 ff.

[2] *Code* 1, 14; 2, 32; 43; 3, 54; 4, 5. Zitelmann, p. 64 and n. 42; pp. 79; 103.

[3] *Code, passim*. Does this imply that in all cases where it is not specified that witnesses shall be free, slaves may be admitted?

[4] *Code* 2, 2 ff.

[5] Zitelmann, p. 64; *Code* 3, 42 ff.; 4, 35 ff.

[6] *Code* 5, 27.   [7] Zitelmann, p. 64.

[8] *Id.*, pp. 114–115.

[9] *Code* 2, 27; 3, 41; 4, 4; cf. Zitelmann, *l.c.*

[10] Zitelmann, pp. 113; 115.   [11] *Code* 2, 2 ff.

[12] Zitelmann, p. 113, from *Code* 4, 3-6.

[13] *Code* 7, 3.   [14] Zitelmann, pp. 108-109.

as has been said, cannot be advanced as conclusive proof concerning the theory of slavery held by the Gortynians, yet the thoroughly regularized and legal status of the slave family is at least a strong indication in favor of the view that the privileges of the Gortynian slave were due chiefly to an admission that these rights were inherent in him as a human being. If this assumption is correct, it is the first example in history of the holding of such a theory, not by a few individuals but by an entire state.

V. POPULAR THEORIES

The examination of the developed legal codes of Athens and Gortyna has revealed the 'popular theory,' if it is proper to speak of such a thing, in practically its final form. In discussing these codes at this stage the chronological treatment of the subject has been abandoned in the hope of securing greater clarity. It still remains, therefore, to discuss the fragmentary evidence bearing on the development of the views seen in the two codes. Unfortunately, since there was no single line of development culminating in a single, universally accepted belief, it will be necessary to insert in their chronological places certain divergent theories, some of which seem to have neither predecessor nor follower. After this development has been traced to the time of the formation of the legal systems, the later popular expressions of the usual theory will be followed; the more complete and systematic justifications of Plato and Aristotle will be discussed in the sixth and seventh sections, and after these the arguments against the institution will be set forth.

In the Homeric world slaves were simply accepted as facts. The master was aware of his unlimited power and used it when he thought fit, but there is no evidence that he ever sought to justify it with a theoretical basis. Since it rested purely on force, it follows that the slave was not assumed a priori to be inferior in any other quality but that;[1] for this reason association with slaves in

---

[1] Plato's opinion (Legg. 776e–777a) notwithstanding: cf. Wallon, Esclavage, I, p. 361; Meyer, Sklaverei, p. 184.

household tasks was not deemed condescension.[1] It was fully recognized that a slave could possess the highest virtues,[2] but unless a slave had earned respect by individual merit, he was regarded as merely a piece of property.[3] It was during the rise of the aristocracies that the new element entered which was to be so characteristic of almost all later thought. As has been seen, an attitude of contempt for labor and a classification of certain tasks as 'slavish' grew up during this period, and it was now that the theory appeared that a slave was by nature fitted for slavery and nothing else. This belief was amazingly confused with ideas on the physical appearance of slaves, and that was taken to be proof of their character.[4] By Solon's time slavery had come to be looked on as worse than death.[5]

Some time after this Heraclitus propounded a unique theory. Holding that strife was necessary for existence, he believed that in the sociological field this strife must take the form of war, and slavery, the universal concomitant of war, was thus justified.[6] τῷ μὲν θεῷ καλὰ πάντα καὶ ἀγαθὰ καὶ δίκαια, ἄνθρωποι δὲ ἃ μὲν ἄδικα ὑπειλήφασιν ἃ δὲ δίκαια.[7]

There is no further evidence for this theory, and until the latter part of the fifth century all that can be found are further illustrations of the usual contempt for slaves, important because it was to be the real basis of the later theory of natural slavery. In 472 Aeschylus in his *Persae*[8] shows the effect of this common feeling

---

[1] Incidents illustrating this: Hom. ζ 71 ff.; π 140 ff. A slave raised with the owner's own daughter: ο 363 ff.; σ 322 f. Warm affection between slave and master: ρ 31 ff.

[2] E.g., ο 351; 365; 370.

[3] Odysseus, in complaining of the damage done by the suitors, puts the damage to the house first, the rape of the maids second: Hom. χ 35-37.

[4] See especially Theognis 535-538.

[5] Punishment by enslavement was abolished, although many offenses were still punished by death: Daremberg et Saglio, IV, p. 1261ab. Cf. the oath before the battle of Plataea, if it is genuine: οὐ ποιήσομαι περὶ πλείονος τὸ ζῆν τῆς ἐλευθερίας: Lycurg. 1, 81. Cf. Plat. *Gorg.* 483b. Compare with this attitude Achilles' famous speech to Odysseus: Hom. λ 488-491.

[6] Gomperz, I, pp. 60 ff. See especially Heraclit. ed. Diels, *Frag. Vorsok.*[5], frg. 53 (I, p. 162).

[7] Heraclit. ed. Diels frg. 102 (I, p. 173).   [8] 355.

when he calls Themistocles' messenger to the Persian king an ἀνὴρ
Ἕλλην, 'als wäre es zu viel Ehre' for a slave [1] 'als Träger einer so
folgenschweren Mission von der Bühne herab genannt zu werden.'[2]
In the next generation Sophocles, in his earlier plays, follows the
lead of Aeschylus and makes the slave roles unsympathetic. In
the *Ajax*,[3] for example, Agamemnon voices the greatest contempt
for all slaves. But already the attacks on the institution were com-
mencing; the period had ended in which there was only a state of
mind concerning the slaves and the time had begun when definite
theories, incomplete as they might be, were gaining general acceptance. There is no longer, therefore, a consecutive development of
any sort, and the remainder of this section will be taken up with a
discussion of the various schools.

The beginnings of the theory of 'natural slavery' [4] lay in the
early scorn of the physical appearance of slaves, combined with
which was the belief that the tasks performed by slaves were in
themselves both physically and morally degrading. These two
factors — both, of course, utterly illogical confusions of cause and
effect — led to generalizations concerning the whole class of slaves
such as that found in Euripides,[5] who as usual presents both sides
of the case:

οὕτω γὰρ κακὸν δούλων γένος·
γαστὴρ ἅπαντα, τοὐπίσω δ' οὐδὲν σκοπεῖ.

The character of the slave was completely without honor, shame, or
any sound element at all (ὑγιὲς οὐδέν).[6] So evil was his nature that
Charon even refused to carry a slave in his ferry, according to
Aristophanes,[7] and in Sparta the slave was considered baser than
thieves and criminals.[8] It was admitted, of course, that occasion-

[1] Hdt. 8, 75, 1.
[2] J. Schmidt, *Der Sklave bei Euripides* (Prog., Grimma, 1892), I, p. 95.
[3] *Id.*, p. 99. Soph. *Ai.* 1228 ff.; 1235; 1289.
[4] This term is used to mean that theory which held that an individual was definitely designed by nature for either slavery or freedom.
[5] Frg. 49 N²; cf. *Or.* 1115; frg. 86.
[6] Plat. *Legg.* 776e; Dem. 8, 51; [Dem.] 10, 27.
[7] *Ran.* 190.
[8] Isoc. 12, 214.

ally cases occurred where a person deserving of freedom was en-slaved,[1] but obviously these did not prejudice the theory.

Of course, the rule of a natural inferior by his superior should result in mutual advantage,[2] and mutual advantage should bring satisfaction on both sides. This common benefit was taken by some to be the only justification of slavery, and the presence of good will was the proof of its presence. The Pythagoreans had first pro-claimed [3] that τοὺς μὲν . . . ἄρχοντας . . . οὐ μόνον ἐπιστήμονας ἀλλὰ καὶ φιλανθρώπους δεῖν εἶναι, καὶ τοὺς ἀρχομένους οὐ μόνον πειθηνίους ἀλλὰ καὶ φιλάρχοντας. An echo of this doctrine appears in Gorgias,[4] and Xenophon frequently expresses[5] the opinion that the master must rule so as to make the slave εὔνους to him. A group of men mentioned by Aristotle appear, if it is possible correctly to inter-pret his confused account of their doctrines, to have held that a just rule of slaves was marked, not by the conditions under which it was established or by the character of the parties involved, but by the presence of εὔνοια.[6] Thus the essence of this doctrine is not that εὔνοια per se justifies slavery, but that its presence proves that the relation is advantageous to both parties, and hence, practically by definition, is just.

From the theory that certain men, and only these men, were naturally fitted for slavery, there was bound to arise the belief that those who were not slaves by nature should not, even could not, be enslaved. The natural belief that the group of which one is a member is superior to other groups, and thus unfit for slavery,[7] tended to make this inference effective first in opposing the enslave-ment of one's fellow-citizens; the results in this field have already been observed.[8] But there has also been observed the growth of a feeling that all the Greeks formed one nation, and it was thus in-

---

[1] Soph. frg. 854 N²; Eur. frg. 831 N².
[2] [Plat.] 1 Alcib. 135bc; Menan. frg. 1093 K. (III, p. 265).
[3] Aristox. frg. 18 Müller, F H G, II, p. 278a.
[4] Plat. Phil. 58b.
[5] Mem. 1, 2, 10; Cyrop. 3, 1, 28; 8, 2, 4.
[6] See Appendix.
[7] Dem. 8, 60; [Dem.] 10, 62.
[8] E.g., in the growing restrictions on the enslavement of citizens for debt and in the right of the ransomed prisoner to purchase his freedom.

evitable that there should come a conviction that no one should enslave a fellow-Hellene. It is to be noticed that this opposition to the enslavement of Greeks is a product of the theory of natural slavery and not of the theory of the injustice of all slavery. Callicratidas' statement[1] at the siege of Methymna in 406, that no Greek would be enslaved if he could prevent it, shows at least that there were at that time a large number who would approve such a course. Plato adopted this theory definitely and emphatically.[2] Epaminondas and Pelopidas enslaved no Greeks,[3] but freed the Messenians.[4] There was general compassion for the Greeks enslaved by Philip at the capture of Olynthus,[5] and dislike for anyone who accepted any of them as a present;[6] the Athenians probably prohibited by law the purchase of any freeman so enslaved.[7]

The opposite of this theory of natural slavery is the admission that the institution rests on nothing but superior force. This, however, is by no means equivalent to an admission that it is unjust. Already about the time of the Persian wars Pindar was proclaiming the rule of the stronger to be just.[8] The enslavement of the Helots and Messenians was admittedly based purely on force and it was an enslavement of Greeks, yet in Plato's time many approved it as εὖ γεγονυῖα.[9] The Athenians who argued [10] against the Melians in 416 and a large group of lawyers and σοφοί of Aristotle's time [11] would certainly have held that slavery — or practically anything else — was justified by the ability to enforce it. Against these were ranged, with Plato[12] and Isocrates [13] at their head, another group of lawyers and σοφοί who denied flatly that mere superior force gave any title whatever to rule.

The strongest proponents of the doctrine of the rule of force were the Sophists, whose general position was that everyone had

[1] Xen. *Hell.* 1, 6, 14. [2] See below, p. 191.
[3] Plut. *Pelop. et Marc. Comp.* 1, 1.
[4] Paus. 4, 26. [5] Aeschin. 2, 156.
[6] Dem. 19, 305-309.
[7] [Plut.] *Vit. X Orat.* 7 Lycurg. 12 (*Mor.* 841f); Meier, *Vit. Lycurg.*, pp. 39-41; cf. above p. 176, n. 3.
[8] Plat. *Legg.* 690bc; *Gorg.* 484b. [9] Plat. *Legg.* 776c.
[10] Thuc. 5, 89. [11] See Appendix.
[12] *Legg.* 690c. [13] 8, 69.

the right to follow his own inclinations if he had the power.[1] Callicles affirms violently and repeatedly that the stronger is identical with the better and that his rule over the weaker is according to the only just law, that of nature.[2] But as Socrates here points out to Callicles, this doctrine becomes hopelessly self-contradictory if it is not restricted to individuals; if Callicles had been dialectically pressed, he would probably have said that it was just for an individual to keep other men enslaved, but unjust for a state to keep a group in slavery.

There remain two justifications, so simple as scarcely to deserve the name of theories. The first is an application of the basic assumption of ordinary Greek ethics, that one should requite both wrongs and benefactions in kind.[3] On this principle it would be eminently just to enslave one's enemies, and Socrates states this as if no reasonable man could be expected to raise a question.[4] Another school, probably a small one, advanced an argument identifying justice and legality; since there was no doubt that it was legal to enslave prisoners of war, it was *ipso facto* just.[5] Both these theories can be extended to include slaves other than prisoners of war by application of the principle that the normal relation between all states was that of war.

Thus until the enlightenment of the later fifth century there was no attempt to formulate a theory of slavery. At first a slave was looked upon much as any other human being, whose esteem was regulated by his merits. With the growth of scorn for certain tasks as slavish, there soon arose the need for a justification of the practice of forcing certain men to perform these tasks, and chief among the theories advanced was that based on the common prejudice against the barbarian, the theory of 'natural slavery,' to which both Plato and Aristotle adhered. But before examining the positions of these two, the curious and unique verses of Philemon[6]

[1] Zeller, I ii⁶, p. 1395.
[2] Plat. *Gorg.* 483d; 488b; 488d.
[3] E.g., Eur. *Med.* 807–810; Sol. ed. Diehl frg. 1, 5–6.
[4] Xen. *Mem.* 2, 2, 2.
[5] See Appendix.
[6] Frg. 31 K. (II, p. 486).

should be noted, where the entire universe is viewed as a hierarchy of slavery, in which one's place on the scale mattered but little.

Ἐμοῦ γάρ ἐστι κύριος μὲν εἶς ἀνήρ·
τούτων δὲ καὶ σοῦ μυρίων τ' ἄλλων νόμος,
ἑτέρων τύραννος, τῶν τυραννούντων φόβος.
δοῦλοι βασιλέων εἰσίν, ὁ βασιλεὺς θεῶν,
ὁ θεὸς 'Ανάγκης. πάντα δ', ἂν σκοπῆς, ὅλως
ἑτέρων πέφυκεν ἧττον', ὧν δὲ μείζονα.
τούτοις ἀνάγκη ταῦτα δουλεύειν ἀεί.

VI. PLATO

Plato, as has been said, is an adherent of the school believing in 'natural slavery,' but his conception of the natural slave differs greatly from that of most of the other members of the school. It is not, as Aristotle later stated,[1] ὅσων ἐστὶν ἔργον ἡ τοῦ σώματος χρῆσις, καὶ τοῦτ' ἔστ' ἀπ' αὐτῶν βέλτιστον, but τοὺς δὲ ἐν ἀμαθίᾳ τε αὖ καὶ ταπεινότητι πολλῇ κυλινδουμένους whom his statesman εἰς τὸ δουλικὸν ὑποζεύγνυσι γένος.[2] In his *Republic*,[3] those who are without the θεῖον ἄρχον, but not sunk in an excess of moral baseness, are to be citizens, not slaves. Thus three classes are distinguished, the highest of which is subdivided in the state into two parts. The first class, which includes the rulers and soldiers in his *Republic*, possess full moral excellence and are capable in private affairs of self-rule; those not possessing this capability are to be ruled by the wise and good,[4] but the closeness of the rule will vary with the degree of incapability. To Plato, the βάναυσος is capable of personal self-rule, but not of the higher activities of politics and government; the slave is capable of neither. The inferior character of both these classes and the superior character of the full citizens tend very strongly to be hereditary;[5] exceptions, however, do occur[6] and, at least in the case of the artisans and probably in that of the slaves, provision is made to remedy any maladjustments.[7]

[1] *Pol.* 54b17 ff.
[3] 463ab; cf. 442c; 552a.
[5] *Crat.* 394a.
[7] *Rep.* 415.

[2] Plat. *Polit.* 309a.
[4] *Id.* 590cd, comparing 463ab.
[6] *Ib.*

Although Plato concurred with the common views of his time in holding that as a rule Greeks should not be enslaved by Greeks, still he differed from most others in holding this theory with reservations and for different reasons than usual. The Greeks, he believed, were all one nation and hence a war among them, being between οἰκεῖοι καὶ ξυγγενεῖς, was στάσις and not πόλεμος. For this reason any such war should be prosecuted with the greatest moderation and ended as soon as possible. All permanent damages, even to property, should be avoided. In fact, all except the ringleaders of the opposing faction are really the friends of those on the just and right side, and hence, when those leaders have been duly punished, no further vengeance should be taken.[1] It is for this reason that Greek prisoners of war are not to be enslaved in a body; there is, however, no evidence to show that Plato believed that no Greek was fit for slavery.

The slave has no 'human rights'; he is lacking in the most essentially human element of the soul. If a man kills his own slave, it is true, he should make expiation; but since the only penalty for killing another's slave is to pay double the value, it would seem that the only reason for the former provision is to delude the citizen into a belief which will prevent intemperance of any sort.[2] For the same reason, and also in order to make the slave population less troublesome in the city, slaves are not to be treated cruelly or flippantly, but firmly and in a dignified manner: by such conduct the character of the master himself is improved.[3]

The superficiality of this discussion of slavery is quite simply explained.[4] The chief end of the Platonic as of the Aristotelian state is the attainment of moral perfection on the part of the citizens — in the case of the *Republic* the two upper classes. Plato is very nearly taking the simple view that whatever contributed to the attainment of this goal is *ipso facto* just and requires no further discussion.

---

[1] *Id.* 469b–471c. On the enslavement of friends cf. Socrates *ap.* Xen. *Mem.* 2, 2, 2.   [2] *Legg.* 868a.

[3] *Id.* 777d–778a.

[4] E. Barker, in *C A II*, VI, p. 522.

VII. Aristotle

Aristotle, as has been shown, followed the common conservative prejudice in admitting to his state only those whose leisure and training were sufficient to enable them to contribute their share to its functioning and to enjoy the benefits which it could confer.[1] For this reason certain tasks were to be given to non-citizen artisans (βάναυσοι), others to slaves; any task unfitting for a citizen would be given to that one of these two classes for which its nature rendered it appropriate. None of the productive industries are to be in the hands of slaves,[2] but they are presumably to be run by free τεχνῖται. The expediency of slavery for society is taken for granted; in fact, almost none of the ancient critics of slavery claimed that it was harmful in any other way than as a violation of the personal rights of the slave.[3]

Since the slave is not to come in any way into direct contact with the state, he is really more a matter of concern for the household, where he is of primary importance.[4] *Oeconomy* is an art with a definite purpose, and like all other arts of that sort requires for its performance its proper tools; but the inanimate tools will not perform their functions by themselves. If they would there would be no need of slavery, but since they will not, the slave, who puts all the other tools into use, is ὥσπερ ὄργανον πρὸ ὀργάνων.[5] Any ὄργανον πρακτικόν, however, is a κτῆμα,[6] and hence the slave is a κτῆμα,[7] although a κτῆμα ἔμψυχον,[8] and part of the κτῆσις,[9] the whole purpose of which is to aid in the enjoyment of life and not in production. The government of slaves is thus a part of the κτητικὴ τέχνη and not connected with that section of *oeconomy* which deals with the government of the other members of the household.[10] And like other tools, the function of the slave is purely physical — in exactly

---

[1] *Pol.* 69a34 ff.; 28b37 ff.

[2] *Pol.* 54a1 ff. But there seems to be an inconsistency when Aristotle (*id.* 30a25 ff.) recommends slaves for agriculture, certainly a productive occupation.

[3] Below, p. 199.　　　　　　　　[4] *Pol.* 53b3 ff.

[5] *Pol.* 53b32 f.　　　　　　　　[6] *Pol.* 54a16 ff.

[7] *Oec.* 44a23 f.　　　　　　　　[8] *Pol.* 53b32.

[9] *Pol.* 56a2 f.

[10] For this whole paragraph, *Pol.* 53b23 ff.

the same class, although differing in certain respects, as the function of beasts.[1]

The man who is qualified to fill this position will be the natural slave,[2] and his qualifications must now be described. Physically he will approach the brute, with strength suited to the tasks he will have to perform, but not with the erect physique of the citizen. This, however, is only of minor importance; the real test of such a person is not so much that he is physically fitted for the task, but that he is mentally and morally unsuited for anything else; and sometimes the soul of a slave may be found in the body of a freeman.[3] Such men are to be slaves, just as men with slave bodies but free souls are to be free.[4]

The definite mark of the slave is his lack of τὸ βουλευτικόν[5] (the faculty of deliberating and considering in advance) and προαίρεσις[6] (the exercise of deliberate choice based on this previous consideration), two qualities greatly different from and much superior to mere cleverness or ingenuity.[7] As to what share in reason the slave actually has, however, Aristotle is inconsistent within the limits of one sentence. He says: [8] ὅσοι μὲν οὖν τοσοῦτον διεστᾶσιν ὅσον ψυχὴ σώματος καὶ ἄνθρωπος θηρίου (διάκεινται τοῦτον τὸν τρόπον ὅσων ἐστὶν ἔργον ἡ τοῦ σώματος χρῆσις καὶ τοῦτ᾽ ἔστ᾽ ἀπ᾽ αὐτῶν βέλτιστον), οὗτοι μέν εἰσι φύσει δοῦλοι· . . . ἔστι γὰρ φύσει δοῦλος . . . ὁ κοινωνῶν λόγου τοσοῦτον ὅσον αἰσθάνεσθαι ἀλλὰ μὴ ἔχειν· τὰ γὰρ ἄλλα ζῷα οὐ λόγῳ αἰσθανόμενα ἀλλὰ παθήμασιν ὑπηρετεῖ. In other words, he simultaneously grants to the slave a participation in reason and denies it to him utterly, making him a mere body. His entire thought on this point is hopelessly confused: the slave was κτῆμά τι ἔμψυχον; now he is

---

[1] Pol. 54b24 ff.   [2] Pol. 54b16 ff.
[3] Pol. 54b27 ff.   [4] Pol. 54b37 f.
[5] Pol. 60a12.
[6] As Newman, Pol. of Arist., III, p. 201, concludes, comparing Pol. 60a12 with Phys. 97b6 ff.
[7] There is no contradiction in the granting to Asiatics of διάνοια (Pol. 27b27 f.) and the denial to slaves of the ability τῇ διανοίᾳ προορᾶν (ib. 52a31 ff.). The difficulty is one of language: the διάνοια of the Asiatics is inventiveness, ingenuity; that of the φύσει ἄρχων is the ability to decide rightly a high moral question.
[8] Pol. 54b16 ff.

I

only σῶμα.¹ But, while he does not fully possess (ἔχειν) reason (λόγος), he participates in it (κοινωνεῖν),² and it is a part of the ψυχή which is involved.³

Criticism is ordinarily directed at Aristotle's remarks on friendship between masters and slaves; they can, as will be shown, be easily explained, and their inconsistencies are only the surface manifestations of the real difficulties and contradictions at the very base of Aristotle's idea of the characteristics of the natural slave. His account can be made consistent by assuming that he meant that the slave is like a man in possessing a part of the ψυχή, like a beast in lacking part of it, and is of neither species completely, but *sui generis*.⁴

The virtue ⁵ of such a partial man will be only a partial virtue. As a tool he has, of course, the ἀρεταί proper to that tool for the performance of its functions; the only question is πότερον ἔστιν ἀρετή τις δούλου παρὰ τὰς ὀργανικὰς καὶ διακονικὰς ἄλλη τιμιωτέρα τούτων, οἷον σωφροσύνη καὶ ἀνδρεία καὶ δικαιοσύνη καὶ τῶν ἄλλων τῶν τοιούτων ἕξεων, ἢ οὐκ ἔστιν οὐδεμία παρὰ τὰς σωματικὰς ὑπηρεσίας.⁶ Since the slave is an animate tool, he must have the moral virtues (ἕξεις) necessary for ἄρχεσθαι καλῶς; his ἀρεταί as a tool are merely those of his physical frame. He cannot participate fully in all the moral virtues, for to do so would be to exhibit that καλοκαγαθία which is the mark of the citizen, and he has no need for this; he needs only such virtues as will enable him to fulfill his purpose: to serve his master without inefficiency caused by ἀκολασία or δειλία. To this extent, then, he will participate in the moral virtues; the master will be the inculcator of these (τῆς τοιαύτης ἀρετῆς αἴτιον), undoubtedly through both precept and example; in the slave they will come to be automatic.⁷

¹ *Eth. Nic.* 61a34 f.; *Eth. Eud.* 41b17 ff.
² *Pol.* 54b22 f.; 60b5 ff.   ³ *Eth. Nic.* 02b23 ff.
⁴ Of course under modern psychology such a distinction is impossible: differences between minds are of degree, not of kind (εἴδει). Aristotle would have recognized that this fact alone would upset his whole theory: *Pol.* 59b36 ff.
⁵ This paragraph largely follows L. Schiller, *Die Lehre des Arist. von d. Sklaverei* (Prog., Erlangen, 1847), p. 10.   ⁶ *Pol.* 59b22 ff.
⁷ The problem of the virtue of the slave is very fully discussed in the long passage (*Pol.* 59b26–60b5) following that quoted in the text.

The slave, being only a κτῆμα, is like a μόριον of the master and thus has no existence apart, but only in reference to the whole.[1] He is apparently a part only of the σῶμα of the master and not of his ψυχή,[2] and thus his rule by his master is that of the σῶμα by the ψυχή, a despotic rule; the rule of the ἄλογον part of the soul by the λόγον ἔχον is, on the contrary, political and royal.[3] It is probably this fact which has led Aristotle into the confusion noticed above concerning the nature of the slave: in relation to his master *qua* master, which is the converse of the relation of the master to the slave *qua* slave, he is ἄψυχος and only a part of the master's body; but in relation to the master *qua* man, the converse of the relation of the master to the slave *qua* man, — the essential point being that here they are considered as two individuals, whereas in the former case they are considered as ὅλον and μέρος, — he is ἔμψυχος. But this explanation, the best I can give, is not adequate: the ἕξεις exist in the ψυχή, not in the σῶμα; but the ἕξεις are necessary for the performance of his functions *qua* slave. This, then, is the ultimate cause of Aristotle's chief error: he tried to alter the common doctrine of slavery by making the slave only a part of the master, and to make one man part of another is, apparently, logically impossible.[4] The necessary granting of ψυχή to the slave really indicates that his relation to his master should have been defined as that of the reasonable part of the soul (λόγος) to the unreasonable (ὄρεξις), absolute (βασιλική) but non-arbitrary (πολιτική).[5]

Thus we come to the problem of the possibility of friendship between the master and the slave. I believe that Aristotle's meaning here is quite simple: it would be also lucid were it not obscured by his contradictions concerning the nature of the slave. The slave, not having part of the soul, is not fully a man; true friendship can

[1] *Pol.* 54a8 ff.; 55b11 f.   [2] *Pol.* 55b9 ff.
[3] Relations of parts of the soul and of the soul and the body: *Pol.* 54b4 ff. Relation of master and slave: *id.* 55b6 ff.; *Eth. Nic.* 60b29.
[4] Newman, *Pol. of Arist.*, I, p. 150, believes the difficulty lies in reconciling the two aspects of man and property. This would cause no trouble; the difficulty enters when Aristotle makes this form of property — which, as has been shown, was not in the common view identical with other forms — exactly like the others in being a part of the owner.
[5] *Pol.* 54b2 ff.

exist only between men and hence not between man and slave. But the slave is also, having part of the soul, partly a man, and in proportion to the extent to which he is a man (καθ' ὅσον ἄνθρωπος) friendship towards him can exist, although it is only the ἀνάλογον of true friendship.[1] The confusion enters because Aristotle thinks of the slave as both having and not having a soul absolutely instead of partially: in his capacity of slave he is ἄψυχος — although, as has been shown, even in that capacity he employs his ψυχή — and hence qua slave there is no friendship; forgetting that to be a slave he must still be a man, Aristotle makes the aspect of man separate and says friendship exists with him only qua man. The underlying thought, however, is clear and simple: it is exactly what we mean when we say we are 'on friendly terms with' a person whom we would never own as a friend.

A final definition of the natural slave may now be advanced; this definition will not be Aristotle's, but it is the essence of Aristotle's doctrine made as consistent as possible. The natural slave is a being having that part of the soul (the παθητικὸν μόριαν; τὸ ἄλογον) which shares in reason (λόγου κοινωνεῖν) to the extent of perceiving it (αἰσθάνεσθαι); he lacks that part (τὸ βουλευτικόν) which possesses reason fully (λόγον ἔχειν) and enables moral choice (προαίρεσις) in advance of action (τῇ διανοίᾳ προορᾶν). Thus he is neither a man, who is distinguished by full possession of the soul, nor a beast (θηρίον), which is distinguished by its absence, but is sui generis. His whole function is to be a tool (ὄργανον) and possession (κτῆμα) of his master; considered in this aspect he is a part (μέρος) of his master; and, since he performs only physical tasks, a part only of the master's physical nature (σῶμα). But since he is a self-acting tool, he differs from other tools, and even in his actions in that capacity employs his ψυχή.

For such a creature to be enslaved is of benefit to him as well as his master,[2] for everything is benefited only by fulfilling its function, by reaching the ἐνέργεια in accordance with its own ἀρετή. No attention, therefore, is paid consciously to the good of the slave; the master looks out for himself alone, but the relation is so intimate

[1] Pol. 55b9 ff.; Eth. Nic. 61a32 ff.; Eth. Eud. 42a28 ff.
[2] Pol. 54b6 ff.

that a harm to one must be a harm to the other and the good of one likewise a good for the other.[1] Such is the natural slave. πότερον δ' ἐστί τις φύσει τοιοῦτος ἢ οὔ, καὶ πότερον βέλτιον καὶ δίκαιόν τινι δουλεύειν ἢ οὔ, ἀλλὰ πᾶσα δουλεία παρὰ φύσιν ἐστί, μετὰ ταῦτα σκεπτέον. οὐ χαλεπὸν δὲ καὶ τῷ λόγῳ θεωρῆσαι καὶ ἐκ τῶν γινομένων καταμαθεῖν.[2] The first part of the proof will, then, be *a priori* and deduced chiefly from analogies.

The distinction of ruler and ruled exists throughout nature, even in inanimate objects and abstract principles.[3] Within an animal, this is the relation between the soul and body, or between reason and the passions.[4] The same relation obtains between man and woman.[5] Since the type of rule naturally depends on the characters of the ruler and the ruled, it follows that if two men differ ὅσον ψυχὴ σώματος καὶ ἄνθρωπος θηρίου, the relation between them should be the same as that between the members of those two pairs.[6] Apparently the argument now continues: All those whose sole function is the use of the body differ from complete men by this much;[7] there are (or, since Aristotle is arguing τῷ λόγῳ, does he mean: there must be?) men whose sole function is the use of the body;[8] therefore there are men who should stand in relation to other men as body to soul. This argument is utterly invalid, and its fallacy lies in the major premise: no man can remain a man and be completely lacking in ψυχή, and therefore no man can differ from the complete man by the difference between σῶμα and χυχή. On the contrary, it has been shown (above, pp. 193 ff.) that men whose sole function is the use of the body employ a part of the soul in performing this function; they differ from complete men, therefore, by as much as the complete soul from the part which only shares in reason. The assumption of the minor premise, that men exist whose sole function is the use of the body, is at least possible. The conclusion will be, then, that there are men fit for the rule

---

[1] *Pol.* 78b32 ff.; cf. 55b9 ff.
[2] *Pol.* 54a17 ff.
[3] *Pol.* 54a21 ff. Cf. Philem. frg. 31 K. (II, p. 486; quoted in text above, p. 190). ·
[4] *Pol.* 54a34 ff.　　　　　　　　[5] *Pol.* 54b13 f.
[6] *Pol.* 54b16 ff.　　　　　　　　[7] *Ib.*
[8] This premise is apparently left to be assumed.

of the reasoning part of the soul over the ἄλογον portion, a rule which is βασιλικὴ καὶ πολιτική.

Aristotle almost fails to take up the proof ἐκ τῶν γινομένων. He has already confessed that a slavish body, easy to distinguish, is no valid test;[1] the nature of the person's soul is to be the only criterion, ἀλλ' οὐχ ὁμοίως ῥᾴδιον ἰδεῖν τό τε τῆς ψυχῆς κάλλος καὶ τὸ τοῦ σώματος.[2] It is no wonder that it is hard to tell: Aristotle has assumed that the slave is completely lacking in a part of the soul, when all that there actually was to differentiate men was a difference in degree of intelligence. This very difficulty should have led him to the realization that no difference εἴδει existed. The differences which he did remark between slaves and freemen, between natural slaves and natural citizens, are rather the effect of slavery or the simple evidence of a low level of culture than signs of native fitness for slavery or unfitness for a higher culture. In reality his only argument is the simple assertion that all barbarians are natural slaves.[3] This assertion, however, in view of its general acceptance by the Greeks, might be called an argument ἐκ τῶν γινομένων valid for his age. But some Greeks are to be enslaved, or at least will be by nature slaves,[4] and how these are to be recognized he does not say. Probably the test would be their ability to perform any function not purely physical. This slavish character tends to be hereditary, but cases occur where good parents have inferior offspring and so perhaps also where slavish parents have free children;[5] in the case of barbarians, however, it is apparently assumed that no exceptions will occur. The entire argument must strike any reader as an evasion. Aristotle concedes to the objectors that some are actually enslaved who should not be,[6] but he does not give the impression of being very greatly interested in bringing about the remedy of this situation, although he was probably

[1] Pol. 54b27 ff.   [2] Pol. 54b38 ff.
[3] Pol. 52b5 ff.; 55a28 f.; see above, pp. 168; 170.
[4] Pol. 55b1 ff.; cf. 83a36 f.
[5] Pol. 55b1 ff. Since, however, all barbarians are slaves by nature, the only chance for a rise in status would be in the children of Hellenic parents who had fallen into the class of natural slaves.
[6] Pol. 55a5 f.

anxious that slaves of really eminent abilities should be freed. His only real concern is to justify the existence in his ideal state of the class of slaves necessary for its proper functioning.

VIII. The Criticism of Slavery

It is impossible to give a satisfactory discussion of those attacks on slavery which were the cause of the various justifications that have been set forth above, for of all these criticisms there are only three surviving scraps: a sentence of Alcidamas, a reference in Aristotle, and an echo in Philemon. And with such scanty material, it is impossible to follow the arguments of the critics; about all that can be done is to show that they existed. Of criticisms of the institution not as unjust but as undesirable socially there is just one: the Phocians violently disliked Mnason, the friend of Aristotle, because his thousand slaves 'deprived so many citizens of their necessary sustenance.'[1] While it might be argued that slavery was responsible for the generally low standard of living of the laboring classes in Greece, nevertheless it is a fact that there is not a single ancient statement of such a belief.

Many writers protested against slavery as it was, without having the least doubt of the justice of the institution if properly applied. Euripides is one of the most vociferous of those who proclaim that the slave is very often better than his master, implying that in such cases slavery is the height of injustice.[2] Since good and able children are often born of slavish parents,[3] all hereditary slavery is probably to be condemned. But most certainly Euripides believed that there existed some whose nature was fit for slavery;[4] thus his divergencies from such a conservative as Aristotle are only the rejection of the inferiority of barbarians as a class[5]

---

[1] Timaeus frg. 67 Müller, *F H G*, I, p. 208a.

[2] Among innumerable passages illustrating Euripides' sympathy for the slave, frgg. 511 and 831 N², *Ion* 854–856, and *El.* 369–372, are especially emphatic.

[3] Eur. *El.* 369–372.

[4] Frg. 57 N²: ὦ παγκάκιστοι καὶ τὸ δοῦλον οὐ νόμῳ (*scripsi col.* Arist. *Pol.* 53b21; λόγῳ *codd.*; τύχῃ Cobet) | ἔχοντες, ἀλλὰ τῇ φύσει (Jacobs; τύχῃ *codd.*) κεκτημένοι.

[5] See above, p. 169.

and the refusal to believe even in a strong tendency for slavishness to be hereditary.

The first[1] of the thinkers categorically to denounce slavery of whom there is an extant record was the rhetor Alcidamas. In his *Messeniac* he defended the liberation of the Messenians by the Thebans in 370, proclaiming:[2] ἐλευθέρους ἀφῆκε πάντας θεός· οὐδένα δοῦλον ἡ φύσις πεποίηκεν. The grounds on which he based this assertion are unknown, but he may perhaps have been one of the apparently very considerable faction to whom παρὰ φύσιν (sc. δοκεῖ) τὸ δεσπόζειν, νόμῳ γὰρ τὸν μὲν δοῦλον εἶναι τὸν δ' ἐλεύθερον, φύσει δ' οὐθὲν διαφέρειν, διόπερ οὐδὲ δίκαιον, βίαιον γάρ.[3] Alcidamas was head of a group which opposed the school of Isocrates;[4] Isocrates entered the Messenian controversy on the opposite side with his *Archidamus*, and it is possible that each was followed in the dispute by his own faction.

Although the Cynics in general disregarded slavery as external and therefore immaterial, Onesicritus, a contemporary of Alexander, held the belief that its abolition would be desirable.[5] His reasons cannot be established, yet it may well be that he objected on grounds of social disadvantage rather than justice. But the widespread influence of the doctrine that slavery was an 'accident' not inherent in the character of the slave is shown by its presence in Philemon, a writer of the late fourth century, who expresses[6] the idea almost in the very words of Alcidamas:

κἂν δοῦλος ᾖ τις, σάρκα τὴν αὐτὴν ἔχει·
φύσει γὰρ οὐδεὶς δοῦλος ἐγενήθη ποτέ,
ἡ δ' αὖ τύχη τὸ σῶμα κατεδουλώσατο.

Such were the attacks upon the institution of slavery, which found its great defender in Aristotle. They are aimed almost ex-

---

[1] J. B. Bury, *A History of Greece to the Death of Alexander the Great*², students' ed. (London, 1913), p. 582, claims that the Sophist Lycophron was the first; there is no evidence for this. He denied the validity of distinctions of birth (Stob. ed. Wach. et Hen. 4, 29, 24), but this implies a rejection only of hereditary slavery.

[2] Schol. in Arist. *Rhet.* 73b6.   [3] Arist. *Pol.* 53b20 ff.; see Appendix.
[4] Pauly-Wissowa, *s.v.* Alkidamas.   [5] Strab. 15, 1, 54, p. 710.
[6] Philem. frg. 95 K. (II, p. 508); cf. frg. 22 (p. 484).

clusively against one theory: that of natural slavishness, innate in the character of the slave. And elaborately as Aristotle might define the character of his ideal slave, it has been seen that he was unable to demonstrate his existence. The entire question turned on a matter of disputable fact, whether there were or were not men whose sole function was the use of the body and who lacked the ability to be their own moral guides. Their existence was affirmed by the defenders, denied by the critics, of slavery. And with this dilemma, probably incapable of settlement, this discussion may stop.

IX. Summary

This final dilemma was a far cry from the beginnings of Greek thought about the slave. In Homeric times mankind had not been separated into Greeks and barbarians, nor had occupations been distinguished as servile or free. The slave, consequently, was thought of as an ordinary human being who had simply had the misfortune of falling under the domination of a master. In the eighth and seventh centuries the exploiting aristocracies in some of the Greek states brought all labor, which was performed by slaves or serfs, under a stigma from which it never recovered and which was reflected later even in some of the writers who belonged to states where this prejudice was not popularly held. In these other states, during the sixth and early fifth centuries, a similar contempt grew up, but was restricted to handicraft and trade. This was especially strengthened after the Persian wars, when many new slaves were acquired. Thus in every state of Greece certain occupations were considered by all, except those so unfortunate as to be engaged in them, as fit only for slaves; the next step was to consider slaves as fit only for these occupations.

Concurrently with this development, beginning with the eighth century, the Greeks were coming to regard themselves as distinct from, and later as superior to, all other peoples. This growth received its greatest impetus from the victory over the Persians; the contempt in which they thereafter held foreigners easily turned into a belief that these foreigners were fit only for servile tasks. Two factors strengthened this conviction: first, the voluntary submission of the Asiatic to absolute monarchy seemed to the Greek the equivalent of voluntary slavery; second, from the fact that most slaves in Greece were actually barbarians the inference was drawn that barbarians were best fitted to be slaves.

By the middle of the fifth century, then, three assumptions were being generally made: certain tasks were fit only for slaves; certain men were fit only for these tasks; all barbarians fell within this class of men (with the corollary that all Greeks were excluded). It remained only to explain the bases of the last two assumptions, and after a beginning made by Plato this explanation was elaborated by Aristotle. For him, the slave was a partial man, lacking the governing element of the soul and consequently needing to be ruled by someone who possessed this element. But already, toward the end of the fifth century, there had arisen an opposing group, who denied the existence of such part-men and refused to admit that anyone was in need of absolute government by another. Others, while not going so far as this, denied at least that race or nationality had anything to do with the determination of character.

Such was the main line of Greek thought concerning slavery. There were at various times divergent theories advanced, but they never received wide acceptance, and at the end of the period under discussion the two chief antagonists in the field were the proponents of 'natural slavery,' and the advocates of liberty for all.

APPENDIX

The passage in Aristotle's *Politics* 1255a5–26 is extremely difficult of interpretation and yet essential for the history of the theory of slavery. The problem comprises two parts: first, the determination of the meaning of Aristotle's words, and second, the separation of the theories which Aristotle is discussing from the adulterations which he has introduced into them. The best treatment is that by Newman in his edition, II, pp. 150–152.

First an attempt should be made to define Aristotle's interpretation. All parties, he thinks, would agree ὅτι τρόπον τινὰ ἀρετὴ τυγχά-νουσα χορηγίας καὶ βιάζεσθαι δύναται μάλιστα, καὶ ἔστιν ἀεὶ τὸ κρατοῦν ἐν ὑπεροχῇ ἀγαθοῦ τινος, ὥστε δοκεῖν μὴ ἄνευ ἀρετῆς εἶναι τὴν βίαν. In other words, this ἀγαθόν τι is at least a form or part of, if not all of or identical with, ἀρετή. Aristotle also believes that everyone would agree that superiority in ἀρετή implies a right to enslave. But now the differences begin.

(1) One party holds that the ὑπεροχὴ ἀγαθοῦ τινος attendant on superior force is *per se* a ὑπεροχὴ ἀρετῆς and therefore confers the right to rule (τοῖς δ' αὐτὸ τοῦτο δίκαιον (*sc.* δοκεῖ), τὸ τὸν κρείττονα ἄρχειν). Aristótle believes that this view, justifying slavery by mere force, is the same as that justifying it by its legality.

(2) The other party holds that this ἀγαθόν τι is only a part of ἀρετή, that the ὑπεροχὴ ἀγαθοῦ τινος implied by superior force does not *per se* imply a superiority in ἀρετή and hence a right to rule. This party, Aristotle thinks, believes that the only proof of the existence of superior ἀρετή in the master is the evidence of εὔνοια between him and his slave (cf. *Eth. Nic.* 67a18).

Aristotle himself gives us the reason for the confusion in his interpretation of these beliefs: he is simply trying to follow his usual ethical and political method, i.e., to prove by the consensus of all thinkers (cf. *Pol.* 55a3; 55b4), and hence to admit that a large number of men were radically in disagreement with him would, in his mind, damage the validity of his conclusion. He must, therefore, assume that a doctrine which differed from his in any real essential would be simply absurd and could not be held by any serious thinker: ἐπεὶ διαqτάντων γε χωρὶς τούτων τῶν λόγων οὔτ' ἰσχυρὸν οὐθὲν ἔχουσιν οὔτε πίθανον ἄτεροι λόγοι, ὡς οὐ δεῖ τὸ βέλτιον κατ' ἀρετὴν ἄρχειν καὶ δεσπόζειν.

Next, the true beliefs of these groups must be separated from Aristotle's adulterations. The starting point is to deny that all would agree that οὔτ' ἰσχυρὸν οὐθὲν ἔχουσιν οὔτε πιθανὸν ἄτεροι λόγοι, ὡς οὐ δεῖ τὸ βέλτιον κατ' ἀρετὴν ἄρχειν καὶ δεσπόζειν; secondly, to deny that all would agree that ἔστιν ἀεὶ τὸ κρατοῦν ἐν ὑπεροχῇ ἀγαθοῦ τινος, ὥστε δοκεῖν μὴ ἄνευ ἀρετῆς εἶναι τὴν βίαν. The theories then are simply:

(1) Force *per se* gives a right to rule, the Sophistic doctrine.

(2) Force *per se* does not give a right to rule. This school splits into two divisions:

(a) Anything based on force is unjust (*Pol.* 53b22: οὐδὲ δίκαιον, βίαιον γάρ); therefore all slavery is unjust.

(b) The origin of slavery neither justifies nor condemns it; it is the character of the rule which does so. A proper and just rule of slaves is one which conciliates the εὔνοια of the slave; this proves the existence of ἀρετή, which is the real justification of the slavery.

(3) Anything legal is just. This is not to be confused with the doctrine that superior force confers the right to rule.

VII

SLAVERY IN PLATO'S THOUGHT[1]

I. SLAVERY IN PLATO'S POLITICAL THEORY

A FORMAL discussion of slavery is nowhere to be found in Plato. We must reconstruct his views from a few casual statements. The most important of these is a simile in the *Laws* (720), where Plato contrasts the free physician in attendance upon freemen with the slave healer of slaves. The free medical man "investigates the origin and the nature of the disease;[2] he enters into community with the patient and with his friends." He is essentially a teacher, but a teacher who also learns from the sick. He gives no autocratic orders, but educates the patient into health. Slaves, on the other hand, are incapable of such reasonable intercourse. The slave doctor's visit is hurried. He "neither gives a servant any rational account (*logos*) of his complaint, nor asks him for any; he gives an order based on empirical belief (*doxa*) with the air of exact knowledge, in the insolent manner of a tyrant, then jumps off to the next ailing servant."[3] Elsewhere (*Laws* 773e), discussing the proper treatment of slaves, Plato sums up the matter in these words: "One must punish slaves justly, not spoiling them by admonition as though they were freemen."[4] And in another context: "Well then, should they discern this, but be unable to give any rational demonstration of it?—Impossible. The state of mind you describe is that of a slave" (*Laws* 966b).

It is clear from such passages that Plato thinks of the slave's condition as a deficiency of reason. He has *doxa*, but no *logos*. He can have true belief, but cannot know the truth of his belief.[5] He can learn by experience (*empeiria*) and external prescription (*epitaxis*). But he can neither give nor follow a rational account. He is *therefore* susceptible to persuasion.[6] This is not

---

[1] Read in substance at a meeting of the American Philosophical Association, December 1939.

[2] 720d: ἀπ' ἀρχῆς καὶ κατὰ φύσιν.

[3] Cf. also *Gorg.* 501a, where scientific medicine is defined in similar terms, contrasting the knowledge of the natural cause (τὴν φύσιν, τὴν αἰτίαν) and the ability to give a rational account (*logos*) with τριβὴ καὶ ἐμπειρία.

[4] Even Aristotle thinks that this is going too far: *Pol.* 1260b 6–8.

[5] See *Tm* 51e 3 and 4.

[6] Διδαχή vs. πειθώ, *Tm* 51e 2. *Peitho* is usually translated "persuasion", and I shall follow this usage here. But "influence" or "suggestion" would be a better rendering. *Peitho* means simply changing another's mind. It puts no strings

evidence of reason, but the reverse. *Nous* is "unmoved by persuasion" (*Tm* 51e 4). The weakness of *doxa*, even of true *doxa*, is that it can be changed.[7] Only knowledge is stable (*monimos*), for he who knows has direct contact with the immutable Forms.[8] This is what the slave lacks. His experience cannot yield true knowledge.[9] In all matters of truth he is, therefore, unconditionally subject to his intellectual superiors.

Now it is an axiom of Plato's political theory that the only one fit to rule is he who possesses *logos*.[10] The good ruler must rule for the good of the state. He can only do this if he knows the form of the Good, and then uses the necessary "persuasion and coercion" to order the state accordingly.[11] Thus government is good for the governed,[12] but does not require their con-

---

on the way this is done. "Persuasion", as ordinarily used in English, ties one down to some kind of intellectual, or, at least, rhetorical, process. You cannot persuade without some kind of argument, though it may be fallacious argument. But Plato can write διδασκάλους πεπεισμένους μισθοῖς (*Laws* 804d) without straining the word. Cf. δῶρα θεοὺς πείθει (quoted in *Rep*. 390e). In Greek usage *peitho* often stands for "bribe".

[7] *Meno* 98a. Plato's educational system aspires to dye the right beliefs into the soul like fast colors into wool. But even fast colors fade. The ultimate guarantee of the stability of the state is not in the early precautions to make the guardians' good convictions proof against persuasion, oblivion, beguilement of pleasure and pressure of fear (*Rep*. 413bc); it is the guardians' eventual acquaintance with the unalterable Good.

[8] *E.g.*, *Rep*. 532a. "Direct" means here "through reason without the mediation of the senses".

[9] It may be asked: What of the slave-boy in the *Meno?* Socrates confidently asserts (85e) that what the boy has done in this instance he could do "in the whole of geometry and in all other lessons". But what has he done in this instance? Socrates makes each successive point so plain that only a half-wit could miss it. Plato never suggested that slaves are stupid. He only says that they lack *logos* or *nous* and cannot apprehend the Forms. One may lack *logos* yet be a paragon of empiric acuteness (*e.g.*, *Rep*. 516c; and 519a τῶν λεγομένων πονηρῶν μέν, σοφῶν δέ, ὡς δριμὺ μὲν βλέπει τὸ ψυχάριον. . .). At the end of the encounter the slave-boy has not discovered the Form "square", "diameter", etc. Socrates gives the pieces of the puzzle and keeps prodding and correcting until the boy has fitted them properly together. The boy then has the answer to this particular problem, but no grasp of the underlying general truth. He knows the true solution, but not why it is true.

Nevertheless I should not conclude that Plato thinks that this slave-boy could not discover the Forms. This point is left undetermined. But, if the slave-boy could master the Forms, then he ought not to be a slave. In a "true" (*i.e.*, Platonic) state he would be a philosopher, and *therefore* at the top, not the bottom, of the social pyramid.

[10] *E.g.*, *Laws* 968a: The highest magistrate "must be able to give a rational account (*logos*) of all that admits of a rational account". Otherwise he cannot be a "fit ruler of the whole state, but only a servant to other rulers".

[11] *Rep*. 518b–e. The phrase πειθοῖ καὶ βία occurs often in the *Laws*.

[12] *E.g.*, Socrates' argument against Thrasymachus in the *Republic*, *I*, maintaining that government is for the benefit of the governed.

sent.[13] A democratically minded theorist like Protagoras[14] holds
that all men have a sense of "reverence and justice"; that they
all share in the "political art".[15] Plato denies this flatly: "Does
it seem at all possible that a multitude in a state could ever
acquire this [sc. political] science?—By no means" (Polit. 292e,
Fowler's tr.). Hence anything like a contract theory of the state
strikes Plato as a pernicious error.[16] How can men who do not
know the nature of justice establish a just state by common
agreement? The only way to get justice is to recognize the fact
that "some men are by nature fitted to embrace philosophy and
lead in the state, while others are unfit to embrace it and must
follow the leader" (Rep. 474c; cf. Laws 690b).

It follows that the absence of self-determination, so striking
in the case of the slave, is normal in Platonic society. The fully
enlightened aristocrats are a small minority of the whole population (e.g., Polit. 292e). All the rest are in some degree douloi in
Plato's sense of the word: they lack logos; they do not know the
Good, and cannot know their own good or the good of the state;

[13] Polit. 293a, 296b–297b. This point is all the more remarkable because it
contrasts sharply with the conception of government which underlies the Crito.
There Socrates thinks and acts as a responsible member of a free republic. It is
because he has himself consented to the laws that they are binding upon him:
παρὰ τὰς ξυνθήκας τε καὶ ὁμολογίας (52d); ξυνθήκας τὰς πρὸς ἡμᾶς παραβάς (54c).
However, it would not be impossible to find a casuistic reconciliation of political
obligation that rests upon consent with political authority that is above consent. Plato's point, I suppose, would be that the good ruler's commands must
be obeyed, consent or no consent; though if his subjects knew the Good as he
knows it (a hypothesis which would abolish the distinction between subject
and ruler in the Republic and the Politicus), they would gladly give their consent.
    [14] It is significant that Pericles entrusted him with the framing of the consti-
tution of Thourioi.
    [15] Prot. 322c, d. It is suggestive to compare Protagoras' myth with the myth of
the Politicus and the comparable passage in Laws 713b ff. In the former the setting
is man's struggle for self-preservation: Prometheus' gift of fire and Hermes' gift of
"reverence and justice" put into man's hands the two weapons that enable him
to succeed. Plato's aristocratic counterblast changes the setting so as to abstract entirely from the principle of human self-reliance and self-help. It harks
back to the age of Cronos where there is no struggle with nature (πάντα αὐτόματα γίγνεσθαι τοῖς ἀνθρώποις, Polit. 271d; ὡς ἄφθονά τε καὶ αὐτόματα πάντα εἶχεν,
Laws, 713c), and where man's social life is directly under the care of divine beings (the "divine shepherd" of the Politicus, the "daemons" of the Laws). Here
reverence and justice (Laws, 713e) are not the condition, but the product, of
good government; and good government means not self-government but government of the inferior by the superior, of the mortal by the divine.
    [16] Rep. 359a, Laws 889a: that justice rests on agreement is mentioned as part
of a dangerous view, destructive of morality and religion. Yet the idea of law
as συνθήκη was so widespread that it invaded even the thought of its opponents:
e.g., Plato himself (Crito 52d, 54c, cited above) and Aristotle (see Bonitz, Index,
729b 53).

their only chance of doing the good is to obey implicitly the commands of their superiors. Thus Plato speaks currently of subjection to the reasonable discipline of rulers, human and divine, laws, parents, and elders as servitude (*douleuein, douleia*).[17] This usage is not without precedent. But Plato goes further in this direction than any earlier writer. It had been the proud boast of Aeschylus for his fellow-countrymen: "They cannot be called the slaves of any man" (*Pers.* 242). It is hard to find an instance in fifth-century literature where *douleia* is used, as Plato uses it, in the sense of virtuous, amicable, and cheerful submission to constituted authority, without any of the grim associations of duresse and dishonor. Yet Plato's genial extension of the word to cover an honorable and even fortunate estate is amply justified by the premises of his own thought: The manual laborer, for example, is "weak by nature in the principle of the best". Left to himself, he could not rule himself, but would be ruled by his appetites. What happier solution could there be than servitude to one who is strong in the principle of the best, "so that we may all be equals and friends so far as possible, all governed by the same principle"?[18]

When Plato speaks so innocently of the artisans of the *Republic* as the "slaves" of the philosophers, he certainly does not mean to be taken literally.[19] He neither means to degrade all artisans to the level of bondmen, nor to raise the social status of

[17] *Laws* 698bc, 700a, 701b, 715d, 762e, 839c, 890a. For some of these references, and for much else in this paper, I am indebted to G. R. Morrow's "Plato and Greek Slavery", *Mind*, April, 1939.

[18] *Rep.* 590cd. (Jowett blurs the point by translating "servant" for *doulos*, much as King James' translators often render "servant" for *doulos: e.g.*, Matthew 20: 27, Mark 10: 44, Gal. 4: 1, Eph. 6: 5. Lindsay's translation is more exact.) This passage has never received the attention it deserves. Bosanquet is the only exception I know. He sees that "this is the essential basis of Aristotle's explanation . . . of slavery", and accepts it in principle: "Plato's general account of the spiritual relation of society to inferior or immature minds, and in some degree to all minds, is unimpeachable" (*Companion to Plato's Republic, ad loc.*). I suppose that in terms of Bosanquet's political theory the philosopher would express the "real will" of the *doulos*. Hegel is more sophisticated on this point. See his stricture on Platonic philosophy: "the principle of subjective freedom does not receive its due" (*Philosophy of Right*, tr. by Dyde, par. 185, note. Cf. M. B. Foster, *The Political Philosophies of Plato and Hegel*, Ch. iii). But it is significant that Hegel does not criticize Plato for his denial of the *objective* freedom of the working classes. Hegel's own political theory would hardly entitle him to make this criticism.

[19] As mistaken, for example, by W. L. Newman, *The Politics of Aristotle*, I, 109–110, in a valuable reference to this passage, suggesting that this was "perhaps the source from which Aristotle derived his theory of natural slavery".

the slave to that of the free laborer. There is not the slightest indication, either in the *Republic*,[20] or anywhere else, that Plato means to obliterate or relax in any way that distinction. The very opposite is the case. Professor Morrow's admirable recent study has shown that Plato's law of slavery is not more but less liberal than current Attic law; and in one important respect less liberal than any known slave legislation of classical antiquity.[21] Then what is the point of speaking so freely of all sorts and conditions of political subordinates as *douloi?* The point is not practical, but theoretical. It underlines the fact that, in principle, there is no difference in Plato's political theory between the relation of a master to his slave and of a sovereign to his subjects; or, as Aristotle put this Platonic doctrine: that "mastership (*despoteia*), statesmanship (*politikē*) and kingship (*basilikē*) are the same thing".[22]

In other words, Plato uses one and the same principle to interpret (and justify) political authority and the master's right to govern the slave, political obligation and the slave's duty to obey his master. His conception of all government (*archē, archein*) is of a piece with his conception of the government of slaves. Is this saying too much? One thinks of any number of important qualifications.[23] Yet substantially the statement is true. One need only refer to the *Politicus* for the explicit statement that there is no other difference between the art of slaveowner (*despotēs*, 259b 7) and king (*basilikos*, 259c 2) than the size of their respective establishments.

Whatever be the refinements of such a theory, it appears at once as a radical denial of democracy. It could no more account for the facts of democratic government in Athens, than the contract theorists could account for the fact of slavery. The

[20] See *Rep.* 469bc. (For barbarian slaves in the *Republic* see 471b and *cf.* with 469b.) It is when aristocracy deteriorates that the free producers are enslaved in the literal sense (547c).
[21] "Plato and Greek Slavery", *Mind*, April, 1939. See pp. 194–198, and especially p. 196. For a more detailed discussion see the same author's *Plato's Law of Slavery* (University of Illinois Press, 1939).
[22] *Pol.* 1253b 18; 1252a, 8. That this is Plato's view is clear from *Polit.* 259bc.
[23] It would be superfluous to detail these here. They are obvious to any reader of the *Republic* and the *Laws,* and I should not wish to belittle them. See especially *Rep.* 547c. All I am suggesting here is that Plato uses one and the same principle to interpret (and justify) authority in the case of both master and statesman and obedience in the case of both slave and subject.

K

contract theorists generalized the government of the state by the *demos* for the *demos*. They verged on idealism at the point where they would substitute "man" for "citizen of Athens"; at that point they did not know what to do with slavery, and played with the subversive view that slavery was unnatural.[24] Plato, generalizing the government of slave by master, was forced into the opposite conclusion that democracy was unnatural. Plato idealized the institution of slavery; the contract theorists the institution of democracy. Their conflicting idealism mirrored the real contradiction in Athenian society: a free political community that rested on a slave economy.

II. SLAVERY IN PLATO'S COSMOLOGY

Can we detect any higher overtones of the master-slave relation? Can we trace it in wholes of a different order than political society: in the human microcosm and the physical macrocosm? One's attention is drawn in this direction by Plato's frequent references to the body as the "slave" of the soul. That this is no mere figure of speech, but is meant to convey a serious philosophical truth, is clear from three considerations. (i) It stands as a formal premise in a metaphysical argument for the immortality of the soul in the *Phaedo*.[25] (ii) It is written into the physiology of the *Timaeus*.[26] (iii) It determines leading ideas

[24] Contract could only be the thinnest of disguises for force, on which slavery so obviously rested (see *Pol.* 1255a 5 ff.). To base slavery on agreement was to suggest the view that this agreement was unnatural and slavery invalid. How many of the contract theorists shared this view? We do not know. In the *Politics* (1253b 21) Aristotle does not name his opponents who flatly maintained that slavery is conventional and contrary to nature. See *Gorg.* 484ab for Callicles' view that "natural justice" may be violated by slavery. Antiphon, the sophist, undercuts the distinction between noble and low birth, between Greek and barbarian ἐπεὶ φύσει πάντα πάντες ὁμοίως πεφύκαμεν (Diels, B, 44, Fr. B, col. 2). The same principle would undercut slavery. Alcidamas, the pupil and successor of Gorgias, is said to have declared: "God left all men free; nature made no one a slave" (*Schol.* on *Rhet.* 1373b, 18). And a fragment of Philemon, the comic poet (ed. Meineke, Fr. 39), runs: "Though one be a slave, he has the same flesh; / By nature no one was ever born a slave."

[25] 79e–80a. It is the necessary link in the analogy of the soul to the "divine" and of the body to the "mortal": "in the order of nature" the body and the mortal are both the slaves of their respective masters, the soul and the divine.

[26] In the head, whose spherical form copies the shape of the universe, is placed "the divinest and holiest part" (45a2), which is "lord (δεσποτοῦν) of all that is in us" (44d). The rest of the body is made to serve (ᾧ καὶ πᾶν τὸ σῶμα παρέδοσαν ὑπηρεσίαν αὐτῷ): it is a vehicle (ὄχημα) for the head, supplementing the soul's two "divine revolutions" (44d) with the "six wandering motions" (44d8; *cf.* 43b). The "mortal" part of the soul is housed apart "for fear of polluting the divine part" (69d); the neck was built as "an isthmus and boundary to keep the two apart" (69e).

in Plato's ethics.[27] Each of these matters deserves detailed discussion. But to keep this paper within reasonable limits, I proceed at once to Plato's application of the slave-metaphor beyond anthropology to cosmology itself.

Let us begin with the scene in the *Phaedo* where the Platonic Socrates explains that he turned away from Ionian physics, because it did not use the right method. The right method, suggested by Anaxagoras' *nous*, but, alas, not followed by this unregenerate Ionian, is defined in the following terms: "If you wish to find the cause of anything . . . , you must find out this about it: How it is best for it to exist or be acted upon or act in any other way" (97cd). Thus a scientific explanation of the shape and position of the earth must prove that it has that particular shape and position because these are "best" for it (97e).

To back this unusual view of scientific method the Platonic Socrates resorts to an analogy: What is the cause of my presence in this prison? It is not bones and sinews that keep me here, but my decision that this is for the best (99b). Physiology is not the "real" cause (τὸ αἴτιον τῷ ὄντι), but only an indispensable condition (ἐκεῖνο ἄνευ οὗ τὸ αἴτιον οὐκ ἄν ποτ' εἴη αἴτιον, 99c). Without apology this argument is transferred from the human organism to the universe at large. The reasoning takes it for granted that teleology and mechanism are related in the world-order as mind to body in man himself. But since the relation of mind to body has already been conceived as analogous to that of master to slave, it would follow that the relation of teleology to mechanism can also be so conceived: that the mechanical cause, mistakenly accepted by the Ionians as the "ruling" cause, is actually only a "slave" cause. This, of course, is so far only an inference. But if we follow the development of Plato's thought

[27] In the beginning of *Laws* v, the whole rationale of virtue is reduced to these terms: "A man's own nature consists invariably of two kinds of elements: the stronger and better are lordly (δεσπόζοντα) the weaker and worse are slaves (δοῦλα); wherefore one must ever honour the lordly above the slavish elements in one's nature" (726). That is, honor the soul above the body and its pleasures and passions. In the *Republic* intemperance is described as insubordination of the appetites against the order of reason. It is "a meddlesomeness and interference and rebellion of one part of the soul against the whole to gain a rule to which it has no right; that part indeed whose nature is such that it ought to be slave, while the other should never be slave, but ruler" (following Lindsay's translation of 444b, except after the semicolon, where he takes τοιούτου ὄντος φύσει to refer to τῷ ὅλῳ instead of μέρους τινός). Similar expression in 442ab.

in the later dialogues we shall find that this is exactly the direction in which it moves.

Physical variables, like hot and cold, dry and moist, which play such an important role in early Ionian thought, appear in the *Philebus* under the category of the measureless.[28] Lacking in order, this realm of being would be full of *hybris* and evil (26b), were measure not imposed upon it[29] by a creative agent.[30] This is *the* cause (τὸ αἴτιον, 26e): the very category that Socrates missed in the Ionians. It is the ordering *nous* of Anaxagoras now taken in good earnest and assigned to its proper place as "king of heaven and earth" (28c). The other principle is its slave: "slave to the cause (δουλεῦον αἰτίᾳ) for the purpose of generation" (27a).

In the *Timaeus* the whole account of man and the world turns on a clear-cut distinction between two kinds of causes:

(1) the "primary" cause, which is "intelligent", "divine", and productive of all that is "fair and good";[31]

(2) The "secondary" cause, which is "necessary", irrational, fortuitous and disorderly.[32]

The modern reader must find something baffling about this blend of necessity with chance in the secondary cause. For us the very idea of necessity implies necessary order.[33] How conceive of necessary disorder without self-contradiction?[34]

---

[28] 25d: τὸ ἄπειρον opposite of τὸ περατοειδές and of τὸ ἔμμετρον καὶ σύμμετρον (26a 6, 7).

[29] Note the force of ἐπ' αὐτοῖς (30c 5).

[30] τὸ δημιουργοῦν (27b), τὸ ποιοῦν (27a), ἡ τοῦ ποιοῦντος φύσις (26e).

[31] τὰς τῆς ἔμφρονος φύσεως αἰτίας. πρώτας (46d), ὅσαι μετὰ νοῦ καλῶν καὶ ἀγαθῶν δημιουργοί (46e), τὰ διὰ νοῦ (47e), τὸ θεῖον (68e).

[32] ἀνάγκη (48a), ἡ τῆς ἀνάγκης φύσις (56c), τὸ ἀναγκαῖον (68e), τὰ δι' ἀνάγκης (47e); ὅσαι μονωθεῖσαι φρονήσεως τὸ τυχὸν ἄτακτον ἐξεργάζονται (46e). *Cf.* with this last *Phil.* 28d 6, 7.

[33] In the ensuing discussion I am not speaking of Plato's concept of necessity as a whole. I am excluding from the discussion logical necessity. Like everyone else, Plato identifies this with rational order. He uses constantly ἀνάγκη, ἀναγκαῖον, etc. to mark the cogency and evidence of a deductive conclusion (*e.g.*, *Gorg.* 475a–c; *Phaedo* 91e; *Phil.* 40c; *Tm* 53c). This kind of *ananke* is at the other extreme from the *ananke* of the secondary cause. Logical necessity is explicitly opposed to verisimilitude (*Theait.* 162e), while verisimilitude is the characteristic mood of all discourse about the material world (*Tm* 29c; and 53d κατὰ τὸν μετ' ἀνάγκης εἰκότα λόγον). This bifurcation of *ananke* into formal order and material disorder is conserved by Aristotle. His view is tersely stated and acutely discussed by D. M. Balme in the *Class. Quarterly*, Oct., 1939: "Ananke does not govern sequences: there is no transeunt causality inherent in the material", p. 130.

[34] In *Plato's Cosmology* (162 ff.) F. M. Cornford throws some light on this problem. He points out that to Plato, as to Aristotle, chance does not mean the

I can think of one clue: "The ideas of *douleia* and *ananke*", writes George Thomson, "are almost inseparable in Greek, the word *ananke* being constantly used to denote both the state of slavery as such, and also the torture to which the slaves were subjected."[35] No one, so far as I know, has ever thought of interpreting the *ananke* of the *Timaeus* on the pattern of slavery. Yet Plato speaks of material necessity as a "servant" (ὑπηρετοῦσιν, 46c 7; ὑπηρετούσαις, 68e 4) who, he also tells us, is "incapable of any *logos* or *nous* about anything" (46d 4). But this, as we have seen, is the defining concept of the slave: a servant destitute of *logos*. Here, I think, is the explanation we need.

The idea of "disorderly necessity" strikes us as a flat self-contradiction because we think of necessity in terms of a mechanical instrument, whose motions follow a strict mechanical order; that order is inherent in the instrument, and we can only use the instrument in so far as we respect its order. Plato thinks of necessity in terms of a "living instrument", whose use does not seem to depend on our understanding of its own intrinsic order, but rather on our ability to "persuade" it to follow our own purpose. In this case the order does not seem to be in the instrument but in us. This is the very image that occurs to Aristotle when he pictures the teleological order of the universe: "But it is as in a house, where the freemen are least at liberty to act at random, but all things or most things are already ordered for them, while the slaves and the beasts do little for the common good, for the most part live at random".[36] The slave does not share of his own accord the order of the common life. Left to himself he would "wander" off into disorder.[37] Order, which

---

opposite of necessity, but the opposite of purpose. Thus a "necessary accident" means to both any unintended, but unavoidable, circumstance involved in the execution of a plan. This does explain the element of compulsion in *ananke*. But it does not explain the element of disorder.

[35] *The ORESTEIA of Aeschylus*, II, 345, (Cambridge, 1938). The association of the two words follows naturally from their obvious meaning. Aristotle defines *ananke* (in the sense of compulsion: τὴν γὰρ ἔξωθεν ἀρχήν, τὴν παρὰ τὴν ὁρμὴν ἢ ἐμποδίζουσαν ἢ κινοῦσαν, ἀνάγκην λέγομεν (*Nic. Eth.* 1224b 11); while the common view of *douleia*, as Aristotle reports it, is τὸ ζῆν μὴ ὡς βούλεται (*Pol.* 1317b 13).

[36] *Met.* 1075a 19. *Cf.* ὅτι ἔτυχεν and τέτακται of this passage with τὸ τυχὸν ἄτακτον of *Tm* 46e 5.

[37] But the slave's behavior is not utter disorder. It is only disorderly from the standpoint of the superior order intended by the master. At the price of in-

he could not originate himself, must be imposed upon him, pre-ferably by persuasion or, failing this, by coercion. The Demiurge, being the wisest of masters, need not resort to coercion at all: he "persuades necessity" (48a 2) and makes it his "willing" slave (56c, 5). The notion of "persuading necessity" and the implied idea of "compelling necessity" make sense only if one keeps steadily in mind the slave metaphor. Persuading the law of gravitation does not make sense. Persuading a slave does.

To appreciate the importance of this development one must see it in historic perspective. The slave metaphor occurs at the very point where Plato turns consciously away from the cosmo-logy of his predecessors.[38] From the very beginnings of Ionian thought *rational* and *immanent* necessity had been an integral feature of the concept of nature. Recall, for example, the saying of Anaximander that things come into existence and perish "as it is ordained; for they make satisfaction and reparation to one another for their injustice according to the order of time."[39] To express natural necessity this early Milesian borrows words from the government of man. But that is, of course, no more than what we must still do to-day when we speak of the "laws" of nature. What is important is rather the absence of any sug-gestion of a superior agency to issue ordinances and enforce reparations. On the contrary, Anaximander excludes the inter-vention of a superior order in the course of nature by endow-ing nature itself with the attributes of divinity: it is infinite, immortal, indestructible.[40] Thinkers as opposed to one another

---

consistency Plato is true to this feature of the slave-metaphor, maintaining that the primordial chaos had crude "traces" of the elegant order that the Demiurge was to impress upon it at creation: τὴν γενέσεως τιθήνην ὑγραινομένην καὶ πυρουμένην καὶ τὰς γῆς τε καὶ ἀέρος μορφὰς δεχομένην, καὶ ὅσα ἄλλα τούτοις πάθη συνέπεται πάσχουσαν (*Tm* 52de). The last clause is particularly important, for it recognizes an order of causal implication *before* the chaos had been "in-formed with shapes and numbers" (53b). Yet Plato can only explain causal implication *through* the Forms: *e.g.*, the necessary connection between fire and heat, snow and cold (*Phaedo* 103c ff.). As P. H. DeLacy has recently put it: "Plato finds no causal relation on the purely physical level. The Ideas are the causes of the qualities of physical objects, for the qualities of particulars exist only in so far as particulars participate in Ideas" (*Class. Phil.*, April, 1939). This is part of a larger contradiction in Plato's thought which I have noted in "The Disorderly Motion in the *Timaios*", p. 76–7, *Class. Quarterly*, April, 1939.

[38] See W. H. Heidel, περὶ φύσεως, *Proc. Am. Acad. of Arts and Sciences*, Jan. 1910.

[39] Diels, B, 1.   [40]*Ibid.*, B, 3.

as the Ionian Heraclitus and the Italian Parmenides[41] preserve
this feature of Anaximander's thought. Some verbal expressions
may suggest the opposite. But a closer examination shows how
firmly they adhere to the notion of autonomous nature. When
Heraclitus says, for example, "The sun will not overstep his
measures (*metra*) else the Erinyes, the assistants of Justice, will
find him out" Justice and the Erinyes stand for no independent
entity; they simply express the inevitability of the pattern that
fire follows in its unceasing transformations, "kindled in measure
(*metra*), and extinguished in measure".[42] Likewise when Parmenides writes, "strong *anankē* keeps it in the bonds of the
limit",[43] *anankē* is neither superior nor inferior to the inflexible
rationality of existence, but simply identical with it.

In the atomism of Leucippus and Democritus this trend of
thought comes to full maturity: "Nothing occurs at random,
but everything for a reason (*ek logou*) and by necessity."[44] Here
is the exact opposite of Plato's doctrine: *logos* and *anankē* are
coupled together; material necessity is rational and it excludes
chance.[45] The inherent motion of matter which seems to Plato
the source of necessary disorder is in the eyes of Democritus
the very meaning of necessary order.[46] And because it is necessary, motion is coeval with matter itself. There is no need for a
"first cause" to set matter in motion.[47] This was the final blow
at the anthropomorphic theory of creation. Its consequences,
writes Cyril Bailey, "were momentous. In the sphere of physical

[41] This connection of Parmenides with Anaximander was suggested to me by
Werner Jaeger's remark: "he also calls it [sc. *anankē*] *dike* or *moira*, obviously
under Anaximander's influence", *Paideia*, Eng. tr., p. 174.
[42] Diels, B, 94 and 30. *Cf.* also B, 80: "strife is justice". The conflict of the
elements ("war") itself produces its own order. So again in B, 53: "War is
father of all and king of all; some he has made gods and some men, some slaves
and some free." A question might arise over B, 41: "the thought (*gnomē*) which
steers (ἐκυβέρνησε) all things through all things." Is this governing thought an
extraneous, superior factor? Clearly not, if one compares B, 64, "the thunder-
bolt that steers (οἰακίζει) the course of all things" with B, 66: "Fire in its advance will judge and convict all things" (Burnet's tr. following Diels): the
"thought" is inherent in the fire; like "justice" above, simply another expression for the relentless orderliness of fire.
[43] Diels, B, 30 l. 31; cf. ll. 14 and 37.
[44] *Ibid.*, 67 B, 2 (Bailey's tr.).
[45] Simpl. 330.14 τὸ δὲ καθάπερ ὁ παλαιὸς λόγος ὁ ἀναιρῶν τὴν τύχην (*Physics*,
196a, 14) πρὸς Δ. ἔοικε εἰρῆσθαι. . . . Dante's reproach, "Democrito che il mondo
a caso pone" rests on a misconception. See Enriques and de Santillana, *Histoire
de la Pensée Scientifique*, III, 40, and Cyril Bailey's elegant argument in *Greek
Atomists and Epicurus*, 141–3.
[46] D. L., IX, 45: τῆς αἰτίας οὔσης τῆς γενέσεως πάντων, ἣν ἀνάγκην λέγει.
[47] Plutarch, *Strom.*, 7 (D. 581).

speculation it introduced for the first time the possibility of a strictly scientific conception of the world."[48]

Why was it that Plato chose to frustrate this possibility in his cosmology?[49] It would be presumptuous to attempt to answer this question within the limits of this paper. But the answer, whatever it be, must reckon with this fact: Plato attacks Ionian physics not only on philosophical, but also on political grounds; so that both the political and the cosmological associations of slavery came into play in his polemic. The issue is the very existence of a philosophy which conceives of the government of the state and the government of the world as analogous to the government of the slave. The *locus classicus* for this attack is the tenth book of the *Laws*.

His opponents are the "modern scientists" (886d; also 888e ff.). He imputes to them not only mechanistic cosmology, but also the contract theory of the state.[50] The first gives rise to the second, and each to atheism. The basic error is the idea that physical bodies "are moved by the interplay of their respective forces, according as they meet together and combine fittingly" (889b, Bury's tr.); in other words, that nature is a self-regulating system, and is not governed by the art of a divine mind. This implies that the stars are products of a natural process, not gods, but inanimate material bodies (886de; 889b). It implies further that legislation (like every other art) is a late product of the same process, so that laws are not absolute commands, but man-made agreements (889c–890e). Instead of deriving the laws

---

[48] *Op. cit.*, 122.

[49] Aristotle is often blamed for importing teleology into physics. The real culprit, of course, is Plato. Aristotle thinks as a Platonist when he repudiates the all-but-universal belief of his predecessors in natural necessity (*Phys.* 198b 12; *de part. Anim.* 639b 21). It was Plato who had led the attack on the Ionian mechanists, foisting on them his own assumption that material necessity is equivalent to chance, and thus forcing them into the absurd position of denying the *de facto* order of the universe because they will not grant the existence of teleological order. This misconception which vitiates the argument for final causes in *Phys.* ii. viii had been anticipated in the *Philebus* (28d–29e) and *Laws* X.

[50] How easily this point may be missed is clear from A. E. Taylor's paraphrase of this passage (in the Introduction to his translation of the *Laws*, lii): "Plato's view is that atheism is the product of two historical factors, the corporealism of the early Ionian men of science . . . , and the 'sophistic' theory of the purely conventional and relative character of moral distinctions." But the text says nothing about "two historical factors". It is the same people (the σοφοὶ ἄνδρες of 888e) whose cosmology is expounded in 889b–d and whose politics is given in 889d–890a.

from the gods, this impious view derives the gods from the laws, and variable laws at that.

To refute all this Plato maintains that the soul is the first cause of all physical motions. His elaborate argument need not be examined here. We need only note that the point of his thesis is to prove that the soul, being "older" than the body, has the right to "rule" the body.[51] And what he means by the soul's "rule" is clear from a parallel passage in the *Timaeus* (34c): soul is *despotis;* it rules the body as master rules slave. If he can prove this, Plato feels he has destroyed Ionian materialism. He can then have everything his own way: that soul or souls direct every bodily motion (896de); that the stars have soul or souls and are divine (898d–899b); and that, in short, "all things are full of gods" (899b). Thus cosmology supports religion by establishing the existence of its gods.[52] And the link between religious cosmology and political religion is the slave-metaphor.

III. PLATO AND ARISTOTLE

Any discussion of Plato's views on slavery invites comparison with the most famous text of antiquity on this topic: the first book of the *Politics*. Aristotle's polemic is mainly directed against those who hold that slavery is contrary to nature.[53] The word "nature" is used here in at least three senses: a moral, a biological, and a cosmological one. The first states the *demonstrandum* of Aristotle's argument; the latter two decide the demonstration. *To prove:* that slavery is natural, in the sense of being good and just:[54] good for the master, to whom it provides a necessary instrument (1253b 23 ff.); good also for the slave,[55] whose intellectual deficiency is supplemented by the master's superior reason.[56] This is proved first by the contention that the

---

[51] E.g., 892a: [ψυχή] ὡς ἐν πρώτοις ἐστὶ σωμάτων, ἔμπροσθεν πάντων γενομένην, whence it is assumed by a simple conjunction (καί) that it rules every bodily change. The inference from superior age to the right to rule is made explicit in *Tm* 34c.

[52] The "gods according to the laws": 885b, 890ab, 904a. Serious confusion results when this limitation is not recognized. *Laws* x does not even attempt to prove the existence of the Demiurge, who is never mentioned among the official divinities.

[53] παρὰ φύσιν τὸ δεσπόζειν, 1253b 20.

[54] βέλτιον καὶ δίκαιον, 1254a 18.

[55] φύσει δοῦλοι οἷς βέλτιόν ἐστιν ἄρχεσθαι ταύτην τὴν ἀρχήν, 1245b 19.

[56] 1252a 31; cf. *Nic. Eth.* 1161a 35–b 1.

difference of master and slave, commensurate with that of soul
and body or of man and beast (1254b 17), is a congenital one:
"some things are marked out from the moment of birth to rule
or to be ruled" (1254a 23). This is the part of Aristotle's argument that has given greatest offence to posterity and thus
attracted widest attention. Yet no less important in Aristotle's
eyes is the metaphysical sanction of slavery. The difference between master and slave, he holds, is natural because it follows
a pattern that pervades all nature: "because in every composite
thing, where a plurality of parts, whether continuous or dis-
crete, is combined to make a single common whole, there is
always found a ruling and a subject factor, and this characteristic of living things is present in them as an outcome of the
whole of nature (ἐκ τῆς ἁπάσης φύσεως)."[57]

Now let us ask: What is there in this argument that Plato too
could not have said in full consistency with his own ideas about
slavery? It is, of course, the A B C of exegesis to distinguish
between what a writer has actually said and what he could
have said or ought to have said. That the Platonic dialogues
give us no equivalent to the first book of the *Politics* points to a
difference of temper between Plato's and Aristotle's views which
must not be minimized. Nevertheless when we have made full
allowance for this difference, we must still observe a fact which
has escaped the notice of many modern interpreters and might
modify their conclusions about Plato's moral and social philosophy: that in every one of these three points Plato would
have to agree with his pupil's argument in defence of slavery:

(1) that slavery is good for the slave (as well as for the
master): better to be ruled by an alien reason, than not to be
ruled by reason at all (Section I of this paper);

(2) that this difference in intellectual and social status rests
on a diversity of native endowment: nature is the original factor

---

[57] 1254a 29–32, Rackham's tr. Other passages too show that Aristotle thinks
of slavery not as an isolated fact but as a special instance of a general relation
which connects slavery with his whole philosophic system: *e.g.*, *Eud. Eth.*
1249b 6 ff., *Nic. Eth.* 1161a 32 ff.
    The analogy of the master-slave to the soul-body relation enables us to con-
nect it with the most general pattern of Aristotelian metaphysics, the relation
of form to matter. Soul is the form of the body, and body the matter of the soul
(*de An.* 412a 16). And since ἐν τῇ ὕλῃ τὸ ἀναγκαῖον, τὸ δ' οὗ ἕνεκα ἐν τῷ λόγῳ (*Phys.*
200a 14), the Aristotelian contrast of mechanism to teleology is, as in Plato,
analogous to the contrast of slave to master.

in differentiating the philosopher from the producer and *a fortiori* from the slave;[58]

(3) that this difference only repeats on the human plane a pattern writ large over the cosmos: the master's benevolent reason persuading the slave's irrational force fulfils a function analogous to that of the Demiurge, persuading towards the Good the irrational *ananke* of the material universe (Section II of this paper).

IV. CONCLUSION

This study does not suggest that Plato deduced his political theory, his psychology, or his cosmology, from his concept of slavery. No such deduction is to be found in his writings, and it is profitless to speculate about the unpublished adventures of his mind. What it does suggest is that his views about slavery, state, man, and the world, all illustrate a single hierarchic pattern; and that the key to the pattern is in his idea of *logos* with all the implications of a dualist epistemology.[59] The slave lacks *logos;* so does the multitude in the state, the body in man, and material necessity in the universe. Left to itself each of these would be disorderly and vicious in the sense of that untranslatably Greek word, *hybris*. Order is imposed upon them by a benevolent superior: master, guardian, mind, demiurge. Each of these rules (*archein*) in his own domain. The common title to authority is the possession of *logos*. In such an intellectual scheme slavery is "natural": in perfect harmony with one's notions about the nature of the world and of man.

There is another world-view that is the antithesis of Platonic idealism, and would be persecuted in the Platonic utopia as false, wicked, impious, subversive.[60] It is associated with Ionian physics[61] and the contract theory of the state. It is scientific in

[58] See the use of φύσις, φύω, etc. in *Rep.* 370ab, 374e–376c, 428e 9, 431c 7, 590c 3; *Polit.* 301e, 309ab, 310a; *Laws* 875c.

[59] I refer to the separation (χωρισμός) of the Forms from the particulars. Attempts to explain this away have been made by Natorp, C. Ritter, and many others. They are not convincing. See F. M. Cornford, *Plato's Theory of Knowledge* 2 ff., and *Plato and Parmenides* 74 ff.

[60] *Laws* 891b; 907d ff. *Cf.* Grote's *Plato* III, 406 ff. in the 1865 edition. See also B. Farrington's *Science and Politics in the Ancient World*, London, 1939. I owe much to this stimulating essay.

[61] Is "Ionian" unnecessarily restrictive? "All the men who have ever yet handled physical investigation" constitute the fountain-head of impious unreason (*Laws* 891c) denounced by the Athenian stranger.

temper, empirical in its theory of knowledge, democratic in its political sympathies. Plato and others of his class complained that democracy was much too lenient with slaves.[62] They never went so far as to charge what seems so evident to us to-day: that a consistent democratic philosophy would repudiate slavery altogether.

QUEEN'S UNIVERSITY
KINGSTON, CANADA   GREGORY VLASTOS

POSTSCRIPT (1959)

IN the twenty years which have passed since I wrote this paper I have learned and unlearned things which would lead me to express myself differently on some topics. I do not mean that there are statements in this paper which I now think false. I mean only that some of them carry different shadings of emphasis than would seem to me proper now, and a few may leave a wrong impression on the reader's mind. For example, I speak of Protagoras (page 291) as a "democratically minded theorist". This is vague enough to fall safely short of saying what I would now believe to be definitely false: that the philosophy of Protagoras provided either necessary or sufficient conditions for holding that democracy is the best form of government possible for Greeks at this time. I could not even now say that Protagoras himself thought that his philosophy provided such conditions. That he was held in high repute by responsible democrats, like Pericles, is certainly "significant", as I say in note 14. It may be taken as evidence of personal sympathy for democracy, but scarcely even of personal commitment to it. Any reader interested in my present assessment of the philosophy of Protagoras (though without explicit discussion of its political implications) may consult my Introduction to Plato's *Protagoras*, Liberal Arts Press, New York, 1956.

I am also uneasy about my remarks on "immanent necessity" in Heraclitus at page 299 and note 42. It is true that the fire which "governs" the world is immanent in the world, since it is a part of the world; and that the orderliness of fire is immanent in fire, since it is the product of its own "wisdom". But then the orderliness

---

[62] *Rep.* 563b; "The Old Oligarch", *Ath. Pol.* I. 10 ff.; Aristotle, *Pol.* 1313b 35, 1319b 28.

of water and earth (the other two main constituents of the Heraclitean world) is somehow imparted *to* them by fire, hence is not purely immanent in *them*; I say "somehow", for the way in which this is supposed to happen is not clear.

As for the "slave metaphor" in Plato, I do believe that it illuminates important aspects of Plato's thought which do not otherwise make sense or as good sense. But I would gladly confess that there are many, and equally important, aspects of Plato's thought which this metaphor does not illuminate. I would not wish to suggest that slavery is *the* key to Plato's philosophy. There are many locks in this marvellously complex and delicate mechanism, and I know of no one key, or set of keys, that opens all of them. Of the statements I make on this topic, the one which stands in greatest need of correction is the following, on page 298: "The notion of 'persuading necessity' and the implied idea of 'compelling necessity' make sense only if one keeps steadily in mind the slave metaphor." If this suggests, as in its context it well may, that the Demiurge *could* have "compelled" necessity had he so chosen, the suggestion would be groundless, indeed inconsistent with Plato's conception of the Demiurge. I should also disclaim the suggestion that "persuading necessity" makes sense *only* in terms of the slave metaphor.

GREGORY VLASTOS.

PRINCETON UNIVERSITY,
PRINCETON, NEW JERSEY.

VIII

Théorie de l'esclavage*

Si l'esclavage, tel qu'il est pratiqué à Rome, nous est relativement bien connu, et que de bonnes descriptions nous en aient été données par des savants modernes, notamment par M. Buckland (1), on peut se demander si la nature même de l'institution a été suffisamment dégagée, si l'on a suffisamment mis en relief les traits fondamentaux de l'esclavage romain le plus ancien, traits que se sont progressivement dégradés de telle sorte que l'institution a perdu à la fin de l'histoire du droit romain une partie de ses caractéristiques essentielles. Il ne paraît pas impossible cependant de les retrouver sans remonter très haut dans le passé et en éliminant seulement les éléments dont nous savons qu'ils sont de date relativement récente. De même il sera possible de le faire en s'en tenant strictement aux éléments assez nombreux que nous offre le droit romain sans utiliser des faits provenant d'autres législations anciennes. Il ne sera fait appel au droit comparé que pour contrôler les résultats obtenus et mesurer ainsi leur degré de généralité.

**
**

De l'ensemble des documents nous permettant de connaître l'esclavage dans le droit romain ancien, me paraît

* **Extrait de la** *Revue Générale du Droit, de la Législation et de la Jurisprudence,* t. 55, 1931, pp. 1-17, reproduit, sous une forme un peu différente, dans les *Travaux de la salle de travail d'ethnologie juridique de la Faculté de Droit de Paris,* t. IV.

(1) W. W. Buckland. *The Roman Law of Slavery* (1908).

se dégager avec la plus grande certitude l'idée que l'esclavage est alors une institution d'ordre essentiellement international, en ce sens que les deux notions d'esclave et d'étranger se confondent. En d'autres termes, à cette époque l'esclave n'est rien autre qu'un étranger sans droits.

Cette manière de concevoir l'esclavage romain ancien peut paraître assez surprenante. Les auteurs que j'ai pu consulter ne semblent pas l'avoir formulée (1). Quant aux Romains eux-mêmes, ils disent à maintes reprises que l'esclavage est une institution du *jus gentium* (2), mais entendent l'expression dans un tout autre sens ; ils veulent dire par là que l'esclavage se retrouve chez tous les peuples connus d'eux.

Dire que l'esclavage romain le plus ancien est une institution d'ordre international, c'est dire que l'esclavage n'existe pas entre Romains, c'est dire, je le répète, que les notions d'esclave et d'étranger se confondent. Et cette proposition, à l'instar d'un théorème, peut s'énoncer sous une forme directe et une forme réciproque que nous examinerons successivement : 1° tout esclave est un étranger ; 2° tout étranger est un esclave.

I

Et, tout d'abord, tout esclave est un étranger, ou, en d'autres termes, aucun Romain ne peut être esclave à Rome.

On aura démontré cette proposition si, en examinant les sources de l'esclavage à l'époque ancienne, on n'en trouve aucune qui puisse s'appliquer à un citoyen romain.

Or, tel est bien le cas, en effet, si l'on prend la précaution de dissiper certaines confusions.

Pour le faire, il faut tout d'abord avoir présent à l'esprit la caractéristique essentielle de l'esclavage. A Rome comme ailleurs, l'esclave est un être privé de droit. Du point de vue juridique c'est une chose ou, si l'on préfère, un ani-

---

(1) M. Buckland, *op. cit.*, p. 5, dit expressément le contraire.
(2) Florentinus au *Digeste*, 1, 5, 4, 1. Cf. Girard, *Manuel élémentaire de Droit Romain*, 8ᵉ éd., p. 102, cité dorénavant : *Manuel*.

mal (1). Le fait est bien connu et je ne le rappelle que parce que les apparences sont parfois contraires. En effet, on a souvent remarqué (2) que la situation de fait de l'esclave est loin d'être en harmonie avec sa condition juridique. Tandis que l'esclave de l'époque impériale, vivant sur de grands domaines et ignoré de son maître, est un être malheureux, souvent traité avec la dernière cruauté alors pourtant qu'un rudiment de personnalité lui est reconnu par le droit, l'esclave de l'époque ancienne, qui n'est protégé par aucune règle légale, vit dans la familiarité de son maître et mène une existence dure et précaire sans doute, mais assez proche de la sienne.

Mais en dépit de cette communauté de vie qui n'est qu'un fait imposé par les conditions économiques, l'absence totale de toute protection caractérise l'esclavage romain le plus ancien. L'esclave n'a pas de famille (3), il n'a pas de patrimoine (4) et quant à son culte, il n'est alors reconnu que timidement (5). En un mot, l'esclave n'a pas de droit.

Cela posé, la distinction apparaît très nette entre l'esclave et certaines catégories d'individus qui se trouvent placés

(1) Tout le régime de l'esclavage romain est fondé sur cette notion. Je n'en donnerai que deux expressions, l'une empruntée à Gaius, 2, 13 : « Corporales (res) hae sunt quae tangi possunt velut... homo » ; l'autre à Ulpien, au Digeste, 50, 17, 32 : « Quod attinet ad jus civile servi pro nullis habentur ». Justinien dit encore, à une époque où cela a cessé d'être absolument vrai : « Servus... nullum caput habet » (Institutes, 1, 16, 4). — Il en était de même en Grèce, l'esclave est considéré comme un outil, ὄργανον ou comme une propriété. Aristote dit : ὁ δοῦλος κτῆμα et ajoute toutefois : Κτῆμά τι ἔμψυχον.

(2) Cf. Ed. Meyer, Die Sklaverei im Altertum (1898).

(3) Son mariage n'est pas qualifié de matrimonium, mais de contubernium. C'est un simple fait. Il s'ensuit que, au moins jusqu'au Bas-Empire, les esclaves conjoints peuvent être séparés et les enfants nés de cette union enlevés à leurs parents.

(4) L'institution du pécule servile, si haut qu'elle remonte, ne contredit pas cette affirmation, car le pécule, bien que laissé en fait entre les mains de l'esclave, reste la propriété du maître ; l'esclave n'a aucun droit sur lui.

(5) C'est, semble-t-il, dans la religion que l'esclave a trouvé le premier élément de protection. Mais cette protection est bien précaire ! Varron parle de Mânes de l'esclave (De Lingua Latina, 8, 9). La première mention du tombeau de l'esclave comme res religiosa est d'Ariston, jurisconsulte du temps de Trajan, chez Ulpien, au Digeste, 11, 7, 2, pr. Du reste, la protection du droit sacré n'implique pas la reconnaissance de la personnalité juridique. Elle s'étend sur les animaux. Cf. Caton, De Re Rustica, 138.

L

dans une situation de subordination vis-à-vis d'autres, en raison d'une obligation qu'ils ont assumée ou d'une décision judiciaire dont ils ont été frappés.

Tels sont, pour l'époque ancienne à laquelle je me place, les emprunteurs qui ont contracté leur dette au moyen du *nexum* et que l'on appelle des *nexi*.

Telles sont encore les personnes qui ont été condamnées en vertu d'une sentence du juge ou qui ont fait l'objet d'une *addictio* du magistrat et qu'on désigne de différents noms : *judicati, damnati, addicti*.

Je n'entre pas dans le détail (1), car ce qui nous importe seulement ici, c'est de fixer qu'aucune de ces personnes, qui sont toutes, au sens large, des débiteurs, n'est un esclave.

Sans doute elles sont privées de ce qui nous apparaît comme le principal attribut de la liberté : la faculté d'aller et de venir. Le créancier les gardera enfermées dans sa prison domestique et pourra les soumettre à un régime très dur sur lequel la loi des XII Tables nous donne des détails circonstanciés, mais tous les textes s'accordent à nous dire que ces individus conservent leur statut d'hommes libres, qu'ils ne tombent pas en servitude. Et une preuve formelle nous en est fournie, comme on sait, par la loi des XII Tables elle-même, laquelle nous dit que le débiteur enfermé pourra, au lieu de recevoir de son créancier les deux livres de farine réglementaires, se faire apporter sa nourriture de chez lui : *si volet, suo vivito* (2). C'est donc qu'il a encore un patrimoine : or l'esclave n'a pas de patrimoine.

Ainsi, les débiteurs prisonniers pour dettes ne sont pas des esclaves : nous devrons donc les laisser de côté. Mais peut-être n'est-il pas besoin d'aller chercher si loin pour trouver des Romains esclaves. Nous savons — tout le monde sait — que le *pater familias* avait sur ses enfants un droit de vie et de mort, *jus vitæ necisque*. Ce droit impliquait la faculté de les vendre, de les manciper. Mais ces fils de famille ainsi mancipés tombent-ils en esclavage ? En aucune

---

(1) Je me borne à renvoyer à Girard, *Manuel*, p. 141.
(2) XII Tables, 3, 4. Disposition rapportée par Aulu-Gelle, *N. At.*, 20, 1, 47.

façon. Les textes prennent soin de nous dire qu'ils sont *in mancipio, in causa mancipii*. Ce ne sont pas des *mancipia*, des *servi*. Et à y réfléchir, cette incapacité du *pater familias* qui peut tuer son fils, mais ne peut faire de lui un esclave, indique nettement qu'il faut voir dans l'esclavage autre chose qu'une peine, un véritable changement du statut personnel qui ne peut être l'œuvre d'une volonté particulière, même toute puissante.

De même, il n'était pas permis à des citoyens libres de se donner en servitude. Sans doute une personne libre pouvait se manciper — la preuve en est dans la *coemptio* réelle ou fiduciaire — mais elle ne tombait pas en esclavage. C'est seulement dans la dernière période du droit romain que l'on vit des personnes libres se vendre, le plus souvent pour tomber dans la condition de colons. La seule manière pour une personne libre de perdre la liberté à l'époque ancienne consistait à se faire rayer des registres du cens, à devenir *incensus*. Mais précisément l'*incensus* perdait à la fois la liberté et la cité. Il devenait étranger.

Après avoir ainsi écarté ces cas qui présentent une certaine analogie apparente avec l'esclavage, mais qui en sont, en droit, profondément distincts, examinons les sources de l'esclavage véritable. Nous constaterons qu'il n'en est aucune qui puisse s'appliquer à des citoyens romains, à l'exception d'une seule, l'esclavage à titre de peine, *servitus pœnæ* ou *pœnæ nomine*. Examinons-la en premier lieu.

Certaines dispositions législatives comminent l'esclavage comme une peine attachée à certains actes criminels. Ainsi la femme libre qui, à l'insu du maître, entretient des relations avec l'esclave d'autrui, tombe en esclavage en vertu du Sénatus Consulte Claudien (52 ap. J.-C.) (1). Certaines constitutions impériales font tomber en servitude des individus condamnés à des peines particulièrement graves : à mort, aux bêtes, aux mines (2). Enfin, un édit du pré-

---

(1) Tacite, *Ann.*, 12, 53. Paul. *Sent.*, 2, 21 *a*, 17.
(2) Sur cet esclavage attaché à certaines condamnations, cf. Mommsen, *Droit Pénal Romain*, t. II, 290 s. ; Buckland, *op. cit.*, p. 403, s.

teur qui date de la fin de la République privait celui qui s'était frauduleusement fait vendre comme esclave, du droit de faire reconnaître sa liberté (1).

Voilà donc, semble-t-il, notre principe en défaut. Voilà des Romains qui tombent en esclavage. Sans doute, mais une observation est de nature à retirer à l'argument toute sa portée : ces dispositions sont toutes de date récente, même la règle de l'Edit, qui vise d'ailleurs un cas tout à fait particulier. Elles ne sauraient dont être retenues pour fixer le caractère de l'esclavage ancien.

En dehors de cette source qui n'existe pas à l'époque ancienne, il ne nous est signalé que deux sources d'esclavage : la naissance et l'acquisition.

En vérité, cette façon de s'exprimer est très défectueuse. On ne saurait tout d'abord considérer la naissance comme une véritable source de l'esclavage. Mode de recrutement, certes, mais non pas source, car lorsqu'un enfant naît esclave, cela suppose que l'un de ses auteurs, la mère, est déjà esclave. De sorte que la question de la source véritable de son esclavage se trouve reculée et non résolue. Comment cette mère elle-même a-t-elle pu devenir esclave ? Elle pourra être tombée en servitude que par le seul mode originaire connu à l'époque ancienne : l'acquisition.

Mais ce terme demande à être précisé. On peut acquérir par différents moyens : par des moyens légaux et juridiques, comme une vente, une donation, un legs, ou par des moyens anormaux, comme la guerre ou la piraterie. Les premiers ne sont pas, à vrai dire, des sources d'esclavage, car ils supposent que celui qui fait l'objet de l'acte juridique a déjà la qualité d'esclave, à moins qu'il ne s'agisse de la vente de populations conquises qui tomberont en esclavage par la vente *sub hasta*. Mais il s'agit alors précisément de la vente d'étrangers. La seule source originaire véritable de l'esclavage est donc la guerre ou la piraterie,

---

(1) Ulpien au *Digeste*, 40, 12, 14, pr. Cet édit était déjà connu de Q. Mucius Scaevola, d'après Paul, au *Digeste*, même titre, 23, pr.

ce qui revient à dire que les esclaves ne peuvent être que des non-Romains (1).

Le principe est d'ailleurs certain. Quel que soit le mode d'acquisition, l'individu acquis à titre d'esclave ne peut être un Romain, car un Romain ne peut être esclave à Rome. C'est là, dit Girard (2), une idée élevée, qui a été abandonnée par le droit romain postérieur. Nous verrons plus loin que loin d'être une idée élevée et particulière aux Romains, ce n'est que la conséquence d'une règle très générale et très archaïque.

Si un Romain ne pouvait être esclave à Rome, il ne s'ensuit pas qu'il ne pût d'aucune manière tomber en servitude. Sans parler du cas de l'*incensus* que j'ai signalé tout à l'heure, des citoyens romains pouvaient être réduits à l'état d'esclaves, non à Rome même, mais à l'étranger. Vendus à Rome, à des Romains, ils gardent leurs droits de citoyens, leur personnalité juridique. Vendus hors des frontières, à des étrangers, ils cessent d'être des hommes libres et ils sont des esclaves. La chose nous est attestée pour le cas du débiteur adjugé à son créancier. Ce dernier peut le tenir en chartre privée. Il peut, au bout de 60 jours, le mettre a mort, mais ce droit de mise à mort n'implique pas plus pour lui que pour le *pater familias* le droit d'en faire un esclave. S'il veut le faire tomber en servitude, il devra le vendre à l'étranger, *trans Tiberim* nous dit la loi des XII Tables, c'est-à-dire hors des frontières, en Etrurie (3).

Ainsi, les esclaves romains anciens — ou plus exactement les esclaves des anciens Romains — ne pouvaient être que des étrangers ou des descendants d'étrangers, par cette raison péremptoire qu'à cette époque il n'y avait pas d'autre source d'esclavage. Mais dire que l'esclave est un étranger, c'est dire que la servitude est un caractère de l'esclave attaché en quelque sorte à sa personne et non pas un simple

(1) On peut noter que les esclaves vendus sur le marché devaient porter un écriteau désignant leur nationalité (D., 21, 1, 31, 21).

(2) Girard, *Manuel*, p. 111.

(3) Aulu-Gelle, *Noct. Att.* 20, 1, 47 : « Tertiis autem nundinis capite poenas.

rapport juridique, qui pourrait affecter une personne quelconque. Si je ne craignais de forcer un peu le sens des mots, je dirais que l'esclavage a un caractère ethnique et par là-même indélébile.

Divers traits de l'esclavage viennent confirmer cette vue.

Tout d'abord, l'état de servitude est héréditaire. L'enfant d'un esclave est esclave. Sans doute ici, comme dans toutes les unions hors mariage, la descendance qui est prise en considération est celle de la mère, mais cela ne change rien à l'affaire, car il arrivera très rarement que l'esclave mâle ait des relations avec une femme libre, et le cas inverse est beaucoup plus fréquent, pour ne pas dire normal. Anciennement, l'homme marié, qui avait une ou plusieurs *ancillæ* avait deux sortes d'enfants dont les premiers, ceux nés de la femme légitime, étaient appelés *liberi* pour les distinguer de ceux qui naissaient de ses femmes esclaves et qui étaient des *servi*. Quant aux enfants nés d'un père et d'une mère esclaves, ils étaient naturellement esclaves.

D'autre part, cette servitude était en principe définitive. Il est possible qu'anciennement on n'ait pas connu de moyen de faire passer un esclave en état de liberté. En tout cas, c'était là une opération compliquée, qui requérait la collaboration du maître et de l'Etat.

Les trois procédés d'affranchissement de l'ancien droit romain, la *vindicta*, le cens et le testament ont tous trois ce caractère. Dans la *vindicta*, le magistrat ratifie par une *addicto* la volonté du maître (1) ; dans le cens, c'est le censeur (2) ; enfin, dans le testament, c'est le peuple assemblé dans ses comices.

---

(1) On admet généralement que l'affranchissement *vindicta* est un procès fictif (cf. Girard, *Manuel*, p. 131). Je crois avoir démontré, dans une communication aux *Journées d'Histoire de Droit de Bruxelles* (juin 1930), qu'il est tout autre chose [cf. *L'affranchissement par la vindicte*, *infrà*, pp.   ]. Mais, que l'on se tienne ou non à la théorie courante, l'affranchissement *vindicta*, requérant l'*addicto* du magistrat, n'est pas un acte purement privé, quoique semble dire M. Ch. Appleton (*L'Affranchissement par la vindicta*, *Mélanges Paul Fournier*, 1929, p. 5).

(2) On a tort, à mon sens, de considérer l'affranchissement par le *cens*, comme une opération fictive, comme un moyen détourné (Cf. Girard, *Manuel* p. 130). Aucun texte latin ne nous le présente comme tel. L'inscription d'un esclave sur le registre du cens à titre de citoyen n'offre pas plus le caractère d'un « subterfuge » que ne le présente de nos jours, l'inscription

Ainsi, comme en matière de naturalisation, l'autorité publique vient s'ajouter à la volonté de l'intéressé et en même temps la contrôler. Sans doute, l'affranchissement n'est pas une véritable naturalisation, mais les deux institutions ont beaucoup de points communs. Nous reviendrons un peu plus loin sur ce sujet (1).

Un dernier trait, encore plus significatif, vient attester que la condition servile est attachée à la personne de l'esclave et ne résulte pas d'une appropriation. C'est une solution certaine qu'un esclave abandonné par son maître, n'acquiert pas la liberté, si longtemps qu'ait duré cet état d'indépendance de fait (2). L'esclave est simplement un *servus sine domino* dont le premier venu peut s'emparer. Ce n'est donc pas la domination, la *dominica potestas*, qui fait l'esclave. Rien ne saurait mieux prouver que la servitude est une tare. Sauf un acte de la puissance publique, on peut dire : « *Semel servus, semper servus* ».

Je crois avoir démontré qu'à Rome tout esclave est un étranger. Mais peut-être avons-nous affaire ici à une singularité du droit romain. Le moment est venu de confronter cette conclusion avec les solutions données sur ce point par d'autres droits de l'antiquité.

En Grèce, à l'époque homérique, il semble bien que les faits d'esclavage doivent recevoir la même interprétation qu'à Rome. Non seulement les esclaves portent le nom de δμῶες de δαμάζω, dompter, mais Timée nous fait savoir que les anciens Grecs ne se servaient pas d'esclaves achetés à prix d'argent (3). D'autre part, à une époque beaucoup plus récente, une règle vient confirmer ce trait originel de l'esclavage. « La vente comme esclave, nous dit Beau-

---

d'un étranger naturalisé sur la liste des nationaux. S'il en avait été autrement, l'esclave devenu libre par ce moyen détourné eût joui de toutes les prérogatives du citoyen alors qu'il n'a que la condition d'un affranchi. D'autre part, il n'y a aucune bonne raison de sous-estimer l'importance du contrôle exercé par le censeur dans cette opération.

(1) Cf. *infra*, p. 28.

(2) Cf. Girard, *Manuel*, p. 104. L'acquisition de la liberté par prescription ne date que d'une époque récente. C. 7, 22, 2 (Constitution de Dioclétien et Maximien, a. 300).

(3) Timée, fr. 67 ; éd. Didot, p. 207.

chet (1), figure sur l'échelle pénale du droit attique, mais cette mesure ne frappe que les étrangers. » L'Etat ne peut pas transformer un homme libre en esclave, à plus forte raison un particulier ne le peut-il pas. Le droit grec le plus ancien ne paraît pas avoir connu, plus que le droit romain ancien, l'esclavage de ses nationaux (2). Un papyrus nous atteste le même régime à Alexandrie (3).

Dans le droit juif, l'esclavage ne s'applique qu'aux étrangers (4). Seule la servitude pour dette, très différente de l'esclavage, peut frapper les Juifs. L'exclusion de toute endo-servitude est ici incontestable.

Il paraît en être de même chez les anciens Germains, d'après Tacite (5) et César (6).

Il apparaît donc que la répugnance à considérer un national comme esclave, loin d'être spéciale à Rome, soit au contraire un fait d'une très grande généralité, au moins dans les sociétés basées sur la cité. En tout cas, nous tiendrons pour acquis qu'à Rome tout esclave est un étranger.

II

La réciproque est-elle vraie ? Peut-on dire que tout étranger est un esclave ?

Je n'hésite pas à répondre par l'affirmative, à condition toutefois de donner au mot étranger son sens fort, de voir en lui un homme absolument en dehors de l'Etat romain.

Partant de là, nous écarterons naturellement les Latins,

---

(1) *Le droit privé de la République Athénienne*, t. II, p. 416.

(2) Naturellement, cette notion de l'esclavage a pu s'altérer en Grèce comme à Rome, et plus tôt encore qu'à Rome.

(3) *Pap. Hal.* I, 119 : « Ὁ Ἀλεξανδρεὺς τῶ Ἀλεσχ[ν]δρεῖ μὴ δουλευέτω μηδὲ ἡ Ἀλεξανδρὶς τῶι' Ἀλεξανδρεῖ μηδὲ τῶι Ἀλ [ε] ξανδρίδι. Cf. le commentaire de Brassloff, in *Hermes*, t. 57 (1922), p. 472 et s.

(4) Farbstein, *Das Recht der unfreien und der freien Arbeiter nach judischen talmudischen Recht verglichen mit antiken, speciell mit dem romischen Recht*, 1896 : « Nur ein Nichtjude kann Sklave sein ; ein Jude nur Schuldknecht. » De même, Winter, *Die Stellung der Sklaven bei den Juden :* « Sklave konnte ein Israelit uberhaupt nicht werden. »

(5) Tacite, *German.*, c. XXIV : « Servos condicionis hujus per commercia tradunt, ut se quoque pudore victoriae exsolvant. » En notre sens le commentaire de Brassloff, *loc. cit.*

(6) César, *Bell. gall.*, IV, 15, 5. Ce texte m'a été signalé par M. L. A. Constans, professeur à la Sorbonne.

qu'une communauté d'origine unit aux Romains et que ces derniers considèrent comme frères de race. Nous écarterons aussi les non-Romains sujets d'Etats unis à Rome par des traités. A partir de la fin de la République, c'est la condition normale des étrangers. La plupart des pays conquis se sont trouvés, après la conquête, soumis à ce régime. On ne saurait dire qu'alors un Egyptien, un Grec, un Gaulois, soient pour les Romains des étrangers, au sens plein du mot. Plus anciennement, au contraire, il y a tout lieu de penser que le mot *hostis* signifiait tout aussi bien étranger et ennemi et que les deux notions se confondaient. Certes, Rome a conclu dès une époque reculée des traités avec ses voisins, mais, pour la période ancienne, ils étaient assez rares.

S'ensuit-il qu'un individu non Romain, ni Latin et n'appartenant pas à une de ces *civitates* qui avaient conclu un traité de paix avec Rome, ne pourrait pénétrer dans la ville sans risquer de tomber en servitude ? Il avait encore un moyen de l'éviter : c'était de se mettre sous la protection d'un chef de *gens*, de devenir son client. Il se formait alors entre eux un contrat engendrant des obligations à la charge des deux parties : obéissance de la part du client, protection de la part du *pater gentis*. Si obscure que soit encore notre connaissance de la clientèle, il paraît hors de doute que le client n'était pas un esclave (1).

Si nous éliminons, comme n'étant pas de véritables étrangers ceux qui se trouvent associés à Rome par un contrat individuel de clientèle, ou par un contrat collectif ou traité, les autres étrangers'étaient sans droit aux yeux des Romains. Or, l'individu sans droit, nous l'avons dit, c'est un esclave.

Mieux encore que sur le raisonnement, cette assertion peut s'appuyer sur des textes. En voici un particulièrement topique. Il est de Pomponius, au *Digeste*, 49, 15, 5, 2.

« *In pace quoque postliminium datum est ; nam si cum gente aliqua neque amicitiam neque hospitium neque foedus*

---

(1) Sur la clientèle, v. notamment Bonfante, *Histoire du Droit Romain*, t. I, p. 80 et s. En tout cas, à Athènes, le métèque, qui est un étranger domicilié, est vendu comme esclave lorsqu'il n'a pas ou lorsqu'il n'a plus de προστατης.

amicitiæ causa factum habemus hi hostes quidem non sunt,
quod autem ex nostro ad eos pervenit eorum fit et liber
homo noster ab iis captus servus fit et eorum ; idemque est
si ab illis ad nos aliquid perveniat. »

Cet texte est extrêmement significatif. J'ai peine à croire
qu'il corresponde exactement au droit du temps de son auteur, c'est-à-dire du II⁰ siècle, encore moins à celui de Justinien qui l'a cependant accueilli dans sa compilation. Mais
quand il ne ferait que témoigner d'une survivance, son intérêt n'en serait pas diminué.

Il dit expressément que lorsqu'il n'existe entre Romain et
étranger ni traité de paix, ni amitié (entendez rapport d'hospitalité), ils peuvent impunément se dérober leurs biens, et
si l'un d'eux s'empare d'un autre, ce dernier devient son
esclave, *servus fit*. Et le jurisconsulte a pris soin de nous
marquer dans sa première phrase que cela se produit en
dehors de toute guerre, en pleine période de paix, *in pace*.
On ne saurait trouver confirmation plus nette de l'assertion
proposée, suivant laquelle tout étranger est (virtuellement)
un esclave.

Le *postliminium* se rattache à la même idée comme l'atteste d'ailleurs ce même texte de Pomponius. On sait en quoi
consiste cette institution : un citoyen romain est fait prisonnier par l'ennemi. S'il revient dans les lignes romaines, il
est réintégré dans tous ses droits et est censé ne les avoir
jamais perdus. C'est dire que la loi étrangère n'existe pas
aux yeux des Romains. Comme le dit Mommsen, « ce qui
constitue la règle en face de l'étranger, c'est l'absence réciproque de droit (1) ».

L'étranger ne jouit pas à Rome de son droit national.
D'autre part, le droit romain ne lui est pas applicable. C'est
donc un être sans droit : un esclave.

Nous arriverons à la même conclusion — c'est-à-dire à
l'affirmation de l'identité foncière entre l'étranger et l'esclave — en examinant la conception que se faisaient de la
liberté les Romains. Pour eux, nous l'avons vu plus haut,

_____

(1) Mommsen, *Droit Public Romain*, VI, 2, 206.

la liberté ne consiste pas dans la faculté de se déplacer à sa
guise, ou du moins cette manière toute matérielle de concevoir la liberté, qui est la nôtre n'est apparue à Rome que
relativement tard (1). Anciennement, la liberté était une
notion d'ordre essentiellement juridique et consistant dans
la jouissance des droits civils. En d'autres termes, elle ne
se distinguait pas du droit de cité. On en peut apporter deux
preuves, l'une directe, empruntée à la théorie de la *capitis
diminutio*, l'autre indirecte, tirée des effets de l'affranchissement.

Il paraît hors de doute qu'anciennement, il n'existait pas
trois sortes de *capitis deminutio*, mais seulement deux, la
capitis deminutio maxima se confondant avec la *capitis
deminutio media*, qu'en d'autres termes, le citoyen romain
se voyait privé de ses droits, par la perte de la *civitas
libertasque* (2). Des textes nombreux nous le prou-
vent (3). Comme le dit très bien M. Desserteaux (4) : « A

(1) *Sic*, Betti, *Corso di Istituzioni di Diritto Romano*, I, Padoue, 1929, p. 100.
La première expression s'en trouve à ma connaissance dans ce passage de
Cicéron, *Parad*, V, 1 : « Quid est libertas ? Potestas vivendi ubi velis. » Il y
a tout lieu de supposer qu'il l'avait empruntée aux Grecs.

(2) Desserteaux, *Etudes sur la formation historique de la capitis deminutio*, I, 1909, pp. 104, 180 ss.

(3) Cicéron, *Pro Caecina*, 34 : « Qui enim potest jure Quiritum liber esse
qui in numero Quiritum non est » Tite-Live, 45, 15. Neque enim si tribu
movere posset, quod fit nihil aliud quam mutari jubere tribum, ideo omni-
bus quinque et triginta tributus movere posse id ad civitatem et libertatem
eripere. » Plaute fait dire à un de ses personnages avant un affranchissement : « Facere ut sit civis atque liber. » (*Poen*, 2, 159). « Jusqu'à la fin de
la République » conclut M .Desserteaux, *op. cit.*, p. 188, « la liberté n'appa-
rait que comme une conséquence nécessaire de la Civitas. »

D'accord avec M. Desserteaux sur l'indistinction primitive de la *libertas* et
de la *civitas*, je m'écarterai de lui quant à l'évolution qu'a subi le premier
de ces termes. Au lieu de considérer que « le mot *libertas* a commencé par
n'avoir pas de sens technique » et signifiait tout état de liberté par opposition aux contraintes diverses qui peuvent entraver en fait et en droit, je
dirai au contraire que le mot *libertas* avait anciennement un sens technique
très défini, le même que *civitas*, ces deux mots formant un doublet. Au
temps de Cicéron seulement, *libertas* prend un sens plus vague, plus philo-
sophique, et s'oppose à la contrainte, ce qui permet à Cicéron de dire de
Clodius, donné en adrogation (*Pro domo*, 29) qu'il perd la *libertas* tout en
demeurant *civis*. Cette conception du mot *libertas* se répand et se vulgarise
même chez les juristes au point qu'un texte juridique qui date au plus tôt
du IIe siècle, le *Fragment* de Dosithée, parle d'esclaves qui vivent en état de
liberté : 5 « Hi... qui domini voluntate in libertate erant manebant servi. »
Cf. Pomponius, *D*, 40, 12, 28.

(4) Desserteaux, *op. cit.*, p. 118.

l'époque de Cicéron et *a fortiori* en remontant plus haut dans le passé, la *libertas* apparaît comme l'accessoire de la *civitas* : on ne peut perdre séparément ni la *civitas*, ni la *libertas.* » Réciproquement, tout étranger, puisqu'il n'a pas la *civitas*, est également privé de la *libertas* : c'est donc un esclave.

L'examen des effets de l'affranchissement vient confirmer ces vues. Les affranchis n'acquièrent pas immédiatement le statut d'un citoyen complet. Bien que libres, ils ne sont pas de tout point comparable aux ingénus, mais si on étudie leur condition, on ne peut pas ne pas être frappé du fait qu'ils acquièrent selon les cas, la même condition que des individus auxquels le droit de cité est accordé d'une manière partielle. Certains prennent la condition de Latins (Latins Juniens) ; d'autres enfin, tout au bas de l'échelle, reçoivent le statut juridique des déditices. On a tendance à ne voir là qu'une assimilation plus ou moins artificielle, établie par la loi pour fixer la condition des affranchis. Je crois, avec M. Betti (1), qu'il faut y voir quelque chose de plus. Si les divers degrés d'affranchissement varient comme les différents degrés du droit de cité, plus ou moins libéralement accordé, c'est qu'il y a plus qu'une analogie, une véritable confusion originelle entre la liberté et la cité, de telle sorte que toute modification de la première se traduit naturellement en termes d'ordre et de nature politique. L'affanchissement est une naturalisation plus ou moins complète (2).

De cette indistinction primitive entre la cité et la liberté résulte avec certitude que tout étranger non intégré d'une façon quelconque à l'Etat romain est privé de liberté. On peut dire, sans forcer le sens des mots, que c'est un esclave, puisque ce qui caractérise l'esclave ce n'est pas l'appropriation, mais l'absence totale de droit. Ou si l'on aime mieux, l'étranger est un out-law, un être dont chacun peut s'emparer et user à sa guise, que l'on peut tuer impunément.

---

(1) Betti, *op. cit.*, p. 103.

(2) De même à Athènes, « la condition des affranchis est exactement celle des étrangers domiciliés. Ils paient le μετοίχιον. Ils n'en diffèrent que par le paiement du triobole. » Beauchet, *op. cit.*, p. 483.

C'était là sans doute son sort le plus fréquent avant que des considérations d'ordre économique n'eussent conduit à penser que l'on pouvait utiliser sa force de travail, exactement comme on eut la pensée de domestiquer les animaux au lieu de les mettre à mort.

Sur ce point encore, la solution à laquelle nous aboutissons n'est point particulière au droit romain. Elle est en harmonie avec le droit de tous les peuples archaïques. On sait le rôle essentiel qu'ont joué le traité et l'hospitalité dans les relations internationales, l'une et l'autre institution reposant sur une idée de communion, de contact. En dehors de cette intégration collective ou individuelle de l'étranger, ce dernier est un ennemi que l'on peut tuer, ou, dans le cas le plus favorable, réduire en esclavage.

Les exemples de faits de ce genre sont trop nombreux et trop connus pour qu'il soit nécessaire d'en citer (1). Il s'agit ici, en réalité, d'un phénomène absolument général, qui ne peut s'expliquer que par des causes ayant elles-mêmes un caractère très général.

Pourquoi le national ne peut-il tomber en servitude ? Pourquoi tout étranger est-il au contraire, par définition même, esclave ? L'explication ressort implicitement de ce qui a été dit. Il s'agit seulement maintenant de la dégager.

Toute la différence entre l'esclave et l'homme libre con-

---

(1) Sur l'hospitalité en droit comparé, cf. Thurnwald, v. *Gastfreundschaft* in *Reallexikon der Vorgeschichte*, de Max Ebert, t. IV, p. 173.

(2) Bien que l'on ne doive utiliser en ces matières la philologie qu'avec une grande prudence je serais porté à croire que l'étymologie des mots *servus* et *liber* peut être invoquée en faveur de ma thèse. Pour le mot *servus*, il n'est pas douteux que les juristes romains le considèrent comme formé de *servatus* et lui donnaient le sens originel d'ennemi « épargné ». Pomponius, D. 50, 16, 239, 1 : « Servorum appellatio ex eo fluxit, quod imperatores nostri captivos vendere ac per hoc servare nec occidere solent. » Cf. Florentinus, D. 1, 4, 3 : « Mancipia vero dicta quod ab hostibus manu capiantur. » En faveur de cette étymologie, cf. Beseler, *Zeitschrift der Savigny Stiftung für Rechtsgeschichte, Romanitsche Abteilung*, t. 49, 1929. *Contra* : Walde, *Lateinisch-Etymologisches Wörterbuch*, p. 568 ; Bréal et Bailly. *Les mots latins*, p. 343. [Mais cf. *infra*, p. 54, n. 1]. — Quant au mot *liber*, il paraît bien avoir désigné anciennement l'homme du groupe. D'après Schrader, *Anzeige für Indogermanische Spache und Altertumskunde*, IX, 172, *liber* et ἐλεύθερος apparentés au vieux haut allemand *liut* et anglo-saxon *leod* : allemand *leute* signifierait originellement membre de la collectivité (Volksgenosse) par opposition aux autres hommes.

sistant dans l'absence de droits refusés au premier, accordés au second, il est naturel et fatal que l'étranger qui est sans droit dans le groupe soit esclave. Qu'est-ce en effet que le droit dans les sociétés de citoyens, sinon un rapport, muni de sanction, un lien, *vinculum juris*, entre deux ou plusieurs personnes éventuellement soumises à une même autorité ? Pour qu'un rapport de ce genre s'établisse, il est nécessaire qu'une certaine communauté au moins virtuelle existe entre elles. Or, entre le national et l'étranger — si cet étranger n'est pas intégré d'une façon quelconque — aucune communauté n'existait à l'époque ancienne. Les relations juridiques ne s'appliquent donc qu'aux membres du groupe.

Aujourd'hui, dans les sociétés de notre type de civilisation, l'on peut dire qu'une communauté morale existe entre tous les hommes. Un homme a certains droits, voit sa personnalité reconnue, du seul fait qu'il appartient à l'espèce humaine. Mais cette notion est relativement récente, et nombreuses sont encore les sociétés où elle n'a pas pénétré. Là où elle n'existe pas, l'étranger est nécessairement sans droit, et, étant sans droit, il est une chose. On peut s'en emparer, le tuer, ou, si les conditions économiques le permettent ou l'exigent, le réduire en servitude. En d'autres termes, en dehors du traité ou du contrat, la mise à mort et l'esclavage sont le sort normal de l'étranger dans les sociétés basées sur la cité, qui ne connaissent pas l'idée d'humanité, de même que, sous la même réserve, la guerre et la piraterie sont les seules relations internationales possibles dans ces mêmes sociétés. Ce sont là les conséquences fatales et logiques de ce fait incontestable, qu'anciennement chaque cité a son droit particulier qui ne dépasse pas les limites de la cité et qui ignore le droit des autres cités.

Mais ce que le droit perd alors en étendue, il le gagne en intensité. Tous les membres du groupe sont protégés par les prescriptions du droit. Tous jouissent des mêmes droits, même s'ils sont en fait dans l'incapacité d'exercer ces droits. Tant qu'ils demeurent dans le groupe, nul ne peut leur retirer leurs droits, pas même le groupe lui-même. Il ne peut les en priver qu'en les expulsant de son sein, en les bannissant. Un membre du groupe ne peut donc pas être esclave, puisque, s'il tombe en servitude, il sort du groupe. Ainsi le veut l'ancienne conception du droit considéré comme un lien purement interne, mais unissant très fortement tous les membres du groupe (1). Ainsi s'explique l'identité que nous avons trouvée dans l'ancienne Rome entre la liberté et la cité. Tout citoyen est libre par définition même.

De cette conception suivant laquelle l'esclave ne peut être un national, est nécessairement une personne étrangère à la collectivité au sein de laquelle il vit, il est resté des traces jusqu'aux temps modernes. A une époque où l'esclavage est en butte à de vives attaques, on ne le tolère plus, que si l'esclave se présente sous un aspect physiquement différent du national, si la distinction ethnique apparaît à tous les yeux. C'est ainsi que l'esclavage qui persista le plus longtemps au moyen âge fut celui des Arabes, et au XIXᵉ siècle, l'esclavage des nègres en Europe et en Amérique. Ici, comme il arrive souvent, c'est sous son aspect essentiel que l'institution manifeste le mieux sa vitalité.

Pour en revenir à Rome, ce régime de droit strictement national, dont les anciennes règles de l'esclavage, comme nous l'avons vu, nous ont gardé la trace fidèle, ne s'est pas conservé longtemps dans toute sa pureté. C'est que deux influences, du reste étroitement unies, venaient la battre en brèche : les idées humanitaires d'une part, et de l'autre les progrès économiques.

Dès la fin du IIIᵉ siècle avant notre ère, Térence et Plaute, dans leurs comédies, exprimaient des idées singulièrement hardies qui leur venaient de leurs modèles grecs. Au cours des siècles suivants, le stoïcisme et sa morale humanitaire se répand dans la société cultivée romaine (2), de telle

(1) De même au moyen âge, dans les villes, l'idée qu'un bourgeois pût être serf était inconcevable.
(2) On connaît la lettre si souvent citée de Senèque à Lucilius 47. 95 : « Servi sunt, Immo homines... » Cf. Id., *De Benef.* 3, 18.

sorte qu'on est bien obligé de reconnaître à l'esclave une personnalité, au moins au regard du *jus naturale* (1).

Cette reconnaissance des droits de l'esclave se trouvait corroborée par la plus grande initiative que les nouvelles conditions de l'économie romaine, devenue commerciale, étaient amenées à lui accorder. Parmi les esclaves, il y en eut qui eurent à remplir des fonctions importantes et délicates. Il fallut, par mesure de compensation, augmenter leur capacité juridique (2).

On ne pouvait dès lors s'en tenir à cette idée ancienne que l'esclave est un être radicalement et ethniquement différent des Romains, et cette idée une fois écartée fit place à une conception différente de l'esclavage, celle qui voit en lui une déchéance sociale. Entre l'esclave et l'homme libre, il n'y a plus différence de nature, mais de degré (3). Pour les Romains de la fin de la République, l'esclave est un homme dégradé, déconsidéré, et lorsque cette conception fut entrée dans les esprits, on n'eut plus scrupule à faire de l'esclavage un châtiment. On en vint alors, mais alors seulement, à frapper de servitude *pœnæ nomine*, des citoyens qui avaient commis certains délits.

En devenant ainsi une peine, et une peine d'ordre interne, susceptible de s'appliquer à des citoyens, l'esclavage s'éloignait de sa nature originelle et se rapprochait inévitablement de certaines situations où l'individu est privé de la faculté de se déplacer librement. Dans cette nouvelle acception, l'esclavage continue à s'opposer à la liberté, mais la

(1) Différents textes juridiques reconnaissent à l'esclave une demi-capacité caractérisée par des obligations dites naturelles. Cf. notamment Ulpien au *Digeste* 50, 17, 32. Cependant ces divers textes ont été récemment soupçonnés d'interpolation par M. Siber. *Naturalis Obligatio* dans *Gedenkschrift für L. Mitteis*, 1925, pp. 17-51.

(2) Cette nouvelle conception produisit des conséquences variées en ce qui concerne la protection de la personne même de l'esclave, la reconnaissance d'un rudiment de droit de famille et même le germe de certains droits patrimoniaux. Sur tous ces points, cf. Girard, *Manuel*, pp. 106, ss. On peut y ajouter ce trait significatif que le meurtre de l'esclave d'autrui anciennement considéré comme un dommage causé au patrimoine, finit par être regardé comme un homicide et puni comme tel. Cf. Mommsen, *Droit Pénal Romain*, t. 2, p. 329.

(3) C'est pourquoi le passage de l'un à l'autre, l'affranchissement, devenu plus aisé, put se faire désormais par un acte de simple volonté privée.

liberté cessa d'être, comme jadis, la jouissance des droits
civils pour prendre le sens matériel que nous lui donnons
aujourd'hui. Cette modification est accomplie sous l'Empire.
Dès lors, la situation de l'esclave ne présente plus guère de
différence avec celle du prisonnier pour dettes que l'on appelle même parfois esclave pour dette. Mais il suffit d'ana-
lyser soigneusement les deux institutions pour constater
qu'elles sont, originairement, profondément distinctes et que
l'esclavage est essentiellement — comme des faits abondants
et précis nous ont permis de le voir avec évidence — une
institution de caractère international (1).

(1) Ces conclusions laissent complètement de côté la nature de l'esclavage
dans des sociétés de type différent comme les tribus africaines ou les grands
Empires asiatiques.

M

IX

THE NATIONALITY OF SLAVES UNDER THE EARLY ROMAN EMPIRE.

By MARY L. GORDON, M.A., B.Litt.(Oxon).

Assistant Lecturer in Classics, University College, Exeter.

The Roman master who visited the slave-market to buy a new slave had little difficulty in solving the important question of nationality. He could read the label attached to each man, on which name and origin were recorded, or listen to the crier who announced the nationality of every slave in turn, as the law required ; and if he feared the ' tricks of the trade,' which were innumerable, he could observe for himself whether the appearance and speech of the slave chosen corresponded to the place of origin ascribed to him. Our difficulties in approaching the same problem are much more formidable. A very large number of Roman slaves and freedmen are known to us by name, but of these only a small minority come to us with labels attached in the form of an explicit statement of origin ; and though these ' labelled ' examples have been collected,[1] and form a body of evidence which is not without interest and value, they are too accidental and isolated, and too widely diffused chronologically and otherwise, to bear the weight of very far-reaching conclusions. Are there then any other indications which may throw light upon servile nationality, and help us towards a more vivid and accurate picture of the slave population of the Roman empire ?

Such an enquiry must necessarily begin by recalling the little that is known to us concerning the routes and centres of the slave trade. It is important to remember that the Romans did not originate this trade, but inherited it from the Phoenicians and Greeks, who from their settlements along the coasts of the Mediterranean trafficked in slaves with the peoples of the interior, or obtained them as captives in conflicts with their neighbours. The Greek slave-dealers, as we see from the inscriptions of Delphi and other evidence, threw their nets very wide : slaves reached Greece from Italy, Illyria, Armenia, Arabia, Palestine, Egypt and even Ethiopia. But the great majority of barbarian slaves came from two principal regions, the one comprising Asia Minor and Syria, the other Thrace, the valley of the lower Danube, and the northern coast of the Black Sea.[2] In Asia Minor, the trade in slaves was a natural outcome of the commercial relations of the Asiatic Greeks with the interior ;

---

[1] Bang, ' Die Herkunft der römischen Sklaven,' Röm. Mittb. xxv (1910), p. 223.

[2] Wallon, Histoire de l'esclavage, Bk. ii, ch. 2, p. 38.

Ephesus, in particular, through its connection with Sardis, the earliest centre of the trade in these parts, became an important slave market, and remained so in the days of Varro. The most highly valued barbarian slaves were obtained from this first region. But the northern route was even more important as providing large numbers of slaves for rougher work of all kinds, and its pre-eminence is clearly shown by the fact that Byzantium preceded Delos as the great centre of the slave-trade for the Aegean.[1] The traffic was promoted by the prevalence of piracy in the Black Sea,[2] and by the custom of selling their children which persisted among the Thracians and their Asiatic kinsfolk until Roman times. When the Romans began to import slaves in large numbers, they must have purchased originally from Greek slave-dealers; and when Italian merchants turned to this lucrative and perhaps congenial form of commerce, they would naturally compete with their Greek predecessors in the same districts. The development of Delos into a great trading centre proceeded rapidly after the battle of Pydna, and reached its climax about 130 B.C.; until the middle of the last century of the Republic it was the chief market of the slave trade, and no doubt derived its goods from the old sources, though the increased demand for the type of slave who might be classed among those Graeco-Oriental luxuries which formed the chief merchandise of Delos, and the new abundance of western slaves for less ornamental purposes, probably altered their relative importance. Asia Minor and Syria became the favourite haunt of slave-dealers; piracy in the eastern Mediterranean reached incredible dimensions, and the oriental peoples of the south-east, Syrians, Jews, Egyptians, Arabians and even Parthians, were preferred to the uncivilised barbarians of the north-east. It is significant that the pirates established their headquarters in Cilicia, and not, as of old, along the coasts of the Black Sea. We have clear evidence, however, that slaves were still obtained from Thrace and the other northern districts, probably in considerable numbers.[3]

The vast and picturesque activities of Delos as a slave-mart were of short duration. The massacre of 87 B.C. and the second destruction of the town by pirates in 69 B.C. ruined its prosperity, and though trade revived after each disaster, it was soon killed by the competition of Italian ports; after 48 B.C. Delos practically ceased to exist commercially.[4] Many of the slave-dealers appear to have moved westwards, some perhaps to the resuscitated Corinth and Carthage of imperial times, but most to the ports of Italy, Ostia and Puteoli (called a ' little Delos '), while Rome itself became the centre of the

[1] Speck, *Handelsgeschichte des Altertums*, vol. II, ch. xi, §482, p. 490.

[2] Strabo, xi, 495-6.

[3] Tacitus, *Ann.* xii, 17. Seneca, *Ep.* 80, 9. Martial, vii, 80. Juvenal, ix, 142.

[4] Homolle, ' Les Romains à Délos,' *Bull. de corr. hellén.* viii (1884), p. 75.

slave trade, as of every other commercial activity. The fall of Delos seems to mark a corresponding change in the history of the trade among the Romans; it is no longer a mere development of Greek slave-dealing, but has a range and character of its own. In the first place, Rome was the heir, not only of the Greeks but of the Phoenicians, who had preceded them as traders in slaves throughout the Mediterranean : Carthage had long been an important centre of the slave trade,[1] and the Romans inherited its traffic in slaves from the tribes of the interior, from Mauretania, and from the countries of its European empire. Doubtless the Italian merchants followed the routes and pursued the methods of their Carthaginian predecessors. Moreover in the west as in the east Rome conquered peoples who were themselves slave-owners, and must have absorbed the slave population, not only of Carthage, but of Spain and Gaul. Above all, her conquests in the west and north flooded the slave-market with new nationalities. The Thracians, Scythians, Phrygians and the rest, who had been hewers of wood and drawers of water to Hellenic civilisation, were supplemented if not superseded by vast numbers of Ligurians, Sardinians, Spaniards, Gauls, Germans and other races. Every addition to the empire brought a new extent and variety to the slave population, as we see from Cicero's jesting allusion to the illiterate Britanni.[2] When the empire ceased to expand indefinitely, a corresponding change came over the servile class ; it became a more or less completed entity, a strange epitome of the *orbis terrarum*, evolving like its prototype into the Graeco-Roman *urbs*. Its ranks were kept full chiefly by slave-breeding and kidnapping within the empire itself, and the slave-dealer became if possible more ubiquitous and less respectable.[3]

Even this slight survey of the vicissitudes of the slave trade is sufficient to dispel the illusion, promoted by Juvenal and others, that the slave population of the empire was chiefly or predominantly oriental.[4] The most ' oriental ' element in that melting-pot of races was composed of Syrians, Jews and Egyptians. To these we may add the inhabitants of Asia Minor (though possessing a strong western admixture), and the Punic minority in Africa. To include Greek slaves, even Asiatic Greeks, among ' orientals ' is misleading. Thus the permeation of Roman society by men of servile stock was by no means equivalent to an orientalising of its population or ideas. This conclusion, based upon the large contribution levied by conquerors and slave-merchants from the north, south, and west, is confirmed by the study of a different type of evidence ; servile nomenclature in its origin and development is likely to bear some traces, however scanty and obliterated, of the countries from which the slaves

---

[1] Speck, vol. iii, ch. i, § 606.
[2] Cicero, *ad Att.* iv, 16.
[3] Bang, *Röm. Mitth.* xxvii (1912), 189 ff.
[4] Juvenal, iii, 60-85.

originally came; and such servile names occur in great abundance on inscriptions, especially in the form of the cognomina of freedmen. A general idea of the commonest Greek and Latin slave names may be very easily obtained from vol. xv of the *Corpus* (*Instrumentum domesticum*), or from such a list as that of 'Augustales' given in Ruggiero's *Dizionario Epigrafico*, vol. i. But for our present purpose those dating from the close of the Republic and the beginning of the empire are most useful. Examples of these may be found in the historical index to Cicero's works in Nobbe's edition, the first volume of the *Corpus*, the inscriptions from the Columbarium of Livia in vol. vi, and the early instances cited by Oxé in his article on the development of servile nomenclature.[1] With these may be compared the numerous inscriptions of imperial slaves and freedmen from two cemeteries at Carthage, dating from the end of the first century A.D. to the reign of Antoninus' Pius, which are collected in vol. viii.[2] The evidence supplied by such names may be meagre, but at least it brings us into immediate contact with the slaves themselves, and prevents the problem of their origin from becoming too abstract. Ancient slavery is mercifully remote and unfamiliar to us; but *Felix Caesaris n. ser. pius vixit ann. II* has an almost startling reality.

The physical characteristics of slaves, which might throw some light upon their nationality, are seldom revealed by the evidence available to us. Roman art does not distinguish the slave in dress or appearance from the free man. It is noticeable that on a sepulchral monument recently acquired by the British Museum, which depicts an elderly freedman with his wife and daughter, the three faces, apparently realistic portraits, have nothing suggestive of the fawning oriental or *Graeculus esuriens* about them, but are strong, shrewd, and decidedly Roman. Servile names do not often take the form of nicknames derived from physical peculiarities, doubtless because they were bestowed by the man's superiors and not by his fellow-slaves. The chief exception is Rufus or more often Rufio, a genuine nickname, as its form shows, which is employed by Cicero as a typical slave name, and occurs commonly at the end of the Republic.[3] The red wig worn by slaves in Roman comedy is merely a legacy from the Thracian slaves who must have been a familiar sight in Greek households; but the comparative frequency of Rufio and similar names suggests that Thrace continued to supply the slave-market in large numbers. Flavus on the other hand hardly ever occurs among slaves, and Fuscus only occasionally.[4] Bassus as a

[1] Oxé, 'Zur älteren Nomenklatur der römischen Sklaven,' *Rhein. Mus.* 1904, p. 108.

[2] *C.I.L.* viii, Suppl. i, p. 1301; cf. iv, p. 2479.

[3] Cicero, *pro Milone*, xxii, 60; *C.I.L.* i, 728, 737, 1032, 1068; ii, 4970, 440; iv, 1847; vi, 6514, 4632; xi, 6700, 597; xv, 5651-5663. Cf. *Rufa*: *C.I.L.* i, 1034, 1094, 1102, 1242, 1260; vi, 3927; ix, 3527.

[4] *Flavus*: *C.I.L.* vi, 14023; xii, 5686, 364. *Fuscus*: vi, 4276, 4716, 13911; viii, 12748, *Fusca*: 13112, 13042.

slave-name may sometimes be an ethnicon.[1] Such names as Celer
or Callistus, which refer to the utility or beauty of the slave, are
naturally frequent but quite useless for our purposes.

It might be supposed that dedicatory inscriptions offered by
slaves would give some clue to the nationality of the dedicants : but
while offerings to a ' barbarian ' deity may confirm other evidence,
they are insufficient of themselves to prove anything as to race. A
slave or freedman might well desire to propitiate the gods worshipped
by his master, or to emulate his betters in adopting a fashionable
cult ; still more would he be attracted, whatever his own nationality,
by those rites which admitted men of servile birth to an equality
with the free. For similar reasons, such names as Isidorus, Sera-
piodorus, Heliodorus, have no racial significance, and nothing can be
inferred from the popularity of Greek theophoric names such as
Dionysius, Apollonius, Aphrodisius, although they may occasionally
have a local explanation. On the other hand, Menophilus and
Tyrannus, the former a common slave name at the end of the
Republic, may, since they are derived from the less widely diffused
cult of Mên Tyrannus, be accepted as evidence for a strong Phrygian
element in the slave population.[2] Many servile names seem to have
originated from the epithets of gods, such as Parthenius, Pannychus,
Eleutherius, Anicetus, and the very favourite early slave name
Nicephor[3] ; Chrysaor, the epithet of the Carian Zeus, may give a
clue to the nationality of the father and son so named in *C.I.L.* vi,
4493. Occasionally slaves bear the names of foreign deities, such
as Ma, the Phrygian goddess (*C.I.L.* vi, 4244), and Arpochra, from
the Egyptian Harpechrot (*C.I.L.* vi, 4493). Latin theophoric names,
which are not frequent among slaves, may reproduce similar native
names through the common identification of Roman with barbarian
deities. Thus, among the slaves and freedmen at Carthage,
Saturninus is probably the Latinised form of a name derived from
Baal ; and it is possible that Mercurius, Martialis and Silvanus
sometimes represent names formed from those of Celtic gods. The
dearth of such names in Latin may have encouraged the assumption
of Greek theophoric names to take the place of native names so formed.
On the other hand, Fortunatus and Primigenius, which are among
the most popular of Roman servile names, especially the former,
may have been originally inspired by the name of the great goddess
Fortuna Primigenia of Praeneste.[4] A different form of local allusion
is to be found in the assumption of historical names, especially those
of Alexander and his successors, by slaves. Philippus rarely occurs,

---

[1] *Bassus : C.I.L.* vi, 4337, 4338, 4342, 13552,
13526. *Bassa :* 4067, 13529. The Bassi were a tribe
in Belgium. Cf. however also Dessau 2196, *P. Ael.
Basso nat. Bessus.*

[2] *Menophilus : C.I.L.* i, 623, 1067, 1068, 8070 ;
vi, 13754, 3939, 4356, 4228 ; xi, 6700, 453.

Tyrannus : vi, 13807, 13908, 14203, 3985, 4012,
4423. Cicero, *ad Att.* iv, 8, *Tyrannio.*

[3] *C.I.L.* i, 1028, 1032, 1041, 1102, 1129 ; vi,
3930, 14176. Cicero, *ad Q. fratr.* iii, 1, 5.

[4] Cf. *C.I.L.* x, 6261 (*Ianum Fortunae*), *Fortunia
Fortunata.*

but Alexander appears everywhere, and Antiochus is common among the earlier slave names. Seleucus, Demetrius, Antigonus, and other such names also appear, and it is possible that Philetaerus and Philadelphus originated in the same way.[1] Such names in general only remind us that Rome inherited the slave trade from the Hellenistic east, though the frequency of Antiochus (the name assumed by Eunus, the Syrian slave-king) reflects the pre-eminence of Syria among the slave-producing provinces.

.The only servile names which appear at first sight to give a clear indication of nationality are those derived from the names of races, countries, cities, and geographical features generally. Such names occur occasionally among Roman slaves, though ethnic names seem to have been less popular with Roman masters than with Greek. As evidence of origin they require to be used with caution. Sometimes they were mere nicknames; more often they were used to designate occupations typical of certain nationalities; above all, they might lose their meaning as completely as the English surnames French or Fleming, and be used indiscriminately as ordinary proper names. Most misleading of all are those apparent ethnica which are really barbarian personal names, just as Germanus may be merely the Latin adjective. So in *C.I.L.* vi, 3195 (*M. Aurelio Bitho nat. Thrax M. Aurelius Surus frater*) Bithus and Surus are Thracian proper names.[2] When with these precautions in mind we turn to the examples of apparently genuine ethnica among Roman slaves, two facts emerge. In the first place, occasional and isolated examples occur of ethnica derived from almost every part of the empire and beyond it: Gallus, Germanus, Baeticus, Afer, Maurus, Ponticus, Phryx, Lydus, Cilix, Araps, Parthus, Persicus and others, showing that the slave population was an epitome of the empire, or even of the known world.[3] Nor can it be inferred that the rarity or absence of any particular ethnicon implies a corresponding racial lacuna. The most valued nationalities would be most likely to be recorded in nomenclature, while unpopular races such as the Sardinians or Egyptians would naturally not be emphasised by ethnic names. In the second place, side by side with these comparatively infrequent ethnica, there appears a distinct class of such names, more often found among the servile part of the community, which

---

[1] *Antiochus :* Cicero, *Pro Caecina*, viii, 22; *Pro Flacco*, xxxvi, 89; *C.I.L.* i, 571, 602, 725, 815, 1095, 1131, 1156, 1477. *Seleucus :* i, 1065, 1483; vi, 12752. *Antigonus :* vi, 4079, 4171, 4328. *Philotaerus :* i, 570; vi, 13592. *Philadelphus :* vi, 3971, 4012.

[2] *Nicknames :* cf. Donat. *ad Ter. And.* i, 3, 21; 'Lesbia, velut ebriosa'; sunburnt girl nicknamed Σύρα, Theocr. x, 26. A free Greek might receive the name Σκύθης from his red hair or snub nose. *Occupations :* Germanus, guardsman; Numida, courier; Thraex, gladiator. Cf. *C.I.L.* vi, 10197,

Macedo Thr(aex) tiro Alexandrin(us). *Proper names :* Cf. Celtic names : Caricus, Indus, Araps.

[3] *C.I.L.* i, 1180, *Gallus ;* vi, 14006, *Galla ;* v, 1362, *Germanus ;* vi, 10909, *Germana ;* vi, 13499, *Baeticus ;* viii, 13053, *Getulicus ;* 13188, *Libycus ;* 2888, *T. Iulio Mauro sive Ruzerati liberto ;* 2237, *Affra ;* vi, 10860, *Ponticus ;* vi, 4042, *Phryx ;* vi, 155, 3976, *Lydus ;* Cicero, *ad fam.* iii, 1, *Cilix ; C.I.L.* viii, 12621, *Cilix ;* vi, 8868, *Araps ;* 29112, *Parthus ;* 1877, 13979, *Persicus.*

attach it closely to Graeco-Roman civilisation. Siculus, Campanus, Etruscus, and even Latinus may be genuine ethnica ; but Romanus implies either that the slave is city-born, or that he displays the true Roman virtues and culture : it is analogous, in fact, to such cogno‧ mina as Verna (' cockney '); Urbicus, Urbanus, Civilis, Priscus.[1] The name Sabinus, not rare among slaves, may often be of Celtic origin. Sometimes it is a true ethnicon, as in the case of the imperial messenger *cui Latiae gentis nomen patriaeque Sabinus.*[2] But it may also have been given with an ethical significance corresponding to that of Priscus.[3] The commonest of such names are those which mark the slave as a product of Hellenistic culture : Atticus, Graecus, Asia, Asiaticus, Syrus.[4] These slaves from Greek or Graecised cities were the most expensive and highly prized, and their names are expressive of their value. In their implications they do not greatly differ from such names as Philomusus, Philologus, Epaphroditus or Tryphon. It by no means follows that such slaves were the most numerous, rather the contrary. Servile names derived from Greek cities, such as Chios, Lesbia, Smyrna, Laudica (Laodicea),[5] which are not infrequent among the earlier slave names, belong to the same class, and recall the interesting passage in which Varro describes how a master might name his slave Ephesios because he had bought him at Ephesus.[6] If this is the origin of the slave name Corinthus, it supports the view that the slave trade shifted in part to Corinth after the fall of Delos.[7] Slaves who were named from the place of purchase might, of course, be of any nationality ; and all slave names which claimed Greek or at least Hellenized origin for their bearers may have been applied with cultural rather than racial significance. ' Caecilia Graecula, natione Hispana.'[8] may have been born in Spain as a *verna* of Greek parentage ; but we may suspect that many an Atticus had never visited Athens. This emphasis upon civilisation in

---

[1]*Romanus :* vi, 1819 (*Urbanus* and *Romanus*) ; 3151, (*M. Aur. Romani . . . n. Sur. M. Aur. Romanus frat.*) ; 11935, (*Romanae et Urbico parentibus*) ; 13780, (*Caecilio Urbico, Caeciliae Romanae*) ; vi, 3970, 10935, 11015, 11212 ; xiii, 10009, 293 ; viii, 24698, 13118, 13119, 14687.

[2] Brambach, 780. For Sabinus as a slave-name compare also *C.I.L.* vi, 3938, 3940, 4446, 11221, 13221, 14257.

[3] Cf. Cicero, *ad Fam.* xv, 20. ' Oratorem meum Sabino tuo commendavi. Natio me hominis impulit, ut ei recte putarem : nisi forte, candidatorum licentia hic quoque usus, hoc subito cognomen arripuit : etsi modestus eius vultus sermoque constans habere quiddam a Curibus videbatur.'

[4] *C.I.L.* vi, 4033, 12705, *Atticus* ; 12708, *Attica* ; 4252, 13290, *Attice* ; 14160, *Athenais* ; v, 1014, *Graeca* ; viii, 24703, *Ionicus* ; iii, 4870, *Asiaticus* ; vi, 3952, *Asia* ; viii, 24711, *Asia Aug. ser. Asiaticus p. et Cupita m.* ; vi, 2223, *Fannia Ɔ. l. Asia* ; *Fannia,*

Ɔ. l. *Sura mater* ; i, 602, *Surus* ; 1316, *Surisca* ; vi, 13754 ; xi, 577 ; xiii, 2106, *Surus* ; viii, 24826, *Syria* ; 13145, *Surus.*

[5] *Chius :* vi, 1952, 4051, 4234 (*Chius and Homerus*), 3937 (*Chio Homeri frat.*) ; *Lesbia :* vi, 4025, 4606 ; *Lesbius :* 4155, 4527 ; *Zmyrna :* vi, 3989, 4600, 4650, 4656, 10254, 12914 ; *Laudica :* i, 1212 ; vi, 13754, 6483 ; *Laudica Cilicissa, Pergamis :* vi, 13729.

[6] Varro, *de Ling. Lat.* viii, 21. ' Sic tres cum emerunt Ephesi singulos seruos, nonnunquam alius declinat nomen ab eo qui uendit, Artemidorus, atque Artemam appellat, alius a regione quod ibi emit, ab Ion<i>a Iona[m], alius quod Ephesi, Ephesium, sic alius ab alia aliqua re, ut uisum est.'

[7] *Corinthus :* *C.I.L.* v, 1305 ; vi, 11541, 3956, 4454.

[8] *C.I.L.* vi, 13820, 'Caeciliae Graeculae natione Hispana . . . P. Aelius Menophilus coniugi.'

preference to nationality, which can be traced in servile nomenclature, is very characteristic of Rome, and indeed reveals one of the
chief *arcana imperii*, the secret perhaps of both the strength and
the weakness of the Empire.

Another manifestation of the same tendency may be found in a
different class of servile names, in which the slave retains either in an
unaltered or in a disguised form the barbarian nomenclature of his
original home.[1] The familiar instance of Spartacus shows that a
prisoner of war might keep his native name after enslavement : and
the earlier inscriptions record slaves with barbarian names from
both east and west.[2] Cicero mentions a Phoenician temple-slave
named Banobal, and the elder Pliny tells of an Arabian giant whose
name was Gabbara.[3] Oxé gives examples of the Celtic name
Alaucus as an early slave name, occurring on potters' stamps and
other inscriptions ; and it is interesting to find Ambactus, a Celtic
name meaning ' captive,' ' slave,' among the members of a Roman
household.[4] Such names appear as a rule but rarely, like the
ethnica to which they correspond. Amid the interminable iteration
of Felix or Hilarus, Eros or Alexander, their strange and ' barbarous '
syllables arrest the attention and refresh the mind. But names of
this sort were not likely to persist or spread. If the slave sometimes thus preserved his native name unchanged, it seems highly
probable that he much oftener retained it in a Graecized or Latinized
form. The native name might, for example, be translated, just as,
in the bi-lingual countries of the east, the free provincials often
adopted a Greek equivalent of their native name. We are reminded
at once of Dorcas (Tabitha) and of Thomas called Didymus. It has
been suggested that Vitalis, a name found among slaves, may be
a translation of the Celtic name Venobius,[5] and it is conceivable
that Primigenius sometimes translates Cintugnatus or Cintugenus.
A more frequent and natural method of civilising the native name
would be to replace it by a Greek or Latin name of similar sound.
Both processes of change were familiar to us in war time, when
Schneider became Taylor, and Bethmann Bateman.[6] Thus
Dorimachus, which has such an entirely Greek appearance, is said to

[1] Cf. Strabo, vii, 304.

[2] *Pharnaces :* Cic. ad Att. xiii, 44 ; C.I.L. i,
602, 1035, 1064 ; vi, 13754, 14065, 14184 ; *Tiridas :*
vi, 4393, 12902 ; *Mabes :* vi, 13706 ; *Barnaeus :*
Cic. ad. Att. xiv, 19 ; C.I.L. i, 973 ; vi, 4289, 4597 ;
Malchio : i, 1087, 1091, 1300 ; vi, 3999, 4710 ;
Martha : i, 1058, 1229 ; v, 1295 ; *Bargates :*
i, 1029 ; vi, 12692 ; ix, 8214 ; *Bitbus :* vi, 3969,
4373, 4578, 10652, 11652, ; *Dasius :* i, 1044 ;
Sasa : vi, 4183, 4371 ; *Lullu :* vi, 4171, etc.

[3] Cic. in Verr. ii, 3, 39. Plin. N.H. vii, 74.

[4] *Alaucus :* C.I.L. i, 1406 ; ii, 4970, 15 ; xiv.
3367, etc. *Ambactus :* vi, 13402.

[5] Rhys, Proc. Brit. Acad. 1911-12.

[6] Cf. Prof. E. Weekley, *The Romance of Names*,
ch. v, ' The Absorption of Foreign Names,' p. 51.
' We have many official lists of these foreigners,
and in these lists we catch the foreign name in the
very act of transforming itself into English. This
happens sometimes by translation, e.g. . . . a refugee
bearing the somewhat uncommon name Petitoeil
transformed himself into Little-eye which became
in a few generations Lidley. But comparatively
few surnames were susceptible of such simple treatment, and in the great majority of cases the name
underwent a more or less arbitrary perversion which
gave it a more English physiognomy. . . This occurs
most frequently in the case of Jewish names of
German origin.'

be really the Thracian name Drimachus, and Acme is the Syrian Hacma.[1] In the west, such assimilation was rendered easy by the close kinship between the Celtic and Latin languages. Iullus could become Iulius or Audagus Audax without any sense of having lost his identity. There was obvious convenience in retaining at least approximately the name by which the captive was accustomed to be called ; and such an expedient would be in accordance with the Roman lack of inventiveness, acceptance of existing conditions, and practical temperament. Perhaps the merchant or the master had a prejudice against Greek, and had already exhausted his slender stock of Latin servile names ; the man proclaimed himself as Iantumarus : why not call him Ianuarius and have done with it ? If scenes of this kind really took place in the earlier days of Roman slavery, it is clear that the nomenclature of Roman slaves must conceal many barbarian names which would give a clue to the original nationalities of the slave population.

There is one supposed indication of origin which is generally accepted as valid and which requires very careful consideration. Professor Tenney Frank in his article on ' Race Mixture,' and again in his *Economic History of Rome*,[2] draws attention to the extraordinary predominance of Greek cognomina in the sepulchral inscriptions of the lower classes, both in Rome itself and in the chief towns of Italy and of the provinces, and infers that they are derived from servile stock imported from the eastern provinces of the empire. ' When the name is Greek, as a very large proportion of slave and freedmen names actually are, we may infer that the bearer came from or at least by way of that part of the slave-producing world in which Greek was the language of commerce, i.e., Asia Minor and Syria.' In the former article, he analyses a collection of 5,000 slave-names drawn from the indices of the *Corpus*, and finds that of these 2,874 are Greek names and 2,126 Latin. It is generally assumed that all slaves and freedmen bearing Greek names were either Greeks or orientals ; and since Latin names might also be bestowed upon such slaves (Felix the brother of Pallas is an obvious example), it is inferred that the eastern provinces supplied the main bulk of the slave population. ' The whole of Italy as well as the Romanized portions of Gaul and Spain were during the Empire dominated in blood by the East.' In this fact the writer finds a clue to the advance of absolutism, the spread of oriental religions, the decline of Latin literature, and the disappearance of Roman capacity for government. Such conclusions show the importance of the problem which here confronts us : Do the Greek names borne

---

[1] Lambertz, ' Die griechischen Sklavennamen.' *Progr. Staatsgymn. Wien*, viii, 1907, note 109, p. 68. Friedländer, vol. i, ch. 2, §4, Freedwomen. Jewess Acme (Hacma = ' clever '), slave of Livia.

[2] ' Race Mixture in the Roman Empire,' *Amer. Hist. Rev.* xxi (1916), p. 689. *Economic History of Rome*, ch. x.

by so many slaves and freedmen (70% in Rome, 64% in Latium, and 46% in Cisalpine Gaul, according to Professor Tenney Frank), imply a Graeco-oriental origin ? And did Trimalchio and the *Graeculus esuriens* combine to destroy insidiously ' the grandeur that was Rome,' much as the secret ravages of an insignificant beetle may reduce the timbered roofs of our most ancient and majestic buildings to a powdery nothingness ?

That large numbers of slaves were obtained from the countries east of Italy, and that most of these slaves would naturally have Greek names, cannot be questioned ; but it is by no means certain, either that they greatly outnumbered those slaves who came from the west, or that western slaves never received Greek names. Professor Tenney Frank himself refers to the vast quantities of captives obtained through wars in the west, and is driven to find various explanations for the supposed preponderance of orientals. The most satisfactory of these is the reason usually given, that the western captives were used in ways which led to their rapid extermination. There can be little doubt that Rome in her wars of conquest made reckless use of the human material so acquired.[1] Very large numbers were employed as gladiators and, as the western provinces became increasingly Romanized, the demand for these and for the other victims of the arena grew with the growth of ' civilization.' Wholesale butcheries were sometimes exhibited, in which the prisoners fought with and massacred each other. The revolt of Spartacus throws light upon the fate of barbarian captives ; he and his followers were chiefly Gauls and Thracians, who had escaped from the gladiatorial schools and the *ergastula*. Captives who were not exhibited in the arena by victorious generals, or sold to private trainers, were largely employed on the estates of the great land-owners, where slave-breeding did not become customary until the seemingly inexhaustible supply of human booty began to run short. Thus as the prey of wild beasts in the arena, as gladiators, as workers in the mines and galleys, or upon such public works as the cutting through of the isthmus of Corinth (for which Vespasian sent 6,000 prisoners to Nero),[2] as chained workers on the plantations and as solitary shepherds, the great hordes of western captives dwindled and in large part perished without leaving descendants or trace. The growth of the empire had a background of human suffering which is unimaginable in its degree and extent. It is not to be supposed, however, that slaves and captives from the east were treated with greater humanity or on more enlightened economic principles. Titus distributed most of his Jewish prisoners among the provincial amphitheatres for destruction[3] ; and the

---

[1] Cf. Koeser, *de captivis Romanorum*, Diss. Giessen, 1904.

[2] Josephus, *B.J.* iii, 10, 10.

[3] *Ibid.* vi, 9, 2.

Syrian 'kingdom' of Eunus shows how recklessly oriental slaves
were employed on the Roman plantations in Sicily. The nationality
of the slave mattered little, so long as his physical strength sufficed
for the most exacting work. (Syrians, for example, were proverbially
strong). If such labour killed him prematurely, the Roman master
of Republican times might say with the concise brutality of Tacitus,
uile damnum : there were plenty more.

This reckless waste of human life, however, does not by any
means account for all the enormous numbers of Rome's prisoners
of war. Some found a more tolerable fate through local sale, as the
conditions laid down by Augustus on a particular occasion show ;
Cicero came across Corinthian captives in the Peloponnese who had
become indistinguishable from their purchasers.[1] Others became
serui publici, with a reasonable chance of survival and even offspring,
and many more were bought by private masters for domestic and
industrial slavery. It is to be remembered that only the minority
of prisoners would be suitable for the arena and the ergastulum.
Of the 44,000 Salassi sold by Augustus, only 8,000 were men capable
of bearing arms.[2] The women and children of the enemy, and
non-combatants generally, were normally enslaved, not butchered.
They were sometimes employed in the mines, more frequently on
the great estates and as public slaves. Though their ranks were
doubtless decimated by ill-treatment and hardship, a large remnant
must have survived in domestic slavery and have perpetuated their
race.

If, then, the hard conditions adverse to survival were not confined
to western slaves, and if the vigorous western stocks resisted
extermination, we are confronted anew by the problem of Greek
servile names : Do they, after all, provide a safe criterion for oriental
descent ? A conspicuous instance to the contrary is furnished by
the German captives of Germanicus and other members of the
emperor's bodyguard of Germans, among whom we find Phoebus,
Gnostus, Alcimachus, Chloreus, Diadumenus, and Nereus.[3] The
inscriptions collected by Bang, in which the slave's place of origin
is recorded, include various slaves from Spain and other western
regions with Greek names.[4] It is possible, of course, that some of
these are the descendants of imported Greek slaves ; but this explanation is not applicable to Phoebus, alias Tormogus[5] or to any of the
German guardsmen, who are explicitly described as *natione Bataus*,
etc. The problem may best be solved by considering precisely
how the naming of slaves was carried out. As the name and origin

[1] Suetonius, *Augustus*, 21. Cicero, *Tusc. Disp.*
iii, 22, 52.
[2] Strabo, iv, 205.
[3] Dessau *Ins. Sel.* i, p. 352.
[4] *Spain :* Phoebus, Eros, Philocyrius, Carpime ;
Gaul : Syntropus, Phoebe ; *Dalmatia :* Pempte ;

Sardinia : Charito ; *Africa :* Helpis. Cf. *C.I.L.*
vi, 9709 : *T. Flavius Genethlius nummul. de basilica
Julia natione Bess.*

[5] *C.I.L.* vi, 10184, *Phoebus qui et Tormogus
Hispanus.*

of a slave were announced in the slave-market, we must suppose that the slave-dealer provisionally named his own wares, or retained the names with which they were already endowed. The master, however, could re-name the slave at his pleasure, as arbitrarily and fancifully as we name our pet animals or ' villa residences.' *Vernae* were no doubt always named by their master, though, as family life developed among the servile class, the names and even the wishes of the parents may have influenced his choice. Not only do the children of freedmen often bear the name of one or other parent, but the same practice is sometimes observable before manumission : for example, Euodion is the father of *Aurelia Euodia Aug. lib.* (*C.I.L.* vi, 13927) and Tyrannus of *Tyrannus Actes l. verna* (*C.I.L.* vi, 1867a). In the case of bought slaves, the master must have frequently, if not generally, saved himself trouble by retaining the name already borne by the slave, which, if bestowed by the slave-dealer, was probably some popular servile name, suggesting good luck or valuable qualities. As the slave trade doubtless remained largely in the hands of Greeks, whether free merchants or freedmen agents, great numbers of slaves might thus receive Greek names irrespective of nationality. Varro gives an instance of a master naming his slave Artemas after the dealer Artemedorus from whom he was purchased [1] ; the Greek name of a well-known slave-merchant might thus become a commonplace of servile nomenclature. Where the master exercised his own invention, and did not merely choose any popular slave name which happened not to occur among his household, his personal character and interests might be reflected in the names of his slaves. So in *C.I.L.* vi, 13663, Felix the master of Hermes, Euplus, Euangelus, and Abascantus, may have been a merchant, though Philumene and Atticus do not carry the same suggestion. A master who affected Greek culture would be likely to give his slaves Greek names. It has been suggested that in the earlier period of Roman slavery, names may have been borrowed from the *fabula palliata.* [2] We know also that certain names were considered appropriate to particular occupations, and these were applied without any reference to race. Examples of such names have been collected by Friedländer in Appendix xxxix to his *Roman Life and Manners.* Actors often assumed the names of famous predecessors, Pylades, Bathyllus, Paris, Memphis, or names in some way appropriate to their profession, such as Apolaustus, Lepos, Thymele, Favor. The name Amoebeus was thus bequeathed by a celebrated citharoedus, Antigenidas and Glaphyrus by flute-players of note. The recurrence of similar names among gladiators may perhaps point to the same custom. The popularity of Asclepiades among doctors is well-known, and here also the names of famous predecessors were some-

[1] See note 6, p. 99. [2] Lambertz, *Gr. Sklavennamen*, p. 6.

times adopted, such as Erasistratus and Themiso.[1] We have no reason to suppose that Roman masters felt any linguistic scruples in applying Greek names to slaves who were not imported from the Greek-speaking provinces. The Greek language was much more familiar to the average Roman than is French to the average Englishman ; and in the study of servile inscriptions it is noticeable that the master as well as his slave or freedman frequently has a Greek name. So for example the master of the *vernae dulcissimi* Agathe, Helicon, and Eutychus in *C.I.L.* vi, 11222 is called A. Iunius Gamus ; of Elpis in 11650, D. Anicius Philetus ; Grattia Cypare in 4574 names her home-born slave Agathocles. In industrial or commercial slavery especially, the master would usually be either a provincial from the east or much more commonly a freedman with a Greek cognomen. Such a freedman might or might not be Greek-speaking ; but in any case he might well bestow a similar name upon his slave. What was good enough for the master was good enough for his servant.

We may conclude that the prevalence of Greek names among slaves was due to several causes, chief among which was the fact that the organised trade in slaves came to Rome from the countries east of Italy. Greek was the original language of the slave trade, and this is reflected in servile nomenclature, much as the use of French on modern menus and in the names affected by dressmakers suggests the history and associations of particular trades. It was for this reason that Greek cognomina had a servile taint, and were avoided or discarded by families with social ambitions. A contributory cause lay in the attitude of Rome to ' barbarian ' tongues and peoples. The ordinary Roman knew no foreign language but Greek ; his native Latin was unprolific in name-formation, and the Celtic and other languages of the west offended the ears of Graeco-Roman civilization. Meanwhile slaves poured into Italy in ever-increasing numbers, and rendered necessary a corresponding abundance of servile names, such as was only provided by Greek, though in course of time a large number of Latin and Latinised slave names came into being. The inter-marriage of Greek and oriental slaves with those from the west must have further extended the range of Greek nomenclature : Greek and Latin names are not only used indiscriminately in the same household but occur side by side in members of the same family. Thus Callistus and Severa are the children of Alexander and Callistrate, Protus and Hilara of Januarius, Felix and Caletyche of Felicula ; Agathopus and Iucunda name their sons Proclus and Iucundus, Callistus and Silvana have a son Silvanus, Asiaticus and Cupita a daughter Asia. The servile world as revealed in inscriptions is a medley of Greek

---

[1] *C.I.L.* xiii, Pt. iii, vol. 1, p. 601.

and Latin. That large numbers of slaves and freedmen possessing Greek names derived their origin wholly or in part from the eastern provinces, cannot be doubted ; but the possession of a Greek name by a slave is not in itself proof of Greek or oriental nationality.

The Latin names bestowed upon slaves in themselves suggest a problem : Why and how did a people who showed such singular parsimony or lack of invention in coining personal names for their own sons and daughters create a numerous and varied nomenclature for their servants ? Professor Tenney Frank in his investigation of 5,000 examples of servile names finds 2,126 Latin, of which Felix, Hilarus, Faustus, Saluius, Fortunatus, and their feminine equivalents account for over 400, Primus, Secundus and Tertius for 193, Auctus, Vitalis and Ianuarius for over 100, while the remaining two-thirds are composed of a large variety of Latin names. To understand the significance of these, it is necessary to trace the development of servile nomenclature at Rome. In the earliest days, the slave had, officially speaking, no name, but was a mere item in the family property, to which the gentilicium of the family was applied adjectively. But practical necessity and the growth of the household gave the slave, like the dog, a name. The first slaves, being Italian prisoners of war, probably retained the names which they possessed when free ; while the acquisition of large numbers of Greek captives in the south of Italy, and the growing custom of purchasing slaves from the east, soon made Greek names very common among the slave population. The oldest examples of such Greek names are to be found in a list of freedmen from Delos—Heras, Diodotus, Apollonius, Prepon and Nicandrus.[1] Among the earliest instances quoted by Oxé are Pilemo, Pilonicus, Pampilus, Pilotimus, Pilomusus, Pilotaerus, Dipilus, Timotheus, Xenodorus. Compounds of P(h)il- are also numerous in the first volume of the *Corpus*, where Greek servile names preponderate, as also among slaves and freedmen named by Cicero.[2] Nicephor seems to have been a specially favourite early slave name, and Lambertz may be right in thinking that it, together with certain Thracian names such as Auluphor, influenced the formation of the curious cognomina formed from the master's praenomen.[3] Eros Aurelius, i.e. the Eros belonging to the Aurelii, was further described, with the development of individual ownership, as *Marci puer*, the slave of Marcus. Early servile nomenclature, thus emphasised the identity, not of the slave, but of his owners. If Eros was so fortunate as to be enfranchised, and so to become a Roman citizen, he originally dropped

[1] *C.I.L.* iii, 14203.

[2] *P(h)ilemo* : *C.I.L.* i, 570, 571, 602, 734, 1094, 1095, 1104, 1241, 1269 ; *Philargyrus* : i, 721, 726, 729, 1034, 1087, 1203, 1241, 1268, 1305, 1393 ;

Pamphilus, Philetaerus, Philotimus, Philogenes, etc., also occur.

[3] *Nicephor* : Cic. *ad Q. frat.* iii, 1, 5 ; *C.I.L.* i, 570, 1028, 1032, 1041, 1102, 1129 ; vi, 3930. Cf. Lambertz, *op. cit.* note 9, p. 6.

his Greek name, adopted a Latin praenomen in its stead, and con-
verted the final words of his official designation into a cognomen,
Marcipor, much as *seruus publicus* provided the gentilicium *Publicius.*
Oxé in his interesting article on this whole subject[1] has shown how,
from about the time of Sulla, the originally adjectival gentilicium
was assimilated to the master's name in the genitive case, so that Eros
became Eros Aureli M(arci) s(eruus), Eros Aureli and finally, in
imperial times Eros, M. Aureli ser(uus). On the other hand, the
enfranchised Eros became M. Aurelius M. lib. Eros, adopting the
praenomen of his master and securing at once continuity with the
past and distinct identity in the present by retaining his former
slave name as a cognomen. When *puer* had given place to *seruus,*
and this practice of retaining the servile name prevailed, such names
as Marcipor disappeared from among the cognomina of freedmen.
Perhaps the most important and interesting fact in this development
is the transformation of servile names into personal cognomina ;
the gradual process by which the cognomen superseded the praenomen as a personal name began among the freedmen class, and for
this reason many, if not most, of such Latin cognomina are of servile
origin, although some seem to have quickly acquired universality
and respectability, while others never lost the suggestion of slavery.[2]

How, then, did these servile cognomina originate ? Lambertz
describes them as ' in most cases ' translations or synonyms of Greek
slave names, but this is much too sweeping a statement.[3] Felix
may, indeed, correspond to Eutychus, Amatus to Philetus, Venerius
to Aphrodisius, and so on. Primigenius may sometimes translate
Protogenes, and Spes was probably inspired by Elpis. We are
reminded of Caletyche the daughter of Felicula, and of Phosphorus
the son of Lucifer.[4] But the majority of Greek slave-names were
not adapted for such translation, and names of similar meaning
could easily arise quite independently : Geminus is not necessarily
or even probably a translation of Didymus, nor Primus of Protus.
Some slave names (like the old family cognomina), were given as
nicknames, such as Rufio or Capito, which are also found among the
earliest personal cognomina of free men ; while others illustrate the
favourite Roman practice of numbering. (More original was the
expedient of Herodes Atticus, who for educational purposes named
his son's slaves after the letters of the alphabet !)[5] When Italian
slave-merchants and masters began to coin slave-names in their
own language, they showed a strong preference for names indicative
of good luck. These are more likely to have arisen spontaneously

---

[1] See note 1, p. 96.

[2] Schulze, ' Zur Geschichte lateinischer Eigen-
namen,' *Rom. Mitth.* 1904 ; Schwab, ' Nomina
propria Latina a participiis,' etc. *Jahrb. f. class.
Philol.* supp. Band xxiv, p. 637.

[3] Lambertz, *Gr. Sklavennamen,* p. 6.

[4] *C.I.L.* viii, 12941, *Aelia Felicula Felix et
Caletyche fil. mvtri* ; vi, 8724, *C. Iulio Luciferi
filio Pospboro architect. Aug. Claudia Stratonice
uxor uiro optumo.*

[5] Philostratus, *Vit. Soph.* ii, 1, 23.

than by deliberate translation or imitation of such names as Eutyches, Calitychus, Abascantus. Other names indicated the qualities, physical and moral, of the ideal slave : Celer, Vitalis, Hilarus, Iucundus, Suauis, Laetus, Modestus, Pudens. More interesting are the many names without special appropriateness to slaves, among which the participial form of name is prominent. These names derived from participles have been collected and discussed by two German writers, [1] who suggest that the past participle preceded the present in the formation of such names, most of which came into use, like the majority of personal cognomina, at the end of the Republic and the beginning of the Empire. Names derived from the past participle are first found among the slave class, and many of them retained their servile character. Donatus, Datus, Extricatus, Honoratus and others are commonest in Africa; Exuperatus, Exoratus, Expectata, Mandatus, Mansuetus, in Cis-Alpine Gaul and neighbouring countries; Cupitus is characteristic of Noricum, and Avitus of Spain. Some of these names are found most often in Rome itself, such as Acutus, Adauctus, Auctus, Cogitatus, Inventus, Paratus. As such names passed from freedmen to *ingenui* and finally to the Romanized provincials, this evidence of their distribution, being confined to no one period, tells us little of their origin. We may, however, connect such names in Africa with the numerous Carthaginian names derived from those of deities, signifying ' Baal has given,' ' Baal has freed,' ' Melcart has saved,' etc., which also appear with the name of the god unexpressed, as in Muttun, 'given,' (for Muttunbaal). [2] Professor Reid gives Donatus and Rogatus as examples of Latin names which are translations from the Punic, and adds that ' words of good omen taken from Latin, such as Crescens, Faustus, Honoratus, etc., all have their counter-parts' in the language of the Carthaginians. [3] It is perhaps not accidental that such names as Felix, Felicitas, Fortunatus, Faustus, are peculiarly frequent in the two cemeteries of imperial slaves and freedmen at Carthage mentioned above, among whom Donatus, Rogatus, Extricatus, and other participial names also occur. The translation of native names among slaves or provincials in the time of the empire does not, however, concern us here, except in so far as it suggests that some, at least, of the Latin cognomina which first came into use in Republican times by way of the slave-market may have originated in the same way. But this is pure conjecture. A much more probable source of slave-names is to be found in the assimilation of native, particularly Celtic, names to Latin in sound rather than sense. The curious participial names Cogitatus, Dubi-

[1] Schwab and Otto, *Jahrb. f. class. Philol.* suppl. Band xxiv, p. 637.
[2] Gsell, *Histoire ancienne de l'Afrique du Nord*, vol. iv, p. 221, 227. Compare also Arishat,

' betrothed ' (of Baal), with *C.I.L.* vi, 4190, *Sponsa Liviae l.*

[3] *Municipalities of the Roman Empire*, p. 251.

tatus, Restitutus or Restutus suggest the Celtic prefixes Cogi,-
Dubo-, Restu-, and it is conceivable that Mansuetus and
Exuperatus may have been inspired by Celtic names in Masu- and
Esu-. These polysyllabic names, inconvenient for slaves, recall
the cadences of what were possibly their Celtic prototypes. Aucus
would very easily become Auctus, and Ambactus, which occurs
in the form Ambatus, may even have given rise to Amatus.
M. Publicius Sedatus (*C.I.L.* xv, 638) is the namesake of a Pannonian
deity Sedatus ; and other Celtic names, such as Carus, Regina and
probably Albanus, could figure as Latin without any change at all.
The curiously inappropriate and not uncommon slave name Ingenuus
or Ingenus may perhaps be an imitation of some Celtic proper name.[1]
It is possible also that Celtic names were sometimes Graecized by
slave-merchants from the east : for example, Cenomannus would
easily become Cinnamon. Many slaves and freedmen with Celtic
names are recorded in Holder, *Alt-celtischer Sprachschatz* ; and
many more have names which look like Latinized (or less commonly
Graecized) forms of Celtic originals.[2] The Celtic element in the
slave population may well have been much larger than is generally
realised. During the age of imperial expansion, the sale of western
prisoners took place on a vast scale : the wars in the valley of the
Po, Liguria, Corsica, and Sardinia, have been described as mere
slave hunts ; Caesar is said to have captured a million prisoners in
Gaul ; the continual wars in Spain must have poured captives into
the slave market, and whole tribes were sometimes sold into slavery
at one time. It is true that such western slaves, especially the
Spaniards and Sardinians, were apt to prove intractable ; but the
freedom-loving spirit would hardly descend to children reared
in slavery. On the other hand, the slaves of western origin were not
inferior in physical strength, good looks, or intelligence to their
oriental fellow-servants, nor, indeed, to their increasingly mongrel
masters. The majority of them were by no means mere savages.
The Celtic races, who proved so receptive of Graeco-Roman
civilisation in the provinces, must have been assimilated even more
rapidly as slaves, who lived and grew to manhood in an Italian environment. It is certain that they were not all incorporated in the
familia rustica, for which, indeed, the inhabitants of the eastern

---

[1] *Ingenuus* : *C.I.L.* vi, 4278, 4610, 4656 ; *Ingenus* :
v, 1170 ; vi, 3207 ; *Ingenuos* : vi, 13877. Cf.
Dottin, *La langue gauloise*, glossary : *enigeno* :
cf. Irish *ingen* (' daughter '), Ogam *inigena*.
[2] *E.g.*, *Bambix Publ. lb.*, *Craxsantus Barbi
P(ublii) s.*, *Postumia P. l. Battu*, *A. Titio A. l.
Bellico*, *P. Occius P. l. Dunomarus*, . . . *us M. l.
Epicatus*, *Iantulle nuri*, *M. Heluius W. lib. Marsua*,
Sassus Ouincii ; C. Catellius C.l. Licinus, *Reginus
uerna Augustorum*, *C. Iulius Karicus l.*, *M. Valerius
M. l. Cissus*, *L. Furio L. l. Lalo*, etc. Slaves with

purely Celtic names are naturally to be found
chiefly in the Celtic-speaking provinces ; but
Holder includes as of possibly Celtic origin many
apparently Latin or Greek cognomina, such as
Blandus, Dubius, Ilarus, Lasciuos, Cupitus,
Speratus, Macarius, Marturus, and even Pilemo
(to give but a few instances out of many). The
abundance of such names at least shows that the
Celtic stems used in name-formation must have
readily suggested Latin and sometimes Greek
equivalents.

provinces, with their traditional skill in the cultivation of the vine and olive and in other branches of agriculture, were at least as appropriate. The slaves obtained from Asia Minor, Syria and even Greece were by no means all elegant and debased representatives of Hellenistic culture; the general mass of them must have been ordinary workers, some of whom were a byword for their stupidity. Certain western races were found to be specially appropriate for certain tasks, e.g., Gauls for the management of horses[1]; and the artistic skill of Celtic workmen must have been of great value to industrial owners. That slaves from the west might attain to a high degree of culture and even fame is shown by the familiar instances of Terence and Caecilius, and by Licinius, the slave of Caesar, who was destined to be the governor of his native Gaul.

The elusiveness of servile nationality, intensified as it is by the rarity of ethnica and the Latinization of native names, has in itself a highly important significance. On a few inscriptions we find a slave rather pathetically described as *natione uerna.*[2] This was the fate which ultimately overtook the slave population of the empire. Inter-marriage produced a complete inter-mixture of races, and environment quickly obliterated almost all traces of 'barbarous' nationality. The typical slave of the early empire belonged to neither east nor west : he was a product of Graeco-Roman civilisation, an example of Rome's strange power of absorbing and assimilating aliens. His name was Greek or Roman; his speech, Latin; his talk was chiefly concerned with gladiators and chariot-races, the ancient equivalents of 'the pictures'; his ambitions followed humbly or daringly after those of his master. His characteristics were not oriental but servile, resulting from the abnormal conditions of slavery. This denationalisation of the slave played its part for good and evil in the history of the empire. An increasingly large proportion of the free citizens of Rome and Italy, and to some extent of the larger cities of the provinces, came to consist of freedmen and their descendants. Hence precisely that portion of the Roman world from which its government, its culture and its ideas proceeded, was derived to a great extent from a servile class, of no nationality and of a civilisation not their own. The conventionality, the waning literary and artistic inspiration, and the general creeping paralysis of ancient culture may find part of its explanation here.

On the other hand, the slave was by no means merely his own avenger and the destroyer of Rome. He lost the great gifts of nationality, its inheritances and inspirations, its vigorous creativeness, its unique, individual quality ; but he also escaped the limitations of race and tradition, and found it easy to become a citizen of the world. He had one great advantage over the free man—the

[1] Marquardt, *Privatleben*, i, 4, p. 246. [2] *C.I.L.* vi, 10049, 14208, etc.

habit of hard work, and, through the hope of emancipation, a constant incentive to work diligently and well. Work was the saving salt which kept the slave class from utter corruption, and gave it a certain unacknowledged dignity of its own. Moreover, the innumerable sepulchral inscriptions, on which freedmen and their sons record the loss of parent, wife or child (*pater carissimus, coniunx incomparabilis, filius dulcissimus*), suggest that home ties must have had a peculiar preciousness to one who had emerged from the forlorn degradation of slavery.[1] The slave had no *patria*, but emancipation gave him not only a city but a home ; as a freedman, he could contract a legal marriage, his children were citizens, and he could found a Romanised and respectable family. How eagerly this privilege was accepted, how much affection and hope surrounded the children so born, and how tragic was their loss, is revealed even in the abbreviated and laconic grief of ancient grave-stones. It is perhaps not a mere accident that the most charming and beautiful picture of the filial relation in Latin literature is given to us by Horace, *libertino patre natus*. And if the home and its affections—that ancient foundation of Roman greatness—renewed its sacredness in the servile population, it was this same despised and degraded class which first received and transmitted the religion of ἀγάπη. The earliest Christians were for the most part of humble and probably servile descent. It is as the first recipients of the new religion that the slaves and freedmen of the early empire have a claim to the highest historical importance. To Christianity they brought their traditionless cosmopolitanism, their discipline of work and suffering, and that family affection which still smells sweet and blossoms in their dust ; while from Christianity they received at once an inspiration greater than that of race, and a spiritual emancipation as daring as it was triumphant : ' Art thou called, being a slave ? *Care not for it.*'

---

[1] E.g., *C.I.L.* vi, 10791 : d.m. T. Aelius Aug. lib. Saturninus et Aelia Glyconis infelicissimi parentes hunc munimentum comparauimus nobis et T. Aelio Saturnino filio nostro dulcissimo qui uixit annis vi, mensibus viii, dib. xvi, horis vi.

X

SLAVERY IN EARLY GERMANY

WHAT was the character of slavery in pre-Migration Germany, i.e., in the period from Julius Caesar to, say, A.D. 400? What is known of the sources of slavery? And of the slave trade inside Germany? And of the extent of slavery? There is very little evidence bearing on these questions. It is hardly possible to treat the problem of Germanic slavery historically and to show the rise and development of the institution in the different parts of the country. But, such as it is, the evidence will be considered in the following pages. We shall not concern ourselves, however, with the enslavement of Germans in the Greco-Roman world, where they were bought and sold as early as the middle of the second century B.C.[1] Nor shall we deal with the barbarian kingdoms of Gaul in the fifth century A.D. for which the Burgundian and Visigothic Law Codes give us comparatively abundant information: the conditions of slavery there were entirely different from what they had been beyond the Rhine and the Danube.

I.

The division of labour among pastoral peoples the world over is usually very primitive. So it was, too, among the pastoral Germans described by Caesar and Tacitus and among their slaves. Indeed, there is no evidence that domestic slavery existed on any appreciable scale among the Germans, and Tacitus denies that it existed at all.[2]

[1] Fiebiger-Schmidt, *Inschriftensammlung*, nos. 5–6. Comparative studies of slavery in general are few, but there are interesting facts in H. J. Nieboer, *Slavery as an Industrial System* (The Hague, 1910), and G. Landtman, *The Origin of the Inequality of the Social Classes* (London, 1938).

[2] *Germ.* xxv. 1. Observe that xx. 2 proves nothing: the fact that slave and free children grew up together is inconclusive for the existence of domestic slaves, cf. Homer, *Od.* xv. 363 ff. In Seneca, *Ep.* xlvii. 10 the MSS. reading is *Mariana*. The first reference to male domestic slaves in Germany dates from the fourth century: see no. 26 below. For females see Salvian, *Epistle* i. 6, who also mentions a domestic servant hired by Frankish women living inside the Imperial frontier.

But in this the historian undoubtedly exaggerates: women could be, and unquestionably sometimes were, put to spinning and weaving and to the heavy task of grinding corn. But there was little that could profitably be done in the households by adult male slaves, though a *princeps* would, no doubt, highly prize a Roman slave with specialized knowledge, and particularly a Roman with some skill in metallurgy. The overwhelming majority of such male slaves as existed were put to work on the land; and when Tacitus speaks of the character of Germanic slavery he suggests that it was wholly agricultural and pastoral. Hence, for a reason which we shall mention later (p. 23, below), each slave was given his own house or indeed ' home ' (*penates*), as Tacitus puts it, and of this he was in practice the master. His obligation to his owner was confined to paying him at unspecified intervals a quantity of grain, cattle, or cloth. Accordingly, he had an interest in developing his land and could presumably profit from an increase in production. But although in some ways he resembled a Roman tenant farmer he was in fact a real slave, and it is misleading to refer to him as a serf. True, whipping and binding were rare by the standards of developed Roman slavery, but the German slave could be whipped and bound and he could be sold and killed with impunity at his owner's whim.[3] And he passed in inheritance along with cattle, horses, and other forms of property.[4] But the slaves did not work in the gangs with which the Romans were familiar, nor did they work on the land side by side with their masters and the free women-folk. The omission of reference to slaves in Tacitus, *Germ.*

[3] Tacitus, *Germ.* xxiv. 4, xxv. 1–2, cf. Agathias, *Hist.* ii. 7. Incidental references to slavery will be found in Tacitus, *Germ.* xxxviii. 2, xl. 5, xliv. 3. Early forms of slavery should not be idealized: idem, *Ann.* xiv. 44. 4 ' suspecta maioribus nostris fuerunt ingenia servorum etiam cum in agris aut domibus isdem nascerentur caritatemque dominorum statim acciperent ' —the fact is implicit in the very nature of slavery.

[4] Idem, *Germ.* xxxii. 4 *familiam.* But Anderson on xxv. 1 (p. 129 of his edition) goes beyond the evidence when he says that ' the serf [*sic*] was bound to the soil and passed ... with the estate '.

xv. 1, is not an accident or an oversight. The historian
says there that the bravest warriors took no part in agricultural work, but left the care of their fields to the
womenfolk, the elderly, and the weak (i.e., children, the
maimed, etc.). There is no reference to slaves, though
these warriors were the very persons who were most likely
to own slaves. The fact is that the only form of agricultural
slavery of which Tacitus had knowledge is that which he
describes in *Germ.* xxv. 1,[5] whereby the slave was given
his own *penates* and largely lived his own life.

II.

As for the sources of slavery, there was no enslavement
for debt, for loans on interest were unknown.[6] The
enslavement of gamblers who had staked their freedom
on the throw of a dice can hardly have supplied more than
a small proportion of the slaves who could be found in
Germany.[7] Leaving aside those who were born into slavery
—and our authorities never certainly refer to them [8]—
there can be no doubt that warfare, which is by far the
chief source of slavery in primitive societies, provided the
majority of the slaves who existed in Germany in the times
of Caesar and Tacitus; and frequent reference is made in
Roman literature to Romans who had been enslaved in
Germany after having been captured in war.[9] But when

[5] Somewhat similar forms of slavery to that described by Tacitus,
Germ. xxv. 1, have been observed in Africa: Landtman, op. cit. 272.

[6] *Tacitus, Germ.* xxvi. 1.

[7] *Ibid.* xxiv. 4. Similar phenomena have been observed in several parts
of the world: Landtman, op. cit. 233 f., R. H. Barrow, *Slavery in the Roman
Empire* (London, 1928), 247, so that the doubts of R. Much, p. 229 of
his Commentary, are unnecessary.

[8] Tacitus, *Germ.* xx. 2, is not necessarily evidence for the breeding
of slaves: compare the passage with Homer, loc. cit.

[9] Tacitus, *Ann.* xii. 27. 4, cf. i. 61. 6 *vincula elapsi*, Dio Cassius, lvi.
22. 4, lxxi. 13. 2, who also speaks (*ibid.* 16. 2) of the sale of Roman prisoners
by the non-Germanic Iazyges, a pastoral people. With the trick mentioned
in the second of these passages of Dio cf. Helmold, *Chron. Slavorum* i. 56
' de captione hominum relaxaverunt omnes senes et inutiles, ceteris retentis,
quos servicio robustior aptaverat etas '.

primitive societies go to war they usually fight against their neighbours, and so their prisoners come from homes which are not very far away. Hence they cannot easily be prevented from escaping from their servitude unless they are first sold to slave-dealers, who will transport them to some distant region or people whence escape will be difficult. Generally speaking, before there can be substantial numbers of slaves at work in primitive societies there must be a slave trade.[10]

III.

In Caesar's day the Suebi allowed foreign traders to enter their territory so as to sell them the booty which they had taken in war.[11] It is probable that this booty consisted in the main of their prisoners, for articles of personal adornment would usually be kept by the warrior who picked them up, while captured cattle too would tend, for the most part, to be retained in a society where cattle were the measure of wealth and prestige. It appears to follow that a slave trade with the outside world, with Gallic merchants, had developed by the middle of the first century B.C. It also appears to follow that the supply of slaves taken in Suebic wars might exceed the demand for them at home. It does not necessarily follow, however, that the use of slave labour by the Suebi was very small, probable though this may be on general grounds, for the Suebi too were a predominantly pastoral people. Caesar's remark, in fact, seems to supply evidence for the export of slaves by the Suebi, but not for their use at home or for their importation into Germany.

Such information as exists about the slave trade inside Germany itself shows the slaves being sold from one people to another until at last they were sold to the Romans on

[10] On this point see esp. Nieboer, op. cit. 209 f., 287 ff., 408 ff.

[11] Caesar, B.G. iv. 2. 1. For the export of slaves from the Empire to Germany see Digest, xlix. 15. 27, where we learn that Roman brigands would sometimes kidnap Roman slaves who would subsequently arrive among the Germans across the frontier.

the Rhine.[12] Several cases are known to anthropologists
of peoples in various parts of the world who, while not
themselves keeping slaves, nonetheless procure slaves in
war and sell them to neighbouring powers that do keep
slaves.[13] The existence of a slave trade in Germany, then,
may have been a pre-requisite, as we have said, for the
substantial use of slaves, but it is not in itself proof of the
existence of large numbers of slaves there. In·the cases
of which we have knowledge little or no effort seems to
have been made to put the slaves to work in any of the
communities through which they passed. The slaves were
bought for ré-sale, and the general movement of the trade
was towards the Roman frontier: the slaves gravitated
towards the Rhine. There were good prices to be had for
slaves on the Roman frontier, so that a German might well
calculate that it would be more profitable for him to sell
his slave to the Romans than to try to keep him at home
in the conditions described by Tacitus. And it would
also be tempting to sell him to the Roman merchants,
who were coming into Germany in the first century A.D.,
in return for some of the new and attractive commodities
which they were offering for sale.

IV.

Some Germanic peoples killed off their prisoners, or at
any rate, their adult male prisoners, after a campaign.[14]

---

[12] Tacitus, *Agric.* xxviii. 5, *Ann.* ii. 24. 5, cf. Ambrose, *de Officiis* ii.
137 (Migne, *P.L.* xvi. 148 f.). Note also the incident of the ' Indians '
reported by Pliny, *N.H.* ii. 170, and Pomponius Mela, iii. 5. Other passages
relating to the slave trade in Germany are Tacitus, *Germ.* xxiv. 4, and Amm.
Marc. xxix. 4. 4, where Severus crosses the' Rhine in 371, reaches Wiesbaden,
' et quia suspicabatur venalia ducentes mancipia scurras [what is the
precise meaning of that word?], casu illic repertos, id quod viderant, excursu
celeri nuntiare, cunctos mercibus direptis occidit '. The traders were
evidently Germans, and since the slaves were spared they may have been
Roman provincials. But who were the prospective purchasers?

[13] Landtman, op. cit. 259 f., with references.

[14] Tacitus, *Ann.* xiii. 56. 6, Amm. Marc. xxviii. 5. 13, Ambrose, loc.
cit., Orosius, v. 16. 6, Zosimus, v. 5. 6.

Now it is an exceedingly common practice among primitive people to kill the warriors of a beaten enemy and to enslave the womenfolk and the children. But this practice is common only at the lower stages of agricultural development. At the higher stages the frequency of the custom drops sharply and is replaced by an equally sudden rise in the practice of enslaving the captured warriors: the technique of agriculture has now become so advanced that it is possible and profitable to put able-bodied men to work as slaves on the land in considerable numbers, and machinery has come into existence for retaining the slaves in their bondage.[15] The inference would seem to be that the Germanic economy and with it the means of repression were at some places and times throughout the Roman period too primitive to absorb and retain considerable numbers of slaves.

But could a Germanic people have kept numbers of Germanic slaves? These would probably understand the language of their owners, of their fellow-slaves,[16] and of the surrounding peoples. If they were prisoners of war their kinsmen might live not very far away and so would not be altogether inaccessible. Since there were vast areas of uncultivated land and of forest and marsh a fugitive could very often elude his pursuers and make his escape to his own people.[17] In these conditions how could masses of Germanic slaves be prevented from combining and escaping if they were not chained in gangs? But in the absence of large estates and of constant, extensive building and mining operations there is no likelihood that gangs of

[15] See some interesting statistics in L. T. Hobhouse, G. C. Wheeler, and M. Ginsberg, *The Material Culture and Social Institutions of the Simpler Peoples* (London, 1930), 232 f.

[16] On this point see Plato, *Legg.* 777 C (cf. Athenaeus, vi. 87), Synesius, *de Regno* 24 B.

[17] For a case where the Romans removed newly caught barbarian prisoners to overseas provinces far from the frontier where they had been captured, see *Cod. Theod.* v. 6. 3, Sozomen, ix. 5. 6. But even the Romans sometimes made mistakes in this connexion: Dio Cassius, liv. 5 and 11.

slaves existed in Germany.[18] The chances of a slave's escaping are reduced if he is marked or mutilated on the face, hand, or the like, so that he is easily recognised to be a slave. But there is no evidence for such mutilation in early Germany (though the free Suebi distinguished themselves from their slaves by a distinctive hair-style).[19] It follows that it cannot normally have been easy to prevent slaves from escaping unless they were Romans or unless they belonged to some other non-Germanic people. This is not to deny, of course, that there were *any* German-born slaves in Germany. The outlaw, the man whose dialect differed markedly from that of the region in which he was enslaved, the man whose kin had been annihilated, the member of a retinue whose leader and fellow-*comites* had been wiped out—these and anyone who for any reason was without protection could easily enough be enslaved, and they could be retained in their slavery provided that they were given some interest in the land—and slaves in Germany were given precisely such an interest (p. 18, above). When the slave-owner gave a ' home ' to his slave, this was not due to any innate mercifulness on his part: it was a necessity if the slave were to be kept at all, particularly a German slave. There was no other machinery for holding him in bondage. We may conclude that, although the existence in Germany of a trade in slaves facilitated the task of enslaving Germans, it scarcely looks as if anything like a majority of the slaves were Germans.

It does not follow, however, that every Roman prisoner who was carried off into Germany was inevitably enslaved when he was not put to death or sacrificed to the gods or sold or ransomed. In the great raids of the mid-third century, the Visigoths carried off a large number of Roman

---

[18] If the embankment mentioned by Tacitus, *Ann.* ii. 19. 3, has been correctly identified at Leese on the Weser it was a structure 1,800 metres long, 2½ metres high, and 10 metres broad : see G. Bersu and others, *Prähistorische Zeitschrift*, xvii (1926), 100–31. Was this built by war prisoners? If so, they may have been put to death on the completion of the work.

[19] Tacitus, *Germ.* xxxviii. 2.

provincials, many of whom were Christian; [20] and their descendants continued in the faith. But these descendants, and, therefore, presumably the original captives, do not all appear to have been slaves. When the Visigothic leaders decided to persecute the Christians in their country in 369–72 they 'expelled' them from Gothia and drove them into the Roman provinces.[21]   But slave-owners would not have driven away their own property gratuitously; and it seems a reasonable inference that a number of Roman prisoners were kept in conditions which could not be described as slavery. We do not know whether they cultivated a given proportion of their holdings for the benefit of the Visigothic optimates. But if they settled on the land and worked it they would enhance its value and so would increase the wealth and manpower of the community; and they would, therefore, be of service to the Visigothic leaders.

V.

We can only argue on the basis of such evidence as exists, however trifling it may be. In view, then, of the restriction of household slavery to females, the tendency of the slave trade to convey slaves from the interior of Germany to the Roman frontier for sale to the Romans, the known cases of the killing of prisoners or, at any rate, of adult male prisoners, the total absence of chain gangs, and the difficulty of preventing large numbers of Germanic slaves from escaping—in view also of the constant demand for slaves on the Roman frontier, and the ease and profit with which they could be disposed of there, it seems fair to conclude (a) that the number of slaves in pre-Migration Germany was small, and (b) that such slaves as did exist

[20] Philostorgius, *H. E.* ii. 5, Syncellus, p. 716, ed. Bonn, cf. Zosimus, i. 28. 1.
[21] Jerome, *Chron.* a. 371.

there were largely non-Germanic. Whether there was at
any time a prestige value in owning slaves, as there was
in owning cattle, is unknown; but it may be thought that
the keeping of slaves was for the most part confined to
the *principes*, for owing to their activities in the *comitatus*
they would have more opportunities than the common
warriors of obtaining prisoners of war from among distant
peoples, and they would also be better able to afford to
pay a Roman trader the price of a slave. It is worth noting
that during the actual Migrations themselves the general
picture was probably not very different. Poor Roman
freemen might occasionally be enslaved by the barbarians:
they would be useful for carrying burdens.[22] And in 406
the more well-to-do, at least, of the Visigoths owned slaves
who served in wartime with their masters.[23] But few
prisoners can have been kept permanently as slaves by the
rank and file of the warriors, for in the conditions of the
invasions, when food was often in short supply and the
means of producing it were often limited, a slave would
have been little more than another hungry mouth to feed.
The great value of prisoners was that they could sometimes
be ransomed or even sold off to Roman slave dealers, who
did not hesitate to buy and enslave Roman freemen who
had been taken prisoner by the barbarians.[24] Even when
the invasions were at their height in the fourth and fifth
centuries the age-old export of slaves from the German
camps to the Roman dealers still continued.

[22] *Carmen de Providentia Divina*, 57 f. (Migne, *P.L.* li. 618).

[23] *Cod. Theod.* vii. 13. 16. Stilicho was able to set free a considerable
number of enslaved Romans in 402 when he captured the Gothic camp at
Pollentia: Claudian, *B.G.* 83 f., 616–22, cf. Amm. Marc. xxxi. 16. 3 *captis*,
Prudentius, *In Symm.* ii. 732–5.

[24] Ambrose, *de Officiis* ii. 70 and 137 (Migne, *P.L.* xvi. 129, 148 f.),
with which cf. Digest, xlix. 15. 6. See also *Cod. Theod.* v. 7. 2, *Const.
Sirmond.* xvi. For this sort of slave trade with the Vandals in 439, see
Theodoret, *Ep.* lxx. (Migne, *P.G.* lxxxiii. 1240), and for similar trade with
the Huns in 452, see Maximus of Turin, *Homily* xcvi. (Migne, *P.L.* lvii.
475 ff.), cf. *Nov. Valentin.* xxxiii. For other ways in which a barbarian
invasion could lead to the enslavement of Roman by Roman, see *Cod.
Theod.* v. 6. 2, x. 10,. 25.

VI.

If it is true to suppose that the number of slaves in Germany, as a whole, was small, it is also true that there were two areas where we may suspect that this was not always the case. There is evidence which seems to suggest that there were large numbers of slaves among the Marcomanni and Quadi north of the middle Danube towards the end of the second century A.D. and also among the Alamanni in what had once been called the Decumates Agri in the middle of the fourth century. In a treaty with the Marcomanni, M. Aurelius once demanded the return of 13,000 prisoners of war and deserters; and this was not the total number of them who were among the barbarians at that time. On another occasion the Quadi undertook to restore no fewer than 50,000 prisoners; and it is known that some prisoners of the Quadi were enslaved, though others were sold.[25] The keeping of such enormous numbers of prisoners suggests a widespread use of slave labour. As for the Alamanni, the Caesar Julian tried again and again during his campaigns in Gaul to recover the Roman provincials who had been carried off in the great invasions of 354-5 and on other occasions.[26] Men, women, and children alike, had been carried off and enslaved ; [27] and the aged were put to death, an indication that the Alamanni did not take prisoners merely in order to hold them to ransom. Some of the prisoners appear to have been kept behind in Gaul to work as slaves in the fields which the Alamanni had occupied there before Julian's arrival, though, on the whole, the settlers proposed to work the

[25] Dio Cassius, lxxi. 11. 2, 13. 4, cf. lxxii. 2. 2, 3. 2, Amm. Marc. xvii. 12. 16.

[26] Amm. Marc. xvii. 10. 4, 7, xviii. 2. 19, Libanius, *Or.* xii. 50, xviii. 77, 78, 89, Eunapius, frag. 13 (who reports that an Alamannic tribal chief carried off 3,000 prisoners in a single raid), Zosimus, iii. 1. 1, 4.4, 5. 1, *Paneg. Lat.* iii (xi). 4. 1, cf. Eugippius, *Vita S. Severini* xix. For the possession of domestic male slaves by the Alamannic optimates, see Amm. Marc. xviii. 2. 13, xxvii. 10. 4.

[27] Libanius, *Or.* xiii. 31.

land with their own hands.[28] And in the end Julian wrote
that he recovered no less than 20,000 Romans from the
barbarians.[29] No doubt many of these prisoners would
have been sold to other parts of the Germanic world or
even to Roman slave-dealers; but the evidence is so
remarkable that we can scarcely resist the conclusion
that there was a demand for slaves among the Marcomanni
and Quadi and among the Alamanni at these times which
was far greater than anything that we might justifiably
assume for the Germany of which Caesar and Tacitus
speak.

But these are precisely the two areas which were far
more advanced socially and politically than any other parts
of contemporary Germany. It is hardly necessary to argue
the point. The Marcomanni and Quadi had been romanized
to a degree which was unknown elsewhere among the
northern barbarians in the period of the early Empire.
Indeed, their culture was so highly developed that it ' set
its stamp on the whole of the archaeological material of
northern Europe during the beginning of the first century ',
and the Marcomanni ' must be given a prominent position
during the Early Empire which can only be compared to
that of the Goths during the Later '.[30] It was among the
Marcomanni that the old system of social organization
described by Tacitus was overthrown for the first time
(so far as we know) in Germany and was replaced by the
monarchical rule of Maroboduus. Again, although the
majority of the Alamanni lived in hovels or in homes
with ' frail enclosures ', often grouped in villages,[31] an
invading Roman army came upon a more striking
phenomenon in one region of Alamannia close to the

[28] Idem, xii. 48, xviii. 34, *Paneg. Lat.* iii (xi). 4. 1.

[29] *Epist. ad Athen.* 280 C. The figure of 11,000 is mentioned by Zonaras,
xiii. 10, p. 204.

[30] G. Ekholm, *Cambridge Ancient History*, xi, 57 f.

[31] Amm. Marc. xviii. 2. 15, 19, xvii. 10. 7, SHA. *Maximin.* xii. 1, cf.
Herodian, vii. 2. 3 f., and see also P. Reinecke, *XVIII Bericht d. röm.-
germ. Kommission* (1933), 166, cf. Amm. Marc. xxxi. 10. 12 f.

o

Rhine. When Julian penetrated into this district in 357 his men were able to plunder ' villas rich in cattle and crops ' and ' dwellings carefully constructed in the Roman fashion ', no doubt in stone; and before burning them the troops rescued some Roman prisoners from them.[32] Now, as used by so excellent an authority as Ammianus Marcellinus, who had himself served on the Gallic frontier in 355–6, this word *villa* has a very definite meaning: it indicates that there were economic units here of an unexpectedly high degree of development and complexity. Apparently some Alamanni lived on large estates, and the presence here of Roman prisoners suggests that some at least of the labour employed on these estates was provided by slaves. These villas may well have been confined to this one part of Alamannia, and there is evidence that among the Alamanni the land (or some of it) continued to be held communally by the kindreds for many centuries after Julian's time.[33] But the estates found there by Julian will have formed nuclei from which the use of slave labour radiated out over much of the country. The anomalous position of the Alamanni in this respect is due to the fact that they lived in what had once been Roman territory, and to some extent they had inherited Roman social ·relations.

The two areas of the Germanic world, then, where slavery was comparatively highly developed, at any rate for a time, are precisely the two areas where Roman influence was most extreme, and the economy and the social organization most advanced. Hence it would be illegitimate to generalize about the extent of slavery in Germany as a whole from what can be inferred about slavery in Marcomannia and Alamannia. These two exceptional cases, however, may serve as a reminder

[32] Idem, xvii. 1. 7. These villas have not been revealed by archaeology, which attests only untiled, wooden or mud houses and none in which stone or plaster were used: so Reinecke, art. cit. 167, cf. Herodian, loc. cit.

[33] *Lex Alam.* lxxxiv.

that even in other parts of Germany slavery may have shown a temporary increase after a war with the Romans in which it had been possible to take numbers of Romans prisoner. But the increase could only have been temporary, for there was no place in the primitive Germanic economy for droves of slaves. There is no reason to suppose that slave labour was the characteristic form of labour inside pre-Migration Germany. It was sporadic and exceptional and was not an essential part of the social system.

E. A. THOMPSON

XI

COMMENT ET POURQUOI FINIT L'ESCLAVAGE ANTIQUE[1]

Dans le monde romain des premiers siècles, l'esclave était partout : aux champs, à la boutique, à l'atelier, à l'office. Les riches en entretenaient des centaines ou des milliers ; il fallait être bien pauvre pour n'en posséder au moins un. Non certes que la main-d'œuvre servile eût le monopole d'aucune activité, si humble fût-elle ; beaucoup d'artisans étaient de condition libre ; d'innombrables champs étaient cultivés par des paysans, petits propriétaires ou fermiers, qui n'avaient jamais été la chose d'un maître ; c'était au libre prolétariat de Rome que Vespasien réservait les rudes besognes qu'il refusait aux machines. Il n'en est pas moins vrai que ni la vie matérielle des sociétés gréco-romaines, ni leur civilisation même, dans ce qu'elle eut de plus exquis, ne sauraient se concevoir sans le secours de ce travail forcé. Les Germains eux aussi avaient leurs esclaves, serviteurs ou ouvriers de culture. L'Europe des temps modernes, par contre, à quelques rares exceptions près, a ignoré, sur son propre sol, l'esclavage. Pour sa plus grande part, cette transformation, une des plus profondes qu'ait connues l'humanité, s'est opérée très lentement, au cours du haut moyen âge.

I

A l'époque des invasions et aux premiers temps des royaumes barbares, il y avait encore, dans toute l'Europe, beaucoup d'esclaves, davantage selon toute apparence qu'aux premiers temps de l'Empire.

La grande source de l'esclavage avait toujours été la guerre. C'étaient les expéditions victorieuses des légions qui, au temps de la Conquête romaine, avaient peuplé les ergastules de l'Italie. De même, à partir du IVe siècle, les luttes incessantes de Rome contre ses ennemis, les combats

---

1. Nous publions ce bel article tel que nous l'avons trouvé dans les papiers de Marc Bloch. Avec ses lacunes. « — Que vous auriez pu et dû combler ? » *Pu*, non, et *dû*, pas le moins du monde. Nous avons soumis le texte de Bloch à l'une des plus hautes autorités de notre pays en matière de médiévisme : impossible, nous dit-il, sans refaire un travail formidable, de substituer aux blancs laissés par Bloch à la page 36 le nombre absent des tenanciers de Saint-Germain ou de Saint-Rémi qu'il devait posséder par devers lui — et par conséquent d'établir les proportions que Bloch comptait établir. Dans ces conditions, le parti de publier le beau texte de Bloch en respectant ses lacunes était le seul qui s'imposât.

N. D. L. D.

que ceux-ci se livrèrent souvent entre eux, les brigandages des soldats régu-
liers ou des bandits professionnels (pas plus que dans la Chine actuelle, la
distinction n'était toujours aisée) accumulaient aux mains tantôt d'un parti,
tantôt d'un autre, ce butin de chair et d'os qui, lorsque la fortune chan-
geait de camp, n'était que bien rarement rendu. « Il n'est pas de maison,
si médiocre soit-elle, où l'on ne trouve un esclave scythe », — entendez,
conformément au vocabulaire habituel de l'auteur, un esclave goth, —
écrivait, vers l'an 400, l'Africain Synésius. Il pensait aux régions orientales de l'Empire, les seules qu'il connût par expérience. Mais remplaçons
goth par un terme plus général, tel que barbare ; nul doute que, sous
cette forme, l'observation ne conservât sa vérité pour tout le monde encore romain. Quant aux envahisseurs eux-mêmes, nous savons qu'un
grand nombre d'habitants de la *Romania*, de tout rang, avaient été
réduits par eux en servitude. Dans la vie de saint Séverin, qui donne
comme le journal de siège des petites villes danubiennes, sans cesse me-
nacées par les peuplades germaines établies aux alentours, ces razzias de
captifs apparaissent à l'état d'incident courant. Au hasard des textes,
nous entrevoyons quelques destinées tragiques, auxquelles beaucoup d'autres ont dû ressembler : songeons à cette grande dame de Cologne, qui,
prisonnière des Barbares, les servit longtemps comme esclave, ou à cette
autre dame gallo-romaine qu'enlevèrent des brigands : ils la mirent en
vente sur le marché de Clermont. Le sort des fuyards n'était pas toujours
meilleur ; parmi les errants que le malheur des temps avait jetés sur les
routes de la *Romania*, plus d'un, victime des populations mêmes auprès
desquelles il avait cherché refuge, tomba dans l'esclavage.

L'homme de guerre, à qui son épée gagnait des captifs en grand
nombre, ne les gardait pas tous à sa suite ; le principal profit qu'il en
attendait était d'en faire commerce. Des Barbares venaient aussi offrir,
sur la terre restée romaine, des esclaves de sang romain : le cas était si
fréquent qu'en 409 une loi impériale ne put que reconnaître la validité
de ces ventes — mais sous réserve que l'esclave puisse toujours racheter
sa liberté, soit en remboursant à son nouveau maître la somme dont il
avait été payé, soit en le servant durant cinq années. L'invasion de
l'Illyrie et de la Thrace avait, au dire de saint Ambroise, dispersé dans
« le monde entier » des hommes à vendre. Plus tard, Grégoire le Grand
put voir les Lombards emmener, « la corde au cou, comme des chiens »,
les prisonniers qu'ils avaient faits au cours d'une expédition sur Rome,
et pour lesquels ils pensaient trouver acquéreurs dans le royaume des
Francs. Les grands troubles de l'Europe avaient eu pour effet une recru-
descence de la traite. La pauvreté des populations agissait dans le même
sens. En dépit des lois romaines, les pères vendaient leurs enfants : le fait
est signalé au VIᵉ siècle, en Corse. Alors qu'au Iᵉʳ siècle de notre ère,
période de paix et de prospérité, Pline le Jeune se plaignait que la main-
d'œuvre servile se fît rare, — alors qu'au IIIᵉ siècle encore, l'esclave coû-
tait assez cher, — au début du moyen âge la marchandise humaine était
redevenue abondante et de prix accessible.

Le commerce s'en poursuivit, très actif, pendant toute l'époque des
royautés barbares et jusqu'aux temps carolingiens. Grands négociants
devant l'Eternel, les Juifs y prenaient une part importante, mais ils
n'étaient pas, tant s'en faut, les seuls à le pratiquer. Les vies des saints,
les lois, les formules en font constamment mention. La Grande-Bretagne,
en particulier, déchirée par des guerres fréquentes — celles des rois

anglo-saxons entre eux ou contre les populations de langue celtique, elles-mêmes en proie à des luttes intestines — fournissait au continent beaucoup d'esclaves : jusqu'en Provence et à Rome même. Sur les terres des riches, des esclaves de toute origine se coudoyaient : barbares aussi bien que romains. Objets d'échanges courants, ils servaient de prix dans les transactions, alors si nombreuses, où la monnaie ne paraissait point, sinon comme étalon et parfois comme appoint. Les textes nous montrent tel Gallois acquérant un champ contre remise d'une épée, d'un cheval et d'une femme saxonne. Enumérant les principales « espèces » qu'ont coutume de vendre les marchands, un capitulaire cite l'or, les étoffes, les esclaves. Non seulement d'un pays à l'autre de l'Europe on voyait circuler les caravanes des traitants ; mais, dans sa balance commerciale, le bétail servile comptait parmi les principaux produits d'exportation ; elle en envoyait de grandes quantités vers l'Espagne musulmane ; elle en expédiait, en moindre nombre, peut-être, par Venise, mais aussi par les plaines de l'Est, vers l'Orient grec ou arabe.

A y regarder de près cependant, des symptômes très clairs attestent que, dès le ixe siècle, l'esclavage était loin de tenir dans les sociétés européennes une place comparable à celle qui, précédemment, avait été la sienne. Pour comprendre et peser ces signes de décadence, il faut d'abord s'efforcer de retracer les vicissitudes que connut, depuis la fin de l'époque romaine, l'utilisation économique de la main-d'œuvre servile.

⁎

Deux méthodes s'offraient au maître désireux de tirer parti de la force vivante que le droit mettait à son entière discrétion. La plus simple consistait à entretenir l'homme, comme on fait d'un animal domestique, et, de même encore que pour l'animal, à user, en tout arbitraire, de son travail. Mais l'esclave pouvait aussi être établi à son propre compte ; le maître, en ce cas, lui laissant la charge de son entretien, prélevait, sous des formes diverses, une part de son temps et des produits de son activité. Or, dès les derniers siècles de l'Empire, ce second procédé se répandit de plus en plus.

Jusque dans l'industrie, les deux procédés étaient entrés en concurrence. Les riches, qui possédaient de grandes troupes d'esclaves, avaient toujours recruté dans leurs rangs des ouvriers domestiques, s'épargnant par là, pour beaucoup de travaux et d'objets, le recours au salariat ou au commerce ; l'usage persistait au ixe siècle. Mais, une fois satisfaits les besoins de la maison, disposait-on d'un surplus de main-d'œuvre dûment qualifiée ? De tout temps on s'était efforcé de lui trouver, dans la production pour le marché, un débouché rémunérateur. Ce pouvait être en instituant de vastes ateliers, où les esclaves que le propriétaire de l'outillage faisait vivre peinaient sous ses ordres et à son seul profit. On rencontre çà et là, dans le monde romain des premiers siècles de notre ère, de véritables manufactures : telles, en Gaule, les célèbres fabriques de poterie de la Graufesenque et de Lezoux ; il est probable qu'à côté d'ouvriers libres, elles comptaient des travailleurs serviles qui, tantôt appartenaient à l'employeur, tantôt étaient loués par lui à d'autres maîtres. Ces établissements déclinèrent à partir du iiie siècle. Non qu'il ne subsistât encore beaucoup d'ateliers seigneuriaux ; mais ils ne fournissaient plus guère que le domaine lui-même. Les ateliers impériaux, de même, ne livraient leurs produits qu'à l'Etat. Les demandes du marché avaient toujours été couvertes surtout par la petite entreprise ; celle-ci désormais ne trouva plus de concurrent. A ce régime d'artisanat, le maître, en mal d'emplois pour des bras qu'il ne pouvait souffrir de laisser oisifs, devait forcément se plier. L'esclave exerçait sa profession pour le public, se nourrissait et se vêtait sur ses gains, et versait au maître le reste sous des formes diverses, souvent fixées à l'avance. Cette pratique, vieille comme le petit métier, était devenue assez générale pour qu'il eût paru nécessaire de régler le problème juridique qu'elle soulevait : dans le monde barbare lui-même, la loi des Burgondes s'en préoccupe.

Mais ce fut surtout dans l'agriculture que la transformation s'avéra profonde. Les petites exploitations rurales, indépendantes ou non, avaient toujours occupé une large part du sol de la *Romania* — sa plus large part, probablement, sauf dans quelques régions de l'Italie. Leur personnel servile était naturellement très restreint. A côté d'elles, au début de l'ère chrétienne, d'immenses domaines que cultivaient, par bandes, de véritables armées d'esclaves, comparables aux nègres des plantations coloniales modernes. Vers la fin de l'Empire, ce système fut généralement abandonné. Les grands propriétaires, prélevant sur leurs biens de vastes espaces, les morcelèrent en une multitude de petites fermes, dont les occupants, sous des formes diverses, payaient loyer. Parmi les bénéficiaires de ces lotissements figurèrent un grand nombre d'esclaves, enlevés aux équipes centrales, pour être chacun pourvu, sous sa responsabilité propre, de ses champs particuliers. Certains avaient été affranchis, au moment même de leur établissement. Beaucoup d'autres, tout fermiers qu'ils étaient devenus, demeuraient juridiquement dans leurs conditions premières. Assurément, le type de l'esclave-tenancier n'était pas de tous points inédit. Il se rencontrait, notamment, depuis longtemps, sur les moyennes propriétés, dont les possesseurs ne pouvaient guère courir le risque de trop vastes entreprises. Mais sa généralisation était un fait nouveau.

Morcellement du *latifundium*, déclin des manufactures serviles, ces phénomènes, s'ils intéressent au premier chef l'histoire de l'esclavage, la dépassent évidemment de beaucoup. Ils se ramènent en somme au triomphe de la petite sur la grande entreprise. Lequel d'ailleurs ne saurait à lui seul rendre compte de tous les changements qui affectèrent alors l'emploi de la main-d'œuvre servile. Rien ne serait plus inexact que de parler d'un anéantissement total de la grande entreprise rurale. La création de petites fermes avait considérablement amoindri l'étendue des réserves d'exploitation directe ; elle ne les avait pas fait disparaître. Vers la fin de l'Empire, et jusqu'au IXe siècle, la plupart des grands seigneurs fonciers conservaient encore sous leur administration propre d'importants terrains de culture. Or, là même, les procédés de mise en valeur s'étaient modifiés.

Certes, le maître n'avait pas cessé de nourrir, loger et vêtir des esclaves, sans cesse à sa disposition, qui l'aidaient à cultiver ses champs. Mais ils suffisaient de moins en moins à la tâche ; ce fut aux tenanciers, dont les terres étaient placées sous la mouvance du domaine principal, que fut désormais demandé, sous forme de services obligatoires, le plus clair du travail nécessaire à sa prospérité : les uns sans doute, petits paysans, anciennement habitués à vivre sous la dépendance d'un puissant détenteur du sol ou qui graduellement y étaient entrés ; les autres, depuis peu établis sur les nouveaux lotissements. En abandonnant une partie de son fonds, le grand propriétaire s'était, par là même, assuré les forces humaines qu'exigeait le reste. De ces tenanciers de date récente, beaucoup, on l'a vu, étaient des esclaves. Ils continuaient à peiner pour le maître ; mais ils n'étaient plus entretenus par lui, pas plus qu'un patron, aujourd'hui, n'entretient ses ouvriers ; la terre qui leur avait été cédée — soumise en outre à des redevances, qui ne nous importent pas ici — était comme leur salaire, dont ils devaient vivre.

**

Quelles considérations avaient donc engagé les possesseurs d'esclaves, gardant en main d'aussi vastes exploitations, à préférer désormais le système détourné de la corvée au procédé, en apparence plus pratique, de l'utilisation directe du bétail humain ?

Dans toutes les sociétés qui ont fait usage du travail servile, en grand et sous sa forme la plus simple, — celle des *latifundia* romains, celle des plantations aux Indes Orientales, — son emploi a répondu à des conditions toujours pareilles, qu'imposait impérieusement sa nature même. L'esclave est mauvais travailleur ; son rendement a partout été estimé assez bas. Il représente, en outre, un capital essentiellement périssable. Le patron qui, aujourd'hui, par mort ou maladie, se voit privé d'un ouvrier, aura peut-être, si le marché de la main-d'œuvre est défavorable, quelque difficulté à le remplacer ; mais s'il le remplace, il n'aura subi aucune perte, puisque le salaire, quel que soit l'homme, demeurera égal à lui-même. Le maître, dont l'esclave mourait, tombait malade ou tout bonnement vieillissait, devait au contraire en acheter un autre ; il perdait, tout net, la somme dont il avait payé le premier. Certes, on pouvait, pour combler quelques vides, faire fond sur les esclaves nés dans la maison même. Non pour les combler tous. De tous les élevages, celui de l'homme est le plus délicat. Ces inconvénients n'avaient pas grande gravité aussi longtemps que la marchandise servile restait abondante et donc de prix peu élevé. Pour faire peu de besogne, on gaspillait beaucoup d'esclaves ; l'un d'eux venait-il à manquer, il n'était ni malaisé ni coûteux de lui trouver un substitut. Tel était l'état de choses qu'avaient créé, vers le début de l'ère chrétienne, tant de guerres victorieusement poursuivies par Rome ; il explique l'existence de grandes équipes serviles. Mais, bientôt, le recrutement des esclaves se fit plus difficile. Leur valeur s'accrut. *Ce fut alors qu'on se tourna vers le régime de la tenure.*

Supposons l'esclave établi à son compte sur une petite ferme. Comme il vit en familles mieux organisées, sa race se perpétue plus sûrement ; sur les champs qui lui sont cédés, son travail est de qualité meilleure ; car les redevances devant, bon gré mal gré, être payées, c'est de sa propre peine que dépend le surplus de produits, auquel est attachée sa vie. Restaient les services obligatoires sur les terres du maître. Leur rendement n'était sans doute pas excellent, et peut-être fut-ce là une des causes qui, bien plus tard, à partir du xe siècle, amenèrent, à leur tour, leur abandon ? On pouvait du moins espérer que, désireux de ne pas se voir enlever cette tenure, qui ne lui était attribuée que moyennant l'exécution de ces corvées, l'esclave-fermier s'acquitterait de sa tâche moins mal que celui qui mangeait au râtelier commun. Le renouveau de la traite, à l'époque des invasions, provoqua-t-il çà et là un retour à l'ancien usage, par vastes ateliers ruraux, de la main-d'œuvre servile ? Les documents sont trop imprécis pour nous permettre de l'affirmer ou de le nier. Le certain est qu'il n'y eut pas de révolution de grande ampleur. Le pli était pris.

Aussi bien les chefs germains, aux mains de qui tombèrent, à ce moment, tant de beaux domaines étaient-ils préparés à adopter ou à continuer le système de l'affermage ? Ils le trouvaient dans les traditions de leurs peuples. Dans l'ancienne Germanie, les conditions économiques générales n'étaient pas favorables à la grande entreprise, quelle qu'elle fût. Le noble, le riche y disposaient de beaucoup de terres, où abondaient les friches, et d'esclaves nombreux, souvent conquis à la guerre ; pour mettre en valeur tant bien que mal ces vastes étendues, pas d'autre moyen que de les morceler ; pour nourrir tant d'hommes, qu'il n'eût pas été commode d'entretenir au foyer du maître, force était de leur assigner à chacun un lot. A une époque où l'esclave-fermier était encore une rareté en Italie, Tacite en notait déjà la fréquence au delà du Rhin.

Or, cet esclave-fermier restait bien, sans doute, par son statut personnel, un esclave. A l'époque carolingienne encore, les monuments législatifs s'efforcent de mentionner la distinction entre le *servus* et les autres dépendants de la seigneurie, tels que les colons. Sur beaucoup de terres, alors que les corvées dues par les hommes libres étaient généralement fixes, le seigneur se réservait le droit d'exiger des tenanciers de condition servile leur travail toutes les fois qu'il le jugeait bon, « quand il leur serait commandé » ; leurs femmes — et leurs femmes seules — semble-t-il, étaient convoquées à l'atelier seigneurial, pour y ouvrer ensemble, aux ordres du maître, et seules lui fournissaient des étoffes de lingerie. En pratique, cependant, la destinée de l'esclave, ainsi établi sur une petite exploitation dont la conduite lui était confiée, différait beaucoup de celle qu'évoque le mot même d'esclavage. Il ne versait au maître qu'une part des produits de son activité ; il ne lui donnait qu'une part de son temps (car, lors même que les corvées étaient théoriquement illimitées, la nécessité, où le maître était de laisser au corvéable les loisirs nécessaires pour tirer de la tenure et de quoi vivre lui-même et de quoi payer les redevances, empêchait évidemment qu'elles n'occupassent toutes ses journées). Il ne vivait pas toutes ses heures sous les ordres d'un autre homme ; il avait son toit à lui et son foyer ; il dirigeait lui-même la culture de ses champs ; s'il était particulièrement ardent à la besogne ou particulièrement adroit, il se nourrissait mieux que son voisin — ou bien, dans la mesure où il y avait un marché, il y vendait des denrées. Les institutions juridiques elles-mêmes ne tardèrent guère à reconnaître les particularités de son sort. Comme il était un de ces travailleurs du sol, dont l'effort importait avant tout à la prospérité de l'Empire, les lois du IVe siècle défendaient au maître — comme elles le faisaient pour le fermier libre — de l'enlever à sa tenure. Sans doute cette règle de « l'attache à la glèbe » ne fut-elle que peu de temps observée ; elle sombra dans la ruine de l'Etat impérial qui l'avait proclamée. Mais, entre les esclaves « chasés » — c'est-à-dire pourvus chacun d'une maison (*casa*) et des terres attenantes — et ceux qui ne l'étaient point, le droit carolingien marque une distinction qui n'est point sans importance : les premiers sont tenus pour biens immobiliers, les seconds rangés parmi les meubles. Les règles qui présidaient à leur aliénation étaient donc fort différentes. Surtout, dès la seconde moitié du IXe siècle, la coutume de la seigneurie, qui, dès longtemps, à défaut de loi écrite, passait pour régler les rapports du seigneur et des dépendants de condition libre, étend sa protec-

tion à l'esclave-tenancier ; au pouvoir arbitraire du maître se substitue
l'empire d'une tradition locale, souvent très dure, mais qui, en principe,
s'imposant au supérieur comme à l'inférieur, prévient ou devrait prévenir
les oppressions nouvelles. Même au regard du droit strict, la condition du
servus casatus différait beaucoup du pur esclavage. Du point de vue de
l'économie, l'emploi qui était fait de ses forces ne répondait plus du tout
à la définition ordinaire de la main-d'œuvre servile.

***

Il y a plus. Non seulement le genre de vie de beaucoup d'esclaves
s'était de bonne heure écarté du type ancien. Leur nombre même dimi-
nua très rapidement. Pour saisir le phénomène, c'est au ixᵉ siècle qu'il
convient de se placer. Trouée de lumière, ou, pour mieux dire, de clair-
obscur, entre deux grandes nuits, il nous offre, dans ses censiers seigneuriaux, les éléments d'une statistique bien imparfaite encore et surtout bien fragmentaire ; mais ni les siècles qui le précèdent ni ceux qui
le suivent ne nous en rapportent le moindre équivalent. Des esclaves non
chasés, nous ne possédons, à vrai dire, aucun dénombrement. Quelques
textes — le règlement de l'abbaye de Corbie ou l'état des biens de Notre-
Dame de Soissons — énumèrent les serviteurs qui recevaient d'un maître la pitance journalière ; mais, préoccupés avant tout de fixer l'ordre
des distributions, ils négligent de marquer, à l'intérieur du personnel qui
y participait, les différences de statut. En ce qui regarde, par contre, les
esclaves chasés, les renseignements sont précis à souhait. Sur les terres
de Saint-Germain-des-Prés, vers la fin du règne de Charlemagne ou le
début de celui de Louis le Pieux, vivaient   tenanciers de
tout sexe et de tout âge ;   seulement appartenaient à la condition servile. Sur les terres de Saint-Rémi de Reims, vers le milieu du
siècle, la proportion était de   sur   Sans doute ces
données ne valent que pour la Gaule et l'Italie. Des indices sûrs nous
permettent cependant d'affirmer qu'en Germanie la situation était ana-
logue. Pour l'Angleterre, il faut, si l'on veut disposer de chiffres certains, descendre jusqu'à l'époque du Domesday Book, c'est-à-dire l'année
1078. Comme l'évolution de la société anglaise semble avoir été sensiblement en retard sur celle du Continent, — où en 1078, nous le verrons,
on n'eût presque plus trouvé d'esclaves, — ce décalage dans la date des
documents n'a pas grand inconvénient. Le Domesday Book ne dénombre
en tout et pour tout, que...

Réduits à ces données, rien, à la vérité, ne nous permettrait d'affirmer que les esclaves tenanciers aient vu, au cours des temps, leurs rangs
s'éclaircir. Elles laissent, en effet, la porte ouverte à une autre interprétation : ces rangs n'avaient-ils pas été en tout temps clairsemés ? Mais pous-
sons plus loin nos observations. Sur les seigneuries de la Gaule franque et
de l'Italie, la plus grande partie du sol abandonnée aux petites exploitations, dépendant du domaine central, était découpée en tenures indi-
visibles, qu'on appelait généralement des « manses ». Ceux-ci n'étaient
pas tous de même nature : diverses catégories s'opposaient, soumises cha-
cune à des charges caractéristiques. La classification la plus répandue
prenait son point de départ dans le statut personnel de l'occupant ; selon
que celui-ci était esclave ou de condition libre, le manse — pour nous en
tenir ici à l'essentiel — était dit servile ou ingénuile, et imposé en conséquence. Du moins tel avait été le principe originel. A partir d'une

époque que, pour des raisons dont on trouvera l'exposé plus loin, on peut estimer avoir coïncidé, en gros, avec la chute de l'Empire romain, on cessa de maintenir entre la condition de l'homme et celle de la terre cet exact parallélisme. Quelle que fut la situation juridique du tenancier, le manse conserva dès lors sa qualité première, ingénuile ou servile selon les cas, et demeura astreint aux obligations que cette épithète exprimait : en sorte que la répartition des manses entre leurs différents ordres subsistait comme le témoin géologique d'une répartition de personnes, depuis longtemps effacée.

Or, sur les terres de Saint-Germain-des-Prés, au ix⁰ siècle, de manses serviles   seulement étaient réellement aux mains d'esclaves ; sur celles de Saint-Rémi de Reims, les chiffres sont d'une part   , de l'autre   . Evoque-t-on l'hypothèse d'un simple va-et-vient des tenures entre des groupes humains qui seraient demeurés chacun d'une importance égale ? De fait, on rencontre des manses ingénuiles qui ont passé à des esclaves : mais ils sont en quantité beaucoup plus faible :   sur un total de   à Saint-Germain ;   à Saint-Rémi. Visiblement c'était bien le nombre des esclaves tenanciers, dans leur ensemble, qui avait diminué : à ce point que beaucoup des lots qui avaient jadis été constitués en leur faveur se trouvaient maintenant occupés par des hommes libres. Que s'était-il produit ? Il serait absurde de penser que parmi les tenanciers d'autrefois on ne sait quelle mystérieuse déchéance physiologique eût atteint les esclaves, et les esclaves seuls. Très certainement les hommes libres qui exploitaient des manses originellement créés pour des esclaves étaient, en grande majorité, les héritiers directs des détenteurs primitifs. Mais, à un moment donné, la famille avait reçu sa liberté. Et sans doute — puisqu'aucune relation obligatoire n'existait plus entre la qualité de la terre et celle de son possesseur — parmi les tenanciers de manses ingénuiles s'était-il glissé, à côté d'esclaves encore attachés à leur servitude, des descendants d'esclaves, dorénavant affranchis.

Aussi, bien que les affranchissements aient été, à l'époque des royautés barbares, extrêmement nombreux et qu'ils se soient appliqués à des groupes très étendus, c'est ce que les textes mêmes, malgré de terribles lacunes, ne nous permettent pas d'ignorer. Non seulement il n'est guère de type d'acte dont les recueils de formules à l'usage des notaires nous offrent plus de modèles ; mais nous en connaissons assez d'exemples, pris à la vie même, pour ne pouvoir douter de leur fréquence ni de leur ampleur. D'où vient que tant d'esclaves aient alors reçu leur liberté ?

II

La nécessité de répondre à cette question nous amène à faire intervenir un facteur dont l'influence sur la pratique sera toujours infiniment délicat à peser : les représentations d'ordre religieux.

A vrai dire, une circonstance favorable va, pour une fois, simplifier notre tâche : nous plaçant au seuil du moyen âge, nous avons la chance de ne plus trouver devant nous une doctrine en devenir, avec tous les mouvements contradictoires que ce stade ne manque jamais de comporter. Dès ce moment, le christianisme occidental avait fixé ses positions vis-à-vis de l'esclavage ; telles elles étaient au temps des grands conciles contemporains de la Paix de l'Eglise ou lorsqu'écrivait Grégoire le Grand, telles pour l'essentiel (et en dépit des modifications de forme introduites par la renaissance de la dure sociologie aristotélicienne) nous les retrouvons inspirant la pensée d'un Thomas d'Aquin, d'un Luther ou d'un Bossuet. Le problème avait deux aspects, selon qu'on envisageait les sources de l'esclavage ou l'institution déjà formée. On ne pouvait omettre de se demander dans quelles conditions il était légitime — s'il l'était jamais — de réduire une créature humaine en servitude. Cette première difficulté résolue, l'existence, dans la société, de nombreux esclaves qui, dès longtemps (et souvent à titre héréditaire), étaient attachés à leur condition, demeurait une indéniable réalité : en face de cet état de fait, quelle ligne de conduite adopter ? Réservons le premier point. Envers les esclaves d'ores et déjà asservis, l'attitude de l'opinion religieuse la mieux autorisée se résuma en quelques préceptes très nets, que voici.

Que l'esclavage en soi fût contraire à la loi divine, nul n'en doutait : tous les hommes ne sont-ils pas égaux en Christ ? Dans cette thèse primordiale, les païens passés au christianisme pouvaient reconnaître une idée que leurs philosophes et leurs jurisconsultes leur avaient rendu familière, et qui d'ailleurs n'avait pas été sans action sur la pensée chrétienne elle-même ; seulement, là où l'Eglise parlait de loi divine, le paganisme avait dit droit naturel. Le parallélisme était si évident que dès l'époque carolingienne on voit les théologiens tendre à identifier les deux notions. Gardons-nous de sous-estimer la valeur pratique du principe d'égalité ainsi proclamé. Mais, s'il pouvait entraîner à mieux traiter les individus, voire même à les traiter d'une façon qui contrastait avec l'emploi classique de la main-d'œuvre servile, il fallait, bien entendu, qu'il n'attaquât point l'institution elle-même dans ses racines. A le prendre à la lettre, c'est l'édifice social tout entier qui eût croulé : toutes les hiérarchies et la propriété même n'étaient-elles pas frappées de la même condamnation théorique ? Sans doute, devant Dieu, l'esclave était l'égal de son maître, tout de même qu'en pleine conformité avec les leçons de l'Eglise l'empereur Louis le Pieux, dans un capitulaire, se disait l'égal de ses sujets. Le maître, pas plus que le souverain, cependant, ne songeaient à abdiquer leur autorité et personne ne l'exigeait d'eux. Le droit naturel avait toujours été conçu comme susceptible d'être corrigé par les règles propres à chaque Etat. Quant aux accommodements auxquels devait se plier la loi divine, les théologiens avaient, dès les premiers siècles, appris à les justifier par le mythe de la Chute. La loi n'avait régné sur terre qu'avant la grande tragédie du couple ancestral ; tous les méfaits de la société étaient la suite du péché originel. « Ce n'est pas la nature qui a fait les esclaves », écrivait, sous Louis le Pieux, l'abbé Smaragde de Saint-Mihiel, mêlant ainsi les deux vocabulaires, païen et chrétien, « c'est la Faute » ; et déjà au VIe siècle, Isidore de Séville : « La servitude est un châtiment infligé à l'humanité par le péché du premier homme. » La pensée de saint Augustin, pénétrée jusqu'après sa conversion d'éléments dualistes, a dominé le moyen âge, dont la religion, même maintenue dans les chemins prudents de l'orthodoxie, n'a jamais — dans la conception du diable notamment — répudié je ne sais quel tour manichéen. La Cité du Diable seule est de ce monde ; la Cité de Dieu appartient à l'au-delà : tel était bien, en effet, toute idéologie mise à part, le sentiment profond qui exerçait son empire sur les âmes. Puisque la vie présente n'est qu'un lieu de passage transitoire, et par définition mauvais, puisque la grande affaire ici-bas est de se préparer à la Vie Eternelle, entreprendre de réformer, de fond en comble, l'ordre social établi, dans l'espoir d'amener le triomphe d'un bonheur en lui-même impossible, ne saurait être qu'une œuvre vaine ; bien plus, un gaspillage sacrilège de forces qui devaient être réservées pour une tâche plus urgente et plus haute. A qui se penche sur la mentalité médiévale — qu'on l'envisage dans la pensée ou dans l'action — il convient de ne jamais perdre de vue cet arrière-plan mystique ; toutes les consciences n'y étaient point également sensibles, ni surtout n'en percevaient la présence avec une intensité égale, à tous les moments de la vie ; il n'en donnait pas moins constamment aux réalités qui nous semblent par excellence la matière concrète de notre effort (la nature, la société) le caractère à la fois fantomatique et fugace d'un décor prêt à tomber.

Ce n'est pas à dire, bien entendu, que, dans les cas traditionnels, la pratique des vertus chrétiennes ne fût impérieusement commandée. Mais chaque condition avait les siennes et le devoir était d'en accepter le tour particulier. La parole de saint Paul demeurait la loi de l'Eglise.

Par là même, la légitimité de l'esclavage était reconnue. Elle paraissait si évidente à saint Augustin que, rencontrant sur sa route la règle du droit hébraïque, d'après laquelle l'esclave de religion juive doit être affranchi d'office, au bout de six ans de service, il se donnait beaucoup de mal pour expliquer comment la Nouvelle Loi en empêchait l'application à l'esclave chrétien. Les conciles de l'époque franque bornent leurs ambitions à interdire l'exportation des esclaves, — surtout leur vente au delà des mers, c'est-à-dire chez les musulmans ou les païens, — et à interdire aux Juifs la possession ou le commerce d'esclaves chrétiens, dont il fallait, contre des conversions possibles, protéger la foi. Aussi bien, les membres du clergé à titre individuel, et l'Eglise elle-même devenue, en tant qu'institution, un très grand propriétaire, possédaient des esclaves en grand nombre. Çà et là sans doute, quelques isolés avaient de la notion d'égalité première tiré des conséquences plus hardies. On prit soin de les condamner. En 324 (?), dans un canon que reproduiront inlassablement les collections occidentales, le Concile de Granges avait proclamé : « Si quelqu'un, sous prétexte de pitié, engage l'esclave à mépriser son maître, à se soustraire à la servitude, à ne pas servir avec bonne volonté et respect, qu'il soit anathème. » La vie pratique posait aux prêtres des cas de conscience ; les autorités ecclésiastiques leur donnèrent des solutions conformes, à la fois, à la charité chrétienne et à l'ordre établi. Est-il loisible, demandait-on à Raban Maur, de dire des messes pour un esclave fugitif, mort pendant sa fuite, en état de péché par conséquent ? Certes, répondit Raban ; mais il convient en même temps de ne pas oublier que tant que l'esclave vit, les docteurs du Christ ont pour obligation de l'exhorter à retourner près de son maître. En 916 enfin, le concile d'Altheim, se référant d'ailleurs inexactement à un texte de Grégoire le Grand, ne craignait pas d'assimiler l'esclave fuyant son maître au clerc qui abandonnait son église — pour les frapper tous deux d'un égal anathème.

Il y a plus. L'existence même de masses importantes d'esclaves posait devant l'Eglise, en tant que corps, un problème délicat. Devait-on les admettre à la prêtrise ? La question ne semble pas avoir été évoquée avant le IVᵉ siècle. Dès le moment où elle le fut, la réponse apparaît ce qu'elle devait demeurer toujours : uniformément négative. Le principe d'égalité avait fléchi devant des considérations d'ordre disciplinaire, dont le clergé, sous peine de mentir à sa mission, ne pouvait faire fi. Comment un homme, que la loi plaçait sous la domination absolue d'un maître, eût-il conservé l'indépendance nécessaire aux dispensateurs des sacrements ? Le danger avait été d'autant mieux ressenti que, malgré les prescriptions répétées des papes et des conciles, les ordinations d'esclaves ne manquaient pas de se produire, en pratique, de temps en temps, et que leurs conséquences fâcheuses étaient par là constamment présentes aux yeux. Ce souci de dignité, sinon l'horreur de je ne sais quelle tare originelle, attachée à la servitude, était si bien le motif véritable de l'interdiction qu'on la voit pareillement appliquée, dans le royaume mérovingien, aux colons, qui étaient juridiquement des hommes libres, mais étroitement soumis à un grand propriétaire ; aussi bien l'affranchissement suffisait à la lever — à moins qu'en vertu des conditions mêmes de l'acte l'ancien esclave ne demeurât dans une sujétion trop rigoureuse vis-à-vis de son maître de naguère. Il n'en était pas moins vrai qu'en barrant ainsi aux esclaves l'entrée des ordres l'Eglise une fois de plus accentuait l'esclavage.

⁎

Ce n'était cependant pas une petite chose que d'avoir dit à « l'outil pourvu de voix » (instrumentum vocale) des vieux agronomes romains : « tu es un homme » et « tu es un chrétien ». Ce principe avait inspiré la législation philanthropique des empereurs, au temps du paganisme, comme après le triomphe de la foi nouvelle. L'Eglise ne l'oublia point. La maxime de saint Paul, après tout, était à double tranchant ; elle s'adressait aux maîtres comme aux esclaves. Sans doute ne savons-nous pas très bien dans quelle mesure les maîtres écoutèrent l'avertissement et, si l'on en juge par les textes des conciles et des pénitentiels, l'effort des ecclésiastiques pour le rappeler aux oublieux ne semble pas avoir été très soutenu. Au ixᵉ siècle, Réginon de Prum invite les évêques à se préoccuper, dans leur tournée pastorale, de la conduite des possesseurs d'esclaves ; mais c'est seulement pour les exhorter à priver de la communion, pendant deux ans, ceux qui auraient tué sans jugement ; les mauvais traitements courants lui paraissent vraisemblablement indignes d'attention. Un peu plus tôt, en Grande-Bretagne, le Pénitentiel dit de Théodore, renouvelant en quelque sorte la législation romaine sur le pécule, défendait au maître d'enlever à l'esclave l'argent que celui-ci avait gagné au prix de son labeur : symptôme significatif de l'évolution sociale, qui tendait à assurer à la main-d'œuvre servile un sentiment d'indépendance économique. Tout cela n'allait pas très loin. Un fait beaucoup plus important fut la validité religieuse reconnue aux mariages que contractaient les esclaves. Par là la législation ecclésiastique consolidait ces ménages organisés que multipliaient, sur les grands domaines, les nécessités de la vie pratique ; au mouvement général qui transformait l'esclavage, elle apportait son aide. Surtout, l'affranchissement, que la morale païenne des derniers siècles avait toujours tenu pour un geste miséricordieux, passa au rang d'œuvre pie. Puisque Dieu avait fait tous les hommes originairement égaux, puisque, par surcroît, le Christ avait souffert pour tous également et qu'au prix de son sang il les avait à sa façon affranchis de la servitude du Péché, donner la liberté était pour le maître, non un devoir impérieux, mais du moins un acte infiniment recommandable, par où le fidèle, se haussant jusqu'à imiter la vie parfaite du Sauveur, travaillait pour son salut.

A en croire, en effet, les préambules des chartes de « manumission » que nous a laissés en grand nombre l'époque barbare, nul autre motif n'en eût inspiré les auteurs. Chacun sait que cette phraséologie ne doit jamais être prise à la lettre. Les raisons qu'un homme donne publiquement de ses actes ne sont pas toujours, tant s'en faut, celles auxquelles il obéit dans le secret de son cœur. Aussi bien, face à face avec un problème pratique précis — l'affranchissement de ses propres esclaves — l'Eglise elle-même dut se préoccuper de mettre fin à des générosités intempestives ; ses biens étaient en principe inaliénables et il n'appartenait pas à un de leurs administrateurs provisoires d'en disposer, fût-ce pour satisfaire au souci, en l'espèce égoïste, de son propre salut. Deux canons de concile, cités par Réginon de Prum et sans cesse reproduits par la suite, défendent à l'évêque, s'il ne dédommage d'abord son église sur ses biens personnels, d'en affranchir les esclaves, et à l'abbé d'octroyer la liberté à ceux qui avaient été donnés à ses moines. Il serait puéril cependant de nier que l'idée de l'autre monde, de ses peines et de ses récompenses ait contribué à inspirer plus d'un affranchissement. Parmi ceux que nous avons conservés, beaucoup font partie de dispositions testamentaires. L'usage était déjà en faveur à l'époque romaine ; nul doute pourtant que le christianisme n'ait grandement contribué à le répandre. A l'heure où l'angoisse de l'au-delà étreint avec une force inaccoutumée l'âme prête à s'échapper, où l'homme aussi considère avec plus d'indifférence que par le passé ces biens temporels dont il ne jouira plus, il était naturel que, fût-ce aux dépens de ses héritiers, le riche possesseur d'esclaves songeât à se procurer le bénéfice d'une charité finale. Ces considérations eussent-elles cependant suffi à bouleverser l'ordre social ? On le croira d'autant plus difficilement que, si libérer des esclaves était incontestablement bien agir, les conserver sous sa domination n'était pas, après tout, mal agir. Les affranchissements, une bonne œuvre : incontestable vérité ; mais, à elle seule, impuissante à en expliquer la fréquence : si celle-ci a été à ce point considérable, c'est qu'en même temps qu'une bonne œuvre — caractère auquel les maîtres étaient loin d'être indifférents — l'affranchissement constituait une opération à laquelle les circonstances économiques du moment avaient retiré tout danger, pour ne laisser à découvert que ses avantages.

**

Rien de plus complexe, en apparence, que le droit de l'affranchissement, à l'époque barbare. Les formes de l'acte ne variaient pas seulement selon les pays ; elles présentaient, à l'intérieur de chacun d'entre eux, une grande diversité. C'est que sur les sociétés de ce temps pesait l'héritage de passés juridiques multiples. Tantôt on usait de procédés venus des vieilles coutumes de la Germanie ; tantôt — fût-on personnellement d'origine et de loi germanique — on avait recours à ceux du droit romain qui, toujours vivant dans l'ancien Empire, Grande-Bretagne exceptée, unissait de lui-même les apports de la législation et de la doctrine classiques avec des pratiques nouvelles, répandues par le christianisme. Chaque tradition offrait ses rites propres, plus ou moins transformés au cours des temps ; la tradition latine, par surcroît, une phraséologie stéréotypée qui, traversant les âges, devait s'appliquer, après les esclaves du haut moyen âge, aux serfs des siècles postérieurs. Mais si, négligeant le détail des modalités juridiques, nous nous en tenons aux suites concrètes de l'acte, nous voyons les différents types se grouper en deux grandes catégories : les recueils de formules les distinguent sous les noms expressifs d'affranchissements avec ou sans obéissance, *manumissio cum* ou *sine obsequio* : le seul contraste qui, du point de vue de la structure sociale, importât véritablement.

Il pouvait arriver que le maître, faisant de son esclave un homme libre, le déchargeât à jamais de toute obligation envers lui. Il lui ouvrait, comme disent certains actes, les quatre voies du monde. Le cas était rare. Ni la tradition romaine, ni la tradition germanique ne lui étaient favorables.

A Rome, non seulement la descendance de l'affranchi devait, avant d'avoir accès au droit de cité, attendre que deux générations se fussent écoulées ; l'usage du patronat la maintenait, à l'ordinaire, presque à l'infini, dans la dépendance de l'auteur de l'affranchissement et de ses successeurs. Chez un grand nombre de nations germaines — Francs, Saxons, Lombards, Bavarois — l'esclave, débarrassé de la servitude, n'entrait pas, pour cela, de plain-pied dans le peuple même. « Lite » ou « alduin », il demeurait, de père en fils, confiné dans une situation juridique inférieure, en même temps qu'attaché au maître de naguère et à sa postérité ; pour l'arracher à ce statut, il fallait, si on le jugeait bon, un nouvel affranchissement. Aussi bien, dans une société troublée comme celle des royaumes barbares, au sein d'Etats où la protection, théoriquement exercée par le pouvoir central, semblait, en pratique, si lointaine et presque dérisoire, l'absolue indépendance risquait d'être le plus souvent tout autre chose qu'un avantage : l'homme alors (surtout l'homme du commun) répugnait moins à accepter un chef qu'il ne redoutait de se trouver dépourvu de défenseur. Et pour qui l'isolement eût-il été plus redoutable que pour l'ancien esclave, dépourvu de famille légale ?

Une charte lombarde, donnant la parole aux affranchis eux-mêmes, met dans leur bouche ces mots : « Vulpo, Mitilde, leurs fils, leurs filles et leur descendance ont dit qu'ils ne voulaient pas des quatre routes et se contentaient, pour leur liberté future, de la recevoir sous la tutelle et protection des prêtres et diacres de Sainte-Marie-Majeure de Crémone. » Les formules de cette sorte sont rarement tout à fait sincères ; on peut croire cependant qu'ici le notaire n'était pas un trop infidèle interprète de la pensée de Vulpo et de beaucoup de ses semblables... L'intérêt des affranchis comme celui des possesseurs d'esclaves contribuait à généraliser la manumission « avec obéissance » — une obéissance qui revêtait, bien entendu, un caractère héréditaire. Tantôt c'était l'ancien maître lui-même qui se réservait le bénéfice de ces pouvoirs nouveaux ; tantôt il cédait ses droits à un tiers qui, le plus souvent, se trouvait être une église. OEuvre de piété en lui-même, l'affranchissement le devenait, dans ce dernier cas, doublement, puisqu'il s'accompagnait d'une donation aux serviteurs de Dieu. L'*obsequium* ne consistait pas seulement dans un devoir général de sujétion, aux contours plus ou moins vagues, avec, pour contre-partie, une promesse de soutien. Il comportait ordinairement des charges très précises, tantôt spécifiées par l'acte d'affranchissement lui-même, tantôt prescrites par une coutume de groupe connue de tous. Traditionnellement, les affranchis de droit franc, les « lites » et probablement leurs congénères des autres droits germaniques versaient à leur pa-

tron, tête pour tête, une sorte d'impôt annuel — en nature ou en argent
— fixé une fois pour toutes. Dans les sociétés barbares, ce chevage prit
peu à peu une valeur très générale ; on s'habitua à l'exiger de toutes
sortes de dépendants — en toute première ligne des affranchis, sans distinction entre les modalités de la manumission. Fréquemment le patron
se réservait une certaine part des successions ; parfois aussi il prélevait
une taxe à l'occasion des mariages. Surtout l'esclave libéré avait le plus
souvent été, dès le temps de son esclavage, un tenancier ; sorti de servitude, il conservait naturellement sa tenure, soumise aux obligations coutumières ; ce pourquoi affranchir un esclave s'exprimait parfois dans les
textes sous cette forme : en faire un colon, entendez un tenancier, de condition libre, mais encore soumis très étroitement au maître de la terre.

Or, de tout temps sans doute, dans le monde romain comme en Germanie, les maîtres avaient su apprécier les profits divers, dans l'ordre
des revenus matériels comme dans celui de l'influence sociale, que leur
réservait, octroyée par leurs soins, une liberté si judicieusement donnée.
Est-il besoin de rappeler la part des affranchis dans les clientèles, soutien,
à Rome, de la grandeur de l'aristocratie ? Mais les conditions propres
à la société du haut moyen âge rendaient ces avantages plus sensibles
que jamais, en même temps qu'elles tendaient à atténuer les inconvénients qui en avaient été longtemps la contre-partie. De plus en plus,
c'était sous la forme détournée de redevances et de corvées que l'on s'ha-
bituait à utiliser la force du travail servile ; affranchi, le tenancier ne
rapportait pas moins, en pratique, qu'au temps de sa servitude. Le chevage, les droits sur la succession et le mariage compensaient vraisemblablement les services qu'il était d'usage de ne réclamer qu'aux esclaves.

Aux affranchissements, les maîtres parfois demandaient-ils plus que
de ne leur rien coûter ? Faisaient-ils d'aventure payer la liberté ? Avides
de voir tomber la barrière juridique et morale qui les séparait des hommes libres, disposant d'ailleurs, pour peu qu'ils fussent chasés, d'un
petit pécule personnel, les esclaves probablement n'étaient pas incapa-
bles d'acheter un bien à leurs yeux si précieux. Les chartes de manumission, à vrai dire, ne semblent pas signaler jamais de prix versé ; mais
l'exemple de ce qui plus tard devait se passer pour le servage nous
apprend que, dans ce genre d'actes, auxquels on tenait à conserver les
apparences d'une œuvre pie, on répugnait beaucoup à introduire des
mentions aussi terre à terre, alors même qu'elles répondaient à la réalité. Il n'est donc pas impossible que les affranchissements aient quelquefois fourni à leurs auteurs l'occasion d'ajouter aux rentes périodiques
dont ils chargeaient l'homme et sa terre un gain supplémentaire, une
fois perçu ; on ne saurait pourtant affirmer qu'il en fut ainsi, ni surtout
déterminer une fréquence. Ce qui est sûr, c'est que, de ces générosités,
apparentes ou réelles, le maître tirait des bénéfices d'une autre sorte qui,
pour ne pas comporter une évaluation en argent, n'en étaient pas moins
tenus pour fort appréciables. Dans la société, à beaucoup d'égards
anarchique, de ces premiers siècles du moyen âge, les liens de sujétion
personnelle avaient pris une importance extrême. Grouper autour de soi
un grand nombre de dépendants, — non des esclaves, mais des hommes
libres, aptes à siéger dans les assemblées judiciaires et qualifiés pour
paraître à l'ost, — la puissance et le prestige étaient à ce prix. L'affranchissement « avec obéissance » prenait place dans la gamme, très variée,
de ces relations de seigneurs à suivants, et fournissait même certains

P

de ses traits à plusieurs d'entre elles, dont la raison d'être première était autre. Tout poussait donc à les multiplier : l'intérêt bien entendu, le souci d'être un chef, le soin de la vie future. Comment s'étonner s'ils étaient très nombreux ?

Ainsi l'esclavage était comme un réservoir qui, constamment, se vidait par le haut, à un rythme accéléré. Mais, pour qu'il cessât d'y avoir des esclaves, il fallait évidemment que ces pertes manquassent à être compensées, ou du moins atténuées, par un afflux à la base, en d'autres termes que le recrutement même de la population servile vînt définitivement à se tarir. Car, ne nous y trompons pas, si les maîtres ne trouvaient certainement pas le même intérêt que jadis à l'entretien de grandes troupes d'esclaves, ils n'en continuaient pas moins à employer des domestiques, des artisans domaniaux et, sur leurs réserves, des garçons et filles de ferme, pour ne pas parler des concubines : personnel qu'il était tentant de demander à la traite. Il est probable que celle-ci, dès l'époque carolingienne, avait sensiblement ralenti ses apports. Mais seuls les siècles suivants la virent, sinon s'interrompre tout à fait (ce ne devait jamais être le cas au moyen âge), du moins diminuer dans une mesure telle que, dans la plus grande partie de l'Europe, l'esclavage pratiquement disparut et, là même, où il subsista, se trouva réduit, comme source de main-d'œuvre, au rôle d'un assez insignifiant appoint.

(*A suivre.*)   † MARC BLOCH.

COMMENT ET POURQUOI FINIT
L'ESCLAVAGE ANTIQUE[1]

III

Arrivés à ce moment de l'évolution[1], il importe tout d'abord de prévenir une équivoque ; les sources ne s'y prêtent que trop bien. Feuilletons les chartes du xı^e et du xıı^e siècle. Fréquemment nous y verrons apparaître, désignant une classe d'hommes, ce vieux mot de *servus*, que les dictionnaires, à juste titre lorsqu'il s'agit de textes antiques, nous ont habitués à traduire par « esclave ». Les langues vulgaires, de leur côté, nous parlent, le français de « serf », l'italien de *servo*, et leur accord avec le latin des actes nous assure que, toujours suspects d'excès de purisme, les notaires, cette fois du moins, en continuant d'appliquer à une réalité de leur temps un terme classique, ne faisaient que se conformer à l'usage vivant.

Plus généralement, sous des noms divers, — rien de plus variable toujours que le vocabulaire juridique du moyen âge, — toute une population d'humbles gens, beaucoup plus nombreux que ne l'avaient jamais été les *servi* de l'époque franque, se révèle à nous dans ces textes comme privée, disait-on, de la « liberté », comme plongée dans la servitude. Elle manquait dans certaines contrées, où le développement de la structure sociale avait suivi de tout autres chemins : par exemple dans les basses terres qui, de la Frise au Dithmarschen, bordent la mer du Nord, ou encore dans la péninsule scandinave. Mais elle était répandue sur de très vastes espaces, en Allemagne et en Italie aussi bien qu'en France et en Angleterre. Dans son sein étaient venus se fondre des groupes humains de provenance très diverse. Tantôt, à la suite d'expresses donations de soi-même, prétendument spontanées, mais dont la plupart n'avaient été consenties que sous la pression de la menace, du besoin de protection, ou plus simplement de la faim, tantôt et plus souvent sans doute par l'effet d'un lent glissement, beaucoup de descendants de libres colons y avaient rejoint la postérité des esclaves tenanciers et celle de nombreux affranchis « avec obéissance ». Elle était d'ailleurs loin de posséder une absolue unité juridique ; en Allemagne notamment, on y distinguait bien des sous-classes, définies par des caractères juridiques différents. Mais une caractéristique commune dominait ces nuances : la séparation, très nettement ressentie d'avec les hommes qualifiés de « libres ». Était-ce donc que l'esclavage avait marqué depuis le ıx^e siècle d'immenses progrès ? Non certes. Ce qui avait changé, c'était le contenu même de la notion de liberté. Et de servitude, qui n'en est que l'antithèse : de sorte qu'une foule d'hommes qui, naguère, eussent passé pour libres voyaient désormais leur condition traitée de servile.

Les troubles constants, la rupture des anciens groupes consanguins ou censés tels, la faiblesse déjà sensible des pouvoirs publics avaient grandement développé, dans les sociétés issues des invasions, les relations de dépendance personnelle. La carence définitive de l'État, à partir du xi⁰ siècle, fit d'elles, pour plusieurs siècles, à côté des rapports familiaux — la parenté était désormais bornée à un petit cercle de proches — le seul ciment social qui comptât. Il était naturel que, pour fixer la place de l'individu dans la société, on s'attachât avant tout à la tonalité particulière de la sujétion où il était tenu, invariablement, envers un plus puissant que lui. Or, parmi les liens humains, d'origine multiple, que l'on vit alors naître ou se procréer, on s'habitua rapidement à distinguer deux catégories : les uns que l'homme nouait, en principe, à son gré, quitte à ne plus pouvoir, sa vie durant, les briser ; tels, dans les hautes classes, ceux du vasselage, dont la transmission de génération en génération, en pratique très fréquente et presque normale, ne fut jamais en droit obligatoire ; — les autres qu'il trouvait tout formés dès le ventre de sa mère et auxquels il n'avait plus, jusqu'à sa mort, qu'à se plier, pour en léguer, son tour venu, à ses enfants l'inéluctable charge. Parmi les paysans, il y en eut toujours, en toute contrée, qui, tenant leurs champs d'un seigneur, vivant sur le territoire où ce chef exerçait ses pouvoirs de commandement, astreints par suite envers lui à des charges souvent fort lourdes, n'étaient cependant ses sujets qu'en raison de circonstances — possession, résidence — qui ne touchaient en rien la personne ; s'ils abandonnaient la tenure, — et l'abandon était licite, — l'attache se rompait totalement ; ces « hôtes », ces « manants », ces « vilains » (*Gäste, Landsassen*, disait de même le droit allemand) étaient tenus pour libres.

Rien de plus caractéristique, en sens inverse, que le cas des descendants d'affranchis. Les pères avaient été dotés d'une liberté conditionnée d'obéissance : parce que la soumission ainsi acceptée était héréditaire, les fils cessèrent un beau jour d'être rangés parmi les hommes libres. Quant aux esclaves-tenanciers, l'effacement, dans leur condition, des caractères juridiques de l'esclavage, déjà apparent, au seuil du moyen âge, n'était que la suite à peu près inévitable de leur situation de fait qui les mettait si loin de l'esclave. Il n'est guère étonnant qu'on ait perdu progressivement l'habitude de leur faire une place à part parmi les dépendants d'autres origines, dont la subordination pareillement s'accentua : d'autant que les institutions de droit public ou disparues ou profondément altérées manquèrent désormais à maintenir l'antique barrière entre l'homme libre, seul membre qualifié du peuple, seul apte au recrutement des tribunaux et de l'armée — et l'esclave étranger à la cité. Fidèle miroir de ces confusions d'idées, où l'historien découvre bien souvent la trace de la lutte du vieux contre le neuf, le langage courant, dès l'époque franque, atteste un grand relâchement de la terminologie. Des notaires d'instruction médiocre traitent les tenanciers libres de *servi* ; le palais carolingien lui-même se laisse un jour aller ; la loi visigothique, un concile espagnol ne craignent pas de qualifier de « servitude » la condition de l'affranchi qui a un patron. Mais les documents officiels, en général, se surveillent mieux. Il existait encore un droit presque savant capable d'imposer, avec quelque succès, le respect des anciens classements juridiques. Plus tard, l'absence de toute législation, de tout enseignement du droit, de toute centralisation judiciaire en favorisèrent au contraire le renouvellement.

**

Cette extension de la notion et du mot de servitude à toutes les dépendances qui pesaient sur l'homme dès sa naissance et en vertu de celle-ci se fit, bien entendu, sans qu'on en prît nettement conscience. Elle s'explique sans peine. Car l'esclavage forma en quelque sorte le prototype des relations de cet ordre. Non que les charges spécifiques du serf, dans leur détail, remontassent au statut des esclaves ; elles furent beaucoup plutôt empruntées à celui des affranchis avec obéissance. Ce fut l'hérédité même qui suggéra l'analogie. Attaché à sa condition par une fatalité en quelque sorte physique, le serf, comme l'esclave, ne pouvait attendre sa libération que du consentement exprès de son seigneur ; on gardait à cet acte le vieux nom d'affranchissement, et, dans les détails de son formulaire, il continua longtemps de reproduire certains des traits des manumissions d'esclaves de l'époque franque, voire de l'époque romaine. Il n'était pas jusqu'à l'espèce de défaveur sociale, invinciblement attachée, semble-t-il, à l'épithète de servile, qui n'en facilitât l'application à tout sujet héréditaire d'un autre homme : car cette absence même de choix semblait une marque d'infériorité. On fit subir à l'ensemble des serfs certaines des incapacités civiles ou ecclésiastiques dont l'esclave autrefois avait été frappé : refus d'accepter son témoignage contre les hommes libres, refus de l'admettre dans les cadres sacrés. Le nom de serf était une injure, que les tribunaux punissaient lorsqu'elle était lancée à tort. On était avant tout le serf d'un seigneur ; on était aussi, en soi, un serf tout court, c'est-à-dire le membre d'une classe placée tout au bas de l'échelle des valeurs humaines. Et certes la sujétion ainsi qualifiée était d'une rigueur singulière. Le langage courant lui rendait pleine justice lorsqu'il attribuait au serf ces noms pleins de sens : en France « homme de corps », en Allemagne « homme tenu en propriété par un autre », en Angleterre « homme lié » (bondman). Elle se traduisait par des charges diverses : leur poids, au total, était incontestablement très lourd.

Pourtant ce serf, si méprisé et placé dans un état de si étroite dépendance, n'avait rien d'un esclave. Il n'en présentait pas les caractères juridiques, puisqu'il pouvait posséder la terre à titre de tenure ou même en pleine propriété, donner, vendre et, sous certaines conditions, hériter ; puisqu'il servait à l'ost et siégeait dans les tribunaux ; puisque, surtout, ses obligations étaient, en principe et sauf violence, strictement limitées par la coutume. Moins encore en présentait-il les caractères d'ordre économique. Car sa force de travail n'appartenait pas à son maître. En tout pays, à vrai dire, certains seigneurs persistèrent longtemps à revendiquer le droit de réquisitionner, en cas de besoin pressant, le labeur de leurs serfs ; ceux-ci, entre tous les dépendants de la seigneurie, n'étaient-ils pas obligés à un devoir d'aide particulièrement impérieux ? L'exigence pouvait être à l'occasion redoutable : elle ne prétendait cependant, en elle-même, qu'à une application par définition exceptionnelle ; et l'on ne voit pas qu'elle ait été bien souvent suivie d'effets. Les serfs devaient sans nul doute à leurs seigneurs une large part de leur temps ; mais

— les corvées spécifiquement serviles étant exceptionnelles — c'était le plus souvent beaucoup moins à titre de serfs que de tenanciers, et au même taux que leurs voisins, les tenanciers libres, lorsque la classe des tenures était pareille.

Surtout, quelle que fût l'origine juridique de ce travail obligatoire et son étendue, il était, comme toutes les autres charges, fixé dans sa durée et parfois dans la nature de son emploi par des normes coutumières propres à chaque seigneurie, — normes qui, dès l'époque franque et peut-être dès l'époque romaine, modifient en pratique la condition de l'esclave-tenancier. Les *Tageschalken* allemands, dont la corvée était quotidienne, semblent au premier abord tout proches de l'esclave ; et c'étaient en effet de bien humbles gens, à peine « chasés », presque des valets de ferme, dont la tenure, semble-t-il, se réduisait à leur chaumière avec son jardin. Là même, cependant, la similitude n'était qu'apparente. Voyait-on vraiment chaque *Tageschalk*, quel que fût son sexe ou son âge, venir chaque jour prendre place dans l'équipe seigneuriale ? Ou n'était-ce pas plutôt chaque ménage de cette classe — hommes, femmes, enfants, peut-être déjà adultes — qui, quotidiennement, devait fournir un ouvrier ? Le point est obscur, encore que la seconde solution, qui est la plus éloignée de l'esclavage, demeure la plus vraisemblable.

Aussi bien, de pareilles charges étaient-elles très rares ; en France, je n'en connais pas d'exemple. Quelques journées par semaine, voilà presque partout les corvées les plus lourdes. En un mot, le servage, ou mieux le système seigneurial dont le servage n'était qu'un des aspects, avait beau mettre à la disposition des seigneurs une somme de main-d'œuvre qui resta longtemps très appréciable, voire même très élevée, le capital travail ainsi offert constituait une quantité inextensible. L'esclave avait été un bœuf à l'étable, sans cesse aux ordres du maître ; le corvéable, fut-il serf, était un ouvrier qu'on voyait arriver à certains jours, pour repartir sitôt la tâche terminée.

IV

Que le servage fût quelque chose de très différent de l'esclavage, les destins mêmes des mots suffisent à nous en assurer. *Servus* et ses héritiers romans avaient, on l'a vu, glissé peu à peu à une acception fort différente de leur contenu ancien. La dissolution des vieux cadres sociaux avait pareillement porté atteinte à divers termes équivalents, dont l'évolution obéit d'ailleurs à des lignes assez différentes ; le germanique *Knecht* et *Schalk*, son synonyme, avaient passé sur le continent au sens atténué de serviteur ; en Angleterre, *knight* a celui de suivant armé et, plus tard de chevalier ; le gallo-romain *vassus* ou *vassallus*, celtique d'origine et qui, sans conteste, avait jadis désigné l'esclave, en arriva à s'appliquer au recommandé libre, notre « vassal ». Dans leur valeur prégnante première, ces noms durent être relayés par une création sémantique nouvelle ; ce fut, sous des formes phonétiques variables, le mot même qui, en français moderne, a donné esclave.

Son histoire est fort obscure, en elle-même et faute d'études assez poussées. Il semble avoir fait son apparition au xᵉ siècle, à peu près simultanément en Allemagne et en Italie, et de là s'être répandu sur le reste de l'Europe, assez lentement d'ailleurs, pour des causes que nous verrons. Naturellement — et c'est là une des raisons qui rendent ce développement si difficile à retracer — il fut adopté beaucoup plus rapidement par les parlers populaires que par le latin des chartes ou des chroniques, conservateur par essence et obstinément attaché à l'usage classique. Son introduction dans le vocabulaire courant marque, de toute évidence, le moment où l'on commença à sentir nettement la différence entre le servage nouveau modèle et une condition qui, selon le schéma ancien, faisait vraiment d'un homme la chose d'un maître. Elle atteste en même temps qu'à côté des serfs il existait encore des esclaves au sens plein du mot.

Ces deux constatations n'épuisent d'ailleurs pas les leçons que nous pouvons demander à l'usage de la linguistique. Le mot d'esclave n'est devenu que secondairement l'étiquette d'une classe. C'était auparavant un nom ethnique. Aussi bien l'avons-nous conservé, en français, dans sa valeur première, mais sous une forme légèrement différente : quand il s'agit de peuples, nous parlons de Slaves. Certainement, le détournement de sens s'explique par l'origine d'un grand nombre des hommes soumis à cette condition. On peut dire, plus généralement, que, s'il y avait encore quelques esclaves dans l'Europe occidentale et centrale aux xi⁰ et xii⁰ siècles, ces esclaves presque tous étaient des étrangers.

*
* *

Le fait, à vrai dire, n'avait en lui-même rien de contraire aux habitudes les mieux enracinées. Sous réserve de quelques cas exceptionnels, comme l'esclavage pénal, l'esclavage pour dettes ou encore, là où la puissance paternelle était la plus forte, la vente de l'enfant par le chef de famille, ni le monde méditerranéen, ni le monde germanique n'avaient jamais tenu pour licite l'asservissement d'un concitoyen. La plupart des esclaves y étaient captifs ou fils de captifs, venus souvent de tout près, au temps où ces sociétés se trouvaient fractionnées entre une foule de petits peuples, ou bien, sous l'Empire romain, puisés dans le vaste réservoir de sa ceinture barbare. La nouveauté fut qu'au moyen âge la notion d'étranger prit une couleur différente, toute confessionnelle.

Les États s'étaient morcelés à l'infini. Mais, au-dessus d'eux et englobant d'immenses masses humaines, une cité nouvelle était née, la *civitas christiana*, la chrétienté, dont tous les membres appartenaient, moralement, à une seule nation. Certes, la paix n'y régnait point, tant s'en faut. La loi de l'Église, cependant, et, plus profondément, la conscience religieuse n'admettaient point que le vainqueur réduisît en servitude le vaincu, lorsque celui-ci était son frère en Christ. Nous touchons ici à l'action la plus forte que le christianisme ait jamais exercée, d'une façon à la vérité quelque peu indirecte, sur les progrès de la liberté humaine, et peut-être sur la structure sociale en général. Tout en favorisant les affranchissements, il n'avait pas condamné l'esclavage ; il ne cessa jamais d'accepter qu'on l'imposât aux païens, aux infidèles, voire dans la catholicité aux schismatiques, considérés comme privés de la véritable communion chrétienne ; il toléra que l'on maintînt sous le joug les esclaves baptisés, pour peu qu'eux-mêmes ou leurs ancêtres eussent été, lors de leur asservissement, étrangers à la vraie foi. Mais, en limitant aux espaces qui s'étendaient au delà des frontières du monde catholique l'aire où les maîtres et les trafiquants pouvaient légitimemént se pourvoir, s'il ne tarit pas tout à fait le recrutement de l'esclavage, il en réduisit au moins la source à un très mince filet.

Certes, la pratique ne se conforma qu'avec beaucoup de lenteur à ces sentiments, dont l'influence se heurtait naturellement aux vieilles traditions de la razzia et aux conseils de l'esprit de lucre. Rien n'indique que les esclaves *barbaricini*, — probablement des Sardes, — dont il se faisait grand commerce dans l'Italie du vi⁰ siècle et qu'achetait Grégoire le Grand, ne fussent pas chrétiens. Si l'abbé de Saint-Michei, Smaragde, croyait devoir inviter Charlemagne à interdire que dans son Empire « il ne se fît de nouvelles réductions en captivité », c'est sans doute que des faits de cette sorte lui avaient passé sous ls yeux. Lorsque les Anglo-Saxons furent devenus chrétiens, les luttes intestines, qui si souvent opposaient les uns aux autres leurs divers royaumes, n'en continuèrent pas moins pendant bien des années à jeter sur le marché des captifs, parfois de haute race. Aussi bien l'Angleterre fut-elle assurément, dans toute l'Europe occidentale, le pays où l'esclavage proprement dit conserva le plus longtemps une place importante dans la vie économique.

Une guerilla continuelle y sévissait entre Saxons et Celtes, chrétiens certes, mais que leurs adversaires tenaient volontiers pour étrangers à l'orthodoxie romaine. Ce n'est pas hasard si l'on y voit tant d'esclaves et d'affranchis porter des noms celtiques ou des surnoms tels que le Scot, ni si — selon un usage qui d'ailleurs remonte peut-être au temps où les conquérants germains de l'île professaient encore le paganisme — le mot de *Wealth* (Gallois) finit par prendre, dans la langue courante, le sens d'esclave. Alimenté ainsi par la présence, toute proche, d'une population dont l'asservissement paraissait légitime, l'esclavage anglo-saxon dut aussi sa longue durée aux caractères propres à l'évolution générale de la société. Le développement des relations de dépendance personnelle en un système régulier, capable de se substituer presque entièrement aux autres liens sociaux, y fut beaucoup plus lent que sur le continent et n'atteignit pas, avant l'arrivée des rois normands, son plein achèvement. Les institutions de droit public germanique témoignaient d'une plus grande force de résistance. Le classement traditionnel des conditions humaines — entretenu d'ailleurs par la continuité du droit écrit et de la législation — tomba moins vite en désuétude. Au vrai, le *theow* anglo-saxon fut jusqu'au bout cet être juridique devenu, de l'autre côté de la Manche, si exceptionnel : un esclave. Pas plus que le régime du fief et de la vassalité — la coïncidence est significative — le servage qui, là comme ailleurs, devait absorber tant d'anciens esclaves, ne se constitua guère avant la conquête normande.

La guerre n'était pas seule à en fournir la matière première : les pères, souvent, nous dit-on, mettaient en vente leurs propres enfants. La traite conservait une grande activité. Au moment où des clercs venus de France rédigeaient le Domesday Book, on se souvenait fort bien du temps où, sur divers marchés de l'intérieur, on « vendait des hommes ». Mais l'île, ₐu x⁰, au xi⁰ siècle, exportait aussi, vers l'Italie, l'Irlande (par Bristol notamment) — peut-être vers l'Espagne. Des garçons, des filles, en grand nombre : ces dernières préalablement engraissées, parfois, pour en augmenter la valeur marchande. De même, une fois converties, les hordes marines de la Scandinavie ne cessèrent d'écumer le littoral frison et barbaresque des terres nordiques, d'y ravir un butin humain ; les lois de la Frise, au xiᵉ siècle encore, tiennent de pareilles mésaventures pour un fait normal, dont les conséquences juridiques doivent être envisagées.

Peu à peu, cependant, l'action des idées nouvelles — ici plus tôt, ailleurs plus tard — fit son chemin. Il est très caractéristique que les guerres qui déchirèrent le monde occidental depuis les dernières années de Louis le Pieux ne semblent guère avoir amené des réductions en esclavage. Sans doute, le bétail servile demeurait une des marchandises les plus activement échangées en ce temps d'échanges assez rares. On n'en trafiquait pas seulement de pays à pays à l'intérieur de la chrétienté latine et germanique. Celle-ci en faisait commerce au dehors : mais ce n'étaient plus des catholiques d'origine que l'on vendait ainsi. De quels pays étrangers l'Europe (au sens restreint où nous employons ici ce mot) tirait-elle donc, soit pour les garder, soit pour en faire argent, ces esclaves exotiques ?

Beaucoup, la plupart sans doute, à l'époque que nous étudions, lui arrivaient par voie de terre, des confins orientaux de l'Allemagne. Celle-ci, il convient de le rappeler, était alors fort loin de son étendue actuelle ; vers l'Est, elle ne dépassa guère, jusqu'au xᵉ siècle, une limite jalonnée en gros par l'Elbe, la Saale et le Böhmerwald ; les conquêtes de la dynastie saxonne, au cours de ce siècle, n'aboutirent qu'à reporter la ligne de défense — non certes la frontière des parlers — de la Saale au cours moyen de l'Elbe, et à élargir un peu sur la rive droite de ce fleuve la zone de protection des postes qui en tenaient les bords. Au delà commençait le monde, le plus souvent hostile, des peuples de langue slave.

Deux Etats indigènes s'y étaient formés dès le xᵉ siècle, assez vastes, relativement bien organisés et, par surcroît, de bonne heure chrétiens : la Bohême et la Pologne. Mais, en dehors d'eux, et pour la plus large part entre la Pologne et l'Allemagne même, de larges espaces subsistaient, qu'occupait une poussière de peuplades, demeurées presque en totalité païennes, sans cesse en guerre entre elles et surtout avec les chrétiens. Cette terre bénie des razzias fut un admirable réservoir à esclaves. Les seigneurs des marches allemandes n'utilisaient pas seulemnt, à leur profit, leurs captifs, faisant d'eux des ouvriers agricoles, des tenanciers, des domestiques, et prenant parmi les captives leurs concubines ; ils en vendaient, et tiraient de ce commerce de beaux bénéfices. De même, les princes slaves déjà convertis. Prague, au dire des voyageurs arabes, était, au xᵉ siècle, un des grands marchés de la traite.

**

L'apport de ces contrées lointaines alimentait un commerce à large rayonnement. A dire vrai, il ne semble pas qu'à l'intérieur de la chrétienté occidentale elle-même l'aire d'expansion de ces esclaves d'outre-Elbe se soit étendue beaucoup au delà du Rhin. En France, je ne crois pas en avoir jamais relevé ni vu signaler aucune mention dans les textes. N'ayons pas l'imprudence d'en conclure que réellement personne n'en possédait. Ce ne serait pas seulement nier la possibilité de découvertes nouvelles, d'autant moins invraisemblables que la recherche est difficile et qu'on n'a pas beaucoup cherché. A supposer même que le silence des documents soit irrémédiable, ni leur abondance ni leur précision, hélas ! ne sont telles que des faits isolés n'aient pu passer à travers leurs mailles. Il n'en est pas moins frappant que le mot même d'esclave — comme terme juridique, mais comportant encore à l'origine une forte saveur ethnique — n'ait pénétré dans le domaine français que très tardivement ; il n'y apparaît guère qu'au xiiie siècle, et s'applique alors à des individus de condition servile, qui étaient peut-être des slaves, mais n'étaient certainement pas nés sur les frontières de l'Allemagne.

Tout indique que les captifs de cette dernière origine, s'il s'en trouvait en France — nous n'en savons rien — y étaient en tout cas en très petit nombre. Sans doute cette marchandise, qu'il fallait faire venir de trop loin, paraissait-elle trop chère ; et la rareté même de la main-d'œuvre servile avait déshabitué de son emploi le commun des maîtres auxquels la société du temps offrait d'autres moyens de se procurer les forces de travail nécessaires. Sur le Rhin, en revanche, et jusqu'aux alentours de l'an 1200 — c'est-à-dire à un moment où les progrès de la conquête allemande et de la christianisation commençaient à restreindre singulièrement les territoires de chasse — on rencontrait encore, souvent comme esclaves, dans les maisons nobles, des filles de race slave. Vers l'an mille, des hommes et des femmes, *servi ancillae*, figurent parmi les marchandises importées que taxent, allant vers l'Italie, les péages des Alpes. Étaient-ce des Slaves ou des Anglais ? Comment décider ? Le curieux est que, si les châteaux de la France n'hébergeaient guère de captifs faits dans les marches allemandes, certains chemins de caravane, qui traversaient le pays de part en part, en voyaient assez souvent passer. Car, au xe siècle au moins et au xie, un bon nombre étaient exportés vers l'Espagne musulmane, riche et habituée à l'usage du travail servile ; Verdun, à mi-route, était un des centres actifs de ce commerce ; ses marchands, avant d'expédier au delà des Pyrénées les jeunes garçons qu'ils avaient achetés, fréquemment les châtraient, afin d'en rehausser le prix aux yeux des maîtres des harems. D'autres, très probablement, étaient vendus dans le Levant. Parmi les esclaves que Venise embarquait sur ses navires, pour Byzance et sans doute aussi pour l'Egypte, il est difficile de croire qu'il n'en était pas de cette provenance.

Exportateurs de chair humaine, les ports de la Méditerranée occidentale et de l'Adriatique s'en faisaient-ils aussi, à l'occasion, les introducteurs dans leur arrière-pays ? A partir du milieu du xiie siècle, point de doute. L'esclave, dès lors, sera pour les longs courriers de l'Orient et de l'Afrique un des éléments ordinaires de leurs cargaisons de retour. Slaves ou Tartares razziés sur les bords de la mer Noire, Syriens ou Berbères « olivâtres », Noirs du Maghreb viendront aussi, plusieurs siècles durant, peupler de leur humble présence les maisons bourgeoises de l'Italie, de la Provence ou de la Catalogne.

Ce sont certainement des gens de cette sorte que, vers ce temps, des documents, tous méridionaux, qualifiaient, pour la première fois en France, du nom d'esclave. Mais les conditions du trafic méditerranéen avaient alors profondément changé. Désormais les métiers des villes occidentales expédiaient aux consommateurs d'au delà des mers leurs produits, dont la vente permettait, en retour, l'acquisition de toutes sortes de marchandises, la marchandise humaine entre autres. Antérieure à cette révolution des courants économiques, les échanges n'étaient pas seulement beaucoup moins actifs ; la plus lourde gêne, pour l'Occident, naissait de la rareté des frets d'exportation. Pour se procurer les denrées exotiques dont il avait un impérieux besoin, il devait soit sacrifier son or, soit céder, précisément, ses propres esclaves. Il ne pouvait guère en importer. Sans doute arrivait-il malgré tout, de ci de là, à s'en procurer quelques-uns. Le raid sur la côte esclavonne, toute proche, aidant à alimenter le marché de Venise, qui vraisemblablement n'en expédiait pas, vers l'Ouest, tout le butin. A la fin du xiᵉ siècle, les croisades familiarisèrent les grands seigneurs avec l'esclavage. Un des étonnements des Latins avait été de trouver, en Syrie, sa pratique largement répandue : Guibert de Nogent s'en scandalisait avec d'autant plus de véhémence que beaucoup de ces esclaves étaient chrétiens ; plus tard, Beaumanoir croyait devoir réserver, dans sa description des statuts juridiques, une place à ce *servus* des « terres estranges », si différent de celui qu'il connaissait par expérience. Imitant ces exemples lointains, quelques hauts personnages, comme l'évêque de Laon Gaudri, prirent plaisir à entretenir dans leur suite des esclaves nègres. Tout cela était bien peu de chose. Guerrière, l'Europe pouvait demander un peu de main-d'œuvre servile aux confins slaves, que ravageaient ses soldats : économiquement encore très faible, elle ne pouvait en attendre, en quantités appréciables, du commerce international.

Mais les pays au delà de l'Elbe n'étaient pas la seule terre où elle se trouvât en contact direct avec des civilisations étrangères au christianisme. Songeons à l'Espagne musulmane, cette Espagne dont la lente reconquête fut un des grands faits de l'histoire. Certes, les habitants des terres soumises n'étaient pas, à l'ordinaire, réduits en servitude. Par contre, la plupart des prisonniers faits sur le champ de bataille l'étaient, des deux parts. Les chrétiens exportaient-ils certains de ces *cautivos* hors du pays ? Il est difficile de le savoir. Incontestablement, ils en gardaient un grand nombre pour eux, les faisant travailler dans la maison ou aux champs, et les soumettant à une condition qui était bien, au propre, celle de l'esclave. Les royaumes ibériques, qui devaient tant faire pour répandre, dans le nouveau monde, l'esclavage, l'avaient, de tout temps, connu sur leur propre sol.

.*.

Ainsi, l'Europe de l'Occident et du Centre, dans son ensemble, n'a jamais été, pendant le haut moyen âge, sans esclaves. Mais ceux-ci, du ixᵉ au xiiᵉ siècle, demeurèrent toujours en très petit nombre — en plus petit nombre même qu'ils ne devaient l'être par la suite, après la reprise du grand commerce méditerranéen. Des régions entières, comme la France, pratiquement les ignoraient. Là même où ils étaient relativement abondants, des affranchissements rapidement venaient éclaircir leurs rangs : car les mêmes raisons qui, à l'époque précédente, avaient multiplié ces concessions continuaient à faire entendre leurs voix. Ni les seigneurs des marches allemandes, ni ceux du Léon, de la Castille ou de l'Aragon, n'entretenaient de grandes exploitations, capables d'occuper de nombreuses équipes serviles, et l'on sait combien aisément l'esclave tenancier cesse, par la force naturelle des choses, d'être un véritable esclave. Là où les conditions particulières du pays permettaient, sans enfreindre le veto de l'Eglise, d'asservir des captifs, l'esclavage permettait aux gens aisés de satisfaire, à bon compte, les besoins de main-d'œuvre de la maison, peut-être, quelquefois, de l'atelier. Il a par ailleurs fourni au négoce une marchandise commode, qui l'aidait à entretenir, avec l'extérieur, d'utiles échanges. Comme force de production, il ne comptait plus.

Profonde et lente transformation des soubassements mêmes de la structure économique : il importe d'observer que certaines de ses conséquences dépassent le plan de l'économie. Quelle qu'ait pu être la misère de certaines classes et le mépris où les heureux de ce monde les tenaient, — mépris entretenu, pour certaines d'entre elles, par la survivance même de l'épithète de « servile », détournée, on le sait, de son sens juridique ancien, — il n'était sans doute pas indifférent qu'aucun homme, aucun vrai chrétien en tout cas, ne pût être désormais légitimement tenu pour la chose d'un autre. En rompant avec l'esclavage, le moyen âge, dont les mœurs sociales n'étaient pas tendres, n'a certes pas détruit, ni prétendu détruire, les inégalités de fait ou de naissance ; mais il leur a donné, si l'on peut dire, une tonalité plus humaine. Plus aisément saisissables, les conséquences démographiques. L'importance de la main-d'œuvre servile, dans le monde romain, l'ampleur de rayonnement de la traite avaient abouti à un brassage de population, dont on saurait difficilement exagérer l'importance. Combien de familles libres, sur le sol de la Gaule, au IVe ou au Ve siècle, descendaient d'esclaves venus des pays les plus lointains et les plus divers ! Privées de cet afflux exotique, les sociétés sans esclaves virent beaucoup moins souvent se renouveler leur sang. A ce point de vue, comme à beaucoup d'autres, la civilisation européenne s'est, au cours de ces siècles, stabilisée et comme enfermée en elle-même.

† Marc Bloch.

BIBLIOGRAPHICAL ESSAY

A VERY CONSIDERABLE BIBLIOGRAPHY appears in the notes in this volume. The present intention is not to assemble all those references, but rather to organize a number of important ones around a few topics, to comment, to supplement with a few of the most recent publications, and to indicate the more serious lacks. There is no particular concentration on works in English except to cite translations when they exist. However, books and articles in the Slavic and other languages of Eastern Europe have been omitted (with one exception), because they remain inaccessible to the great majority of students. Fortunately, Eastern European work in ancient history, in which slavery is a major subject, is now available in abstracts, usually in German, in *Bibliotheca classica orientalis*, a quarterly published by the Berlin academy since 1956.

Titles are not duplicated in the various sections, and this is especially to be remembered with respect to the general works.

The following abbreviations are used:

J. = *Journal.*   *Z.* = *Zeitschrift.*

Akad. Mainz = *Abhandlungen der geistes- und sozialwissenschaftlichen Klasse* of the Akademie der Wissenschaften und der Literatur, Mainz (Wiesbaden: Steiner Verlag).

SD = *Studia et documenta historiae et iuris.*

GENERAL

The first general survey of ancient slavery in nearly a century is W. L. Westermann, *The Slave Systems of Greek and Roman Antiquity* (Philadelphia: American Philosophical Society, 1955). For all its merits, as C. B. Welles wrote in a sympathetic review in the *Amer. J. of Philology* 77 (1956) 316-18, "this is not the definitive book on slavery which it, in some way, purports to be". Several lengthy and highly critical reviews deserve study in their own right: by H. J. Wolff in *Iura* 7 (1956) 308-15, especially on Roman law; by G.E.M. de Ste Croix in *Class. Rev.*, n.s. 7 (1957) 54-59; by R. E. Smith in *J. of Hell. St.* 77 (1957) 338-39; by P. A. Brunt, in *J. of Rom. St.* 48 (1958) 164-70. More favourable are those of H. Kupiszewski in *SD* 22 (1956) 429-34 and H. Strasburger in *Hist. Z.* 186 (1958) 600-608.

In consequence, the old and often inaccurate three-volume work of Henri Wallon, *Histoire de l'esclavage dans l'antiquité* (2nd ed., Paris: Hachette, 1879), remains useful. There are two monographs on Hellenistic slavery which, though dealing with specialized problems, go on to more general considerations: Iza Biezunska-Malowist, *Quelques problèmes de l'esclavage dans la période hellénistique* (*Eos*, supp. vol. 20, 1949; in Polish, with French resumé pp. 65-69); W. L. Westermann, *Upon Slavery in Ptolemaic Egypt* (New York: Columbia University Press, 1929), an edition with full commentary of portions of a royal ordinance dated *c.* 198-197 B.C. R. H. Barrow, *Slavery in the Roman Empire* (London: Methuen, 1929), will shortly be re-issued in a corrected edition.

Slavery is of course discussed in the general works and manuals on ancient economic history, of which the following may be mentioned: Max Weber, "Agrarverhältnisse im Altertum", in his *Gesammelte Aufsätze zur Sozial- und Wirtschaftsgeschichte* (Tübingen: Mohr, 1924) 1-288: originally published in 1909, this brilliant essay ranges far beyond the agrarian problems indicated by the title; F. M. Heichelheim, *Wirtschaftsgeschichte des Altertums* (2 vols., Leiden: Sijthoff, 1938), now in process of publication in a revised version in English; W. E. Heitland, *Agricola: a Study of Agricultural Life in the Graeco-Roman World from the Point of View of Labour* (Cambridge University Press, 1921), a large work which suffers from a bad principle of organization, according to ancient authors, but which is nonetheless useful in the Roman section; Gustave Glotz, *Ancient Greece at Work* (London: Routledge, 1926); H. Michell, *The Economics of Ancient Greece* (2nd ed., Cambridge: Heffer, 1957); M. Rostovtzeff, *The Social & Economic History of the Hellenistic World* (3 vols., corrected ed., Oxford: Clarendon Press, 1953); A. B. Ranowitsch, *Der Hellenismus und seine geschichtliche Rolle* (Berlin: Akademie-Verlag, 1958), translated from the Russian work published in 1950; Tenney Frank (ed.), *An Economic Survey of Ancient Rome* (5 vols.. and a general index vol., Baltimore : Johns Hopkins Press, 1933-40), particularly valuable for its extensive quotations from sources in translation, but very weak in analysis and interpretation in the first and last volumes, which are devoted to Rome and Italy; M. Rostovtzeff, *The Social and Economic History of the Roman Empire* (2 vols., 2nd ed. by P. M. Fraser, Oxford: Clarendon Press, 1957).

Mention should also be made of the vast German encyclopaedia, *Pauly-Wissowa, Real-Enzyklopädie der klassischen Altertumswissenschaft*, begun in 1894 and finally nearing completion. It contains many articles on aspects of slavery, published under the key words (Greek, Latin or German); the general article, "Sklaverei", was written by Westermann and is in essence an earlier version of his English book. None of the *Pauly-Wissowa* articles is included in this bibliographical essay. Finally, for reviews of books mentioned, consult *L'Année philologique* (Paris: Les Belles Lettres).

NUMBERS AND SOURCES

The size of the ancient slave populations is extensively discussed in this volume. Here it is merely necessary to note that K. J. Beloch, *Die Bevölkerung der griechisch-römischen Welt* (Leipzig: Duncker & Humblot, 1886) remains indispensable, though now outdated especially for the epigraphical evidence. As examples of regional analysis based on inscriptions (both more recent than Miss Gordon's survey), see Jotham Johnson, *Excavations at Minturnae*, Vol. II: *Inscriptions*, Part 1, *Republican Magistri* (University of Pennsylvania Press, 1933); and H. Thylander, *Etude sur l'épigraphie latine* (Lund: Gleerup, 1952) 149-67. The limitations of statistical analysis from such evidence are clearly brought out by F. G. Maier, "Römische Bevölkerungsgeschichte und Inschriftenstatistik", *Historia* 2 (1954) 318-51.

What we lack completely are full-scale investigations into the sources of supply. Studies of war and piracy have been promised by the Mainz academy. In the meantime, note may be taken of an important article on the general attitude by A. Aymard, "Le partage des profits de la guerre dans les traités d'alliance antiques", *Rev. hist.* 217 (1957) 233-49; and of the brief survey by H. A. Ormerod, *Piracy in the Ancient World* (University Press of Liverpool, 1924). No serious study of either slave breeding or the slave trade exists, to my knowledge.

MANUMISSION AND FREEDMEN

A. Calderini, *La manomissione e la condizione dei liberti in Grecia* (Milan: Hoepli, 1908), was a useful collection of materials in its time, but the subject requires complete re-analysis. References to more recent articles on special topics will be found in the general books. Two may be cited here because they throw light on a previously misunderstood and ignored status, half-slave and half-free, so to speak, which was common in many parts of the Greek world (especially after Alexander the Great), and which was often brought about by a qualified manumission: Paul Koschaker, *Über einige griechische Rechtsurkunden aus den östlichen Randgebieten des Hellenismus* (Sächsische Akad. d. Wiss., Phil.-hist. Kl.: *Abhandlungen* vol. XLII, no. 1, 1931); W. L. Westermann, "The Paramone as General Service Contract", *J. of Jur. Papyrology* 2 (1948) 9-50.

For Rome, the standard work has long been A. M. Duff, *Freedmen in the Early Roman Empire* (re-issue with addenda, Cambridge: Heffer, 1958). For special problems one should consult C. Cosentini, *Studi sui liberti* (2 vols., Univ. di Catania, 1948-50). On the interesting Roman phenomenon of manumission leading directly to citizenship, see F. De

Visscher, "De l'acquisition du droit de cité romaine par l'affranchissement . . .", *SD* 12 (1946) 69-85; E. Volterra, "Manomissione e
cittadinanza", *Studi in onore di Ugo Enrico Paoli* (Florence: Le Monnier,
1955) 695-716.

HELOTS AND DEBT-BONDSMEN

A Jena dissertation of 1956 is the first serious modern analysis of the
unfree groups in Greece (such as the helots) who have often, and
erroneously, been called "serfs": Detlef Lotze, *Metaxy Eleutherōn kai
Doulōn: Studien zur Rechtsstellung unfreier Landbevölkerungen in Griechenland
bis zum 4. Jahrhundert v. Chr.* (Berlin: Akademie-Verlag, 1959). For
recent summary accounts of the two best known groups, see H. Michell,
Sparta (Cambridge University Press, 1952) pp. 75-92; R. F. Willetts,
Aristocratic Society in Ancient Crete (London, Routledge and Kegan Paul,
1955) ch. V-VI; Henri van Effenterre, *La Crète et le monde grec de Platon
à Polybe* (Paris: De Boccard, 1948) pp. 84-98.

Debt bondage in antiquity still lacks a systematic investigation. The
bibliography is extensive, but it is heavily concentrated on two famous
cruxes, the legislation of Solon in Athens at the beginning of the sixth
century B.C., and the institution of *nexum* in Rome, which survived until
late in the fourth century B.C. On the former, the best recent discussions
to start with are the interchange between Kurt von Fritz and Naphtali
Lewis in the *American Journal of Philology* 61 (1940) 54-68; 62 (1941)
144-56, and 64 (1943) 24-43; and D. Lotze, "Hektemeroi und
vorsolonisches Schuldrecht", *Philologus* 102 (1958) 1-12. The literature
on *nexum* is too concerned with the purely formal juristic side of the
institution; it is sufficient to cite the articles by G. Dulckeit and
J. Imbert in *Studi in onore di Vincenzo Arangio-Ruiz*, vol. 1 (Naples:
Jovene, 1952) 75-100 and 339-63, respectively; and H. Lévy-Bruhl,
"The Act *Per Aes et Libram*", *Law Q. Rev.* 60 (1944) 51-62. On the legal
aspects of Greek debt bondage, the pioneering study by H. Swoboda,
"Beiträge zur griechischen Rechtsgeschichte. II: Über die
altgriechische Schuldknechtschaft", *Z. d. Savigny-Stiftung f. Rechtsgesch.,
Rom. Abt.* 26 (1905) 190-280, has not been superseded, much as a new
examination of the evidence is needed. Hellenistic material, in
particular, has been given a fresh analysis in the work by Koschaker
already mentioned in the section on freedmen and manumission.

LAW

There is no book on the Greek law of slavery. For Athens, the best
work is G. R. Morrow, *Plato's Law of Slavery in its Relation to Greek Law*
(University of Illinois Press, 1939); more briefly, in the same context,
there is the excellent discussion by L. Gernet in the introduction to the
Budé edition of Plato's *Laws*, vol. I (Paris: Les Belles Lettres, 1951),
pp. cxix-cxxxii. The discursive treatment in L. Beauchet, *Histoire du
droit privé de la république athénienne*, vol. 2 (Paris: Marescq, 1897)
393-545, is useful for the source references, but is otherwise unreliable and
unsophisticated. For Graeco-Roman Egypt there is R. Taubenschlag,
The Law of Graeco-Roman Egypt in the Light of the Papyri (2nd ed., Warsaw:
Panstwowe Wydawnictwo Naukowe, 1955) 66-101. On Rome, the
standard work is W. W. Buckland's massive *The Roman Law of Slavery*
(Cambridge University Press, 1908). The quickest guide to the very
extensive list of articles and monographs which have since appeared
will be found under the appropriate rubrics (*servus*, *libertus*, etc.) in
Adolf Berger, *Encyclopedic Dictionary of Roman Law* (Philadelphia:
American Philosophical Society, 1953).

THEORY AND ATTITUDES

For ancient theories in the more formal, philosophical sense, see the
works of Morrow and Gernet just mentioned (on Plato); the first two
parts (pp. 257-74) of R. Andreotti's article, "Per una critica dell'
ideologia di Alessandro Magno", in *Historia* 5 (1956), with comments by
E. Badian on pp. 440-44 of his "Alexander the Great and the Unity of
Mankind", in *Historia* 7 (1958); W. Richter, "Seneca und die
Sklaven", *Gymnasium* 65 (1958) 196-218. On less formally expressed
attitudes, there is the very difficult question of how to interpret the
treatment of slaves in drama. The evidence in Greek comedy is
carefully assembled by Victor Ehrenberg, *The People of Aristophanes*
(2nd ed., Oxford: Blackwell, 1951) ch. VII. The Mainz academy has
announced a study in preparation on the slaves in Plautus and Terence,
and one on Greek tragedy would be most welcome.

The role of slaves in ancient religions has been almost totally
neglected. There is now Franz Bömer, *Untersuchungen über die Religion der
Sklaven in Griechenland und Rom*, vol. I: *Die wichtigsten Kulte und
Religionen in Rom und im lateinischen Westen* (Akad. Mainz, 1957, no. 7).
A rather negative judgment may also be made of the available work on
the impact of Christianity on slavery, if not with respect to mere
quantity of writing. There is one book, nearly a century old and several
times reprinted, by Paul Allard, *Les esclaves chrétiens depuis les premiers
temps de l'Église* (6th ed., Paris: Lecoffre, 1914), which, though not

without merit, can hardly be said to be adequate or comprehensive. Again it is the lawyers who have been most systematic, insofar as their own interests are concerned. A fair sample of the range of their views is provided by three publications: E. J. Jonkers, "De l'influence du Christianisme sur la législation relative à l'esclave dans l'antiquité", *Mnemosyne*, 3rd ser., 1 (1933/34) 241-80; J. Imbert, "Réflexions sur le Christianisme et l'esclavage en droit romain", *Rev. internat. des droits de l'antiquité* 2 (1949) 445-76; Biondo Biondi, *Il diritto romano cristiano*, vol. 2 (Milan: Giuffrè, 1952) 373-447.

SCIENCE AND TECHNOLOGY

Writing from different points of view and different (and sometimes incompatible) theoretical foundations, most experts seem to be agreed in the present century that slavery was the key factor in restricting scientific progress and particularly in blocking technological advance in antiquity. A convenient introduction to the question is that of Albert Rehm, "Zur Rolle der Technik in der griechisch-römischen Antike", *Archiv. f. Kulturgesch.* 28 (1938) 135-62. For more forceful statements of the impact of slavery, see Benjamin Farrington, *Head and Hand in Ancient Greece* (London: Watts, 1947) ch. I-II; R. J. Forbes, *Studies in Ancient Technology*, vol. 2 (Leiden: Brill, 1955) 78-125. The latter has been much influenced by the works of Ct. Lefebvre des Noëttes, the most important of which is *L'attelage: le cheval de selle à travers les âges: contribution à l'histoire de l'esclavage* (2 vols., Paris: Picard 1931).

For a point of view which rejects this emphasis on slavery, see the review-article, devoted chiefly to a critique of Farrington, by L. Edelstein, "Recent Trends in the Interpretation of Ancient Science", *J. of the Hist. of Ideas* 13 (1952) 573-604. His judgment is apparently shared, though not necessarily with the same vigour or shading, by S. Sambursky, *The Physical World of the Greeks* (London: Routledge and Kegan Paul, 1956) ch. X.

SLAVE REVOLTS

The recent 57-page monograph by Joseph Vogt, *Struktur der antiken Sklavenkriege* (Akad. Mainz, 1957, no. 1) replaces all previous work on this subject, and gives adequate bibliographical references. It is complemented by his article, "Pergamon und Aristonikos", *Atti del terzo Congresso internazionale di epigrafia greca e latina* (Rome: Bretschneider, 1959) 45-54. On slaves in connection with peasant revolts, see E. A. Thompson, "Peasant Revolts in Late Roman Gaul and Spain", *Past and Present*, no 2 (1952) 11-23.

MISCELLANEOUS

Finally, a few works must be listed for their contribution to special subjects (evident from their titles) connected with ancient slavery:

K. H. Below, *Der Arzt im römischen Recht* (Munich: Beck, 1953).

Ettore Ciccotti, *Il tramonto della schiavitù nel mondo antico* (2nd ed., Udine: Edizione Accademica, 1940), with a German translation (Berlin: Buchhandlung Vorwärts, 1910) of the original (1899) edition.

C. A. Forbes, "The Education and Training of Slaves in Antiquity", *Transactions of the Amer. Philological Assn.* 86 (1955) 321-60.

Léon Halkin, *Les esclaves publics chez les Romains (Bibl. de la Fac. de Philos. & Lettres de l'Univ. de Liège*, no. 1, 1897).

Oscar Jacob, *Les esclaves publics à Athènes (Bibl.... Liège*, no. 35, 1928).

S. Lauffer, *Die Bergwerksklaven von Laureion* (2 vols., Akad. Mainz, 1955, no. 12; 1956, no. 11).

L. A. Moritz, *Grain-Mills and Flour in Classical Antiquity* (Oxford: Clarendon Press, 1958) 97-102.

W. L. Westermann, "Industrial Slavery in Roman Italy", *J. of Econ. Hist.* 2 (1942) 149-63.

SUPPLEMENT (MAY 1967)

GENERAL : Joseph Vogt has collected his articles and monographs, with some revisions, in *Sklaverei und Humanität. Studien zur antiken Sklaverei und ihrer Erforschung (Historia*, Einzelschriften 8, 1965). The 93-page first part of Ja. A. Lencmann, *Die Sklaverei im mykenischen und homerischen Griechenland* (Wiesbaden: Steiner, 1966), translated from the Russian, is a critical survey of the modern literature on ancient slavery generally since David Hume. See also the discussion between E. Ch. Welskopf and S. Lauffer in *Acta Antiqua* 12 (1964) 311-63, based on the latter's report to the XIth International Historical Congress, Stockholm 1960, published in vol. II of the Congress *Rapports* and reprinted in *Gymnasium* 68 (1961) 370-95; F. Gschnitzer, *Studien zur griechischen Terminologie der Sklaverei* I (Akad. Mainz, 1963, no. 13); D. B. Davis, *The Problem of Slavery in Western Culture* (Cornell Univ. Press, 1966), ch. I-III.

NUMBERS AND SOURCES: M. I. Finley, "The Black Sea and Danubian Regions and the Slave Trade in Antiquity", *Klio* 40 (1962) 51-9; H. Volkmann, *Die Massenversklavungen der Einwohner eroberter Städte in der hellenistisch-römischen Zeit* (Akad. Mainz, 1961, no. 3); I. Biezunska-Malowist, "Les esclaves nés dans la maison du maître . . . en Egypte romaine", *Studii clasice* 3 (1961) 146-62; L. R. Taylor, "Freedmen and Freeborn in the Epitaphs of Imperial Rome", *Amer. J. Phil.* 82 (1961), 113-32.

MANUMISSION AND FREEDMEN : A. M. Babacos, *Actes d'aliénation en commun* . . . *d'après le droit de la Thessalie antique* (*Séminaire d'histoire du droit, Université de Thessaloniki*, no. 4, 1966); P. R. C. Weaver, "The Slave and Freedman 'Cursus' in the Imperial Administration", *Proc. Camb. Philological Soc.*, n.s. 10 (1964) 74–92, the most general so far of a number of articles he has published on the subject.

HELOTS AND DEBT-BONDSMEN : M. I. Finley, "Between Slavery and Freedom", *Comp. Studies in Society and Hist.* 6 (1964) 233–49; "The Servile Statuses of Ancient Greece", *Rev. int. des droits de l'ant.*, 3rd ser., 7 (1960) 165–89; "La servitude pour dettes", *Rev. hist. de droit*, 4th ser., 43 (1965) 159–84; R. F. Willetts, "The Servile System of Ancient Crete : A Reappraisal of the Evidence", in *Geras* . . . *George Thomson* (Prague : Charles Univ., 1963) 257–71; D. Lotze, "Zu den *woikees* von Gortyn", *Klio* 40 (1962) 32–43; B. Shimron, "Nabis of Sparta and the Helots", *Class. Phil.* 61 (1966) 1–7.

THEORY AND ATTITUDES : Bömer's work on religion and the slaves has now been completed with three further volumes : Akad. Mainz, 1960 no. 1, 1961 no. 4, 1963 no. 10. The promised work of P. P. Spranger, *Historische Untersuchungen zu den Sklavenfiguren des Plautus und Terenz*, has been published (Akad. Mainz, 1960, no. 8).

SCIENCE AND TECHNOLOGY : L. Edelstein, "Motives and Incentives for Science in Antiquity", in *Scientific Change*, ed. A. C. Crombie (London : Heinemann, 1963) 15–41, with discussion, pp. 79–87; M. I. Finley, "Technological Innovation and Economic Progress in the Ancient World", *Econ. Hist. Rev.*, 2nd ser., 18 (1965) 29–45; H. W. Pleket, "Techniek en Maatschappij in de Grieks-Romeinse Wereld", *Tijd. v. Gesch.* 78 (1965) 1–21. Vol. 2 of Forbes's *Studies* has been issued in a revised 2nd ed. (1965).

SLAVE REVOLTS : P. Green, "The First Sicilian Slave War", *Past & Present* 20 (1961) 10–29, with discussion in no. 22 (1962) 87–93; K. M. Kolobova, "The Second Sicilian Slave Revolt" (in Russian), *Eirene* 2 (1963) 111–35; J. C. Dumont, "A propos d'Aristonicos", *Eirene* 5 (1966) 189–96; J. P. Brisson, *Spartacus* (Paris : Club Fr. du Livre, 1959), with more general analysis of slave revolts.

MISCELLANEOUS : W. Beringer, "Zu den Begriffen für 'Sklaven' und 'Unfreie' bei Homer", *Historia* 10 (1961) 259–91, and "Der Standort des *oikeus* in der Gesellschaft des homerischen Epos", *Historia* 13 (1964) 1–20; N. Charbonnel, "La condition des ouvriers dans les ateliers impériaux au IV et V siècles", *Trauvax, Fac. du droit, Paris, Sect. des sci. hist.*, 1 (1964) 61–93; I. Hahn, "Freie Arbeit und Sklavenarbeit in der spätantiken Stadt", *Ann. Univ. Budapest, Sectio hist.* 3 (1961) 23–39; C. Mossé, "Le rôle des esclaves dans les troubles politiques du monde grec . . .", *Cahiers d'hist.* (Lyon) 4 (1961) 353–60; G. Nussbaum, "Labour and Status in the *Works and Days*", *Class. Q.*, n.s. 10 (1960) 213–20; E. Ch. Welskopf, "Einige Bemerkungen zur Lage der Sklaven und des Demos in Athen zur Zeit des dekeleisch-ionischen Krieges", *Acta Antiqua* 8 (1960) 295–307.